Early Childhood Education in English for Speakers of Other Languages

Edited by Victoria A Murphy and Maria Evangelou

ISBN 978-0-86355-782-8

Contents

Foreword

The British Council asked Victoria A. Murphy and Maria Evangelou to put together this wide-ranging book on English language learning in the early stages of education (pre-primary, or ages 0 to seven years) as a result of increased interest and incidence of practice in the area – perhaps the final frontier in the rush to teach and learn English at ever younger ages – combined with a relative lack of specific research and experience sharing.

Quality early childhood education and care (ECEC) has become more and more widespread globally in both state and private sectors over recent years and decades, though there is still lamentably a huge discrepancy in access. Research has shown the added value to later achievements of quality education at this vital pre-primary stage. Equally, there has been an ever-growing demand, especially from parents, to ensure that children leave school with a mastery of English, which is seen as the international language of communication in more and more domains, and a key to social and economic improvement. This volume provides a variety of perspectives on how these two social trends can come together to give children an advantage in their multilingual development alongside physical, emotional, social and cognitive development, in a way that is age appropriate and without the need for a false divide between the world of work and play. The editors tell us that there are no cognitive impediments or negative consequences to learning more than one language in young children when done well, and the contributors show us that doing it well includes having well-prepared teachers, a well-designed curriculum, good resources, considered policies and supportive parents.

A number of core values and beliefs underpin this volume. We believe in quality early childhood education for all. We believe in working tirelessly for increased understanding across cultures, for valuing cultural diversity, and for promoting multilingualism. That means that while we work to develop a wider knowledge of English across the world in response to clear demand, we will never forget the importance of the mother tongue and local languages that mean that children can talk to their grandparents and learn from them, and which carry with them the glorious array of cultures and ways of being that the human race embraces. As the editors say, a world that only speaks English would be bleak indeed. We support an additive bilingual education that supports the home language as well as the wider development of creative and wise global citizens who will look after our planet far into the future.

We hope that this volume will inspire practitioners and policy-makers, and form a part of the classes and reading lists for initial and in-service early childhood teacher education courses. Our thanks go to the editors for their expertise and efforts in putting this innovative collection together, as well as to the many contributors for sharing their experience and wisdom with us.

John Knagg OBE
British Council

Introduction

Victoria A Murphy, Maria Evangelou, University of Oxford

"Viewed freely, the English language is the accretion and growth of every dialect, race and range of time, and is both the free and compacted composition of all."

Walt Whitman

The story of the Tower of Babel is perhaps an interesting metaphor for the international power of the English language. In the tale, humans are reaching for the heavens through the construction of their tower, achievable through their ability to communicate effectively with one another. God was not pleased with this idea, and hence the solution was to confuse the language of the world such that people began to speak many different languages, were no longer able to understand each other, and hence could no longer aim to reach heaven in their earthly lives. This story suggests that if we can communicate effectively with each other, the sky is the limit in terms of human achievement (indeed, in the story of Babel, maybe the sky is not even the limit!). Is the English language the new Babel? The eagerness to learn English that we see around the world does rather suggest that fuelling the desire to learn English is the belief that it will somehow be transformative for people's lives, it being considered a cornerstone of future economic and personal success. While English is the fourth most spoken language by native speakers (after Mandarin, Hindi and Spanish), more people (i.e. total number of speakers) speak English around the world than any other language (approximately one thousand five hundred million, c.f. www.statista.com). While it is not obvious that the whole world speaking English means we will reach heaven, it is clear that sharing such a global lingua franca has direct and specific consequences on numerous aspects of life, including education.

A number of research studies have identified a growing international phenomenon where different forms of education are offered through the medium of English to non-English speakers. One of the main underlying reasons for this expansion of such forms of education undoubtedly lies (in part) in the success of the French immersion programmes established in Canada by Lambert and Tucker (1972). In this programme, primary school children are educated for part of the school day in their native language (English) and in the other part of the day, in the second language (French). Many studies have since shown that immersion is a highly successful form of bilingual education since it promotes higher levels of oral language proficiency in the second language (L2) and higher levels of L2 literacy skills than would be found in more traditional taught programmes (e.g. Genesee, 1987, 2004; Murphy, 2014). As a result of the success of immersion education, immersion programmes have proliferated throughout the world (see Murphy, 2014 for a review). It is likely, therefore, that due to the international success of immersion education in raising achievements in L2 or foreign language (FL) learning, English language education (and particularly English immersion programmes) has similarly escalated. In the sphere of higher education, for example, Dearden (2015) reports on the rapid expansion of programmes offered through English Medium Instruction (EMI) around the world. Interestingly, the general support and feelings for EMI are equivocal – not everyone in Dearden's research (who were British Council staff from 55 countries) felt that EMI was self-evidently a good idea, while some viewed it as potentially controversial and reported feeling that EMI might have potentially negative consequences for lower socio-economic groups or for first language maintenance and/or education. This is an idea we will return to later on.

At the other end of the educational spectrum, Rixon (2013) shows that despite research indicating that successful English language learning is not determined (only) by the age of the learner, many countries have reduced the age at which English as a Foreign Language (EFL) instruction is introduced into the primary, and often the pre-primary, curriculum. She suggests that introducing EFL at young ages can be problematic when the materials, quality teacher education and generally appropriate conditions for learning are not in place. This view is consistent with Murphy (2014) who also argued that it is not the age of the learner that is the most powerful predictor of EFL success but, rather, the context (i.e. nature of the provision, materials, teachers, parental support, and the like). Rixon (2013) also comments that the proliferation of English language teaching is particularly notable in Early Childhood Education and Care (ECEC) settings despite the fact that her research showed that in many contexts resources are either lacking or not sufficient to the task.

At the same time that English language learning is being offered in numerous different educational programmes (from ECEC up to higher education), more and more children are participating in ECEC. The Office for Economic Co-operation and Development (OECD)'s family database shows that between the years 2003–10, all countries in the OECD experienced significant increases in enrolment in formal childcare and pre-school services for children under three years of age as well as increases in enrolment rates of children aged three to five years (OECD, 2014). Additionally, many countries have very high proportions (sometimes close to 100 per cent) of three-to-five-year-old children attending formal pre-school educational programmes (OECD, 2014)[1]. Given that higher numbers of young children are participating in ECEC and, as Rixon (2013) showed, increasingly are being offered English through ECEC, it is timely to examine English language learning through ECEC with children who do not speak English.

This volume brings these two issues – the proliferation of English language education and increased participation in ECEC – together. It provides an over-arching discussion of pertinent issues, research findings and concerns/challenges related to the education of children between 0 and seven years old through the medium of English (EMI) or through EFL instruction. The first section of this volume presents critical discussion of key issues related to specific 'global perspectives' where each continent is represented – except Antarctica, as it is virtually uninhabited. Contributions from North and South America, Europe, Africa, India,

---

[1] Unfortunately, it is also true that many of the poorest children in the world are not able to access good quality ECEC (UNICEF, 2014)

Australia and East Asia from researchers and/or language teaching and learning professionals working within these regions present detailed discussion of central topics specific to these contexts in relation to ECEC in English for non-English speakers. The second section of this volume presents more local discussion of particular projects related to ECEC in English across the world. These 'case studies' are sub-divided into those relevant to the EMI or EFL contexts and show us the considerable variability in how researchers, teachers and other language professionals are working within this growing international area. These discussions range from the very quantitatively research-oriented (e.g. the control trial in Fricke and Millard), to more ethnographic and descriptive projects carried out in English language classrooms (e.g. Ang). While the majority of these case studies are ultimately concerned with the child and their learning of English, some of them focus on the environment in which the child is learning (i.e. the classroom-based environment in Mourão and Robinson) and/or how we can best support teachers (e.g. Ellis), parents and/or other language professionals (e.g. Paradis). One could use the term 'eclectic' to characterise the range of topics and approaches in this volume. We deliberately adopted this multifaceted approach in putting this volume together because we believe that it is important to illustrate the significant diversity of research and areas of discussion and concern in relation to ECEC in English internationally. This diversity is important because we believe the area of ECEC through English for non-English speakers is itself in its early years from a research point of view. We hope, therefore, that this volume will serve as a catalyst for much more discussion and research.

Why are non-English-speaking children aged zero to seven learning English at pre-school?

The chapters in this volume illustrate some of the different reasons underpinning why children aged zero to seven years are being cared for or educated in English in the pre-school years. The United Nations Department of Economic and Social Affairs (UNDESA) reported that in 1990 there were approximately 156 million migrants worldwide. In 2010, this number increased to 214 million (Castles, 2013). In 2013, UNDESA reported that the number of immigrants rose to 232 million. In 2015, at the time of writing, there is an international refugee crisis. It is quite clear, therefore, that one major reason for why some young children are learning English through educational provision is that they and/or their families have emigrated from a non-English-speaking country to an English-speaking one, where the medium of instruction is English. This setting is relevant to the discussion in Genesee's chapter where he examines issues concerning the education of English Language Learners (ELLs) in North America, children whose home language is not English but who, by virtue of living in North America, are being educated through the medium of English. Paradis' chapter also is set within this context, where she discusses the important, and often neglected, issue of children with developmental disorders who are growing up bilingually. She shatters the myth that developing bilingually is somehow detrimental to children with disorders that can affect their linguistic development. Fricke and Millard also present an interesting randomised control trial set within this context of ethnic minority children growing up in England. Many children with English as an Additional Language (EAL) come to school with under-developed oral language skills (relative to native-speaking children) (Dockrell et al., 2010) and Fricke and Millard discuss the results of a successful oral language intervention aimed at helping pre-school children with EAL develop their vocabulary, and other oral language abilities. Murphy, Evangelou et al. (this volume) also include a discussion of children from ethnic minority backgrounds who are being educated through the medium of English. They discuss research, which identifies some of the challenges for very young non-English-speaking children as they begin ECEC in English. One of these challenges is that the parents of children from ethnic minorities in English-speaking countries might themselves not speak very much English, which can then mean that the parents are less equipped to offer support for their children's educational activities, an issue noted in Genesee's chapter. Starting school can be a difficult enough adjustment for young children but doing it through the medium of English, which for many children with EAL is a language they do not understand well, can create a range of different challenges that we need to learn more about so as to offer children from ethnic minority backgrounds the best possible educational experiences. As Genesee notes, young children being educated in these contexts need to learn the dominant, societal language for both social and academic reasons, along with the respective cultural norms (which may be different from the home). Additionally, they have to learn literacy skills along with general and subject-specific knowledge and skills, all through the medium of a language, which, for many EAL and/or ELL children, might be quite unfamiliar. Genesee also reminds us that language-related issues are often not the only, or even perhaps the most serious, challenges that young English learners face at school. Children from ethnic minority backgrounds might have to contend with issues related to poverty, pre-immigrant experiences and/or trauma if they are refugees, cultural differences between home and school, teacher attitudes, and the like. So, while this volume is focused on English language learners, it is important to also recognise that learning through the medium of English is not always young children's biggest challenge.

Another common reason for young children being educated in English that is highlighted in this volume refers to the widespread belief that 'younger is better' when it comes to language learning. Many of the chapters in this volume describe research in contexts where the desire to help children start out 'right' means introducing English as early as possible (e.g. Zhou). De Mejía (this volume), for example, cites Banfi (2015) who reports that it is a widespread belief in the public domain that foreign languages need to be taught at early ages if students are to develop proficient English language skills. This 'younger is better' belief is also highlighted in Murphy, Evangelou, et al.'s chapter where, increasingly, European countries are introducing English in ECEC and, in some countries, it is even now a formal part of the curriculum (e.g. Spain, Poland and Cyprus). It is important to remember, as Rixon (2013) and Murphy (2014) describe, that there is no research carried out in the instructed foreign language learning context that unequivocally demonstrates advantages for younger over older learners, hence it is indeed interesting to note increased numbers of countries introducing English as part of pre-school provision.

In some countries, English can have an official role in the society, hence leading educationalists to introduce English language education into pre-primary settings. For example, Shankar and Gunashekar describe the complex and diverse setting of India where English is a second language, where higher education is offered primarily through English, and where, for historical reasons, there is now an English-speaking elite (residual from Britain's rule). English is seen as the language of opportunity and social mobility in India, as well as in East Asia (Zhou and Ng) and other countries. For example, English is an official language of the Hong Kong Special Administrative Region (HKSAR) of China, and is viewed as a high-status language, which, if learned to sufficiently high standards, can lead to greater economic success.

These issues are also echoed in Gawne, Wigglesworth et al.'s chapter, where they discuss issues of English language education in Australia. Australia is a country with significant linguistic diversity (over 250 different languages represented by Australia's Indigenous peoples alone) and many aboriginal children who speak a home or community language that is not the 'Standard Australian English' (SAE) come to school with different linguistic and socio-cultural conventions and can struggle in learning SAE through educational settings. Mrutu, Rea-Dickins, et al. also discuss the importance of English language learning in Africa, where English is associated with better quality education and, as in other contexts, is seen as an important skill, enabling citizens to have a more successful life. As with India (Shankar and Guneshekar), English is important for older students in Africa given that higher education is offered through English, so the belief is that offering English language education at very young ages sets up the path to success.

Indeed, this notion of 'beliefs' that are held by different elements of society underpins most of the chapters in this volume, and is an issue directly discussed in Genesee's chapter, for example. A common theme that emerges from the discussions here is the pressure from parents. As Enever (2004) noted, there is a strong 'parentocracy' in relation to English language education, where throughout the world parents' beliefs that it is important for their children to learn English at young ages creates an environment where programmes are sometimes hastily put together to meet demand, often without appropriate teacher education and resources/materials (e.g. Zhou and Ng, this volume). This pressure from parents is characterised by a worrying finding described in Wong's chapter where he notes that 49.5 per cent of parents in Hong Kong who participated in his survey would not mind if their pre-school-aged children acquired English rather than Cantonese as their L1 – despite the fact that the respondents of this survey were from Cantonese families. This pressure from parents, therefore, is tangible and, while they have the best of intentions for their children, they could clearly benefit from some evidence-based guidance regarding the benefits of different educational programmes on bilingual development.

Educators', policy makers' and parental beliefs often tend to guide and shape the forces that lead to young children receiving some form of English language education at young ages. Sometimes these beliefs are inconsistent with research and one of the issues that emerges from this volume is the importance of fighting against these beliefs when they contradict the evidence. For example, some of the beliefs that are discussed and dismantled in Genesee's chapter include the notion that learning and using more than one language can be burdensome and has associated costs or disadvantages. Genesee discusses what he refers to as assimilationist, submersion, or "monolingualist" educational policies and practices and how these can be detrimental to young bilingual children's linguistic development. Similar issues are found in chapters throughout this volume.

There are many stakeholders involved in English language education for young children between zero and seven. The contributions in this volume highlight some of the unique and difficult challenges the educators involved in developing and delivering English language education to young learners must resolve.

Teacher education

One of the most prevalent concerns is whether and to what extent English teachers of young children in ECEC contexts have received appropriate teacher education. This is an issue that emerges from a considerable number of chapters here. For example, in de Mejía's chapter about developing appropriate bilingual education programmes in South America, teacher training programmes figure prominently, to encourage teachers to develop skills and knowledge concerning the languages, the cultures, the content, pedagogical knowledge, and general knowledge about bilingualism and bilingual education. Teacher education is a concern in Mrutu, Rea-Dickins et al.'s chapter on Africa, and Zhou and Ng's chapter on East Asia. Zhou and Ng, for example, describe a situation that is prevalent, but not unique to East Asia, where an unqualified native speaker teacher is deemed sufficient, or perhaps even more important, than a qualified, local (but non-native speaking) teacher. These chapters, and others, identify the problems inherent in the mismatch between the demand for native-speaking English teachers, and the numbers of such qualified teachers available. There are, thankfully, some examples of successful collaborative practice discussed in the contributions from de Mejía, Mourão and Robinson, and Ordoñez. It is important to learn from these examples of good practice and do more research on examining the particular variables that lead to successful English language outcomes in young children.

Paradis also raises the issue of teacher education from the perspective of working with children with language and/or developmental disorders. She explains how there is a common misconception that being bilingual exacerbates the difficulties faced by children with developmental disorders. She highlights the need for appropriate teacher education that helps teachers understand that bilingualism does not impede language development in either typically, or atypically developing children.

The lack of multilingual teacher education is a theme from Murphy, Evangelou et al.'s chapter on Europe and Gawne, Wigglesworth et al.'s chapter in the context of Aboriginal children learning the standard dialect of English. For example, Gawne et al. discuss the problem of the 'monolingual mindset in a multilingual context' where neither the policy nor the curriculum acknowledges the linguistic contexts that the child is learning in, and which can actually disadvantage the learner. When teachers are unfamiliar with, or lack understanding of, the differences and similarities between home language and school language and social patterns, difficulties can arise. In Australia, often the teachers who teach young SAE learners have only received this 'monolingualist' perspective as part of their Initial Teacher Education (ITE) and often do not have any real understanding of the linguistic and/or socio-cultural needs of aboriginal children. This can also often lead to high turnover, as non-aboriginal teachers can sometimes find teaching in this context very challenging – not surprising given that they may not have received adequate training for the task.

While a lack of qualified teachers with appropriate training is a common theme throughout this volume, Ellis provides us with an example of a short course for state pre-school teachers in France and illustrates how combining theory and practice, providing theoretical input on children's language development and building on teachers' pre-existing skills can be successfully and effectively transferred to EFL for young children. Ellis' project provides us with an interesting model as to how we can support teachers as they modify their practice to encourage their young pupils to learn English. Furthermore, as mentioned above, Mourão and Robinson, and Ordoñez, all illustrate examples of collaborative practice that seems to have positive consequences on the children's learning and teachers' professional development. One of the themes that emerges from this volume is the lack of research in this area – which means that it is all the more important for us to document and discuss what we conceive of as examples of good practice and to critically examine and identify (preferably empirically) what leads to successful English language education for young learners. The examples in this volume represent an important contribution in that regard (see also Mourão and Lourenço, 2015, as another example of a volume presenting critical discussion of different topics central to early years language learning).

Lack of resources

A recurring theme in Mrutu, Rea-Dickins et al.'s chapter is the lack of resources available to teachers to help support the English language learning of young learners. Of course, Mrutu, Rea-Dickins et al. describe the unique context of Sub-Saharan Africa (SSA) where access to engaging and appropriate resources can be a real challenge for teachers. However, lack of resources and materials is not unique to SSA, as evidenced throughout many of the chapters here. Mohamed illustrates that when there is an imbalance of how resources are allocated (i.e. more towards L2 English than L1 activities), problems can ensue. In the case described by Mohamed, despite policy specifically identifying the importance and role of the L1, resources being allocated more to L2 activities permeated into literacy-based activities in English at potential cost to L1 development. Zhou and Ng also identify a lack of resources appropriate to the learner population as being one of the challenges of educators in the East Asian context.

Curriculum

Developing and implementing an appropriate curriculum is of course inherently connected to both teacher education and resources. A number of chapters in this volume highlight the problem of curriculum. For example, Zhou and Ng note that in many East Asian countries, there is a pedagogical focus on memorisation and copying activities – partly based on the fact that such activities are more straightforward for parents to support outside of school activities (particularly if they themselves do not have high levels of English proficiency). They note that such activities are not generally agreed by educators to be appropriate for young children because they fail to make language fun and communicative or meaningful. Wong also identifies how curriculum planning is typically driven by market forces in East Asia. Furthermore, he highlights how curricula are only very loosely bound by educational policy. This is a common thread throughout many chapters in this volume – where there is either a lack of policy, or a very loose connection between what is implemented in Early Years classrooms in English, and what is dictated by policy. Indeed, policy itself does not figure prominently in this volume, which we assume reflects the fact that policy for English language learning through ECEC is not well developed internationally. This issue is discussed further, for example, in Murphy et al.'s chapter.

From a research perspective, Fricke and Millard show how a focus on oral language skills through classroom-based activities can have manifest benefits on EAL children's development of vocabulary knowledge and skills – which in turn are important predictors of literacy development. Ang also shows, through an ethnographic study, how an integrated curriculum for Singaporean pre-school children (three to six year-olds) can be effective. Ang illustrates how there was an appropriate blend of East and West where children were observed using two distinct languages in context, and actively engaging with and participating in various social and cultural activities. These chapters show how relevant curricular content and activities lead to clear positive gains in developing bilinguals.

Within the EFL context, Samantray suggests that an appropriate curriculum can benefit other skills (e.g. maths) as well as developing English language skills. Navarro Martinez, Coyle and Roca de Larios show how young English language learners can improve their English pronunciation through appropriate pedagogical focus, and Hillyard describes an action research project which illustrates how teachers can engage in enquiry-based professional activities to help guide and support their teaching and EFL children's learning. Therefore, there are a number of interesting and promising examples of how different pedagogical approaches, which of course is intimately connected to curriculum and provision, might be beneficial for young learners of English in ECEC settings. A common but highly relevant refrain, however, is that more research is needed in this area.

Developing the L1

Another major theme common to many chapters in this volume is the concern about promoting the L1 of young English language learners. As countries lower the age at which English language education is introduced, and as ECEC is increasingly offered through English, we have a situation where a foreign language is introduced at a time when the L1 has not yet fully developed. There is no inherent reason for why this should be problematic, as much research has shown that there are no cognitive impediments to learning more than one language in young children (e.g. Genesee, 2006; Murphy, 2014), hence learning English through educational provision does not require the sacrifice of the developing L1. Yet, as evidenced in a number of chapters of this volume, in the zeal to learn English, some educators, parents and policy makers seem to have lost sight of the importance of supporting the L1. This is a particular issue in respect of the minority language context relevant to Genesee's chapter, as well as Paradis, Fricke and Millard, and Murphy, Evangelou et al. When children are being educated in the majority English language, when they have a different home language, there are all sorts of pressures on whether and to what extent the child will be able to develop his/her L1 to a native-like standard. Indeed, often we find that minority language learners switch from being L1 dominant to English dominant when they start learning English in school (Murphy, 2014). Furthermore, unless the parent, school and community actively aim to support the L1, many minority language learners end up with only very limited knowledge at best of their home language. This is why Genesee (and others in this volume, e.g. de Mejía, Ordoñez) advocates additive *bilingual* education that aims to support both languages. Despite the importance and power of English, a world that only speaks English would be bleak indeed. Rather, we are interested in a multilingual world. This means that both of the child's languages need to be developed within and without educational settings.

Paradis also discusses the importance of maintaining the L1 within the context of children with language disorders. As mentioned earlier, often children from ethnic minority backgrounds have parents who themselves do not speak English to a very high level of proficiency. However, in their enthusiasm to encourage English in their children, they may only speak English in the home. This situation results then in the child not receiving an appropriately rich source of linguistic input and can potentially have negative consequences on their language (and bilingual) development, which can be particularly problematic for children with developmental disorders. Paradis urges educators and other language professionals to encourage bilingualism in their pupils, which necessarily requires support of both the L1 and English.

Indeed, the issue of L1 maintenance and/or integration with the L1 is a predominant issue throughout this volume, in almost all of the chapters. However, the concerns are slightly different depending on the context. Minority language learners, who receive no formal instruction in their L1, have a specific and unique challenge if we are to support the maintenance and development of their L1 – which, as discussed in Genesee and Paradis, has positive consequences on their L2. However, when the child is a speaker of the majority language, such as in the context described in Ordóñez, Mohamed, Zhou and Ng, and others, educators (curriculum designers and policy makers) might assume that there does not need to be a focus on developing language skills of the L1 through educational provision. In other words, if the child speaks, for example, Spanish in the home and Spanish is the majority language of the society, the belief is that s/he will naturally learn Spanish, implying that what we need to focus on in educational settings is English. However, as is argued in a number of chapters in this volume, there are tangible concerns about ensuring that English language education programmes that are offered and implemented to young children do not fail to include appropriate provision to help support the development of both of the child's developing languages.

The learner

As well as there being numerous themes which emerge from the discussions in this volume for educators of young English language learners, the learners themselves have a number of issues with which they have to contend. As mentioned above, since 1960 we have seen a big increase in the number of young children attending any type of childcare and pre-school education: *"Today's rising generation in the countries of the OECD is the first in which a majority are spending a large part of their early childhoods not in their own families but in some form of childcare."* (UNICEF, 2008: 3)

A review by Melhuish et al. (2015) on childcare and pre-school education (i.e. ECEC) has affirmed once more the crucial role that pre-school education plays in children's development, especially for those from disadvantaged backgrounds who enter school with fewer academic skills than their more advantaged peers, and they often lag behind in their cognitive development during the later school years (Stipek and Ryan, 1997). Melhuish et al. state that there is:

> *"... clear evidence that cognitive, language and academic skills can also be enhanced by ECEC experience and these are likely to play a role also in the later educational, social and economic success that is often found in well-implemented ECEC interventions."* (Melhuish et al., 2015: 24)

Brice Heath (1994), in her seminal book *Ways with Words: Language, Life, and Work in Communities and Classrooms*, addressed the disparities between the language children use at home and the language they are invited to use when they come to school and what educators should know about it. She reminds us of the challenges young children face when they enter pre-school settings especially when the languages used at home and at the school environment are not shared. One of the most important messages of the book is the need to be aware of the home linguistic skills of every child in our care and build upon these further, rather than seeing them as an obstacle.

The first time a young child attends school is fraught with change; change which not every child will find easy to accommodate. If that educational experience is offered through the medium of a language in which that child has limited proficiency, this can exacerbate those difficulties. For example, in some of the research described in Murphy, Evangelou et al., we see evidence of young children being very quiet and not engaging much with the other children and teachers, partly as a function of having limited English proficiency. In EFL contexts, there is considerable evidence that shows that, in general, young children are enthusiastic and motivated learners of foreign languages (e.g. Murphy, 2014); however, the extent to which this enjoyment persists as the child develops his/her English depends considerably on the teacher and the curriculum/provision being offered. It is critical, therefore, that we find ways to make English language learning meaningful, relevant and enjoyable for young learners. Enever (2011) showed how young primary school children's motivation to learn a foreign language waned over a four-year period, notably in boys. We need to ensure that we help maintain young children's high levels of motivation to learn languages throughout their ECEC experiences and beyond.

As mentioned earlier, for many children there is a concern about bridging the gap between home and school. For example, in Gawne, Wigglesworth et al., they report that the home language of Aboriginal children is not used in school, and the standard Australian variety (SAE) is not directly taught. They illustrate how important it is for the children to develop appropriate proficiency for school-related activities and interaction because the multilingual children's language repertoire is invisible since the focus is only on acquiring SAE in school. This challenge is discussed also in Genesee and in Murphy, Evangelou et al. This gap between the home and school is arguably less of a problem in EFL contexts because, typically, all the children and teachers will speak the majority language. Nonetheless, there are other issues the child has to face. For example, in EFL contexts such as East Asia, (Zhou and Ng, Wong, Ang) we see very highly pressurised environments for children where they are expected to achieve to the highest possible standard. We also see evidence of young children engaging in activities that are not always appropriate for young learners (such as rote memorisation and copying, in Zhou and Ng). One of the important roles of ECEC is to set up a successful foundation upon which further learning can proceed. To illustrate, Whitehead (2004) argues that it is critical that literacy is not concentrated on in a way detrimental to other aspects of the early years environment. Indeed, the research literature shows that literacy itself will suffer if it is not established on a broad and deep foundation of worthwhile experiences of symbolising and representing meanings through skills such as movement, dance, music, listening, talking, drawing, and story-telling, as well as scientific and mathematical investigations. This list of 'literacies' (Edwards, Gandini, and Foreman, 1996) provides a balanced early years education, which can be pursued in ways that are open-ended and sensitive to where children are in their thinking and learning.

If the approach of early childhood practitioners is unpressured and reflects their confidence in children's abilities to reflect and learn for themselves when supported by their peers and adults who care for them, there should be less danger of a work–play split in the early childhood curriculum (Whitehead, 2004; Bruner, 1986). ECEC helps the child prepare for primary school and beyond. If we put undue pressure on young children in ECEC settings we are potentially hampering the facilitative role of pre-primary education. It is important therefore that we put the needs of the child in our central focus in considering successful English language education for young children.

Parents

It has already been mentioned in this chapter that parents have a powerful role to play in the development, implementation and support of English language education for young non-English-speaking children. This is a theme threaded throughout the volume. For example, de Mejía discusses some research carried out on parents' attitudes and expectations towards English–Spanish bilingual education programmes. She notes that while in some cultures parents expect to be highly involved in their children's education, studies from some Latino families have shown that parents are more accustomed to waiting for the schools to take the initiative. Parents do have high expectations in English–Spanish bilingual educational programmes and in most cases have explicitly chosen these forms of education for their young children, sometimes at significant personal expense (true also for many contexts in East Asia where ECEC is almost exclusively run by private companies). De Mejía discusses the importance of parents' contributions to the success of their young children's learning, which is developing through a language that is different from the home language. She discusses the role of parents as educational partners in their children's early learning, and how important it is that this relationship between the home and school, facilitated by the parents, is maximised. Similar issues are discussed in many chapters in this volume (e.g. Mrutu, Rea-Dickins et al.'s discussion of community engagement to support ECEC in English in Sub-Saharan Africa).

While we have seen from many studies that parents have a powerful, facilitative influence in their children's educational achievement, Zhou and Ng (and to some extent Wong) also talk about some of the potentially unintended negative consequences that stem from parental influence. As already identified, parents in East Asia (and many other contexts around the world) are deeply enthusiastic about their young children receiving English through ECEC. They constitute a powerful force, therefore, in the development of EMI and EFL programmes. Zhou and Ng suggest that this has sometimes led to initiatives in English language education being implemented perhaps before they are ready, before policy and curricula have been well considered and before teachers have had appropriate training. It is important that parents have high expectations for their children; however, it is important also for them to be realistic about what young children are likely to achieve through English language programmes in ECEC (see Wong).

Conclusions

We have suggested in this chapter that research on English language learning through ECEC is largely in its infancy. This volume is part of a growing impetus to develop our understanding in this area, which in turn will have positive consequences on the development of appropriate policy, curricula, provision and teacher education for English language learning in young children. The chapters of this volume represent a highly diverse discussion given that many different geopolitical contexts and many different areas of interest and concern are represented. Despite this diversity, there are a number of common themes that emerge, underscoring their importance. These relate to teacher education and how important it is that we develop appropriate guidance and training for teachers of young children learning English; the development of an appropriate curriculum; the importance of maintaining the L1; the needs of the learner; and the role of the parents and wider community. The development and implementation of effective policy is also critical.

Pre-school has been referred to as 'the most important grade' (cf, Barnett and Hustedt, 2003) due to the many long-term benefits that are associated with children attending good quality pre-school provision. High quality ECEC programmes, therefore, represent a solid investment in our future. ECEC provision offered through English, then, needs to be carefully and critically examined to ensure we are providing the best educational opportunities for all our young children. We hope that this volume is a valuable contribution to that endeavour.

References

Barnett, WS and Hustedt, JS (2003) Pre-school: The most important grade. *The First Years of School, 60(7)*, 54-57.

Brice Heath, S (1994) *Ways with words; language, life, and work in communities and classrooms.* Cambridge University Press: USA.

Bruner, J (1986) *Actual minds, possible worlds.* Cambridge, MA: Harvard University Press.

Castles, S (2013) The forces driving global migration. *Journal of Intercultural Studies, 34(2)*, 122-140.

Dearden, J (2015) *English as a medium of instruction – A growing global phenomenon.* London: The British Council.

Dockrell, JE, Stuart, M and King, D (2010) Supporting early oral language skills for English language learners in inner city pre-school provision. *British Journal of Educational Psychology, 80/4*, 497-515.

Edwards, C, Gandini, L and Foreman, G (1996) *The hundred languages of children.* London: Ablex.

Enever, J (2004) 'Europeanisation or globalisation in early start EFL trends across Europe?' in Gnutzmann, C and Intemann, F (eds) *The globalisation of English and the English language classroom.* Tübingen: Narr.

Enever, J (ed) (2011) ELLiE: *Early language learning in Europe.* London: The British Council.

Genesee, F (1987) Learning through two languages: *Studies of immersion and bilingual education.* Cambridge, MA: Newbury House.

Genesee, F (2004) 'What do we know about bilingual education for majority language students?' in Bhatia, TK and Ritchie, W (eds) *Handbook of bilingualism and multilingualism.* Malden, MA: Blackwell.

Genesee, F (2006) 'Bilingual first language acquisition in perspective', in McCardle, P and Hoff, E (eds) *Childhood bilingualism: Research on infancy through school age.* Clevedon: Multilingual Matters.

Lambert, WE and Tucker, GR (1972) *The bilingual education of children: The St. Lambert experiment.* Rowley, MA: Newbury House.

Melhuish, E, Ereky-Stevens, K, Petrogiannis, K, Ariescu, A, Penderi, E, Rentzou, K, Tawell, A, Leseman, P and Broekhuisen, M (2015) *A review of research on the effects of early childhood Education and care (ECEC) on child development* http://ecec-care.org/resources/publications/

Mourão, S and Lourenço, M (eds) (2015) *Early years second language education: International perspectives on theory and practice.* London: Routledge.

Murphy, VA (2014) *Second language learning in the early school years: Trends and contexts.* Oxford: Oxford University Press.

OECD (2014) OECD Family Database www.oecd.org/social/family/database

Rixon, S (2013) *British Council survey of policy and practice in primary English language teaching worldwide.* London: The British Council.

Stipek, D and Ryan R (1997) Economically disadvantaged pre-schoolers: Ready to learn but further to go. *Developmental Psychology,* 33, 711-723.

UNICEF (2008) *The child care transition: A league table of early childhood education and care in economically advanced countries.* www.unicef-irc.org/publications/pdf/rc8_eng.pdf

UNICEF (2014) data.unicef.org http://data.unicef.org/ecd/early-childhood-education.html

Whitehead, MR (2004) *Language and literacy in the Early Years.* London: Sage.

1

Global Perspectives

1.1

North America

Rethinking early childhood education for English language learners: the role of language[2]

Fred Genesee, McGill University, Montreal, Canada

There is an increasing proportion of children in English-speaking countries who grow up speaking other languages exclusively or predominantly during the pre-school years. When these children begin school, they may have virtually no proficiency in English or relatively little. In this chapter, these children will be referred to as English language learners, or ELLs. For example, in Canada, more than 2.2 million families (of which 40 per cent are children or youth) immigrated to Canada between 1991 and 2000, the highest number of any decade during the preceding century (Statistics Canada, 2001); and this number was expected to increase as the Canadian government increases immigration quotas (Canadian School Boards Association Consultation Paper, 2006). In the US, in 2007, about 10.8 million (or 20 per cent) of school-age children spoke a language other than English at home, and this number is expected to increase 50 per cent by 2025 (Passel and Cohen, 2008). There is a number of explanations for these demographic facts, the primary one being increased immigration of families and children from non-English-speaking, underdeveloped regions of the world to more prosperous English-speaking regions. At the same time, many children who come to school with no or limited proficiency in English are not immigrants or the children of immigrants; but rather are born and raised in English-speaking countries and grow up learning only or primarily the families' heritage languages. This, in turn, may reflect a number of different factors, including lack of parental proficiency in the societal language, parental choice to maintain the heritage language by using it in the home during the pre-school years, or "ghettoisation" of children in communities where the heritage language is the lingua franca among community members and, thus, the language to be learned for day-to-day communication.

[2] I would like to thank Kathryn Lindholm-Leary, San Jose State University, California, for insightful comments on an earlier version of this chapter.

Children who come to school with no or limited proficiency in English can face a number of significant challenges. From a linguistic point of view, they must learn the societally dominant language for both social and academic purposes along with the cultural norms that govern its use in school and in the community at large. At the same time, they must learn literacy skills along with general and subject-specific knowledge and skills – in science, mathematics, or social studies, for example, in English. As a result of the growing recognition of the importance of the pre-school years for children's cognitive, social and personal development (Ontario Ministry of Children and Youth Services, 2007), more and more children begin education during the pre-school years. On the one hand, increasing participation in pre-school programmes is to be favoured since it appears to close the achievement gap between ELL and mainstream students (Barnett and Hustedt, 2003; Frede and Barnett, 2011). On the other hand, the linguistic challenges that ELL children typically face at the onset of formal schooling may begin earlier if they attend pre-school programmes.

These are also challenges for parents, childcare workers and educators responsible for raising and educating ELLs because their knowledge and assumptions about how best to promote the educational development of these children may be called into question. There are indeed good reasons to question our assumptions and policies with respect to best practices for educating ELLs, not least of which is extensive evidence in the US, for example, that many ELLs, on average, underperform in school in comparison to mainstream English-speaking students (Abedi et al., 2006; Kim and Herman, 2009). As a result, as adults, they can experience disproportionately high rates of unemployment, poverty, drug- and alcohol-related problems and poor health. While all of these outcomes cannot be explained exclusively in terms of quality of education per se, there is no doubt that success in school can serve to ameliorate the most severe forms of these difficulties (Barnett and Hustedt, 2003).

This chapter focuses on the role of language in the educational success, difficulty or failure of ELL children. While focusing on language makes a great deal of sense given the importance of language in education, it is critical to recognise that language-related issues are not the only or even necessarily the most serious challenges faced by ELLs in school. Depending on the background of specific children or groups of children, their academic success can be jeopardised by issues related to poverty, poor health, trauma linked to immigration and/or pre-immigrant experiences, cultural differences between home and school, school and school district policies and practices (including assessment requirements), the quality of educational materials, instruction and curriculum, teachers' attitudes and inadequate teacher preparation. Of these, socio-economic status has been shown to be particularly potent (National Task Force on Early Childhood Education for Hispanics, 2009; OECD, 2010). Individual ELLs can experience a number of different challenges simultaneously with significant and commensurate effects on their academic outcomes (Lindholm-Leary, 2010). It is also important to recognise that not all ELL students do poorly in school and that the academic performance of ELLs can vary from country to country. Two notable exceptions to the general pattern described above are Canada (Aydemir et al., 2008) and Australia (Cobb-Clark and Trong-Ha Nguyen, 2010). Research has shown that immigrant ELLs in these countries, on average, perform as well or better than native-born students on standardised tests of academic achievement. Explanations for these findings are not entirely clear; but one reason can be found in these countries' immigration policies, which favour relatively highly educated immigrants from middle class backgrounds. Whatever the complete explanation of these between-country differences, suffice to say here that the academic performance of ELLs can reflect complex, national-level factors and that across-the-board stereotypes about the academic achievement of ELLs are to be avoided. Because the educational outcomes of ELLs in Canada are atypical, the focus in this chapter is on issues and challenges in educating young ELLs in the US with secondary references to Canada where useful.

The following sections examine the beliefs and attitudes of North American educators and the public at large with respect to the role of language in early childhood education and during the primary school grades (ages five to seven) because these beliefs have shaped policies and practices with respect to ELLs in significant ways. Empirical evidence that refutes these beliefs is then discussed and alternative strategies for educating ELLs based on this evidence are then considered.

Beliefs about educating ELLs

Policies and practices with respect to educating ELLs have historically been driven largely by beliefs and attitudes with respect to language learning and, in particular, dual language learning (see also Espinosa, 2013). These beliefs and attitudes, in turn, have reflected a combination of what might be called "common sense" as well as scientific theories of what is best for ELLs when it comes to learning English. Socio-political and legislative factors have also played a significant role. For example, in the 1960s, the Office of Civil Rights (OCR) in the US declared that educating ELLs in mainstream classrooms using only English instruction, without special provisions to respond to their special linguistic and cultural backgrounds, was a violation of their civil rights because it was a form of discrimination based on ethnic and/or national origin. The OCR also argued that instruction in English only without special provisions or accommodations effectively precluded ELLs from equal access to the benefits of education in comparison to children who were already proficient in English. It was at that time that bilingual forms of education for ELLs emerged; these programmes are described briefly in a later section. Subsequent legislation in a number of states in the US eroded support for and access to bilingual programmes. For example, in 1998, Proposition 227 in California resulted in state legislation that established a number of administrative requirements that significantly reduced enrolment in bilingual programmes. Several other states subsequently passed English-only legislation. Notwithstanding the importance of such socio-political and legislative factors, this chapter focuses on the important role that attitudes and beliefs about language learning and about the relationship between language and learning in general have played in shaping educational policies and practices with respect to young ELLs.

Generally speaking, educational policies and practices concerning the role of language in the education of ELLs have been shaped by four commonly held beliefs (see Cummins, 1981; Grosjean, 1985; and Cook, 1992 for earlier renditions of these ideas):

1. Learning and using more than one language is burdensome and has associated costs or disadvantages.
2. Young children are effective and efficient (second) language learners.
3. Amount of exposure is a significant correlate of language competence.
4. The languages of bi- and multilinguals are separate neuro-cognitive systems.

Taken together, these beliefs have important implications for thinking about when and how ELLs should learn English – for example, to what extent ELLs should begin to learn English during the pre-school years in order to prepare them for formal schooling in English; the role of the L1 in pre-school and school programmes where English is otherwise used as the only language of instruction; whether ELLs should receive instruction in the home language to ensure acquisition of academic objectives while they learn English; and whether their achievement in non-language subjects (such as mathematics or science) and in English (such as reading and writing) should be assessed in the same ways and, in the case of English proficiency, using the same benchmarks as are used with monolingual native English-speaking students. In fact, these beliefs have been the historically prevalent way of thinking about educating young ELLs and about preparing them for school entry. The influence of these beliefs and attitudes has been most evident in educational programmes during the elementary (primary) and secondary school years, but has also impacted thinking about pre-school education as more and more children attend pre-school programmes.

In brief, these beliefs and 'theories' underlie what might variously be referred to as assimilationist, submersion or 'monolingualist' educational policies and practices (Wiley, 2014). Under these views, for most of the 20th century to the present, most ELLs have attended pre-school and primary school programmes in which they have been educated exclusively in English along with native English-speaking children. They might receive some instruction or support in English-as-a-second-language (ESL) in separate (or pull-out) classrooms by specialist ESL teachers; but, otherwise, formal instruction in language arts and the rest of the curriculum has been and continues to be provided by teachers who often have little or no background on how to teach language or other school subjects to students who are learning through a language they are still acquiring. Individualised instruction (or individual educational programmes, IEPs), a cornerstone of contemporary general education, that reflects ELLs' specific backgrounds has not been commonplace for ELLs, although it has become more common recently.

Belief in the importance of early acquisition of English has extended to families who often think that they should begin to use English with their children as soon and as much as possible so they are prepared for English-only schooling. In fact, at times, parents of ELL children have been encouraged to use English with their children even though they themselves might not speak English well. Wave upon wave of immigrant parents, committed to ensuring the academic success of their children, have abandoned use of the heritage language in the home and made valiant efforts to use English, even when they lacked full proficiency in that language (Wong-Fillmore, 1991). All of this makes sense if the four foundational beliefs presented earlier are valid. Evaluations of the educational outcomes of ELLs during the school years indicate that the approach suggested by these beliefs is not working. To cite one example, the 2005 report of the National Assessment of Education Progress (e.g. see Fry, 2007) indicated that ELLs scored significantly lower than national norms and other learners in the nation's schools (see also Lindholm-Leary and Borsato, 2006, for a review). This then raises the question of the validity of the foundational beliefs that have dominated thinking about educating ELLs.

Examining beliefs

In this section, research is considered that examines the validity of each of the general beliefs presented in the preceding section. This review is necessarily selective and simplified owing to space limitations; but it nevertheless serves to highlight research findings that challenge conventional ways of thinking about educating ELLs and opens the door to considering alternative strategies that might be more effective.

To begin, it has been widely believed that learning and using more than one language is burdensome and has associated costs and disadvantages (Belief 1). However, this commonly held belief runs into empirical obstacles from diverse sources. An assumption of this particular belief seems to be that the human neuro-cognitive capacity for learning and using language is fundamentally monolingual in nature and, thus, learning and/or using two languages requires additional cognitive resources that can stretch learners' capacity and, in turn, limit their linguistic and communicative competence. Indeed, an early theory of bilingual acquisition argued that children who grow up learning two languages during the pre-school years go through an early stage when input from the two languages is treated as part of a single system (e.g. Volterra and Taeschner, 1978). Neuro-cognitive separation of the two languages was thought to emerge only during the third year of life and, thus, it was only after two years of age that these learners were truly bilingual. Bilingual children's use of words or grammatical structures from their two languages in the same sentence or conversation (i.e. code-switching or code-mixing) was taken as evidence in support of this theory.

This view has been rejected by extensive research, and there is now a consensus that young children exposed to two languages from birth are able to distinguish their two languages, functionally and probably therefore cognitively, from the earliest stages of development (e.g., Paradis et al., 2011). That learning and using two languages is not burdensome is also attested by evaluations in the U.S. of the language abilities of pre-school and school-age ELLs in bilingual programmes in which at least 50% of instruction takes place in Spanish and the rest in English (see Genesee and Lindholm-Leary, 2012, for more detailed discussions of these issues). Findings from these studies reveal, that contrary to the above expectations, ELLs in bilingual programmes demonstrate the same or even higher levels of ability in

English as ELLs in English-only programmes, and they similarly attain the same levels of academic achievement as ELLs in programmes in which instruction is provided only in English (Lindholm-Leary and Borsato, 2006).

While there are other sources of evidence that challenge the notion that dual language learning is burdensome, perhaps the most compelling evidence comes from studies of children who grow up learning two language from birth under conditions of neuro-cognitive impairment. Arguably, children with specific language impairment (SLI) or Down Syndrome, for example, who have well documented difficulties acquiring language that are known (in the case of children with Down Syndrome) or thought (in the case of children with SLI) to be linked to genetically-based neuro-cognitive impairments should have greater difficulty learning two languages than one. Contrary to this hypothesis, research on such learners indicates that they do not differ significantly from children with the same impairments who are learning only one language (e.g., Paradis et al., 2003; Kay-Raining Bird, et al., 2005; see also Marinova-Todd and Mirenda, in press, for research on children with Autism Spectrum Disorder), although they do demonstrate more language-related difficulties than children without these challenges. It is difficult to reconcile these diverse findings with the belief that the human neuro-cognitive capacity for language learning is fundamentally monolingual and is challenged when required to learn more than one language.

It is also widely believed that young children are effective and efficient language learners (Belief 2). As a result, it is generally expected that second language (L2) acquisition by young children will proceed quickly and effortlessly and will result in native-like proficiency, largely through untutored, natural exposure to the target language, especially if such exposure involves contact with native-speaking peers. This thinking is based, in part, on the critical period hypothesis of language learning, according to which the human neuro-cognitive abilities that are responsible for language learning are particularly 'plastic' during early development, usually thought to be between birth and 12 to 13 years of age. Accordingly, it is during this critical period when language learning is relatively effortless and results in complete mastery of language (e.g. Long, 1990).

With respect to L2 acquisition, there is evidence that, other things being equal, children are more likely to attain native-like levels of oral proficiency, or at least higher levels of proficiency in an L2 in the long run than learners who begin to learn an L2 when older (Long, 1990). However, there is no consensus on how early is early enough for native-like competence to be acquired and, in fact, whether monolingual native-like capacity is possible among any learners who begin to acquire a language after one or two years of age. In this regard, research conducted in Sweden by Abrahamsson and Hyltenstam (2009) examined the language abilities of immigrants to Sweden who had immigrated at different ages, including during the pre-school years. In comparison to native Swedish speakers, most pre-school-age immigrants in their study did not demonstrate native-like competence in Swedish as an L2 even after more than 20 years of exposure when a battery of diverse and demanding language tests were used. In a similar vein, our own research on internationally-adopted (IA) children from China has shown that they score significantly lower than matched non-adopted children on a variety of standardised measures of language ability, including expressive and receptive vocabulary and grammar (Delcenserie and Genesee, 2013). This was found even though, as a group, the adoptees had begun learning the adopted language between 12 and 24 months of age and even though they had exclusive exposure to the adopted language post-adoption. These children did not show similar delays in general cognitive, socio-emotional or non-verbal memory development, suggesting that their language development was uniquely affected by their delayed exposure. These findings suggest that even when L2 acquisition begins at an early age, it may be more complex and difficult than has generally been thought.

Moreover, commonly held beliefs about how easily young learners can acquire an L2 do not take into account the complexities of language learning in the context of schooling. In this regard, North American education researchers increasingly distinguish between language for social communication and language for academic purposes as a means of understanding the academic development and, in particular, the academic difficulties experienced by some learners. While there is no consensual definition of academic language, for present purposes the succinct definition offered by Chamot and O'Malley (1994: 40) will suffice. According to these authors, academic language is *"the language that is used by teachers and students for the purposes of acquiring new knowledge and skills... imparting new information, describing abstract ideas and developing students' conceptual understanding"*. To expand on Chamot and O'Malley's definition, academic language refers to the specialised vocabulary, grammar, discourse/textual and functional skills associated with academic instruction and mastery of academic material and tasks; it includes both oral and written forms of language.

Emerging evidence indicates that the acquisition of L2 oral language for academic purposes in school-age students is a complex process that takes considerably longer than previously thought. In a review of research on the oral language development of ELLs in the US, Saunders and O'Brien (2006) concluded that ELLs, including those in all-English programmes, are seldom awarded ratings of "generally proficient" (but not native-like) in English even by grade 3. In fact, none of the studies they reviewed reported average ratings of "native-like" in English until grade 5. In a longitudinal study of 24 ELLs (called ESL in the study) in Edmonton, Canada, Paradis (2006) found that after 21 months of exposure to English, only 40 per cent performed within the normal range for native-speakers on a test of grammatical morpheme production (e.g. the use of "s" to pluralise nouns or "ed" to express past tense in verbs), 65 per cent on receptive vocabulary, and 90 per cent on story grammar in narratives. Similarly, Parrish et al. (2006) note that a report of the American Institutes for Research evaluation of the implementation of Proposition 227, legislation that curbed access to bilingual forms of education, concluded that the "current probability of an EL *(English learner)* being redesignated to fluent English proficient status *after ten years in California* to be less than 40 per cent" (p. III-1) (text in italics added by chapter author). They went on to state: "we estimate that 75 per cent of EL students are not redesignated [*as fluent English proficient*] after five years of schooling" (p. III-33).

Their reclassification figure of only 25 per cent is close to the figure reported by Grissom (2004), who found that only 30 per cent of ELLs were reclassified within five years.

Bolstering these results, findings from a number of reviews and individual studies on proficiency levels in English among ELLs indicate that it can take ELLs between five to seven years to achieve proficiency in English for academic purposes (August and Hakuta, 1997; Cummins, 1981; Lindholm-Leary and Borsato, 2006; Thomas and Collier, 2002). In these studies, language proficiency was defined in terms of performance on standardised tests of the type used to assess academic progress and, thus, can be considered measures of language for academic purposes. In a review of research on child ELL learners, Paradis (2006: 401) concluded that *"obtaining oral language proficiency in the L2 on par with native speakers can take most of the elementary school years"* and, moreover, that there is considerable inter-individual variation in rate of L2 development. These estimates contrast with informal impressions that children can acquire highly proficient levels of competence in an L2 for social purposes very quickly.

An equally complex and related issue concerns the expectation that more exposure to English in school will result in greater proficiency than less exposure (Belief 3). Research findings from both minority language ELLs learning English in the U.S. and from majority language students learning in L2 immersion programmes in Canada (e.g., English-speaking students learning French in bilingual programmes; see Genesee, 2004, for a review) indicate that amount of time or exposure alone cannot explain the language learning outcomes that have been reported for students in these programmes. On the one hand, research in the U.S. and Canada has shown that time or amount of exposure does matter when it comes to learning a minority language; for example, ELLs in Spanish-English bilingual programmes with 90% exposure to Spanish achieve higher levels of proficiency in Spanish than ELLs in bilingual programmes with only 50% exposure to Spanish (Genesee and Lindholm-Leary, 2012). On the other hand, studies of the English language development of Spanish-speaking ELLs in the U.S. indicate that the level of proficiency that they achieve in English, the majority group language, is not related to amount of exposure to English in school in a simple correlational fashion (e.g., Lindholm-Leary and Borsato, 2006). In other words, more exposure to and instruction in English in school does not necessarily result in higher levels of proficiency in English. In this regard, Saunders and O'Brien noted that rates of progress in attaining proficiency in oral English by the end of elementary school were "strikingly consistent" for ELLs in different types of programmes, described in more detail in the next section, regardless of how much instruction in English they received. ELLs who receive some instruction in English in the primary grades sometimes demonstrate an initial advantage in English over ELLs with reduced instruction in English; but, these differences disappear by the end of elementary school. Of particular note, similar findings have been found in bilingual (Spanish-English) pre-school programmes for low SES ELLs in the U.S. (Barnett et al., 2007; Lindholm-Leary, 2014; Rodriguez et al., 1995). More specifically, ELLs in bilingual pre-school programmes did not differ significantly from ELLs in English programmes on English language tests; in contrast, the bilingual programme participants showed significant advantages in Spanish in comparison to the English programme participants. Clearly, the minority-majority status of the language matters, with exposure in school being much less important when it comes to learning the majority language, English, than a minority language such as Spanish or French.

This is not to say that exposure is totally unimportant. Below some minimal level of exposure, bilingual children are likely to demonstrate less proficiency or competence than monolinguals (see Thordardottir, 2011, for evidence on simultaneous bilinguals). However, children who are learning two languages do not need as much exposure as monolingual children to attain native-like levels of proficiency. In other words, they can perform as well with less input. That sheer amount of instruction in English is not related in any simple and direct way to achievement in English will probably come as no surprise to most educators who understand that instructional time must be turned into effective teaching and learning to pay off. The question is what constitutes effective instruction for ELLs – pedagogical factors matter, and will be discussed in the next section.

Finally, educators, and to some extent researchers, have long assumed that the languages of bilingual students are separate and, thus, that development and use of each language is independent, what Cummins (1981) referred to as the separate underlying proficiency hypothesis (Belief 4). That this notion is taken seriously is evident in educational programmes for ELLs that traditionally have discouraged and, in some cases, even prohibited ELLs from using their home languages in school. Even most current programmes that use two languages for instruction – as in US bilingual programmes – relegate each language to designated subjects or instructional times on the assumption that using both languages or drawing links between the two is not useful and may even be detrimental to mastery of English. Even in bilingual immersion programmes for majority language English-speaking students in Canada, teachers systematically avoid using both English and French during the same instructional periods, and students are required to likewise use only French during French periods and English during English periods.

To the extent that this hypothesis is true, it would explain, at least in part, the other beliefs under discussion. In particular, it could account for the belief that learning and using two languages is burdensome and that exposure has a significant impact on language proficiency because it would mean that bilinguals need to learn twice as much as monolinguals. In contrast, if the acquisition of two languages is interdependent and, in particular, if acquisition of one language facilitates acquisition of aspects of another language, then these beliefs are untenable or, at least, need to be modified to acknowledge that overlap between two languages can result in savings in the time and cognitive effort needed to learn an additional language.

In fact, there is a growing body of scientific research that the languages of bilinguals are not independent of one another and, on the contrary, that the boundaries between the languages of bi- and multilinguals are dynamic and permeable. For example, as noted earlier, researchers have found that child and adult bilinguals and, in particular, simultaneous bilinguals are able to code-mix without violating the grammatical constraints of either language, most of the time (e.g. Paradis et al., 2011). The ability to interweave two languages during oral discourse without violating the grammatical constraints of either language indicates that bilinguals have access to the grammars of both languages simultaneously and automatically – how else could error-free code mixing be explained? There is also a great deal of evidence of significant and positive correlations between reading skills in one language and reading skills in another in bilinguals; the nature and extent of the interaction depends to some extent on the typological similarity of the languages and their orthographic systems (e.g. Genesee and Geva, 2006). Research on the acquisition, comprehension and production of two languages during second language learning and during proficient bilingual performance has revealed further that both linguistic systems are differentially accessible and activated at virtually all times (e.g. Gullifer et al., 2013). Moreover, the two languages of bilinguals share a common cognitive/conceptual foundation that can facilitate the acquisition and use of more than one language for communication, thinking and problem solving. This research also suggests that competence in two, or more, languages engenders the development of sophisticated cognitive skills for negotiating and minimising cross-language competition (Kroll, 2008). Findings from these studies reveal a highly sophisticated system of cognitive representations, access and use, and they deepen our understanding of the language performance of bilinguals that would go unexamined were researchers focused on the cognitive aspect of language characteristic of monolinguals only.

Implications

Taken together, these findings challenge some traditional widely held views concerning language learning in educational programmes for ELLs. Increasingly, North American educators have been motivated by recent findings to explore alternative possibilities to create more effective, evidence-based policies and practices. Some of the implications of these findings for educating young ELLs are discussed in this section; they will be reviewed with respect to three aspects of early childhood education and instruction: (1) language of instruction, (2) oral language development, and (3) pre- and early literacy instruction.

1) Language of instruction

The most radical innovation to have been tried in educating ELLs in the US involves the language of instruction. More specifically, educators in the US have experimented with the effectiveness of educating ELLs using the heritage language along with English for instruction of significant portions of the curriculum, including literacy- and non-literacy-related subjects. Very briefly, in bilingual elementary school programmes for Spanish-speaking ELLs, for example, between 50 and 90 per cent of the curriculum is taught in Spanish in the primary grades – Kindergarten to Grade 2. Depending on the particular programme, instruction in English increases gradually after Grade 2 so that it is the predominant language or only language of instruction by the end of elementary (primary) school (see Genesee and Lindholm-Leary, 2012, for more discussion). The rationale behind these programmes is that teaching literacy and academic subjects initially in a language ELLs already know will permit them to begin to acquire literacy skills right away and, at the same time, to keep up in academic domains while they are learning English. Once their English skills have advanced sufficiently, then ELLs will be better able to keep up to grade-level standards in literacy and other school subjects taught in English. In brief, this approach is thought to be a better way to increase the chances that ELLs will not fall behind and, in fact, will close the gap with native speakers more readily than if they are taught entirely in English.

Likewise, there are bilingual pre-school programmes that use both Spanish along with English (see Barnett et al., 2007; Lindholm-Leary, 2014; and Rodriguez et al., 1995, for examples). For purposes of this discussion, these programmes will be referred to as bilingual pre-school (three to five year olds) and bilingual elementary (primary) school (five to ten year olds) programmes. The first language of a large majority of ELLs in the US is Spanish, and it is for this reason that most bilingual programmes use Spanish along with English and are the focus of discussion in this chapter. While using ELLs' heritage language is clearly not realistic in many settings because there are too many different heritage languages and an insufficient number of qualified teachers who speak those languages, these alternative models of education for ELLs are worth considering here because they pose the most serious challenge to traditional views on how best to educate ELLs. If it can be shown that bilingual instruction in pre-school and/or elementary school programmes does not compromise ELLs' acquisition of English and/or their general academic development or that, to the contrary, it benefits their language and general academic development, then there would be reasons to question traditional beliefs that favour using English only and from early on and, furthermore, to consider alternative educational strategies besides those that are based on exclusive use of English as the language of instruction.

Five fairly recent meta-analyses have examined the achievement of ELLs in bilingual versus English-only elementary school programmes. They all concluded that ELLs in bilingual programmes scored as well as or often better than ELLs in English-only programmes on tests of literacy and other school subjects (e.g. mathematics) in English (see Genesee and Lindholm-Leary, 2012; and Goldenberg, 2008, reviews); at the same time, the bilingual programme participants performed significantly better on measures of Spanish language proficiency. In their review, Genesee and Lindholm-Leary note that ELLs in English-only programmes generally show an advantage in English in the primary grades (K-3), but differences are no longer evident when students are evaluated in the middle or late elementary grades, once English is used as a language of instruction. Lindholm-Leary and Borsato (2006), in fact, report that evaluations in California, which has one of the highest proportions of ELLs in the US, reveal that, in the long run, ELLs in bilingual programmes often outperform ELLs in English-only programmes on state-mandated tests. Evaluations of bilingual pre-school programmes, while few in number, also report that there is no significant advantage in English among ELLs in English-only programmes in comparison to ELLs in bilingual programmes and that bilingual programme participants demonstrate superiority in Spanish (Barnett et al., 2007; Lindholm-Leary, 2014; and Rodriguez et al., 1995).

In sum, the findings from this research do not provide support for the assumptions that underlie early and exclusive focus on English as the language of instruction during either the pre-school or elementary school years. On the contrary, they demonstrate that bilingual programme participants demonstrate superiority with respect to maintenance of the heritage language and, in the case of elementary school programmes, in domains of achievement related to English literacy and general academic achievement. Thus, use of ELLs' heritage language need not be avoided or discouraged in school and, on the contrary, should be encouraged – where possible, in order to support maintenance of the heritage language and take advantage of cross-linguistic facilitation that has been found among such learners, to be discussed in the section on literacy. A further implication of these findings is that parents or caregivers of ELLs with limited proficiency in English themselves need not be discouraged from using the heritage language in favour of English on the assumption that an early start will be advantageous. On the contrary, parents of ELLs should be informed of the potential advantages of developing the heritage language during the pre-school years, especially when parents are literate in that language and can engage in literacy activities in the heritage language with their children. Parents may need guidance on how to do this. Promoting bilingualism through support of the heritage language along with mastery of English is itself a valuable goal in an increasingly globalised environment.

2) Oral language development

Evidence, reported earlier, from research on the oral English language development of ELLs during the school years indicates that ELLs require many years of schooling to acquire native-like proficiency in English for academic purposes. In fact, many ELLs do not attain native-like or even advanced levels of proficiency by the end of elementary school; these findings are particularly likely among ELLs from low SES backgrounds. This poses serious obstacles to their academic achievement and literacy development because attainment of advanced levels of reading comprehension, which are critical for academic progress as students advance through school, can be impeded by weak oral language skills. Clearly an emphasis on an early start to learning English along with extended exposure to English in school without systematic support do not guarantee the advanced levels of proficiency in oral English that ELLs need to succeed in school in the long run. An important and obvious implication is that ELLs need planned and systematic support in acquiring oral language proficiency in English that is sustained over grades. Support should focus on language for academic or cognitive purposes since most ELLs appear to have little difficulty acquiring sufficient proficiency in English to function socially with their peers and others. The question arises: How can the oral English language development of ELLs be promoted so that, over the long term, they attain advanced levels of proficiency commensurate with the academic demands of the curriculum as they progress through school? Addressing this question brings us to considerations of pedagogy.

The available evidence, albeit limited at present, suggests that a dual-pronged approach is called for. One prong calls for direct instructional support for oral language development. In the US, this form of instruction is often referred to as English Language Development, or ELD. The other prong calls for systematic integration of English oral language instruction with instruction in academic subjects or content. In the US and Canada this is often referred to as sheltered instruction. In contrast to direct language instruction (i.e. ELD instruction), the primary focus of sheltered instruction is to promote general academic achievement by reducing the linguistic demands of the material to be learned. A dual-pronged approach is complementary since language and academic development are inseparable, albeit they may have different primary instructional objectives. Thus, content-based sheltered instruction focuses on advancing ELLs' academic achievement with a secondary focus on advancing their English language development, while ELD instruction aims to directly promote the acquisition of academic language skills that often elude ELLs when no additional support is provided and thereby to enhance ELLs' academic achievement indirectly by making them better able to benefit from academic instruction in English.

Several versions of sheltered language instruction have been proposed for enhancing the general educational outcomes of ELLs in the US: the Sheltered Instruction Observational Protocol (or SIOP, Echevarria and Graves, 2007) is one such approach; the Cognitive Academic Language Learning Approach (CALLA; Chamot and O'Malley, 1994) is another. Both approaches were designed for elementary school-age learners; the SIOP model has been adapted to also apply to pre-school-age learners, but with important modifications (Echevarria, Short and Peterson, 2011). The SIOP Model, which enjoys some empirical support (see Echevarria and Short, 2010, for a review), is a framework for teaching non-language academic subjects (such as social studies) to ELLs using strategies and techniques that make the content of the curriculum comprehensible. At the same time, SIOP serves to promote the development of ELLs' language skills across the four domains of reading, writing, listening and speaking in content-specific domains. In effect, SIOP is a set of pedagogical strategies that seek to circumvent or reduce the linguistic barriers that ELLs face when confronted with academic instruction in English and, at the same time, to enhance ELLs' proficiency in English for academic purposes using the academic curriculum as a vehicle for planning and promoting language development (see Echevarria, Voigt and Short, 2010, and Echevarria, Short and Peterson, 2011, for more detailed discussions of the rationale, empirical justifications for and guidelines for applying this model). SIOP is particularly useful because it conceptualises and considers ELD as part of general educational planning for ELLs and, thus, helps to ensure that ELD instruction is part of a coherent plan for educating ELLs.

Turning to ELD, at present, the research evidence on what constitutes effective ELD instruction is limited but growing, especially when it comes to pre-school learners (see Goldenberg et al., 2013; Saunders and Goldenberg, 2010; and Snow and Katz, 2010, for overviews of what is currently thought to be effective ELD instruction). There are significant areas of overlap in the recommendations emanating from current research and professional discussions of effective education for pre-school-age and elementary-school-age ELLs. With respect to pre-school programmes, current evidence-based views are that high quality pre-school programmes can be effective learning environments for both monolingual English children and ELLs (see Saunders and Goldenberg, 2010, and Snow and Katz, 2010, for specific recommendations for elementary school contexts). Goldenberg and his colleagues (p. 95), for example, concluded that the features of what they refer to as "generic" high quality pre-school programmes "appear to support the learning and development of young DLLs (i.e. ELLs, added by author) as well as monolingual English children". Their conclusions, like those of others, are understandably cautious because of the paucity of research and the lack of a single definition of "high-quality pre-school programme". In short, what we know to be effective early childhood education for monolingual children can serve as the foundation for designing pre-school programmes for ELLs.

At the same time, as Goldenberg and his colleagues and others emphasise, important modifications are called for. At the school and programme level, it is important that a supportive environment be created that is responsive to linguistic and cultural diversity among students in the programme and that such diversity be seen as an asset for both individual learners and the school as a whole. More particularly, this means that: school administrators, education specialists and teachers be knowledgeable about and understand the linguistic and cultural diversity of ELL children in their care; they view ELLs' existing language skills and knowledge as resources to develop; and they know how to harness these resources in the service of their general education. From a language learning point of view, effective early learning environments endorse an additive view of bilingualism and seek to foster development of ELLs' home languages at the same time as they acquire competence in English. In contexts where there are reasonable numbers of ELLs who speak the same heritage languages, this means incorporating those languages in instruction and, as much as possible and appropriate, into the day-to-day life of the classroom. This is advisable not only because research suggests that it will support their acquisition of English and general skills and knowledge, but also because it will create an inclusive classroom environment. Where use of ELLs' heritage language is not feasible, then alternative strategies are possible. For example, partnerships between families, communities and the school can create an additive learning environment by bringing the language and cultural resources linked to students' backgrounds into the school (Roberts, 2009, for suggestions). This can also enhance and enrich the learning environment of mainstream monolingual English learners. Positive teacher attitudes toward diversity and their ELL students and active and positive relationships between parents, the school and teachers have been linked to enhancements in ELL outcomes in pre-school and primary school programmes (Vitiello et al., 2011). In brief, what is important here is that ELLs be viewed in terms of their strengths and that any vestige of attitudes that view language and cultural diversity as problems be replaced with attitudes that support ELLs in their diversity.

Specific modifications to instruction are also called for to enhance the effectiveness of "generic" high quality pre-school programmes. Reviews of research on both pre-school and elementary school programmes for ELLs recommend the following language-related modifications:

1. Intentional or explicit focus on language teaching and, in particular, vocabulary and grammatical features that might be difficult to acquire.

2. Designated times or small group work when language can be the explicit focus of instructional attention.

3. Focus on oral language that is useful for higher order cognitive or academic purposes and is age appropriate, although written forms of language can also be incorporated.

4. Lots of modelling and examples of to-be-learned aspects of language.

5. Plenty of opportunities for children to use and practise targeted language skills.

6. Use of interactive activities that are meaningful and authentic and expand students' opportunities to use language.

7. Pair or small group work with students who are more proficient in English, provided activities are planned carefully to ensure equitable involvement by all members of the group.

8. Use of visuals and realia to make new language, concepts or skills comprehensible and easier to learn.

9. Individualised and adapted instruction to reflect individual ELL's "lived experiences" rather than socio-cultural stereotypes about the ethnolinguistic groups they belong to.

All reviews of research on effective instructional strategies for promoting language and literacy development in ELLs also point to the importance of incorporating ELLs' home languages, where feasible and useful, into instruction; this is particularly true when it comes to pre- and early literacy discussed in the next section (e.g. Goldenberg et al., 2013; Riches and Genesee, 2006; Saunders and Goldenberg, 2010). As noted earlier, use of ELLs' heritage languages for day-to-day instruction may not be realistic in many settings, but strategies for drawing on ELLs' skills and knowledge in the heritage language can include: ELLs with a common heritage language work together using the heritage language on specific tasks and then share their work with other students in English; students bring examples of written language from home to share with other students and the teacher; "bridging time" when teachers work with students to identify similarities and differences between English and their heritage languages (Beeman and Urow, 2012); and teachers teach all students common words or expressions (such as greetings, days of the week) in the various languages of the ELL students in their class. Aside from direct benefits to learning, some of these activities can serve to create a supportive and additive bilingual environment.

3) Development of literacy skills

As noted earlier, extensive research has revealed that there are significant facilitative interactions between the languages of ELLs. While this has been noted in a number of domains of learning, it has been noted most consistently in the acquisition of skills and knowledge related to reading. More specifically, there are significant positive cross-linguistic correlations for phonological awareness, knowledge of the alphabetic principle, word decoding skills, print awareness and general reading ability. Correlations are, of course, larger the more similar the languages. In brief, young ELLs with pre-reading or early reading skills in the heritage language demonstrate better reading skills in English and can acquire reading skills in English more easily than ELLs with no or less well developed early reading skills in the heritage language (see Genesee and Geva, 2006, for an extensive review of the relevant research). In a related vein, evidence from evaluative studies of bilingual pre-school and elementary school programmes for ELLs, discussed earlier, indicates that teaching ELLs to read in the heritage language does not hinder the development of reading skills in English; to the contrary, it can be facilitative (e.g. Espinosa, 2010; Riches and Genesee, 2006). At the same time, literacy instruction in the home language supports biliteracy.

It follows then that when planning literacy instruction for young ELLs, it is helpful if teachers are aware of their ELLs' existing literacy-related skills and of literacy-related practices in the home so that they are better able to individualise instruction that builds on their existing skills. Assuming that all ELLs lack literacy skills is wasteful and may result in students with existing literacy skills in the home language becoming disengaged because instruction does not line up with what they already know and can do. For example, students who already have early decoding skills do not need the same level or kind of support to learn to decode in English as ELLs with no such skills. This can be done even if teachers themselves do not know all of the languages of their students: ask students to identify similarities and differences in sounds, words and grammar in their two languages – even young learners can do this and it helps enhance their metalinguistic awareness, a critical skill in the development of literacy. Similarly, when trying to determine if an ELL might be at risk for reading impairment or reading difficulty, abilities in the heritage language should be taken into account in order to determine whether difficulties learning to read in English are linked to an underlying impairment or are simply a reflection of the student's incomplete mastery of English (Erdos et al., 2014). Teachers, even monolingual teachers, should be encourage to draw on ELLs' literacy skills in the heritage language during literacy instruction (see Lyster et al., 2009, for an example of a biliteracy reading programme). It also follows then that parents who are literate in the heritage language should be encouraged to support their children's acquisition of early literacy skills in the heritage language – by reading to and with their children; by engaging in pretend writing and in sound and word games; and by demonstrating the value of reading and writing in their own use of language in the home. Cloud et al (2009) and Roberts (2009) provide more extensive discussions and practical examples of how to promote the acquisition of literacy skills in ELLs.

Final words

ELLs in many English-dominant countries struggle in school; statistics from countries such as the US indicate that ELLs experience disproportionally high drop-out and failure rates in school. While there is growing evidence that pre-school programmes can enhance children's preparedness for school (Barnett and Hustedt, 2003), if pre-school programmes are designed using the same assumptions and beliefs that underlie current thinking about elementary school education, we risk recreating the same pattern of failure among ELLs in early childhood education programmes as we see in current programmes. This chapter considered how conventional beliefs and attitudes about second language teaching and learning and about dual language acquisition in general may be undermining our attempts to create successful pre-school programmes for ELLs. A growing body of evidence from research in education, psycholinguistics and cognitive science challenges conventional views and, in particular, argues that dual language acquisition is not a zero-sum game and, in fact, that maintenance and development of ELLs' heritage language may facilitate English language development. The challenge now is to reconceptualise strategies for educating young ELLs so that educators draw on their existing language skills in ways that are practical, effective and feasible – even in classrooms with ELLs who speak multiple heritage languages and even when teachers themselves are monolingual. Research has begun to address these critical issues and we have the beginnings of better understandings of how to do this; albeit much still remains to be done.

References

Abedi, J, Courtney, M, Leon, S, Kao, J and Azzam, T (2006) *English Language Learners and Math Achievement: A Study of Opportunity to Learn and Language Accommodation* (CSE Report 702, 2006). Los Angeles: University of California, Center for the Study of Evaluation/National Center for Research on Evaluation, Standards, and Student Testing.

Abrahamsson, N and Hyltenstam, K (2009) Age of onset and nativelikeness in a second language: listener perception versus linguistic scrutiny. *Language Learning*, 59, 249–306.

August, D and Hakuta, K (eds) (1997) *Improving schooling for language minority children: A research agenda.* Washington, DC: National Academy Press.

Aydemir, A, Chen, WH and Corak, M (2008) *Intergenerational education mobility among the children of Canadian immigrants.* Institute for the Study of Labor (IZA) Discussion Paper 3759. http://ftp.iza.org/dp3759.pdf (accessed May 27, 2014).

Barnett, SW and Hustedt, JT (2003) *Pre-school: The most important grade.* Educational Leadership, April 2003.

Barnett, SW, Yarosz, DJ, Thomas, J, Jung, K and Blanco, D (2007) Two-way and monolingual English immersion in pre-school education: An experimental comparison. *Early Childhood Research Quarterly, 22,* 277-293.

Beeman, K and Urow, C (2012) *Teaching for Biliteracy: Strengthening bridges between languages.* Philadelphia: Caslon.

Canadian School Boards Association Consultation Paper (2006) *Meeting the Language Learning and Settlement Needs of Immigrant Children and Youth in Canada's School Systems.* www.opsba.org/index.php?q=system/files/CSBA_Draft_Consultation_SLL.pdf (accessed May 27, 2014).

Chamot, AU and O'Malley, JM (1994) *The CALLA handbook: Implementing the cognitive academic language learning approach* White Plains, NY: Addison Wesley Longman.

Cloud, N, Genesee, F and Hamayan, E (2009) *Literacy Instruction for English Language Learners.* Portsmouth, NH: Heinle & Heinle.

Cobb-Clark, DA and Trong-Ha Nguyen (2010) *Immigration background and the intergenerational correlation in education.* Institute for the Study of Labor (IZA) Discussion Paper 4985. www.iza.org/en/webcontent/publications/papers/viewAbstract?dp_id=4985 (accessed May 27, 2014).

Cook, V (1992) Evidence of multicompetence. *Language Learning, 42,* 557-591.

Cummins, J (1981) 'The role of the primary language development in promoting educational success for language minority students', in *Schooling and Language Minority Students: A Theoretical Framework.* Los Angeles, CA: California Department of Education.

Delcenserie, A and Genesee, F (2013) Language and memory abilities of internationally-adopted children from China. *Journal of Child Language.* http://dx.doi.org/10.1017/S030500091300041X

Echevarria, J and Graves, A (2007) *Sheltered content instruction: Teaching English language learners with diverse abilities,* 3rd Ed. Boston: Allyn & Bacon.

Echevarria, J and Short, D (2010) 'Programmes and practices for effective sheltered instruction', in *Improving Education for English Learners: Research-Based Approaches* (pp. 251-322). Sacramento, CA: California Department of Education.

Echevarria, J, Short, DJ and Peterson, C (2011) *Using the SIOP model with Pre-K and kindergarten English learners.* Upper Saddle River, NJ: Pearson.

Echevarria, J, Vogt, ME and Short, D (2010) *The SIOP model: Making content comprehensible for secondary English learners.* Boston: Allyn & Bacon.

Erdos, C, Genesee, F, Savage, R and Haigh, C (2014) Predicting risk for oral and written language learning difficulties in students educated in a second language. *Applied Psycholinguistics,* 35, 371–398. DOI: 10.1017/S0142716412000422

Espinosa, L (2010) *Getting it right for young children from diverse backgrounds: Applying research to improve practice.* Upper Saddle River: Pearson.

Espinosa, L (2013) PreK-3rd: *Challenging common myths about dual language learners*. Foundation for Child Development, August 2013 #10. http://fcdus.org/ sites/default/files/Challenging%20Common%20Myths%20Update.pdf (accessed June 8, 2014)

Frede, E and Barnett, WS (2011) Why Pre-K is critical to closing the achievement gap. *Principal*, 90(5), 8-11.

Fry, R (2007) *How Far Behind in Math and Reading are English Language Learners?* Washington, DC: Pew Hispanic Center.

Genesee, F (2004) 'What do we know about bilingual education for majority language students?', in Bhatia, TK and Ritchie W (eds) *Handbook of Bilingualism and Multiculturalism* (pp. 547-576). Malden, MA: Blackwell.

Genesee, F and Geva, E (2006) 'Cross-linguistic relationships in working memory, phonological processes, and oral language, Chapter 7', in August, D and Shanahan, T (eds) *Developing literacy in second language learners. Report of the National Literacy Panel on Minority-Language Children and Youth*, pp. 175-184. Mahwah, NJ: Lawrence Erlbaum.

Genesee, F and Lindholm-Leary, K (2012) 'The education of English language learners', in Harris, K, Graham, S and Urdan, T et al. (eds) *APA Handbook of Educational Psychology*, pp. 499-526. Washington DC: APA Books.

Goldenberg, C (2008) Teaching English language learners: What the research does – and does not say. *American Educator, 32*, 8-23.

Goldenberg, C, Nemeth, K, Hicks, J, Zepeda, M, and Cardona, LM (2013) 'Programme elements and teaching practices to support young dual language learners', in *California's Best Practices for Young Dual Language Learners: Research Overview Papers*. Sacramento, CA: CDE Publications and Education Reviews.

Grissom, JB (2004) Reclassification of English learners. *Education Policy Analysis Archives, 12*, 1–38. Retrieved August 3, 2007, from http://epaa.asu.edu/epaa/ v12n36/

Grosjean, F (1985) The bilingual as a competent but specific speaker-hearer. *Journal of Multilingual and Multicultural Development, 6*, 467-477.

Gullifer, JW, Kroll, JF and Dussias, PE (2013) When language switching has no apparent cost: Lexical access in sentence context. *Frontiers in Psychology*, Retrieved March 10, 2015, from doi:10.3389/fpsyg.2013.00278

Kay-Raining Bird, E, Cleave, P, Trudeau, N, Thodardottir, E, Sutton, A and Thorpe, A (2005) The language abilities of bilingual children with Down syndrome. *American Journal of Speech-Language Pathology, 14*(3), 187-199.

Kim, J and Herman, JL (2009) *A Three-State Study Of English Learner Progress*. (CSE Report 702). Los Angeles: University of California, Center for the Study of Evaluation/National Center for Research on Evaluation, Standards, and Student Testing.

Kroll, JF (2008) Juggling two languages in one mind. *Psychological Science Agenda*. Retrieved March 10 2015 from www.apa.org/science/about/psa/2008/01/kroll. aspx

Lindholm-Leary, K (2014) Bilingual and biliteracy skills in young Spanish-speaking low-SES children: *Impact of instructional language and primary language proficiency. International Journal of Bilingual Education and Bilingualism 17*(2), 144-159. doi: 10.1080/13670050.2013.866625

Lindholm-Leary, K (2010) PROMISE *initiative student outcomes*. San Bernardino, CA: Promise Design Center. http://www.promise-initiative.org/research.html

Lindholm-Leary, KJ and Borsato, G (2006) 'Academic achievement', in Genesee, F, Lindholm-Leary, K, Saunders, W and Christian, D (eds) *Educating English Language Learners* (pp. 176-222). NY: Cambridge University Press.

Long, M (1990) Maturational constraints on language development. *Studies in Second Language Acquisition, 12*, 251-285.

Lyster, R, Collins, L and Ballinger, S (2009) Linking languages through a bilingual read-aloud project. *Language Awareness, 18*, 366-383.

Marinova-Todd, SH and Mirenda, P (in press) 'Language and communication abilities of bilingual children with ASD', in Patterson, J and Rodriguez, BL (eds) *Multilingual perspectives on child language disorders*. Bristol, UK: Multilingual Matters.

National Task Force on Early Childhood Education for Hispanics (2009) *Para nuestros niños: The School readiness and academic achievement in reading and mathematics of young Hispanic children in the US*. (www.ecehispanic.org/work.html)

OECD (2010) *Closing the gap for immigrant students: Policies, practice and performance*. ISBN 978-92-64-086876 (accessed May 20, 2014).

Ontario Ministry of Children and Youth Services (2007) *A Framework for Ontario Early Childhood Settings*. www.children.gov.on.ca/htdocs/English/topics/ earlychildhood/early_learning_for_every_child_today.aspx (accessed May 27, 2014).

Paradis, J (2006) 'Second language acquisition in childhood', in Hoff, E and Shatz, M (eds) *Handbook of Language Development* (pp. 387-405). Oxford, Eng.: Blackwell.

Paradis, J, Crago, M and Genesee, F (2006) Domain-specific versus domain-general theories of the deficit in SLI: Object pronoun acquisition by French-English bilingual children. *Language Acquisition, 13*(1), 33-62.

Paradis, J, Genesee, F and Crago, M (2011) *Dual Language Development and Disorders: A Handbook on Bilingualism and Second Language Learning* (2nd ed). Baltimore, MD: Brookes.

Parrish, T, Linquanti, R, Merickel, A, Quick, H, Laird, J and Esra, P (2006) *Effects of the implementation of Proposition 227 on the education of English learners, K–12: Final report*. San Francisco: WestEd.

Passel, JS and Cohn, D (2008) *US Population Projections: 2005–2050*. Pew Research Center. February 11.

Riches, C and Genesee, F (2006) 'Cross-linguistic and cross-modal aspects of literacy development', in Genesee, F, Lindholm-Leary, K, Saunders, W and Christian, D (eds) *Educating English language learners: A synthesis of research evidence* (pp. 64-108). NY: Cambridge University Press.

Roberts, TA (2009) *No Limits to Literacy: For Pre-school English Learners*. Thousand Oaks, CA: Corwin.

Rodriguez, JL, Diaz, RM, Duran, D and Espinosa, L (1995) The impact of bilingual pre-school education on the language development of Spanish-speaking children. *Early Childhood Research Quarterly, 10*, 475-90.

Saunders, W and O'Brien, G (2006) 'Oral language', in Genesee, F, Lindholm-Leary, K, Saunders, W and Christian, D (eds) *Educating English language learners: A synthesis of research evidence* (pp. 14–63). New York: Cambridge University Press.

Saunders, W and Goldenberg, C (2010) 'Research to guide English language development instruction', in *Improving Education for English Learners: Research-Based Approaches* (pp. 21-82). Sacramento, CA: California Department of Education.

Snow, MA and Katz, A (2010) 'English language development: Foundations and Implementations in Kindergarten through Grade 5', in *Improving Education for English Learners: Research-Based Approaches* (pp. 83-150). Sacramento, CA: California Department of Education.

Statistics Canada (2001) Children of immigrants: how well do they do in school? www.statcan.gc.ca/pub/81-004-x/200410/7422-eng.htm (accessed May 27, 2014).

Thomas, W and Collier, B (2002) *A national study of school effectiveness for language minority students' long-term academic achievement*. Santa Cruz, CA: Center for Research on Education, Diversity and Excellence.

Thordardottir, E (2011) The relationship between bilingual exposure and vocabulary development. *International Journal of Bilingualism, 15*(4), 426-445.

Vitiello, VE, Downer, JT and Williford, AP (2011) 'Pre-school classroom experiences of dual language learners', in Howes, C, Downer, JT and Pianta, RC (eds) *Dual Language Learners in the Early Childhood Classroom*. Baltimore, MD: Brookes.

Volterra, V and Taeschner, T (1978) The acquisition and development of language by bilingual children. *Journal of Child Language, 5*, 311-326.

Wiley, TG (2014) Diversity, super-diversity and monolingual ideology in the United States: Tolerance and intolerance. *Review of Educational Research, 38*, 1-32.

Wong-Fillmore, L (1991) When learning a second language means losing the first. *Early Childhood Research Quarterly, 6*(3), 323-347.

1.2

South America

Early childhood bilingual education in South America

Anne-Marie de Mejía, Universidad de los Andes, Bogotá, Colombia

Introduction

Conscious of the processes of globalisation and internationalisation, Latin American governments have increasingly started to implement policies designed to improve foreign language proficiency in their populations (Banfi, 2015). Together with these initiatives, there has been a corresponding emphasis on young learners, as there exists a widespread perception among the general public that *"if foreign languages are not learnt in the early years of schooling, the opportunities for mastery later on are dramatically and negatively affected"* (Banfi, 2015: 2). Thus, bilingual schools catering for pupils from the higher social strata have become increasingly popular throughout the region.

A parallel development has been the implementation of bilingual programmes (overwhelmingly English–Spanish) in state (public) schools. Consequently, in 2008 Mexico launched the National Plan of English for Basic Education (Plan Nacional de Inglés para Educación Básica) incorporating a Content and Language Integrated Learning (CLIL) approach and designed to cater for students from kindergarten up to the end of middle school education (from the ages of five to 15) (Mexican Ministry of Education 2011, cited on the PNIEB website, 2014).

In Argentina in 2001, the City of Buenos Aires, which has a long tradition of foreign language teaching and learning (Banfi, 2013), set out to provide foreign language tuition (mainly in English) in the belief that the learning of a foreign language in the state-run schools, particularly those located in socially disadvantaged areas, would raise educational standards. Furthermore, there was the assumption that introducing a foreign language at an early age, (from the age of six, in this case), would improve the students' academic and employment prospects (Banfi and Rettaroli, 2008). In these bilingual (now officially plurilingual) schools the children are taught by two teachers. On the one hand, there is the class teacher who teaches all subjects (Spanish, Science, Social Science, and Mathematics) in Spanish. On the other, the foreign language teacher teaches the foreign language. However, curricular content is not taught in the foreign language.

A third example is Colombia, where The National Bilingual Programme (Programa Nacional de Bilingüismo), started in 2004 and now renamed The National English Programme (Programa Nacional de Inglés), emphasises the beginning of the learning of English from Grade 1 (five years old). Although the Colombian Ministry of Education has foregrounded the teaching of the language itself, rather than learning through English, the local Education Secretariat in Bogotá has drawn up a programme (Abouchaar et al., 2009) which contemplates the introduction of bilingual education through content teaching and learning in English, beginning in the primary school from Grade 1 onwards.

Thus it can be seen that both local and national policy makers have taken on board the importance of young children being educated through the medium of English, in the hope that by the time they finish secondary education, they will be able to achieve an intermediate or high intermediate level of proficiency in the foreign language. As one school in Argentina, cited in Banfi (2010), proclaims:

> The pupils enter into the world of reading and writing by means of a great variety of activities organised in thematic units which respond to the children´s interests. This bilingual programme provides a solid basis for the continuation of learning in [primary and secondary] education. (p. 38)

> Los alumnos entran al mundo de la lectura y de la escritura a través de una gran variedad de actividades organizadas en unidades temáticas que responden a los intereses de los niños. Este programa bilingüe brinda una base sólida para continuar los aprendizajes en educación básica.

Moreover, as Banfi (2015) notes, there is increasing awareness among politicians as well as educational administrators in the region that beginning learning in a foreign language from an early age leads to results that are *"more clearly and directly perceived [and that makes] it an attractive proposition for those searching for a quick return on their educational or political investment"* (p. 9). However, when we revise regional policy documents, such as a recent report by UNESCO, which refer to the state of education in Latin America and the Caribbean, there is little or no reference to the learning of foreign languages at an early age, even though there is a general recognition that *"Investment in the early years has also been found to be strongly associated with better long-term academic performance"* (UNESCO, 2013: 43).

Bearing in mind this brief contextualisation, this chapter will present certain key issues that characterise early childhood education provision in Latin America carried out through the medium of English for children who are for the most part native speakers of Spanish or Portuguese. There will be special emphasis on three topics: biliteracy, teacher training and parents, as these themes have been found to be of particular interest in the region. Then, there will be a discussion about how far these issues raised in a South American context resonate with the results of studies carried out in North America and in Europe.

Biliteracy

This section will discuss five studies carried out in three different Latin American contexts: Colombia, Ecuador and Mexico. All are concerned with the teaching and learning of reading and writing in two languages with different emphases: code switching in storytelling events, the examination of pupils' similarities and differences in written production in English and Spanish, as well as an analysis of the effect of adopting a biliterate perspective in the teaching and learning of initial literacy processes. The section ends with the consideration of a case study of the biliterate development of a young US–Mexican child.

An early project in Colombia (de Mejía, 1998) focused on code switching in bilingual storytelling in two early immersion classrooms in Cali with pre-school children between the ages of four and five. Using visual supporting material, it was noted that both teachers told, rather than read, the stories to their young learners and switched between Spanish and English throughout the sessions. The teachers generally exhibited rather relaxed attitudes to their own code-switching practices and those of their pupils, as can be seen by this comment in one of the interviews conducted during the study:

> At this moment I'm not worried about the [mixture of languages] and the parents aren't either; on the contrary they told me it was good … it´s been … something very positive that they [the children] integrate little by little the other language into their normal life. (de Mejía, 2004: 37)

> En este momento, no me preocupa [la mescla de idiomas, a los papás tampoco, sino que al contario, me lo comentaban como cosa buena … ha sido … algo muy positivo que ellos [los niños] van integrando poco a poco el otro idioma a su vida normal.

The study found that the classroom code switching functioned not only as a meaning-making device, or 'contextualisation cue' in Gumperz's (1982) terms, but also allowed pupils to collaborate in the story-telling events. Analysis of the code-switching patterns observed in the classroom interaction between teachers and pupils showed how bilingual language use added a further dimension of meaning to the interaction. Through the skillful and flexible use of code switching, the young learners were able to access their first language in the process of learning English, thus helping to maximise learning opportunities in the bilingual classroom. Consequently, according to the results of this research, code switching should be seen as *"a vital communicative resource available to children and teachers who share proficiency in the children´s L1 and not as a practice relegated to a strategy of last resort"* (de Mejía, 1998: 9).

In 2005, Jo-Ellen Simpson published a chapter based on a study of early childhood writing in English and Spanish in an early immersion school in Quito, Ecuador. In this context, English was a foreign language for the majority of students, and in pre-school there was a focus on oral language development along with pre-reading and pre-writing activities. By Grade 1 the children were able to produce short texts in both languages. As Simpson notes, the teaching of writing was primarily carried out in English. Spanish was used mainly in the Spanish language class and in art, music and physical education.

The author justifies the importance of the study by referring to an earlier research review carried out by Reppen and Grabe (1993), which found that writing in Spanish has often been described as being "more ornate and formal" (p.117) than writing in English. These researchers were interested in children's writing in order to locate the source of the "elaborate style" of native Spanish speaking adolescents and young adults tested in earlier studies. After analysing essays from three groups of fifth-grade students, some native English speaking and some native Spanish speaking, it was found that the Spanish-speaking L1 fifth graders (writing in English) have characteristics similar to those of older Spanish-speaking participants from the other studies. Reppen and Grabe (1993) came to the conclusion that this style of writing must be culturally influenced because the children in the study were quite young and had not received much formal training in writing in Spanish.

Simpson was interested in finding out about writers who were six or seven years old, so she decided to examine the writing of first grade students to see if they reflected the same tendencies. This study also discussed the possibility of reverse transfer of writing style — from the foreign language to the native language — due to the fact that the policy at the school was to emphasise reading and writing in English, while the teaching and learning of written skills in Spanish was limited to one hour per day. Ten samples of writing in English and ten samples in Spanish were randomly chosen from first grade portfolios. For the purpose of analysis, these were divided into T-units, defined as *"one main clause with all the subordinate clauses attached to it"* (Hunt, 1965: 20, cited in Simpson, 2005).

The researcher came to the conclusion that the first grade children who participated in the study had similar syntactic ability in both their languages, although they wrote longer narratives in Spanish than in English. Furthermore, the analysis of sentence connectors showed greater variety and number in Spanish than in English, which Simpson attributed to the children´s higher level of oral competence in Spanish. An interesting finding had to do with the analysis of pupil errors in the two languages. It was found that, except for spelling, the errors in the two languages were quite different. For example, there was evidence of a tendency in English to omit words more than in Spanish. In addition, there were twice as many correct T-units in English, suggesting to the researcher that the students had learned a number of simple sentences in English and were able to use them in their own writing. However, when they had to use English in new situations, they made many more mistakes than in Spanish, which showed a consistent level of errors across all T-units. In Spanish the children had to struggle with the correct use of accents and with word spacing. They often divided words that should not be divided, such as: a wela and a guelo for abuela (grandmother) and abuelo (grandfather). According to the results of the study, these differences in the children´s errors in the two languages can be linked to their different experiences writing in each, as indicated above.

With regard to spelling, there was a much greater variety noted in the errors in

English than in Spanish, "including invented sound spellings, such as *animols, warol* (world), and *Mayami*; misspelling of words that they have used and/or read in school, such as *broder* (brother) and *frinds* (friends); and Spanish-influenced spellings, for example *vi* (bee) and *tri* (tree)" (Simpson, 2005: 106). Simpson cites Ammon (1985) in suggesting that *"invented spellings can be a strategy used by young children when faced with the rather daunting task of writing in a relatively unknown language"* (Simpson, 2005: 106). There was no evidence of the 'elaborate' style found to characterise writing in Spanish in the studies reviewed by Reppen and Grabe (1993). Simpson suggests that this is probably due to the young age of the children and the fact that they were just learning to write. She also hypothesises that the intensive instruction in English writing probably had an effect on their way of writing. She notes that in terms of the topical structure analysis, while there was evidence that the children used similar amounts of sequential progression and extended parallel progression in both languages, there was a difference in that it was found that they used more parallel progression in English. Narrative strategies in both languages progressed from *"simple lists with no internal progression in the form of repetition of key terms, through a combination of lists with repetition and true narratives with more topical progression, to true narratives with sophisticated use of repetition of key terms to provide internal coherence"* (Simpson, 2005: 114).

Thus, it may be concluded that the fact that there were more T-units in English without errors than in Spanish in the pupils' writing demonstrates the influence of the training the children had in writing simple sentences in English, showing that they had better control of these familiar words and patterns. However, when it came to writing unfamiliar material in English, the number of errors was much higher. This points to the importance of helping learners to become familiarised with different writing patterns from a young age. The finding that the intensive teaching of writing in English also affected the "elaborate style" traditionally associated with Spanish is also evidence of the effect of the explicit teaching strategies used in the school for initial literacy when transferred to writing in Spanish. Helping teachers to understand the potential benefits and limitations of cross-linguistic transfer (Cummins, 2008) as part of these explicit teaching strategies would provide the learners with the possibility of being able to differentiate increasingly between writing in English and writing in Spanish.

There have been two research projects carried out fairly recently at pre-school level (Transition) and at First Grade level in bilingual schools in Bogotá. The first study (Ortiz Maldonado, 2006) looked at the ways in which teachers were implementing processes of reading and writing in the children's first and second languages and whether there were connections between the two processes. During the pre-school stage, children were expected to develop the basic motor skills and the necessary cognitive abilities to be able to read and write in both Spanish and English (although not at the same level) by the end of Transition (four to five years old). However, there was no joint collaboration between the teachers of the two languages where they could make the necessary connections to ensure parallel development of literacy processes in English and Spanish.

By means of classroom observations and semi-structured interviews with four English and four Spanish teachers from pre-school and Grade 1 and 20 children, Ortiz Maldonado concluded that the teaching styles of the participants were very different, one from the other and were focused on different objectives, which made cross-connections difficult. However, in general, there was evidence from observations of classroom practice, that in both languages teachers adopted a mainly teacher-centred approach where learner participation was limited and controlled and during which the children had little opportunity to ask questions. The English teachers tended towards rather traditional mechanical and repetitive activities, rather than trying to relate learning to the pupils' previous knowledge and to their own contexts. One example of these types of practices observed in the English class was the drawing up of a list of words containing the sound /ee/ without any further use in independent written production by the children. Moreover, in one of the Spanish reading classes observed, the children seemed to be mainly concerned with processes of decodification of the written symbols leading to a slow rhythm of reading production. However, it was also noted that half of the learners (six in Grade 1 and four in pre-school) were able to give a good synthesis of what they had read in Spanish. In the case of English, only five children in Grade 1 were able to give a good summary of the main ideas in the text they had read, while another four were able to say what the topic was.

Ortiz Maldonado concluded that it was difficult to see how the English teachers used the abilities developed in Spanish, such as summarising main ideas, to help children with their reading and writing in the foreign language. Yet there was evidence that teachers in both languages were able to intuitively recognise the contribution of these processes in the first language to the development of the second. She recommends that the school should provide spaces for teachers to discuss their understandings of the processes of reading and writing in two languages and relate these to theoretical conceptions and their implications in classroom practice. Ortiz Maldonado also further foregrounds the importance of analysing the relationships between the two languages in this process and of helping teachers to become aware of the importance of intentionally using these connections in their lesson planning.

We can therefore surmise that if both the Spanish and the English teachers were more conscious of conceiving the development of literacy in two languages (biliteracy) as an integrated process in which the classroom strategies used in both languages could be deliberately implemented to make these connections evident, then the process of learning could be enhanced and made more consistent. However, for this to be possible there would need to be institutional commitment to facilitate spaces for the teachers to jointly establish and plan for an integrated programme of biliterate development for their young learners.

The second study, this time carried out at pre-school level (Transition) by Jennifer Parrado in 2014, furthers the debate on the relationship between Spanish and English initial literacy practices by analysing how the teaching and learning of initial literacy in English can be enhanced by deliberately adopting a biliterate perspective in relation to similar processes in the children's first language

(Spanish). In other words, this research can be seen as a development of some of the questions raised in the previous study.

Five pupils from two Transition classes (ten in total) participated in the study, as well as two Spanish teachers and the English teacher-researcher, author of the study, who were working at this level. The action research project started with a diagnostic test to establish the specific conditions in which the children began their process towards biliteracy. The intervention that followed involved working jointly with the teachers responsible for initial literacy in the first and foreign languages to establish criteria and working strategies mutually agreed on and articulated across the two languages. The teacher-researcher documented the effect of the intervention by means of interviews with the teachers involved in the process, both in Spanish and in English, and a series of classroom observations.

The results showed that it was possible for these young children to successfully transfer what they knew about reading and writing in their first language in a global fashion to help them advance quickly in the process of comprehension. Pupils were able to associate sounds and meaning of cognates, previously studied in Spanish, with their English counterparts. The conscious use of teaching strategies common to the teaching of initial reading and writing in both languages had the advantage of familiarising the children with similar dynamics, habits and routines, so that they felt more confident about taking risks in predicting and in associating words and ideas in the English class. As the researcher observed:

> … the gradual process … which began with a rigorous strengthening of the level of understanding in the foreign language, led us to design and plan for appropriate activities, in which the routines and the setting up of specific working time-framed class dynamics, which respecting the teaching principles in the mother tongue, began with the decodification and representation of messages, but gradually led to a more complex process of comprehensive reading and guided writing. (Parrado, 2014: 37)

> el proceso gradual en los estudiantes, que inicia con el trabajo riguroso en el fortalecimiento del nivel de comprensión en la lengua extranjera, el cual nos llevó a diseñar una planeación de actividades apropiadas, en donde las rutinas y el establecimiento de tiempos específicos de trabajo, enmarcaron la dinámica de las clases, que respetando el principio de enseñanza en lengua materna inicia con la decodificación y representación de mensajes, pero que gradualmente los llevó a un proceso más complejo de lectura comprensiva y escritura guiada.

The teacher-researcher, an English specialist, also recognised that the experience of being able to work together with colleagues teaching literacy in Spanish had helped to widen her vision of the whole process and enabled her to become aware of a number of ways in which both processes could converge for the benefit of the learners.

Thus, it can be seen that here again the notion of transfer (Cummins, 2008) is a vitally important concept in the context of the development of initial biliteracy. Rather than seeing the development of reading and writing as separate, discrete areas in the learners' two languages, an understanding by teachers of how harmonious processes of biliterate development can be facilitated can help pupils to understand and communicate written messages effectively in both English and Spanish.

The final contribution to this section comes from a longitudinal ethnographic case study conducted by a North American father on his young bilingual daughter in relation to her journey towards biliteracy in Mexico and in the US (Smith, 2007). The author describes how Arantza grew up in a small Mexican town until she was two; was four years old when the family moved to Tucson, Arizona where she went to a bilingual kindergarten at the age of five. The family then returned to Mexico when Arantza was six, and she went to a monolingual Spanish-speaking school. Among the sources used to document this case study were the texts produced by the child at school as well as interviews with the teachers and headteacher. At home, the author used audio-recordings to document the interactive biliteracy sessions involving story reading.

The results of the research showed that the abilities characteristic of Arantza´s biliterate practices in the home were generally more sophisticated than those evidenced in school contexts. Moreover, as the father/researcher observes: *"It is possible that a bilingual child, with almost no attention at school to her 'other' language, can continue developing reading and writing in that language* (Smith, 2007: 160) *(es possible que una niña bilingue, sin casi nada de atención en la escuela a su 'otra' lengua, puede seguir desarrollando la lecto-escritura en dicha lengua).* Of course, it must be said that this type of development depends very much on the kind of family background in which the child is brought up. As can be seen in the study cited above, both parents were academics that worked in the field of language teaching and learning and therefore were knowledgeable about ways of promoting bilingualism and biliteracy.

It can thus be seen that these studies carried out on the development of biliteracy among young children in Ecuador, Colombia and Mexico all point to the importance of teacher education and development programmes to enable teachers of young children to understand the processes involved in becoming bilingual and biliterate, as well as be able to design appropriate teaching and learning strategies which build on the young learners' previous knowledge of literacy in their first language and help them use this to facilitate the learning of the new language, English.

Teacher training

In Argentina, in the plurilingual schools of Buenos Aires mentioned above, the foreign language teachers, who work in tandem with the qualified primary teachers, have to attend a one-month training course that introduces them to topics to do with bilingual education. They work with teacher trainers, tutors and carry out class observations.

They also have to submit a formal written evaluation (Banfi and Rettaroli, 2008). According to these authors, there are five basic areas of knowledge for teaching in bilingual programmes. These consist of:

- Knowledge of the languages involved
- Knowledge of the cultures involved
- Knowledge of the content to be taught
- Pedagogical knowledge
- Knowledge about bilingualism and bilingual education.

The results of the study carried out by the authors show that while the content, languages and pedagogical knowledge are generally well covered in these programmes, cultural knowledge and knowledge about bilingualism and bilingual education are not.

In response to this last point, we will briefly turn to a research project conducted in São Paulo, Brazil in 2009, in relation to teacher training programmes for novice teachers in bilingual education programmes for very young children. This is a new development in bilingual education studies in Brazil (and in much of South America) as can be seen by the researcher's acknowledgement that she did not find any previous studies carried out on this topic (Wolffowitz-Sanchez, 2009).

The participants in this collaborative research project were student teachers who were registered on a pre-service teacher-training course in bilingual education, which included critical-reflexive sessions based on classroom videos, both face to face and through emails. The results of the analysis of this data indicates that the participants considered that the emails constituted an important space where they could express themselves, disagree, question and contribute with their own knowledge. There was also evidence that the participants gradually became conscious of themselves as teachers responsible for the different decisions and activities they were involved in. They were greatly helped in this process of consciousness-raising and understanding by the collaborative nature of the project and the co-authorship or co-production of knowledge. As the role of the trainees increased in importance, the role of the teacher trainer became more peripheral. Thus, there was an ongoing movement among all the participants *"from the centre to the periphery and from the periphery to the centre"* (Wolffowitz-Sanchez, 2009: 119) (*do centro para a periferia e da periferia para o centro, movimentos esses que todas as participantes realizaram*).

To sum up, it can be said that these developments in teacher training for bilingual education programmes targeting young learners are relatively recent and not enough work has been done in this area. However, such projects that have been carried out have shown this to be a useful and potentially effective way forward in bilingual education studies.

Parents

In Colombia, there have been various studies carried out by teachers and researchers into parental attitudes and expectations towards bilingual education English–Spanish programmes. An early project (Araújo and Corominas, 1996) focused on parents of children aged five to six years old, in the pre-school section of four English–Spanish bilingual schools in Cali. In this study, the results of a questionnaire sent out to parents of the four schools included in the research showed that the main reason for parents' choice of school was the fact of it being bilingual in English and Spanish, as well as the quality, experience and recognised high academic level of these programmes. However, parents' greatest interest was in their children's development of the foreign language, English, rather than in their progress in their first language, Spanish. For these parents, their children's bilingualism centred on the development of their proficiency in English, due to its importance as a world language, *"for study, work, travel, business and international communications"* (Araújo and Corominas, 1996: 180). Progress in English was helped by the fact that most parents acknowledged that they could speak English and in many families there were other relations, such as uncles, aunts, brothers and sisters, who had knowledge of the language. This clearly shows the high degree of penetration of English in the lives of middle and upper-middle class Colombian families in 1996.

More recently, another study, carried out in Bogotá in 2011, was designed to characterise the previous conceptions and expectations of a sample of parents and teachers about English–Spanish bilingual education (Aljure et al., 2011). In similar terms to the earlier study, it was found that the majority of the parents who participated in the project saw bilingual education as a means of advancement for their children in a globalised world and the possibility of better job opportunities.

A further study, also carried out in Bogotá, this time among teachers and parents from different socio-economic strata (Flaborea et al., 2013), found that most parents surveyed were conscious of the importance of the relationship between school and home. However, many of them did not feel that their level of English was sufficient to enable them to help their children with their homework and therefore considered that it was the responsibility of the school to take this on. As one parent noted:

> *What I would like to emphasise is the topic of teacher participation, to strengthen this work; perhaps they can send us homework as well, maybe as reinforcement, because, from my point of view, it is possible that not all children have access to this support at home.* (Flaborea et al., 2013: 40)

> *No, de pronto lo que sí te quiero reforzar es el tema de la participación con los docentes, de afianzar ese trabajo; de pronto, que nos envíen a nosotros también tareas, bueno, nosé, como refuerzos, porque pues desde mi punto de vista, de pronto no todos los hogares cuentan con el manejo del idioma, y pues no todos los niños cuentan con ese apoyo desde casita.*

However, there was also evidence that the contact between school and parents was often in the "co-operation without contact" mode, involving support for the children, but the lack of contact meant that there was little understanding on the part of the parents of the pedagogical strategies used by the school in teaching and learning through English. This led to parent insecurity and lack of understanding by teachers as to what was happening in the home with regard to family support.

Thus, it can be seen that the parents of Colombian students in all sectors are very positive towards the development of programmes designed to improve the English language proficiency of their children, with a view to increasing their chances of better career possibilities. While in some cultures parents expect to be more highly involved in their children's education, in the studies discussed in this section, parents are accustomed to wait for the schools to take the initiative. It can be seen that parents have high expectations invested in these English–Spanish bilingual programmes and have voluntarily chosen to send their children to these types of school, often at great personal expense. This shows clearly the importance they attach to their sons and daughters being able to become fluent in two or more international languages for their future success in an ever-shrinking world.

Conclusions and implications

In this final section, I would like to place some of the issues and tendencies discussed in this chapter in relation to South America in dialogue with recent trends in early pre-school immersion and bilingual education in North America and in Europe, as revealed in a Special Issue of the International Journal of Bilingual Education and Bilingualism entitled 'Immersion education in the early years' (2014). We find some interesting similarities between the two texts. For example, in the introduction to the Special Issue there is the observation that: *"One of the central issues, noted by several authors, centres on teacher education and ongoing support for educators in pre-school immersion"* (p. 138). This is a field which is in its infancy in South America, but which is beginning to be recognised, particularly in Brazil, as an important way forward to ensure the quality of bilingual early learning programmes.

Another area of convergence relates to teachers' beliefs about L2 teaching and learning. Just as we have seen in Ortiz Maldonado's study (2006) in Colombia on teachers' pedagogical intuitions about the importance of relating the teaching of initial literacy in English to teaching in Spanish, so we note that Hüttner, Dalton-Puffer and Smit (2013, cited in Hickey and de Mejía, 2014), in their exploration of the effect of teachers' 'lay theories' about the nature of language use and language learning on their teaching in Content and Language Integrated Learning (CLIL) programmes, come to the conclusion that these pre-existing beliefs must be taken into account in any successful plans for change.

Finally, we can see that there is reference to the importance of parents' contribution to success of young children learning through a language that is different from their home language. As Patrick Smith (2007) has noted in his study, home practices can complement and enrich both oracy and literacy as developed at school. However, as Kavanagh and Hickey (2013, cited in Hickey and de Mejía, 2014) explain, *"Parents who do not speak the target language of the immersion programme may feel marginalised and unable to offer support for the child's learning"* (p. 140), reflecting the feelings of some of the parents who participated in the study carried out in Bogotá (Flaborea et al., 2013). Nevertheless, as we suggested (Hickey and de Mejía, 2014), parents' involvement as effective educational partners in their children's early learning experiences needs to be maximised if these early language learning and learning through another language initiatives are to prosper.

A trend noted by the Early Language Learning in Europe team (2011) (sponsored by the British Council) in many Asian countries is the decision *"to introduce English from the very start of compulsory schooling, arguing that the global economic benefits of being able to communicate in English are a high priority for true national prosperity"* (p. 10). A similar tendency has been seen in many of the countries in South America referred to in this chapter. Early childhood bilingual education is closely associated with economic development. However, in the words of the Colombian Ministry of Education, I would also like to argue for the importance of making sure that *"the capital and wealth produced for a country by plurilingualism may translate into linguistic capital for each individual and that plurilingualism may become an educational priority"* (Ministerio de Educación Nacional, 1999: 1) (*el capital y la riqueza que le produce a un país el plurilingüismo (se traduzcan) en capital lingüístico para cada individuo y que el 'plurilingüismo (se convierta) en una prioridad educativa*).

References

Abouchaar, A, Fajardo, LA and Vargas, N (2009) *Lineamientos curriculares para los colegios pilotos hacia el bilingüismo.* Unpublished document.

Aljure, LH, Arciniegas, MC, Castillo, MF, Correal, MF, Mejía, ME, Mejía, MV and Rueda, C (2011) Concepciones y expectativas de padres de familia y profesores acerca del bilingüismo y la educación bilingüe en siete colegios de Bogotá y Cundinamarca. *El Astrolabio*, 10(2), 21-32.

Ammon, P (1985) 'Helping children to learn English as a second language. Some observations and some hypotheses', in Freedman SW (ed) *The Acquisition of Written Language: Response and Revision.* Norwood, N.J.: Ablex.

Araújo, MC and Corominas, Y (1996) *Procesos de adquisión del inglés como segunda lengua en niños de 5-6 años, de colegios bilingües de la ciudad de Cali.* Cali: Universidad del Valle. Unpublished MA thesis.

Banfi, C (2010) *Los Primeros Pasos en las Lenguas Extranjeras.* Buenos Aires: Ediciones Novedades Educativas.

Banfi, C (2013) 'The landscape of English language teaching: roots, routes and ramifications', in Renart, L and Banegas, D (eds) *Roots & routes in language education: Bi-multi-plurilingualism, interculturality and identity.* Selected papers from the 38th FAAPI Conference. Buenos Aires: APIBA.

Banfi, C (2015) 'English language teaching expansion in South America: Challenges and opportunities', in Kamhi-Stein, LD, Diaz Maggioli G and de Oliveira, LC (eds) *English Language Teaching in South America: Policy, Preparation, and Practices.* Bristol: Multilingual Matters.

Banfi, C and Rettaroli, S (2008) 'Staff profiles in minority and prestigious bilingual education contexts in Argentina', in Hélot, C and de Mejía, AM (eds) *Forging Multilingual Spaces.* Bristol: Multilingual Matters.

Cummins, J (2008) 'Teaching for transfer: Challenging the two solitudes assumption in bilingual education', in Cummins, J and Hornberger, NH (eds) *Encyclopedia of Language and Education.* Second Edition. Volume 5. Springer.

de Mejía, AM (1998) Bilingual storytelling: Codeswitching, discourse control and learning opportunities. *TESOL Journal* 7(6), 4-10.

de Mejía, AM (2004) Two early immersion classes in Colombia: Reformulation in bilingual storytelling. *The Welsh Journal of Education* 13(1), 30-43.

Enever, J (ed) (2011) ELLiE. *Early Language Learning in Europe.* British Council.

Flaborea, R, Gómez, MT, Roldán, JH, Rodríguez, ML and Henao, MC (2013) Concepciones sobre la relación familia-colegio: fortaleciendo el aprendizaje del inglés. *Voces y Silencios*, 4(2), 30-46.

Gumperz, J (1982) 'Conversational codeswitching', in *Discourse Strategies.* Cambridge: Cambridge University Press.

Hickey, TM and de Mejía, AM (2014) Editorial. Immersion education in the early years: a Special Issue. *International Journal of Bilingual Education and Bilingualism,* 17(2), 131-143.

Ministerio de Educación Nacional (1999) *Lineamientos Curriculares: Idiomas Extranjeros.* Bogotá: Ministerio de Educación Nacional.

Ortiz Maldonado, AA (2006) *Descripción del proceso de desarrollo de la lecto escritura adelantado por maestras de grado transición y primero elemental en un colegio bilingüe de Bogotá.* Maestría en Educación, Bogotá: Universidad de los Andes. Unpublished MA thesis.

Parrado J (2014) *Enseñanza de la lectura y la escritura en la lengua extranjera inglés, teniendo en cuenta el proceso simultáneo en la lengua materna en grado transición (Biliteracy).* Maestría en Educación, Universidad de los Andes. Unpublished MA thesis.

PNIEB. Secretaría de Educación Pública (2014) *National English Programme in Basic Education*. www.sepbcs.gob.mx.

Reppen, R and Grabe, W (1993) Spanish transfer effects in the writing of elementary school students. *Lenguas Modernas, 20*, 113-128.

Simpson, J (2005) 'A look at early childhood writing in English and Spanish in a bilingual school in Ecuador', in de Mejía, AM (ed) *Bilingual Education in South America*. Clevedon: Multilingual Matters.

Smith, P (2007) 'El desarrollo del bialfabetismo en una niña bilingüe: ejemplos de un estudio longitudinal', in de Mejía, AM and Colmenares, S (eds) *Bialfabetismo: Lectura y Escritura en Dos Lenguas en Colombia*. Cali: Universidad del Valle.

UNESCO (2013) *The state of education in Latin America and the Caribbean: Towards a Quality Education for All – 2015*. Regional Bureau of Education for Latin America and the Caribbean, Santiago: OREALC/UNESCO.

Wolffowitz-Sanchez, N (2009) *Formação de professores para a educação infantil bilíngue*. Mestrado em Linguística Aplicada e Estudo da Linguagem, Pontifícia Universidade Católica de São Paulo. Unpublished MA thesis.

1.3

Europe

European perspectives on early childhood education and care in English for speakers of other languages

Victoria A Murphy, Maria Evangelou, Jenny Goff
and Rebecca Tracz, University of Oxford, England

Introduction

Linguistic diversity comes in many forms. Internationally, the most common means of developing knowledge of more than one language tends to be: i) learning a foreign language (FL) as a taught subject through educational provision, ii) learning a second (sometimes foreign) language through participation in some form of bilingual education (such as immersion) and/or iii) being raised bilingually (Murphy, 2014). This final category of being raised bilingually can itself happen in numerous different ways (e.g. see Romaine's (1995) categories of child bilingualism). Often children who develop bilingually are considered 'minority language learners' if the language(s) in the home is (are) not the same as the majority language context, a situation that often arises through immigration. In this chapter we will examine each of these three contexts of learning English as another (additional) language within the context of Early Childhood Education (ECE) (up to age seven) in Europe. We will first discuss the nature of ECE in Europe, including identifying approximately how many children participate in ECE and the basic characteristics of ECE across European countries, regardless of linguistic considerations. We then look more closely at the extent to which other languages, usually English, are introduced into ECE in different European countries. This will be followed by a more in-depth discussion of particular (selective) countries where we have more detailed information about the nature of ECE programmes in English for speakers who do not speak English in the home. We then turn our attention to the English as an Additional Language context in the UK where children are educated through the medium of English, who have a home language that is not English, and where English is the majority language of the wider community. The discussion presented in this chapter should not be considered an exhaustive or systematic review, but rather presents a brief snapshot of the kinds of issues researchers and practitioners are attending to within this context.

Early Childhood Education and Care in Europe

There are over 50 countries in the geographical entity called 'Europe' with more than 40 different languages from different language families (e.g. Indo-European, Semitic, Turkic) spoken by over 742 million people. Europe, therefore, like many continents, is a highly linguistically diverse geographical area. Within the continent of Europe exists the political–economic union of 28 member states that forms the European Union (EU), officially founded in 1993. There are 24 'official' languages of the EU and many others that do not (for one reason or another) enjoy 'official' status, including regional minority languages (e.g. Sami, Scottish Gaelic). This is not an inconsequential number of languages, particularly bearing in mind that as a continent Europe is actually relatively small (Europe being the second smallest continent next to Australia). This linguistic diversity means then that a child in their formative years in Europe is likely to encounter more than one language early on in his/her lifetime. Increasingly for many children in Europe, that first encounter happens during the early years educational setting.

As of 2014, there were 32 million children in Europe who were the appropriate age to participate in Early Childhood Education and Care (ECEC) (Eurydice, 2014). In most European countries the demand for high quality ECEC services exceeds the supply, with the exception of Scandinavian countries (Finland, Norway, Sweden and Denmark) where supply equals demand. This problem of demand exceeding supply in most European countries perhaps reflects the fact that publicly funded pre-primary education tends to be more well developed in European than non-European countries in the Organisation for Economic Co-operation and Development (OECD, 2014) and is a reflection of women's increasing participation in the labour force. Ninety-three per cent of children participate in some form of ECEC in the year (or two) preceding entry into formal primary education; this is nearly at the European Commission's target that 95 per cent of all children between the age of four and the starting age of compulsory education would participate in ECEC by the year 2020. However, in the younger age group, (i.e. under three), participation in ECEC is much lower.

One of the reasons why the European Commission (among others) is keen to support children's participation in ECEC is that international student achievement surveys have consistently shown that children who participate in ECEC tend to have higher academic scores than children who do not (e.g. Programme for International Student Achievement (PISA) and Progress in International Reading Literacy Studies (PIRLS)). For some children, this amounts to as much as the equivalent of one full year's worth of schooling. ECEC generally, therefore, can have a measureable positive impact on developing children's academic performance later on in primary school (Eurydice, 2014). For example, Tucker-Drob, (2012) and Sammons et al (2002) have shown clear links between pre-primary and stronger progress in academic achievement later on in education. One of the factors associated with high quality ECEC is the qualifications of the teachers working in ECEC settings. In Europe, there are typically three levels of staff: i) educational staff who usually have a higher degree (e.g. Bachelor's), ii) care staff with qualifications typically at the level of secondary school or a post-secondary diploma, and iii) auxiliary staff/

assistants who often have no qualifications or, at most, an upper secondary certificate. In two-thirds of the ECEC settings in Europe, educational staff are included on the staff register, and in some countries in Europe, educational staff are required to have a Master's-level degree in order to work with older children. However, some countries do not require their ECEC staff to have more than a secondary school certificate and/or do not set a minimum level of formal education (qualification) for individuals wishing to work with young children.

A lack of sufficient training and qualifications is an issue throughout Europe and indeed a major theme that has emerged from this volume more generally. There is also considerable variability across countries with respect to in-service training (continuous professional development (CPD)). CPD for staff working with younger children is only mandatory in ECEC settings in half of the countries in Europe. It is obligatory in most countries for staff working with older children. This variability both across countries and even within countries with respect to requirements for working with younger versus older children sends a message about the extent to which ECEC is perceived as being an important part of a child's development, particularly for younger children (i.e. less important for younger, more important for older). More important 'educational' work seems to be offered to older children (aged three to six) by more qualified staff, while care seems to be the focus for younger children (0 to three) by less qualified staff. This is potentially an issue since, as mentioned above, numerous studies have demonstrated the positive effect of ECEC on later performance at school.

Children's progress in ECEC in Europe is regularly assessed, particularly with a focus on transition between ECEC and primary level. Indeed, a major focus of European ECEC settings is to facilitate the transition from ECEC to formal primary education. Assessment across many countries is largely diagnostic in that the aim is to determine whether and to what extent the provision is effective, and to identify any difficulties children may be having. Mostly, such progress is carried out through observation accompanied by written records of children's manifest development in key areas such as readiness for school, maturity and language skills (Eurydice, 2014). Results of international studies, which include European countries, have identified that children from more socio-economically disadvantaged families make significant progress in reading as a function of participation in ECEC (Mullis et al., 2012). This is a particularly important finding because as Mullis et al. (2012) report, children from lower socio-economic status families and/or poorly educated/immigrant families were more likely to not have attended ECEC longer than one year. If ECEC is to help "... break the generational cycles of poverty and low achievement" (Mullis et al., 2012), then children from more disadvantaged families need to be able to consistently attend good quality ECEC.

In summary, a significant proportion of young children in Europe attend some form of ECEC, most notably in the year or two leading up to the compulsory starting age of primary education. There is significant variability across countries with respect to the levels of education required for staff working with young children in ECEC settings in Europe. Furthermore, within countries there is often variability about qualification requirements for working with younger vs. older children where, in a number of countries, staff more typically are not obliged to have tertiary-level education if working with children younger than four. Having presented this brief snapshot of European ECEC settings overall, we now turn our attention towards ECEC settings that offer English language instruction – either as discrete sessions or through the medium of instruction.

ECEC in English in Europe

The Eurydice (2012) document *Key Data on Teaching Languages at School in Europe* clearly indicates a general trend across European countries to offer some form of foreign language (FL) instruction in early years settings. A clear theme from this document is the trend for European countries to lower the age at which a taught foreign language is introduced. Indeed, between 1994 and 2011 only nine countries in the European Union did not lower the age for compulsory foreign language learning. Many countries begin formally teaching a foreign language (English usually in non-English speaking countries) between the ages of six and nine and some countries formally introduce foreign language instruction at pre-primary (ECEC) level, sometimes as young as three (e.g. the German-speaking community in Belgium where children are taught French and/or Dutch, and *comunidades autonomas* in Spain). This is contrasted to English-speaking countries (e.g. the UK) where formal FL instruction has only recently been included in the primary curriculum in Year 3 (age seven). Despite the fact that the Eurydice (2012) document presents interesting data from across Europe with regards to different language provision at different levels of education, there is a considerable amount of information that is lacking, particularly with respect to the content of this volume. For example, there is a general lack of information reported which is clearly related to pre-primary (ECEC) provision. In many of the discussions in this report it is unclear whether what is being discussed is true for pre-primary or just primary and beyond. For example, in identifying that 89.6 per cent of foreign language teachers report they are 'fully qualified' to teach the FL, it is not clear whether this is true for ECEC settings, nor even what it even means to be 'fully qualified' for language teaching in ECEC settings. Furthermore, there is very little information on the provision offered in the pre-primary EFL and/or EMI (English Medium of Instruction) settings. There are a few statistics on the inclusion of CLIL (Content and Language Integrated Learning) programmes, which illustrate a general trend that CLIL programmes have proliferated across Europe, but at which levels of education is not clear. Therefore, while the document provides interesting, and often helpful, statistics for FL learning in Europe (which is overwhelmingly English in most countries), it does not really offer much in the way of clear information on EFL and EMI in pre-primary education across Europe.

Another document that is arguably more helpful in trying to ascertain what provision is offered in different European countries for ECEC in English is the 2011 policy handbook produced by the European Commission on language learning at pre-primary school level. This document aims to provide summaries of the nature of provision across a range of different European countries (or regions within countries) and in many respects is an attempt to fill in the significant lack of information available to support language learning through pre-primary settings (Mourão and Lourenço, 2015). Twenty-eight countries (regions) are discussed in terms of language education policy in the early years, the context and organisation of language learning in ECEC settings, and particular challenges faced by a given context together with a discussion of the nature of the resources available (with a particular emphasis on human resources). Furthermore, in many of the country summaries there is a brief inclusion on teaching processes and coherence and continuity, which often addresses (where relevant) the extent to which language education in ECEC is linked appropriately with provision at the primary level. The handbook claims that its primary function is to identify so-called conditions for success, together with 'pitfalls' of early language learning. 'National experts' from these countries met to discuss and exchange knowledge and good practice – which led to the guidelines presented in this handbook. These experts advocate that the second or foreign language should primarily be used as a communication tool in activities rather than being taught as a discrete subject. A communicative approach seems to be widely adopted in that the main aim is to use the language in meaningful and useful contexts. In reviewing the country summaries linked to this document, there are a number of interesting themes that emerge from the handbook itself and the country summaries that are linked within.

Most of the ECEC provision in languages across the 28 countries discussed in the handbook reflects a strong focus on developing L1 skills. This is, of course, appropriate since in the pre-primary age group children are still developing key aspects of their L1 and are (hopefully) establishing the important foundation needed to develop strong literacy skills in their L1. Where there is provision in another language (usually English), the focus tends more to be on developing language awareness and bicultural understanding as much as on actually learning features of English. This seems highly appropriate to us given that developing linguistic awareness is not only beneficial for future foreign and second language learning but also in developing L1 literacy skills. Much research has demonstrated the relationship between metalinguistic knowledge and developing L1 literacy (e.g. Bialystok, 2001) and more recent work has demonstrated that learning a foreign language in the primary school can have positive impacts on developing L1 literacy skills (Murphy et al., 2015). Furthermore, as Hawkins (2005) has also advocated (albeit for older learners than pre-primary), one of the main emphases on early foreign language learning should be on 'awakening of language awareness' (p. 4) to enable learners, among other things, to make informed decisions about their further foreign language learning endeavours. In addition, developing intercultural awareness is an important component of many language learning policy documents, though, as some researchers have identified, developing high levels of this intercultural sensitivity it is not always achieved (e.g. Cable et al., 2012).

Another issue that is immediately apparent in reading the European Commission (2011) document is the wide variability as to what is provided at pre-primary levels (aged three to six) regarding foreign language provision. While most countries offer some form of pre-primary provision in the year immediately preceding the child's entry into formal primary education (and indeed the enrolment rates even at age three in ECEC have steadily risen across many countries in the past ten years

(OECD, 2014)), the extent to which ECEC in or about another language is available beyond that (i.e. in earlier years) is highly variable. In those countries where ECEC is not freely available, the fee is usually waived for this year immediately preceding formal entry to primary education. As mentioned above, English is the most commonly taught FL in pre-primary education across the countries summarised in the European Commission (2011) document, second only to languages with regional consequence (e.g. Estonia where Russian or Estonian is taught, or in Flanders Belgium where French is taught). However, even in these contexts English is also taught as a further (additional) foreign language.

It is clear from the discussion in the 2011 document that parental pressure is a key element in the decision to introduce some form of English instruction at pre-primary levels across countries in Europe. Numerous countries report that as a consequence of parental pressure and desire for their children to learn English (viewed as social capital and a means through which their children will have greater opportunities in life), English is being offered at younger ages across pre-primary contexts in Europe. Enever (2004) coined the term 'parentocracy' to identify the significance of this parental pressure through networks or other lobby groups.

A notable challenge, reflected throughout the document and almost all of the 28 countries included in this handbook, relates to the nature of the qualifications for the teachers of English in ECEC settings. Some countries have very clear standards and guidelines concerning the qualifications required by language teachers in ECEC settings. Unfortunately, many do not, where becoming trained as a fully qualified pre-primary teacher is only just beginning to fall under the remit of tertiary-level education settings. In many countries it seems that simply being a native speaker of English is sufficient to qualify an individual to teach young children English in ECEC contexts, despite a lack of teaching qualifications. In other contexts, specialist FL (English) teachers are brought in to supplement (and complement) the expertise of the teaching staff. These difficulties in teacher education and qualifications are compounded by the challenge many countries have in accessing good quality English language teaching materials.

There is a general lack of data in many countries on numerous issues, particularly with respect to the proportion of different types of educational settings, and the numbers of children being educated through English (or on English) (in those countries with a focus on English). The phrase 'no official data available' is ubiquitous throughout the 2011 review. As also noted by Mourão and Lourenço (2015) there is little evidence of agreed processes or shared understanding across countries, no uniformity of approach or established indices of success. Arguably the largest gap in knowledge concerns the nature of the actual teaching provision that is offered across these 28 countries in the 2011 European Commission review. Very few of the countries which focus on English are able to report on the nature of the English curriculum and how exactly it is implemented. Furthermore, where there is a discussion of the practices in the FL (English), there seems to be relatively little information about programmes where the medium of instruction is English. In some countries, there is mention of whether CLIL or immersion programmes are offered but there is very little data about the proportion of children attending these programmes, the qualifications of the teachers and the nature of the provision.

This lack of information is a problem noted in Buyl and Housen (2014) who discuss the implementation of English immersion in the Francophone community of Belgium. In their study, children's development of English vocabulary was evaluated when children were in pre-school (aged five) after six months of participation in the immersion programme. Testing continued into years 1 and 2 of primary school. Importantly, the children, even after only six months, were able to demonstrate they had learned 'specific and substantive lexical and grammatical knowledge' (p. 14), but Buyl and Housen (2014: 16) argue that *"To date we have had only a fragmentary view of factors, processes and outcomes in immersion education in the Belgian FC"*, and we would say this is true across the European context as well. They specifically warn against automatically assuming immersion programmes will be successful since there is not yet enough evidence, or institutional guidance, to support schools and teachers in this age group. Having a better understanding of immersion education in this early years age group is particularly important since some researchers have identified that children can sometimes have difficulties adjusting to being educated through the medium of language that is not their own. For example, Soderman and Oshio (2008) report on a study carried out in a dual immersion programme (English–Mandarin) that was offered in an international school in Beijing, China. Dual immersion programmes are those where children who speak the majority language (in this case Mandarin Chinese) are educated alongside children who do not, and where two languages are used (often 50-50) throughout the day. In Soderman and Oshio's study, the non-Chinese speaking children came from a variety of different home language backgrounds and nationalities. The focus of their study was on analysing the social behaviour and competence of children as they progressed in their L2 development (English for the Mandarin Chinese-speaking children and Mandarin for the non-Mandarin-speaking children). Interestingly, they report that girls had more difficulty adjusting than boys, a finding which contradicts previous research that suggests girls are more pro-social than boys. Soderman and Oshio (2008) suggest that this is largely due to a lack of receptive and expressive language skills, which hampered the non-Mandarin-speaking girls' abilities to interact with other students effectively. Boys seemed less hampered by a lack of linguistic competence. Importantly, they also demonstrated that as children's linguistic skills developed, their adjustment difficulties decreased. Thus there is nothing inherently problematic with dual immersion programmes, but rather, in line with Buyl and Housen (2014), it is perhaps unwise to simply assume children will automatically thrive from the beginning of participation in dual immersion programmes like these. More research on issues such as this will enable practitioners to be able to predict potential problem areas like those identified in Soderman and Oshio (2008) such that these can be attenuated.

In summary, in attempting to review the state of English language education across ECEC throughout Europe, the European Commission (2011) document offers a helpful start, but unfortunately also highlights the significant gaps in our understanding of what is actually going on in ECEC settings in Europe. This lack of consistent and reliable information makes it very difficult to develop a shared understanding of what constitutes good practice in terms of teacher qualifications, the actual curriculum being followed, and the nature of the materials and resources that are available and used. This lack of information illustrates a lost opportunity to try and establish some coherence across Europe in terms of effective guidelines for English language education in the early years.

A snapshot of some European countries

Fortunately, some researchers are remedying this lack of information described above by carrying out more detailed analyses of ECEC provision in or through English within specific European countries. In this section, we will examine a few such cases.

Italy

A recent report produced by Langé et al (2014) provides a very helpful review of ECE in Italy. The main focus of the report is to present the results of a survey that was carried out in November 2014 on FL (most commonly English) teaching or awareness experiences, together with implementation and effects of FL provision in Italian pre-schools. An online questionnaire was administered to 5,145 state schools and 9,781 non-state schools concerning the main features of existing early years FL experiences. In terms of the kinds of teachers who offer FL provision, the results indicated that 49.4 per cent of the teachers were mostly generalists but that external specialist teachers were sometimes brought in (31.4 per cent) and external native-speakers (14.2 per cent) and voluntary native-speakers (3.5 per cent) were included in some schools. Most of the teachers held a university degree in either primary education studies or foreign languages. Alternatively, teachers held a primary school diploma with a specialist qualification in FL. Most of the teachers who responded to the survey report had participated in in-service courses on FL methodology or had FL teaching certified qualifications. They also report their own competence in the FL as falling between B1 and B2 and in some cases C1 and C2 of the CEFR (Common European Framework of Reference).

As indicated above in the more general discussion of ECEC provision in Europe, 84.8 per cent of the pre-primary schools that responded to the survey in the Langé et al. (2014) report claimed they implement EFL teaching 'experiences' and, within this, 48.7 per cent implement both FL teaching and awareness experiences. Most of the schools reported introducing the EFL around age five, with approximately 30 minutes spent on or in English each week. The provision largely centres around game-based activities (nursery rhymes, role play, etc.) and use of multimedia. The general assessment of this provision is positive where children's families and the pre-primary teachers themselves have positive attitudes about the FL experiences they encounter.

Cyprus

Ioannou-Georgiou (2015) provides details about the ECEC provision in or through English in Cyprus. Pre-primary education in Cyprus is free and compulsory for those children in the year leading up to formal primary education (as indicated above). This happens in the year they turn six years old, if places are available in respective pre-primary settings; however, children are allowed to attend as young as three years old. The curriculum adopted in Cyprus pre-primary settings focuses on developing social, psychomotor, linguistic and cognitive skills, implemented through play and other experience-based approaches to help prepare the child for formal education. Staff in ECEC settings in Cyprus include qualified pre-primary schoolteachers and support staff (such as classroom assistants). Ioannou-Georgiou reports that the policy regarding language learning in pre-primary settings in Cyprus changed in 2010 where L2 (FL) learning was included in the pre-primary curriculum and where (as indicated earlier in this chapter) the language usually offered is English. Furthermore, in September 2015 it became compulsory to teach English in the final year of pre-primary education in Cyprus, and the English teachers have completed in-service training to become English teachers. English is important in Cyprus because, historically, Cyprus was once a British Colony, meaning that English was at one time an official language. Policy makers also felt English was appropriate to adopt as the FL given that they believed most Cypriot teachers to be sufficiently competent in English, thus facilitating its inclusion in the Cypriot pre-primary classroom. Finally, due to the fact that English is taught at primary level, including it at the pre-primary level facilitates this transition.

The predominant emphasis of the English FL programme at the pre-primary level in Cyprus is on the development of positive attitudes towards languages and developing intercultural awareness (consistent with the review of ECE across Europe described above). There are no dedicated English lessons as such, but rather English is included throughout the day in routines and greetings and the like. The main aim is to allow the child to interact with English in regular and systematic ways. Mostly the exposure is relatively limited, up to 30 minutes twice a week, and the focus tends towards the aural/oral approach.

Ioannou-Georgiou (ibid.) describes a pilot project, which essentially is an attempt to examine how the implementation of English in pre-primary settings in Cyprus is developing. Ten pre-primary schools, which included 15 teachers and 550 children, participated in the study, where teachers were given a questionnaire aimed at soliciting their opinions and attitudes towards L2 (English) learning at pre-primary levels. Seven of these teachers were also randomly selected for interview and all teachers participated in focus group discussions. Twelve children were interviewed to help identify children's levels of language awareness and their attitudes towards English FL learning. The general results reported by Ioannou-Georgiou (ibid.) are that despite some initial reservations about how the English language programme was implemented, teachers were generally 'enthusiastic' about the children's achievements and development. Despite finding it initially challenging, teachers reported that they felt more comfortable in their roles as English teachers with adequate training and systematic support. As for the children, they reported positive attitudes towards languages, and language learning more generally, a finding that has been reported consistently in other studies (e.g. Brumen, 2011). Ioannou-Georgiou (2015) suggests that these English FL programmes are successful in the ECEC settings in Cyprus, but she cautions that teachers must have relevant competence in English and that they must receive appropriate training and support through in-service training. These points in particular are relevant not just across Europe, but as seen more generally in this volume, are critical throughout the world.

The Czech Republic

Černá (2015) reports on pre-primary English language learning and teacher education in the Czech Republic, which was introduced at the pre-primary level of education in the 2000s. The inclusion of English in the Czech Republic gained momentum with *The National Plan* – a document aimed at identifying the conditions needed for promoting L2 development. This document was also intended to produce a methodology for pre-primary teaching of English, and aimed to introduce English into the pre-primary teacher education curriculum (at secondary pedagogical schools or faculties of education). The guidelines stipulate that ECEC foreign language education is conceived as a preparatory phase preceding formal primary education, that it offers a foundation for learning foreign languages, that teachers should be trained specifically to teach foreign languages to pre-primary-aged children and that relevant teaching materials and resources, as well as appropriate curriculum time for learning foreign languages (English), should be available. Černá (ibid.) indicates that in a report produced by the Czech School Inspectorate in 2006–07, 635 institutions were inspected and, of these, 47 per cent provided L2 provision at the pre-primary level, and of these, 96 per cent chose English as the L2. There was a reliance on external (peripatetic) language teachers (59 per cent) so English provision was considered an extra curricular activity, and only five per cent of the schools offered English daily. As already indicated in this chapter, Černá (ibid.) notes that many of these initiatives were in direct response to parental pressure – and she further suggests that this parental pressure meant that the implementation of English to pre-primary students was not ideal in that English was often taught by unqualified teachers – highlighting the significant shortage of qualified pre-primary English teachers in Czech Republic. She further suggests that research has had little impact on implementation and development of educational policy in the Czech Republic. One of the reasons for this might be the general lack of shared understanding already referred to in this chapter. One hopes that with increased interest in language learning at the pre-primary level this problem will be remedied over time. As with most of the countries in Europe already discussed in this chapter, Černá reports that in 2015 (eight years on from the initial report) little has changed – including difficulty of ensuring continuity of L2 education between pre-primary and primary. This issue of continuity is a particular concern for not just the European context but internationally as well. Together with the problems of teacher qualifications, there seems to be a number of issues that need to be addressed in the provision of English at pre-primary level in the Czech Republic.

Slovakia

Early L2 learning (mostly English) in Slovakia has steadily increased in popularity as a consequence of the European Union's policy of multilingualism and educational reform that took place in 2008 requiring children to learn an L2 English at primary level and, as already seen, parental pressure on policy makers (Portiková, 2015). Portiková (ibid.) reports that this parental pressure in particular has led to a number of early years institutions developing an English L2 programme in order to be more competitive, but she suggests this raises a number of challenging questions concerning the quality and conditions of these early language learning programmes. While pre-primary education is not compulsory in Slovakia, it is freely available for all children in the year before they begin formal schooling (as with many other countries in Europe) and covers the age range of three to six years. In 2013, there were 2,716 pre-primary institutions in Slovakia that were financially supported by local municipalities. Portiková (ibid.) laments the lack of research that has been carried out on L2 English provision at the pre-primary level, together with the lack of legislative support. There are no laws, no programmes or official documents stipulating the content or methodology for early L2 education, despite the proliferation of L2 provision in early educational settings.

In part as a consequence of this lack of research, Portiková (ibid.) describes the results of a survey that was carried out to examine teacher education in Slovakia and whether it meets the standards of learning an L2 (English) at pre-primary level. The results of this survey, as with the Czech Republic example described above, identified a significant challenge in the lack of qualified pre-primary L2 teachers. This is a challenge that was also identified in the ELLiE *study (Early Language Learning in Europe* (Enever, 2011), which was a four-year longitudinal project looking at L2/FL provision at primary-level education. Portiková also notes the problem of continuity – a common theme in this chapter and indeed the volume more generally – that there is a lack of cohesion between pre-primary and primary-level L2 English provision. One of the main conclusions Portiková (2015) makes concerning the results of the survey is that there has not been a sufficient amount of effort and attention paid to L2 teaching at pre-primary level in Slovakia, and that the lack of legislation has resulted in a non-systematic approach to how languages are taught at pre-primary level. The 'parentocracy' (Enever, 2004) has meant, however, that L2 learning is rapidly evolving in Slovakia, despite no critical assessment of the conditions under which children are developing L2 (English) knowledge.

These brief descriptions of how English is being introduced in four different countries across Europe (Italy, Cyprus, Czech Republic and Slovakia) indicate a number of interesting issues. First, is the notion of variability. While some countries have specific legislation that covers the provision of a foreign language (again, mostly English) at pre-primary levels, others do not. We see from Portiková's (2015) discussion how a lack of legislation can lead to huge inconsistencies in provision. A further issue relevant to all of these countries is teacher qualifications, teacher education and pre- and in-service training. This seems to be a challenge for most countries within Europe that are offering English language learning at the pre-primary level and one that emerged from the European Commission's (2011) policy handbook. The different contexts described above also demonstrate that despite some of these challenges, children themselves are largely positive about learning English as a foreign language at pre-primary level. This positivity is also identified in Brumen (2011) who carried out semi-structured interviews with children aged four to six learning English (or German) as a foreign language in Slovenia. Brumen reports that children are happy to include foreign language into their daily routines and that they were overwhelmingly positive about doing so – i.e. 96.7 per cent of the 120 children sampled responded 'yes' to the question: 'Do you like the foreign language (English or German)?' The discussions in these country-specific descriptions, therefore, seem to be sending the same clear message; namely, that we need far more systematic research on all of these issues of how children in ECE settings across Europe can best develop knowledge and awareness of English (or indeed other foreign languages).

EAL in the UK

Thus far, the contexts described in this chapter relate to English as a foreign language instruction/learning in ECEC contexts in Europe. There has been little discussion of CLIL or other immersion-type programmes, partly due to the fact that in reviewing the documents which attempt to review English language instruction in pre-primary settings, little information is available on these types of bilingual education programmes – apart from a few statements that they are provided in some countries. Exactly how many such programmes, and how many children are enrolled in these, and the precise nature of the provision within these programmes, is not specified. Another context that is relevant for this volume, and for Europe, which has not yet been described is the minority language learner context in the UK and other English-speaking countries in Europe such as Ireland. Minority language learners are those for whom their home language is not the language of the wider, majority society. In the UK, emergent bilingual children (i.e. those children who have the foundations upon which they can develop bilingual language proficiency) from these linguistically diverse backgrounds are referred to as children who have English as an Additional Language (EAL). [Note that in the US they are referred to as English Language Learners (ELL) and in Canada as ESL (English as a Second Language).] Pre-primary children who participate in some form of ECEC in the UK yet who come from non-English-speaking homes fall under the purview of this volume (i.e. ECEC in English for speakers of other languages). It is worth briefly, therefore, examining some issues that emerge for pre-primary school children in the UK who fall in this category.

There are currently over one million pupils in formal education in England who are classified as EAL and who represent over 360 different home languages (NALDIC, 2014) distributed throughout the country, though there are dense proportions of children with EAL in major urban areas such as London. An important issue with children with EAL is that there are observed achievement gaps between them and non-EAL (i.e. native-speaking children) (Strand, Malmberg and Hall, 2015). Strand et al. (2015) illustrate the achievement gap between EAL and non-EAL pupils broken down by age.

Of particular interest for this chapter are the children in the Early Years Foundation Stage Profile (EYFS) who are just entering formal education – which happens in the year the child turns five. By the end of the first year (Reception) of schooling only 44 per cent of children recorded as EAL achieve a 'good level of development' as measured by the Early Years Foundation Stage Profile (EFSP), relative to 54 per cent of non-EAL pupils. The odds of achieving a 'good level of development' for EAL pupils are 0.67 (33 per cent) lower for EAL students relative to non-EAL pupils. As stated in Strand et al. (2015: 27): *"We conclude that, perhaps not surprisingly, at the end of their first year of full-time education children from homes where they may have had less exposure to English on average achieve lower results than those with FLE (first language English)"*. However, as the child develops, the gap between EAL and non-EAL children seems to narrow where, at age seven, the odds ratio analysis is 0.73. There are many variables associated with academic achievement in pupils with EAL, but the strongest predictor is English language fluency (Strand et al., 2015). In light of the research mentioned in the introductory sections of this chapter that experiences in the early years makes a marked contribution to the child's subsequent academic performance (e.g. Sammons et al., 2002), it is worth examining pre-primary (i.e. under five) provision and experiences of children with EAL. Unfortunately, there has been very little research carried out on this population in the UK. Only a handful of studies have been published thus far, some of which will be discussed below. [Note Fricke and Millard's contribution in this volume is an example of an empirical study aimed at supporting the English language learning of pre-primary and early years children with EAL.]

Drury (2013) reports on a qualitative, ethnographic study of one four-year-old EAL child in an early years setting whose L1 is Pahari. She notes that the child experiences some difficulties in making the transition from home to school, marked notably by a complete lack of interaction with any of the other children, and to a large extent even with the teachers. Drury conceptualises this as a 'silent period', which is characterised by a lack of non-verbal behaviours, a lack of gestures or even eye contact with other children or staff. Drury argues that the child investigated in her study uses silence as a strategy to be unobtrusive, but that despite this, there was 'invisible' learning that went on, unrecognised by the nursery school staff, and this lack of recognition contributed to holding back the child's educational progress. As a result of her observations, Drury urges practitioners to i) recognise and build upon bilingual children's linguistic and cultural 'funds of knowledge' in the early years, ii) recognise the role of silence in early learning in the wider socio-cultural context of home and school, iii) create opportunities with bilingual staff to mediate between home and school, and iv) provide explicit and detailed guidance for practitioners working with bilingual children. This final point is important to emphasise because this is precisely what is missing, both in this EAL context in the UK but throughout Europe in relation to English language learning and instruction more generally.

Drury (2000) suggests best practice is to i) provide opportunities for one-to-one discourse with adults, ii) provide opportunities for language learning in teacher-led small group work, iii) reduce potential for stress in the new learning environment and maximise opportunities for participation, iv) seek ways of supporting social interaction, and to v) make rules and routines explicit. She also urges a commitment to avoid mother-tongue language loss because children will be less likely to use the L1 since the message they will pick up in school settings is that they have to focus on English.

Similar issues are raised in Safford and Drury (2013) who point out how bilingual (i.e. EAL) children are often conceived of as a 'problem' in early years educational settings. They report on the fact that there is little space to respond to local language and cultural contexts, so in turn little space for teaching and/or assessment to take account of bilingual children's learning paths. There are numerous difficulties, assessment being one, where bilingual children with less experience and proficiency in English are assessed with the same tests as native speakers. This happens throughout all educational levels in the UK for children with EAL. This means that pupils with EAL (especially if they are new arrivals and have attended education in another country) are labelled as underachievers early on, which often becomes a self-fulfilling prophecy. Safford and Drury (2013) also note that teachers often feel under prepared to address the needs of bilingual pupils – again a similar refrain throughout this chapter and indeed many of the chapters in this volume. A similar message is espoused in Conteh and Brock (2011), who identify the problems faced by educators and policy makers of how to provide best conditions for bilingual children to learn English. They point out that educational policy is confused and contradictory because on the one hand it claims to be supportive of linguistic diversity, while on the other the universal model of language development and assessment is English only (measured against monolingual norms).

One study that focused exclusively on teachers of children with EAL in early years settings was Robertson et al (2014). They carried out some qualitative research on two multilingual practitioners in the early years settings trying to support the learning of three- and four-year-old children. Of particular note in their study was the observed tensions between supporting home language and the need for children to learn English – often perceived (incorrectly) as two opposing and irreconcilable forces within English schools early years settings. They urge that so-called 'funds of knowledge' need to be opened up to inform bilingual pedagogy in the early years where funds of knowledge denotes the idea that there are resources within communities, which, if shared and exchanged, can help support children's learning (e.g. families, culture, and the like).

These studies have some common themes – themes that permeate not just the English language learning contexts in this chapter, but also throughout the whole volume. The research seems to be suggesting a significant problem in terms of the extent to which teachers of emergent bilingual children feel prepared and equipped to both meet policy, and the needs of the children themselves. More guidance, and research, on what constitutes 'best practice' across a range of associated domains within EAL pedagogy would be welcome. One type of research that is particularly helpful in this sense is the intervention study, where researchers identify particular strategies that they believe will be of specific use for teaching pupils with EAL and try them out in a research design that makes comparisons in achievement following participation in the intervention. Importantly, these designs have a comparison group of children who do not participate in the intervention, to enable researchers to associate any improvements with the participation in the intervention programme. We believe there is a need for more intervention studies such as that described in Fricke and Millard (this volume), where they describe an intervention aimed at supporting oral language development of EAL children in pre-primary education and the results indicated a benefit to children who participated in the intervention on measures of vocabulary. Similar results are found in Dockrell et al (2010) who also carried out a study on pre-primary EAL children and showed how specific pedagogy aimed at improving oral language skills can have positive benefits on EAL children's English language development.

Partly in response to some of the issues described above concerning a problem with teacher education, Karemaker, Sylva, Jelley, Kanji and Murphy (in progress) report on an intervention carried out in early years settings aimed at helping support childcare practitioners to develop knowledge and skills for implementing effective emergent literacy activities. In this study, practitioners participated in training on how to improve their literacy activities across four two-hour sessions. The outcome measures were the children's vocabulary, verbal comprehension and phonological awareness scores on standardised assessments. The results showed improvement in children's vocabulary scores for those children who spoke English in the home (i.e. non-EAL) but, interestingly, the children with EAL did not seem to benefit from their teachers participating in the practitioner sessions. This result underscores the importance of developing particular pedagogical strategies to support all children, particularly in contexts in the UK where in some schools there are high proportions of EAL pupils.

In general, just as with the other context reviewed in this chapter, the context of EAL in the UK (and indeed elsewhere) has a number of challenges associated with it, notably teacher education, a lack of research, difficulty with respect to policy (i.e. matching policy to the reality of teaching children with EAL) and funding (the current UK government at the time of writing has removed the funding for the Ethnic Minority Achievement Grant, which was available to help support the learning and teaching of children with EAL).

Conclusions

In making some concluding remarks, we'd like to start with some positives. It is encouraging to see how countries across Europe are committed to providing good quality (and in many cases free) ECEC to children in the years before they enter formal education at primary level. It is also heartening to see that many countries across Europe have in mind the aim to provide foreign language learning experiences as one of the key elements of a pre-primary curriculum. What is less positive, however, is the lack of 'consistent' information available across countries in Europe about how this is implemented, the curricula being offered, the success of FL (English) programmes and the nature of teacher education for teachers of English at pre-primary levels. This lack of general information creates a number of potential problems in this area. First, it is difficult to establish what is actually going on in Europe in ECEC in English for non-English speakers. We have snippets of information, as represented in this chapter, but we do not have detailed or comprehensive (reliable) information that we can feel assured accurately represents the European context. Consequently, it is difficult to share and learn from each other within the European context (though volumes such as this one mitigate against that problem somewhat). It is undeniable that different contexts will encounter different issues and hence the notion of a 'one size fits all' curriculum is unrealistic. Nonetheless, there will also be a lot of similarities across contexts and a lack of coherence in this area means we are less able to take advantage of others' expertise. This is most seriously problematic for teacher education and provision.

From a research perspective, there is also a lack of activity in this area; however, we are hopeful that over time this will change as increasingly researchers are paying attention to the importance of EFL or English as a Medium of Instruction (EMI) at the pre-primary level. At the moment, there is relatively little published research available to support teachers, teacher educators, policy makers and families on English language learning through ECEC in Europe (Mourão and Lourenço, 2015). More research in these areas would help us adopt a more unified approach based on a shared understanding, which would enable the development of a set of guidelines in terms of teacher education, in-service training and curriculum design, among other issues. We look forward to the coming years where, we hope, we will see greater developments in these crucial areas.

References

Bialystok, E (2001) *Bilingualism in development: Language, literacy and cognition.* Cambridge: Cambridge University Press.

Brumen, M (2011) The perception of and motivation for foreign language learning in pre-school. *Early Child Development and Care, 181(6)*, 717-732.

Buyl, A and Housen, A (2014) Factors, processes and outcomes of early immersion education in the Francophone Community in Belgium. *International Journal of Bilingual Education and Bilingualism, 17(2)*, 178-196.

Cable, C, Driscoll, P, Mitchell, R, Sing, S, Cremin, T, Earl, J, Eyres, I, Holmes, B, Martin, C and Heins, B (2012) Language learning at Key Stage 2: findings from a longitudinal study. *Education 3-13: International Journal of Primary, Elementary and Early Years Education. 40(4)*, 363-378.

Černá, M (2015) 'Pre-primary English language learning and teacher education in the Czech Republic', in Mourão, S and Lourenço, M (eds) *Early years second language education: International perspectives on theory and practice.* London: Routledge.

Conteh, J and Brock, A (2011) 'Safe Spaces'? Sites of bilingualism for young learners in home, school and community. *International Journal of Bilingual education and bilingualism, 14(3)*, 347-360.

Dockrell, JE, Stuart, M and King, D (2010) Supporting early oral language skills for English language learners in inner city pre-school provision. *British Journal of Educational Psychology, 80/4*, 497-515.

Drury, R (2000) Bilingual children in the nursery: a case study of Samia at home and at school. *European Early Childhood Education Research Journal, 8(1)*, 43-59.

Drury, R (2013) How silent is the silent period for young bilinguals in early years settings in England? *European Early Childhood Education Research Journal, 21(3)*, 380-391

Enever, J (2004) 'Europeanisation or globalisation in early start EFL trends across

Europe?' in Gnutzmann, C and Intemann, F (eds) *The globalisation of English and the English language classroom*. Tübingen: Narr.

Enever, J (ed) (2011) *Early language learning in Europe*. London: The British Council.

European Commission (2011) *Language learning at pre-primary school level: Making it efficient and sustainable. A policy handbook*. European Strategic Framework for Education and Training (ET2010). http://ec.europa.eu/languages/policy/language-policy/documents/early-language-learning-handbook_en.pdf

Eurydice (2012) *Key Data on Teaching Languages at School in Europe*. Education, Audiovisual and Culture Executive Agency. European Commission. http://eacea.ec.europa.eu/education/eurydice/documents/key_data_series/143en.pdf

Eurydice (2014) *Key Data on Early Childhood Education and Care in Europe*. Eurydice and Eurostat Report. Luxembourg: Publications Office of the European Union. http://eacea.ec.europa.eu/education/eurydice/documents/key_data_series/166EN.pdf

Fricke, S and Millard, G (2015) 'A setting-based oral language intervention for nursery-aged children with English as an additional language', in Murphy, V and Evangelou, M (eds) *Early childhood education in English for speakers of other languages*. London: The British Council.

Hawkins, E (2005) Out of this nettle, drop-out, we pluck this flower, opportunity: Re-thinking the school foreign language apprenticeship. *The Language Learning Journal, 32(1)*, 4-17.

Ioannou-Georgiou, S (2015) 'Early Language Learning in Cyprus: Voices from the classroom', in Mourão, S and Lourenço, M (eds) *Early years second language education: International perspectives on theory and practice*. London: Routledge.

Karemaker, A, Sylva, K, Jelley, F, Kanji, G and Murphy, VA (in progress) *'Ready to Read': Can a professional development programme successfully improve children's language and literacy skills?*

Langé, G, Marrocchi, D, Lopriore, L, Benvenuto, G, Cinganotto, L and Vacca, M (2014) *Esperienze di insegnamento in lingua straniera nella Scuola dell'Infanzia: Rapporto sulla rilevazione effettuata nel November 2014*. Direzione Generale per gli Ordinamenti scolastici e la Valutazione del Sistema Nazionale di Istruzione – Gruppo di lavoro "Monitoraggio esperienze di insegnamento in lingua straniera nella scuola dell'infanzia".

Mourão, S and Lourenço, M (eds) (2015) *Early years second language education: International perspectives on theory and practice*. London: Routledge.

Mullis, IVS, Martin, MO, Foy, P and Drucker, KT (2012) *PIRLS 2011 International Results in Reading*. Boston: TIMSS & PIRLS International Study Center.

Murphy, VA (2014) *Second language learning in the early school years: Trends and contexts*. Oxford: Oxford University Press.

Murphy, VA, Macaro, E, Alba, S and Cipolla, C (2015) The influence of L2 learning on first language literacy skills. *Applied Psycholinguistics, 36,* 1133-1153.

NALDIC (2014) *EAL Pupil attainment, gaps and progress 1997-2014.* Available online at www.naldic.org.uk/research-and-information/eal-statistics

OECD (2014) *Education at a Glance (2014): OECD Indicators.* OECD Publishing. http://dx.doi.org/10.1787/eag-2014-en

Portiková, Z (2015) 'Pre-primary second language education in Slovakia and the role of teacher training programmes', in Mourão, S and Lourenço, M (eds) *Early years second language education: International perspectives on theory and practice.* London: Routledge.

Robertson, L, Drury, R and Cable, C (2014) Silencing bilingualism: A day in the life of a bilingual practitioners. *International Journal of Bilingual Education and Bilingualism, 17(5),* 610-623.

Romaine, S (1995) *Bilingualism, 2nd Edition.* Oxford: Blackwell.

Safford, K and Drury, R (2013) The 'problem' of bilingual children in educational settings: policy and research in England. *Language and Education, 27(1),* 70-81.

Sammons, P, Sylva, K, Melhuish, E, Siraj-Blatchford, I, Taggart, B and Elliot, K (2002) *Measuring the impact of pre-school on children's cognitive progress over the pre-school period.* Technical paper 8a. London: Institute of Education, University of London.

Soderman, AK and Oshio, T (2008) The social and cultural contexts of second language acquisition research in young children. *European Early Childhood Education Research Journal, 16(3),* 297-311.

Strand, S, Malmberg, L and Hall, J (2015) *English as an Additional Language (EAL) and educational achievement in England: An analysis of the National Pupil Database.* London: Education Endowment Foundation.

Tucker-Drob, EM (2012) Pre-schools reduce early academic achievement gaps: A longitudinal twin approach. *Psychological Science,* 23(3), 310-319.

1.4

India

Early childhood education in English in India

Padmini Shankar and Paul Gunashekar
English and Foreign Languages University, Hyderabad, India

Introduction

India is a vast country with 1.2 billion people, 29 states, seven union territories, 22 official languages and 365 recognised dialects[3]. Presenting a profile of early childhood education in English in India is a daunting task because of the plethora of complex issues involved. In fact, there is no single policy that governs the entire country although there are pertinent guidelines in the National Curriculum Framework (NCF, 2005). One reason why India does not have a unitary national policy is that education comes under the concurrent agenda of both the central government and the different state governments, and the latter formulate their own policies based on prevalent political agendas.

At the primary level most government schools offer instruction only in the regional languages. There are no government pre-primary or play schools since the official starting age of school education in India is six years. However, there is a multitude of private pre-schools that offer pre-primary education in the English medium – a phenomenon attributable to the notion that "younger is better". It is evident then that English language education in India at both the pre-primary and primary levels is a complex matter.

This chapter aims to provide a status report on early childhood education in English in India. It is organised in five sections. The first section traces the history and background of English language education in India. The second section throws light on the socio-cultural milieu in which English education happens – the divergent contexts and organisations that are involved in the process. The third section outlines the policy decisions that have influenced the study of English across decades, including the debate on lowering the threshold age for introducing English in school. The fourth section, the thrust of the chapter, turns the spotlight on teaching practice – methodology, materials and testing at the pre-primary level.

[3] www.mapsofindia.com or www.translationdirectory.com/articles/article2474.php

The fifth section, in conclusion, notes the challenges involved in early childhood education in English such as designing child-friendly course materials, devising appropriate classroom methodologies, and addressing teacher education needs. The chapter concludes with suggestions for strengthening early childhood education in English in India.

Historical background to English language education in India

The story of English in India is deceptively simple. It began in the early 17th century with the entry of the East India Company (EIC). However, by the early 19th century what began as trade transformed into imperial possession, and the prime duty of the Company altered from trade to managing India on behalf of the British Crown. The roots of English medium education in India can be traced back to this period. In what came to be known as 'Macaulay's Minute on Education' (1835), Thomas Babington Macaulay strongly advocated that English should be the medium of education in India with the aim of creating a *"class who may be interpreters between us and the millions whom we govern – a class of persons Indian in blood and colour, but English in tastes, in opinions, in morals and in intellect"* (cited in Graddol 2010: 62). Subsequent local recruitment resulted in the availability of well-paid new jobs to English speakers in public service. This alone ensured that higher education became largely English-medium. The British thus successfully created an English-speaking elite.

Over the centuries, English has transformed from the language of the aliens and the elite into the language of opportunity and upward mobility. English is now closely associated with wider social and political aspirations with an ever-increasing demand for it from all sections of society. In the words of Graddol (2010: 64): *"Economic growth means that more jobs require English; the expansion of education means that English is needed by more people for study; and for a growing, globalised, urban middle class English is playing a greater role in both their work and personal lives".*

English was granted 'associate official language' status (though it is still not a language listed in the eighth schedule of the Indian Constitution). According to a study, 75 different languages are used in India's education system with 31 different languages used as media of instruction. The percentage of schools teaching English as a 'first language' doubled between 1993 and 2002 from five per cent to ten per cent in primary schools and from seven per cent to 13 per cent in upper primary schools. English is offered as a second language in 19 states, of which 16 introduce it in Class 1, one in Class 3 and two as late as Class 5. Thirty-three States and Union Territories claim to offer English as a medium of instruction, which is more than any other language used in India (Meganathan, 2011). The National Knowledge Commission believes that *"the time has come for us to teach our people, ordinary people, English as a language in schools. Early action in this sphere would help us build an inclusive society and transform India into a knowledge society"* (GOI, 2007, cited in Meganathan, 2011: 83).

Socio-cultural milieu

English education is viewed as a means of upward social mobility, which has led to the mushrooming of private schools where English is not only taught as a subject but is also used as the medium of instruction in all subjects right from Class 1. A notable trend has been for poor families, in both rural and urban areas, to send their children to private schools. Proficiency in English is developed, as Graddol (2010: 74-75) delineates, in seven locations:

1. The home and community: children who come from homes where English is spoken gain a head start in English, and also are supported in schoolwork. Communities also vary greatly in the exposure they provide children to English out of school.

2. Primary school (compulsory education): English skills, considered to be an important part of a child's general education, have to be acquired by the age of 14, underlining the importance of learning English at primary school, although practice and quality vary greatly.

3. Secondary schools (15-18) have traditionally focused on teaching English as a subject, and/or teaching subjects through English. Neither approach is very effective in developing skills in using the language.

4. Private language institutes, coaching colleges, private tuition: these cater for all age groups, but access is better in urban areas and for richer families.

5. Universities/colleges: focus on 'employability skills' of their graduates and the conduct of courses in English communication skills.

6. Workplace/corporate training: many employers help make up a skills gap by in-house training.

7. Informal life experience – such as overseas study, employment: those who study overseas, mostly richer, middle-class families, for example, can expect to come back with improved English skills.

The Indian Constitution has ensured that children's educational needs are addressed at an early age. For instance, the 86th Amendment to the Constitution (2002) ensures provision of early childhood care and education for all children until they reach the age of six years. The Right to Education Bill (2009) proclaims the right of children to free and compulsory education. For school education, India's flagship schemes are the Sarva Shiksha Abhiyan (SSA, 2001), which focuses on primary education; the Rashtriya Madhyamik Shiksha Abhiyan (RMSA, 2009), which takes care of secondary education; and the Mid-Day Meal scheme (1995), which aims to provide nutritious meals to school children of grades 1 to 5 and in some cases, grades 1 to 7. Between them, they account for 85 per cent of India's school education budget and are aimed to achieve universal primary school enrolment.

This background is important to understand the breadth and spread of English education in India. English is now introduced into schools at an early age and more children are learning through the medium of English. Many state governments are responding to the competition from the private sector by switching schools to English medium, or introducing English-medium streams. For instance, Chennai

Corporation started English-medium classes in selected schools in 2009. The Times of India quoted one mother, a domestic helper:

> I work at three houses, and it is difficult for me to afford a private English-medium school for my child. Still I send my daughter there because I want to hear her speak English. Chennai Corporation is starting English-medium schools. I will definitely consider enrolling my child there. (The Times of India, 22 February 2009, cited in Graddol, 2010: 86)

Parents place a high premium on English-medium education owing to its perceived benefits of upward mobility and the general assumption that younger is better; and governments bow down to the pressure. This has led to the rapid growth of private schooling and the increased shift towards English as a medium of instruction in some government schools. In many states, for instance, even where English medium is not adopted, English is now being introduced into the curriculum of government schools from Class 1. Maharashtra was one of the first to implement such an innovation when in 2000 it began teaching English five hours a week. However, one needs to understand that English medium by itself brings no special magic. If not implemented carefully, English-medium instruction can result in neither English nor much education. In fact, early childhood education in English in India is inextricably linked to universalisation of primary education and it indeed is a challenge to ensure quality education for all.

Early Childhood Care and Education

Early Childhood Care and Education (ECCE) addresses children in the age group 0 to six years. It facilitates the realisation of the goals of Universal Elementary Education (UEE) by helping children develop necessary readiness for schooling – getting children used to attending a centre-based programme away from home; developing certain pre-reading, pre-writing and pre-number skills, concepts and vocabulary which help children negotiate the primary curriculum better; and focusing on their health and nutritional requirements through need-based interventions. The ECCE services in India are made available through three channels – public, private and non-governmental organisations. The major public initiative is the Integrated Child Development Services (ICDS) Scheme, which is co-ordinated by the Ministry of Women and Child Development, Government of India. Private-unaided ECCE services (nurseries, kindergartens and pre-primary classes/sections in private schools) constitute a significant proportion of institutions delivering pre-primary education in the country, especially in urban areas. In addition, several NGOs have been engaged in conducting small-scale innovative ECCE programmes focused on children of disadvantaged population groups.

At the time of Independence in 1947, pre-school education was primarily managed by a few voluntary organisations with little governmental help to reach out to poor and needy children. In 1953 the Government of India took the first initiative in ECCE by setting up the Central Social Welfare Board (CSWB). A committee set up by CSWB in 1960 to study the problems of children below six years of age made the following recommendations:

- A comprehensive plan for children's care and training to be evolved
- Pre-schools to be started by voluntary agencies with adequate assistance from the government
- A cadre of adequately trained child welfare workers to be developed.

CSWB started a grants-in-aid scheme for voluntary organisations and sponsored a composite programme of Welfare Extension Projects in rural areas during the First Five-Year Plan with the creation of women's groups or mahila mandate and balwadis. During the Second Plan, these projects were co-ordinated with programmes for women and children in community development blocks, with education for children up to six years forming an integral part. The Education Commission (1964–66) too recognised the significance of pre-school education in child development and its critical linkage with enrolment, retention and learning outcomes at the primary level. It suggested that pre-school education should be left to voluntary agencies with governmental supervision, guidance, training and research.

In the Third Plan period, the emphasis shifted to the child as an entity with specific developmental needs. Although there were 6,000 pre-schools, their quality was suspect and pre-school education in the government system continued to be dominated by the child welfare concept. There were no specific recommendations regarding language education or the teaching/learning of English. The Fourth Plan started the Scheme for Family and Child Welfare to foster all-round development of the pre-school child. In the Fifth Plan there was a shift in approach from 'welfare' to 'development'. As part of the National Policy for Children (1974), Integrated Child Development Services (ICDS) were set up. In 1980, an expert group on Early Childhood Education was set up to examine problems, particularly with reference to the quality of education. An Early Childhood Education Scheme of grants-in-aid for voluntary agencies working in the educationally backward states was established.

The 1970s and 1980s witnessed not only a rapid growth of a variety of programmes for children but also a sharp polarisation in terms of their target group and content. While the government-supported programmes degenerated into mere feeding or custodial centres for children with no attention to their psycho-social needs, the private sector flourished, establishing nursery schools, initially in the urban areas and later extending to semi-urban and rural areas as well. However, these tended to be *"developmentally inappropriate, academically oriented programmes, which were essentially a downward extension of the primary curriculum. Unfortunately, these also served as pace-setters or role models in terms of programme content, for the other category"* (Kaul 2002: 26).

In 1986, the National Policy on Education (NPE) explicitly recognised the importance of Early Childhood Care and Education (ECCE—nomenclature introduced in the policy itself) and emphasised the need to invest in the development of young children belonging to the poverty group. Programmes of ECCE would be child-oriented, focused around play and the individuality of the child. Formal methods and introduction of the three R's would be discouraged at this stage. The local community would be fully involved in these programmes. A full integration of childcare and pre-primary education would be brought about, both as a feeder and a strengthening factor for primary education and for human resource development in general (http://www.ncert.nic.in/oth_anoun/npe86.pdf). The Eighth Five-Year Plan period from 1992 onwards saw accelerated expansion of ICDS with a view to universalising the programme. The Ninth Five-Year Plan addressed the issue of early childhood care and education more exhaustively than previous plans. While acknowledging the first six years of life to be critical, it recommended the institution of a National Charter for Children, which would ensure that 'no child remains illiterate, hungry or lacks medical care' by the end of the Ninth Plan. Thus, influenced by global thinking, the concept of ECCE has undergone a shift from a *"unidimensional, sectoral concept to a more holistic and developmentally appropriate definition"* (Kaul, 2002: 27).

Policy design, implementation and impact

Education is conceived as an important engine of national development geared to combating poverty and reducing inequality within developing societies. Policies supporting the teaching of English as a means of educational enhancement are not solely based on societal beliefs about the power of English to transform people's lives, rather, there is tangible evidence that knowledge of English is correlated with better overall education in certain contexts (Grin, 2001, cited in Seargent and Erling, 2011: 265). Therefore, the prominent role assigned to quality English education in the education systems of developing countries is partially justified. Also, policy statements reflect people's perception of the power of English and its associations with economic value, education, opportunity and technology. And yet, lowering the age for the introduction of English and imparting learning in English at the primary and even pre-primary levels is to be done with caution. Especially in a multilingual context like India, the L1 should be gainfully employed to teach the L2.

Constitutionally, child development and education are concurrent subjects. This implies shared federal and state responsibility in ECCE service delivery. The provisioning of ECCE services in India entails multiple components.

Table 1 provides details of ministerial charge in the delivery of ECCE services:

Table 1: Ministerial charge in the delivery of ECCE services

Area of Responsibility	Age of Children	Ministry
Nutritional supplementation, nutrition and health education	0-6 years	Department of Women and Child Development (DWCD), Ministry of Human Resource Development (MHRD)
Immunisation	0-6 years	Department of Family Welfare, Ministry of Health and Family Welfare (MOHFW)
Pre-school education	3-6 years	DWCD and Department of Elementary Education and Literacy (EE and L), MHRD
Childcare	0-5/6 years	DWCD, Ministry of Labour
Prevention and early detection	Prenatal onward	Ministry of Social Justice and Empowerment

The National Focus Group on Early Childhood Education (2006) clearly outlines five major dimensions of quality: appropriate curriculum; trained, motivated and suitably rewarded teachers; appropriate teacher-child ratio and group size; a supervisory mechanism; and child-friendly infrastructure. In the private sector, it argues that ECCE is plagued by such problems as: burdensome and boring learning; anxiety ridden admission process through entrance tests; structured and rote learning for which children are not developmentally and cognitively ready; taxing evaluation procedures, heavy homework, lack of adequate and appropriate play material. Children in pre-school should be taught through their L1 because it is more natural for children to communicate using the L1 than to struggle to communicate through the L2 that they have still not acquired. In fact, it is a matter of *"the rights of learners. All individuals have the right to an education in their first language, and this right might be violated with the premature introduction of English into elementary education"* (Nunan 1999).

The National Focus Group on Teaching of Indian Languages (2006) recommends that even at the primary level, learning should be imparted only in the L1: "Primary education is essentially language education. Even elementary arithmetic and early knowledge about society and environment are best acquired through the mother-tongue(s) of learners. The medium of instruction at the level of primary school must be the mother-tongue(s) of learners, building upon the rich experiential, linguistic, and cognitive resources that they bring to schools" (p.30). It may be argued that ECE can be provided in the L2 too but it would require trained and informed teachers and well-written coursebooks coupled with the availability of and exposure to the L2 outside of school. It is worthwhile noting what The National Focus Group on Teaching of English (2006) says: "The level of introduction of English has now become a matter of political response to people's aspirations, rendering almost irrelevant an academic debate on the merits of a very early introduction. There are problems of systematic feasibility and preparedness, for example, finding the required number of teachers" (p.1). What Agnihotri (2008, cited in Mathew, 2012) remarked about primary education is true of pre-primary education too: "First, there are no teachers; if there are some, they don't know any English themselves; and if some do know it, there are no materials and support systems". Mathew (2012: 88) reiterates this point when she states: *"First of all India does not have sufficient English-proficient teachers to teach the millions of children who have made this early start".*

The National Focus Group on Teaching of Indian Languages (2006: 30) holds the view that *"where qualified teachers and adequate infrastructural facilities are available, English may be introduced from the primary level, but for the first couple of years it should focus largely on oral-aural skills, simple lexical items, or some day-to-day conversation ... If trained teachers are not available, English should be introduced at the post-primary stage and its quantum increased in such a way that learners should soon reach the level of their classmates who started learning English early".*

Furthermore, in a multilingual country like India, language teaching is not a straightforward issue. Any Indian language used as a medium of instruction, especially in towns and cities, may cause problems to both children and teachers, and it indeed is a challenge to bridge the gap between the home language/dialect and the school language. To elaborate, we cannot assume that the language of a given State is the L1 of all the children studying in that State. Also, in the border areas, the L1 spoken by the children is not necessarily the same as the state language. For instance, children studying in a Kannada-medium school near the border of Karnataka and Andhra Pradesh may speak Telugu at home, and if Kannada is used as the medium of instruction, they will find it difficult to transact learning. It makes sense, therefore, for children to be allowed to express themselves in their home language while they gradually acquire the regional/ school language through exposure. Prioritising listening and speaking alongside free play with peers should help in this regard. As Mathew (2012: 101) argues: *"Adopting a multilingual approach and addressing other pedagogical issues are extremely important although not easy. For example, L2 literacy skills may have to be introduced gradually and after learners are fairly conversant with oral skills. This means that the first two or three years of instruction would have to largely focus on speaking and listening".*

In a multilingual classroom, children should be encouraged to express themselves in their own language and to pay attention to and learn from each other. This is a natural and easy process in play situations. This argument applies with even greater force to children in tribal areas who enter directly into a primary school that uses the state language totally unfamiliar to them. The National Focus Group on Teaching of English (2006) suggests that multilingualism can help counter some of the problems arising from the early introduction of English such as *"the loss of one's own language(s), or the burden of sheer incomprehension"* (p.1). Indeed, as Cameron (2001) argues, scaffolding L2 learning with the L1 is quite beneficial, especially to young children.

Further, in their craze for English the general public has equated/confused learning English with so-called 'English medium', and the growing popularity of these 'English-medium' schools has lead to rapid privatisation of education at the primary and pre-school levels. To quote the National Focus Group on ECC: *"English has become the line dividing the privileged from the rest, and the base of the continuing dual track in our educational system. These are issues of class, power and social inclusion rather than of pedagogy, and hence have to be approached from a political standpoint"* (p. 32). In fact, the primary education scenario in India is very complicated with hundreds of home languages and many in most classrooms and defies straightforward solutions (Jhingran, 2009, cited in Mathew, 2012). There are government schools that are considered low quality institutions. These schools offer instruction in the mother tongue with English as one of the subjects from Class 1 where English could be the children's fourth language (the first three languages being home language, link/street language and school language). Quite often, these schools do not have teachers who can teach English. There are private schools which offer instruction in English medium in response to parental/societal demands, although a large majority of them, especially in rural/semi-urban areas, do not have English-proficient or qualified teachers. *"It is ironic that the Indian constitution provides for education in the mother tongue at the primary stage, but there is no national language policy that is binding on all the states"* (Mathew 2012: 87).

Pedagogical practices

It is important for policies to consider the complex realities about the role of English and its relation to economic development and education; but it is also important that this is reflected in the pedagogic practices promoted within programmes that aim to teach English as a language for international development (Seargent and Erling, 2011). The years at primary school are extremely important in children's intellectual, physical and social-emotional development. Hence it is important to adopt effective pedagogic practices. Arguing that the pedagogy of primary teachers has always been under-theorised and the complexity of the task under-rated, Eaude (2014: 11) states that the expertise required to teach young children successfully is especially complex and demanding because of the combined effects of: the social and cultural context outside the classroom; the people involved in the classroom and the interactions between them; and how the role and identity of primary school teachers affects, and is affected by, their values and beliefs. Research (Phillips, 1993; Cameron, 2001; Slattery and Willis, 2001) suggests that while teaching young learners we need to:

- use simple, stimulating and achievable activities within children's abilities
- teach through oral and listening activities with minimal writing
- use L1 when needed.

In this regard, it would help to examine some of the pedagogical practices followed in early childhood education. The scenario can be described from three perspectives: how the practice should be in general, how it used to be in India, and how it is now.

What it should be: voices from research

What are some of the characteristics of young learners? According to Slattery and Willis (2001: 4), very young learners:

- Acquire through hearing and experiencing lots of English, in much the same way as they acquire their first language.

- Learn through doing things and playing: they are not consciously trying to learn new words and phrases – for them it is incidental.

- Love playing with language sounds, imitating and making funny noises.

- Are not able to organise their learning. Often they will not realise that they are learning a foreign language. They simply see it as having fun!

- May not be able to read or write in their mother tongue, so it is important to recycle new words and expressions through talk and play.

- Will have their grammar develop gradually on its own provided they hear lots of English and learn to understand a lot of words and phrases.

When we teach children, therefore, we should encourage them to read in English (e.g. stories, comics, reading games), work meaning out for themselves, and use a wider range of language input as their model for language use. In fact, a lot of English can be taught to children while establishing classroom routines and rules; these "build up familiarity and security" (Scott and Ytreberg, 1990: 11). We need not shy away from using the mother tongue since such use offers a sense of security to children, and caters for their need to communicate and puts them at ease (Reilly and Ward, 2003). Cameron (2001) too supports use of the mother tongue in a young learner classroom for such purposes as giving instructions, organising classroom activities and establishing classroom rules. We need to bear in mind that *"offering more opportunities for the linguistic initiative to the child is not an abdication of teacher responsibility if and when the activities are structured carefully, managed effectively and evaluated properly"* (Wood, 1988: 149).

What are the ways to teach a second language, in our case, English, to very young children?

Art and craft

Art, crafts and design render children's limited range of language part of something bigger – something that is strong, rich and has material presence. For example, the word 'me' on its own is worth little or nothing, but written below a self-portrait of a child it becomes meaningful, and is much more likely to be remembered (Wright, 2001: 5). Art, crafts and design activities can help children to appreciate the world around them, be more aware of the five senses, and develop skills in using them. They help children to use language in order to compare, contrast, classify, sequence and organise information.

Stories

Stories and associated activities help children develop a wide range of abilities such as empathising, analysing, evaluating and hypothesising (Wright, 2008). For instance, they help children to: research into the subject matter of the story, reflect on the story and its meaning, predict what might come next in the story, infer what is meant but not said, visualise what the place, people or object might look or sound like, etc. All this helps children not only to put to use the language that they have at their disposal, but also enables them to learn new vocabulary and structures through meaningful contexts.

Drama

Drama activities are very useful for children because drama involves children at many levels, through their bodies, minds, emotions, language and social interaction. They boost children's confidence, address different learning styles, personalise language and contextualise language (Phillips, 1999). Therefore, using drama with very young learners of English helps identify and label emotions and experiences.

Assessment

Although assessment sounds threatening and unsuited to a young child's nature it is a necessary part of teaching and learning. Assessment of young learners should occur in a familiar, "psychologically safe" environment. Texts used in assessment tasks should deal with familiar content – with home and family and school and with familiar, simple genres like children's stories and folktales (McKay, 2006: 9-10). Child-friendly techniques that are compatible with everyday classroom activities have to be used (Pinter, 2006). A variety of techniques have to be used to get a comprehensive picture of young children's language achievement.

What it was: Critiquing the reality (The Yashpal Committee Report, 1993)

Language teaching in the 1980s and 1990s in India left much to be desired. The teaching materials and the activities rarely reflected the world as experienced by children. It was assumed that children would learn to communicate through aimless repetition or rote memorisation (Rampal, 2002: 157).

The National Advisory Committee, 1993 (known as the Yashpal Committee), expressed distress over the academic burden on children and the unsatisfactory quality of education: there is no room for pedagogic experimentation. Education is crippled by large classes, a heavy syllabus, difficult textbooks, and ill-equipped classrooms. Most teachers lack the training as well as the motivation to explain things in detail or ignite young minds. The Committee concluded that English-medium instruction renders learning joyless and demotivating, denying children the privilege of experiencing the world through their mother tongue. Parental demand and craving for English-medium education has led to an increase in the cognitive load/content of the syllabus by advancing the introduction of many topics and subjects in utter disregard of the process of maturation.

The Committee also complained that textbooks are filled with tersely written facts and do not encourage children to think and explore. Textbooks and guidebooks form a tight nexus and sometimes children are compelled to buy the guidebook (or 'key') along with the textbook. Each time the textbooks are revised, new topics are added and the teachability of the textbook – the quotient of content that an average teacher can put across – gets jeopardised. Concepts and information get repeated because of the flawed structure of the syllabus. In the primary classes, ideas and information are presented in a synoptic manner, making the content of the text deceptively simple. In the later classes, the same ideas are repeated, with some elaboration, resulting in a sense of trivialisation and boredom. Curriculum inquiry and reform are not undertaken in a systematic manner and teachers have no role to play in it but for a token involvement of a handful.

The 'catch them young' notion controls the system and pre-school children are burdened with textbooks and the formal learning they represent since parents and teachers feel that unless academic training begins early, children cannot cope with the fast-paced pedagogy and the competitive ethos of the later school years. The Yashpal Committee expresses its deep anguish thus:

> The pernicious grip of this false argument manifests itself in absurd, and of course deeply harmful, practices in pre-schools and primary schools, such as early emphasis on shapely drawing, writing and memorising information. Intrinsic motivation and the child's natural abilities are being smothered at a scale so vast that it cannot be correctly estimated. Our national commitment to the development of human resource is daily challenged in our nurseries and primary schools. (p.14)

What it is: National Curriculum Framework, 2005
In its Position Paper, the National Focus Group on Curriculum, Syllabus and Textbooks (2006) advocated a curriculum framework that emphasises learning with understanding and learning to learn, and one that helps children develop their own understanding based on their lived experiences (p. vii). Curricular knowledge should be selected and organised in view of the aims of education, an epistemological perspective, the child's learning and mental development, and the child's context. Pedagogic practices are to be based on the following principles:

- Understanding that children construct their own knowledge.
- Importance of experiences in learning.
- Active engagement of learners in the construction of knowledge.
- Variety of situations and multiplicity of methods for creating diverse experiences.
- The socio-economic context and identity of the learner.
- An enabling teacher–child relationship.
- The role of and space for parents and community.

The Focus Group made the following observations. Instead of a single textbook, a package of teaching learning material could be used to engage children in active learning, with the textbook a part of this package. The materials should recognise learner concerns; classroom activities should promote in learners a clear sense of self-worth; textbook tasks should direct learners to the goal of personalisation; and textual context should reflect the uniqueness of India's multiculturalism. A large number of packages should be developed at the state and district levels with adequate provision for cluster- and school-level modifications and supplementary materials. The examination system should be revamped and continuous comprehensive evaluation is to be implemented with the collective effort of children, teachers, parents and institutions. Further, the learning experience itself must be evaluated, and not only its outcomes.

It is important to understand that in the first year in which English is introduced as a subject, the learning goal is to develop the basic abilities of listening, speaking, reading and writing in children (see Table 2 below):

Table 2: Learning goals in English in the first year of English teaching in primary schools in India

Letters			
Listening	Speaking	Reading	Writing
Small and capital letters introduced with words and pictures. Many textbooks are similar to workbooks where practice writing can be undertaken in the book itself.			
Words			
Listening	Speaking	Reading	Writing
Building up of vocabulary is done with sets of words from familiar contexts such as home, animals, family, school, etc. Sets of similar sounding words are often used. In most cases, the introduction of the alphabet is done with words and pictures to facilitate letter and word recognition.			Practice in writing words. (Usually copy and write.)
Sentences			
Listening		Speaking	
A number of different activities including recitation of poems so that children can listen and repeat. Listen and repeat sentences after the teacher. Greeting. Instructions and a few basic sentence structures are practised.			

(Source: Banerji and Bobde, 2013: 29)

In its Position Paper, the National Focus Group on Teaching of English (2006), while strongly recommending a pre-literacy curriculum, states that irrespective of the particular class in which English is introduced (Classes I–III or Class IV, or Classes V–VI), the aim at the initial levels (the first, or first two years of English) is to *"build familiarity with the language (through primarily spoken or spoken-and-written input) in meaningful situations, so that the child builds up a working knowledge of the language"* (p. 6). It suggests that "comprehensible input" be provided that includes textbooks, other print material such as Big Books, class libraries, parallel materials in more than one language, and media support (learner magazines, newspaper columns, radio/audio cassettes, etc.), and the use of "authentic" or "available" materials.

Mention must be made here of the welcome change that has been occurring in English language teaching at the pre-primary level. Primers with colourful artwork and attractive layout have been designed that offer a multi-sensory learning experience to young Indian learners of English. These primers reflect the understanding that at the kindergarten stage, children need to learn the rudiments of a variety of life skills: eye-hand co-ordination; ability to colour, sketch and draw; ability to perform activities involving cutting, sticking and folding; ability to solve puzzles and do activities involving the recognition of similarities and differences; the essential skills of identifying, sorting, classifying, matching and recognising the odd one out; conceptualisation of character, quality, position, size and amount; and the ability to follow chronological order. The role of the primers during this stage is to help children develop in all these life skills and to prepare the ground for the more formal kind of teaching that will follow in primary schools. The primers therefore focus on providing an array of interesting language tasks and activities intended to develop the psychomotor, cognitive and affective skills of the young learner. In other words, the goal is to enable the very young learners to actively construct meaning using a range of verbal and non-verbal cues as well as visual and context-embedded clues. Oxford University Press' New Broadway primers – with their rich content of children's songs, nursery rhymes, mini-stories, games and activities and with a happy blend of the Phonic, the Whole Word, and the Whole Sentence methods to introduce the young learners to the basics of reading – are a case in point.

Conclusion

To reaffirm the point, the primacy and supremacy accorded to the English language in the socio-cultural and economic ethos of India stays unquestioned and both the government and non-government organisations have been investing efforts and resources towards improving pedagogical practices. And yet, there are issues that still plague us: large class size, the pressure to 'cover the syllabus' and to teach what will be tested, lack of time and resources to truly implement activity-oriented learning, incompatibility vis-à-vis teaching materials and methodology and testing content and format, excessive workload coupled with non-academic chores for teachers, and teachers' own low proficiency and competence in English. Elaborate training programmes and the need for scaling up teaching skills are the concerns to be immediately addressed. Further, constant dialogue between all stakeholders – teachers, trainers, parents and policy makers – can help plug loopholes. Such attempts at communication can *"tailor English language education to the local needs of communities attempting to engage fully in a rapidly globalising world"* (Seargent and Erling, 2011: 269). Additionally, there is a need for a two-pronged measure: attitudinal makeover (in both the teaching community and the general public) and pedagogic training. To elaborate, lack of early achievement in English, especially in the case of children from rural or underprivileged backgrounds, should not be equated with lack of potential to learn. Massive teacher training programmes, offering attractive pay cheques to teachers, exploring indigenous models of development, and bridging the gap between research and teaching practice are the measures that could strengthen early childhood education in English in our country.

References

Banerji, R and Bobde, S (2013) 'Evolution of the ASER English tool', in Berry, V (ed) *English Impact Report: Investigating English Language Outcomes at the Primary School Level in Rural India.* Berry, V (ed) London: British Council, 27-32.

Cameron, L (2001) *Teaching language to young learners.* Cambridge: CUP.

Curtain, HA and Dahlberg, CAP (2000) *Planning for Success: Common Pitfalls in the Planning of Early Foreign Language Programmes.* ERIC®DIGEST EDO-FL-00-11 DECEMBER 2000.

Eaude, T (2014) What makes primary class teachers special? Exploring the features of expertise in the primary classroom. *Teachers and Teaching: Theory and Practice, 20(1),* 4-18.

Graddol, D (2010) *English Next India.* British Council.

Kaul, V (2002) 'Early childhood care and education', in Govinda, R (ed) *India Education Report: A Profile of Basic Education.* New Delhi: OUP, 23-34.

Mathew, R (2012) 'Young learner English language policy and implementation: A view from India', in (pp.83-106)', in Spolsky, B and Moon, Y (eds) *Primary School English-Language Education in Asia: From Policy to Practice.* New York and London: Routledge, 83-106.

McKay, P (2006) *Assessing Young Language Learners.* Cambridge: CUP.

Meganathan, R (2011) 'Language policy in education and the role of English in India, From library language to language of empowerment', in Coleman, H (ed) *Dreams and realities: Developing countries and the English language.* London: British Council, 59-87.

Ministry of Human Resource Development (1986) *National Policy on Education.* Government of India. www.ncert.nic.in/oth_anoun/npe86.pdf

Ministry of Human Resource Development (2009) *Right to Education Act.* Department of School Education and Literacy, Government of India. http://mhrd. gov.in/rte

National Council of Educational Research and Training (2005) *National Curriculum Framework.* www.ncert.nic.in/rightside/links/pdf/framework/english/nf2005.pdf

Nunan, D (1999) Does younger = better? *TESOL Matters,* 9(3), 3.

Phillips, S (1999) *Drama with Children.* Oxford: OUP.

Phillips, S (1993) *Young learners.* Oxford: OUP.

Pinter, A (2006) *Teaching Young Language Learners:* Oxford Language Teachers' Handbook Series. Oxford: Oxford University Press.

Position Paper of National Focus Group on Curriculum, Syllabus, and Textbook (2006). New Delhi: NCERT.

Position Paper of National Focus Group on Early Childhood Education (2006). New Delhi: NCERT.

Position Paper of National Focus Group on Teaching of English (2006). New Delhi: NCERT.

Position Paper of National Focus Group on Teaching of Indian Languages (2006). New Delhi: NCERT.

Rampal, A (2002) 'Texts in context: Development of curricula, textbooks, and teaching learning materials', in *India Education Report: A Profile of Basic Education*. New Delhi: OUP, 153-166.

Reilly, V and Ward, SM (2003) *Very young learners*. Oxford: OUP.

Report of the National Advisory Committee (1993) *Learning without Burden*. New Delhi: Govt. of India.

Scott, WA and Ytreberg, LH (1990) *Teaching English to Children*. New York: Longman.

Seargent, P and Erling, EJ (2011) 'The discourse of 'English as a language for international development': Policy assumptions and practical challenges', in Coleman, H (ed) *Dreams and realities: Developing countries and the English language*. London: British Council, 255-274.

Slattery, M and Willis, J (2001) *English for Primary Teachers*. Oxford: OUP.

Wright, A (2008) *Storytelling with Children*. Oxford: OUP.

Wright, A (2001) *Art and Crafts with Children*. Oxford: OUP. http://en.wikipedia.org/wiki/Pratham (accessed on 8 December 2014).

1.5

Africa

Beyond ABC: the complexities of early childhood education in Tanzania

Nipael Mrutu, Pauline Rea-Dickins, Fortidas Bakuza, Shelina Walli, Aga Khan University, Institute for Educational Development, East Africa

Alan Pence, University of Victoria, Canada

The importance of early childhood care and education has gained increasing recognition in Tanzania, resulting in various transformations in the education landscape in the country. Without disregarding the developmental milestones that the provision of education has undergone over the years, this chapter, based on data collected from 14 regions in the country as part of the *Tuwaendeleze Watoto Wetu (TWW)*, Let Us Develop our Children study, describes some of the complexities in the provision of early childhood education in Tanzania. The project[4] was designed to contribute to what is known about effective approaches to support young children's development and education in Tanzania. Early childhood care and education in Tanzania is mainly provided by private institutions, including religious institutions, and in some cases community-owned pre-schools. The language of instruction in privately run early childhood centres tends to be English while in public schools, including pre-primary centres and classes, the language of instruction is Kiswahili, the national language. This divide between public and private education providers is also associated with the quality of education where English, on the one hand, is associated with a higher quality education and Kiswahili, on the other, is viewed as weak and therefore a poor medium of instruction when it is associated with the quality of education. Drawing on the relationship between language competency and literacy in the early years and the findings from the TWW study, this chapter highlights a situation whereby the pursuit of ensuring the right to education for Tanzanian children may lead to the creation of injustice and inequalities for the majority of young children. While we

[4] This research, one of several related studies in the area of early human development, was made possible through funding from the Department for Foreign Affairs Trade and Development (DFATD) within the Programme for the Advancement of Human Development in Africa and Asia.

acknowledge the importance of exposing young children to rich experiences and the right to choice in the provision of early childhood education (ECE), it is argued in this chapter that there is a need to examine the disparities and differences that exist in the provision of ECE created through language issues in Tanzania.

Introduction and background

The challenges facing Tanzania are not unique. Early childhood care and education[5] services have expanded dramatically in many Sub-Saharan Africa (SSA) countries since 2000. In 2000 it was estimated that only a few countries had ECE policies in place while, by 2008, 19 countries had tabled Early Childhood Development[6] policies, with another 20 countries engaged in preparations to do so (UNESCO BREDA, 2012). This increase relates to a number of initiatives, both global and SSA in scope.

Globally, ECE has benefitted not only from the presence of international conventions highlighting the rights and developmental needs of children, such as the Convention on the Rights of the Child (United Nations, 1989), but also through the World Declaration on Education for All (EFA), launched in Jomtien, Thailand in 1990 (UNESCO, 1990). The EFA was revisited at the World Education Forum held in Dakar, Senegal in 2000, at which point early ECE emerged as the first of six priority goals:

> *"(i) expanding and improving comprehensive early childhood care and education, especially for the most vulnerable and disadvantaged children."*
> (The Dakar Framework for Education for All, 1990: 8)[7].

Such conventions and initiatives have been joined by a dramatic increase in the profile of ECE as a key tool for broader social and economic development (e.g. Heckman, 2006; Heckman et al., 2006; Engle et al., 2011[8]).

Within SSA, initiatives such as the African International Early Childhood Development Conference series (1999, Kampala; 2002, Asmara; 2005, Accra; 2009, Dakar) brought ever-larger numbers of political leaders into interaction with technical specialists and advocates, helping to spur the dramatic increase in policy developments noted earlier and summarised in Table 1 below (Pence and Benner, 2015).

---

[5] In this chapter we use ECE – Early Childhood Education – to cover a range of provision for young children, which variously is referred to elsewhere as ECCE (Early Childhood Care and Education, or ECD (Early Childhood Development). Our focus here is primarily on education and we therefore use ECE throughout
[6] These policies cover ECE, ECCE, ECD
[7] http://unesdoc.unesco.org/images/0012/001211/121147e.pdf)
[8] www.thelancet.com/pdfs/journals/lancet/PIIS0140-6736%2811%2960889-1.pdf

Table 1: Location, size and scope of African ECD conferences

Conference Location and Theme	Date	# of Attendees	# of SSA Countries	# of Presenters	African-based participation	African Government Representation
Kampala, Uganda Showcasing ECCD: Innovation and Application in Africa	1999	200	19	35	75%	3 national ministers
Asmara, Eritrea Health, Nutrition, Early Childhood Care and Education, and Children in Need of Special Protection	2002	200	28	60	80%	6 national ministers; 1 international minister
Accra, Ghana Moving Early Childhood Forward in Africa	2005	300	39	80	85%	6 national ministers; 27 international ministers/ delegates
Dakar, Senegal From Policy to Action: Expanding Investment in ECD for Sustainable Development	2009	600	42	146	89%	35 national ministers; 113 international ministers/ delegates

These activities were supplemented by SSA multi-country professional capacity development initiatives such as the Association for the Development of Education in Africa's support for the Working Group on ECD (ADEA-WGECD; see www.afdb. org/en/news-and-events/article/africa-launches-platform-to-enhance-collaboration-between-countries-for-the-delivery-of-quality-early-childhood-development-programmes-13956/; http://www.adeanet.org/portalv2/en/news/ africa-launches-inter-country-quality-node-on-early-childhood-development)[9], the Early Childhood Development Virtual University (University of Victoria, Canada), and a host of internationally supported initiatives within specific SSA countries[10].

---

[9] ADEA's Working Group on Early Childhood Development (WGECD) was created in 1998, superseding a group known as the Early Childhood Development Network in Africa (ECDNA). The WGECD, with funding through ADEA, supported ECD in Africa through its activities in areas of research, dialogue, advocacy and networking. As from February 2015, WGECD responsibilities have been passed to the Inter-Country Quality Node on Early Childhood Development (ICQN-ECD). The ICQN-ECD has been created at the instigation of the Ministry of Education and Human Resources, Higher Education and Scientific Research of Mauritius, which has taken the responsibility of its leadership. Its main objective is to improve ECD policies and practices, so that "every African child gets a good start in life through the implementation of effective ECD programmes."

[10] One such event was the Inaugural Conference and Official Launch of the Institute for Human Development, February 14–15, Nairobi, East Africa. There were 220 participants from 22 countries, many of which were from Sub-Saharan Africa. The theme of the conference was: *Investing in Early Childhood Development for a Better World* (see also www. aku.edu/ihd/Pages/home.aspx).

Examples of these in the context of this chapter include:

Conference Location and Theme	Date	# of Attendees	# of SSA Countries	# of Presenters	African-based participation	African Government Representation
Arusha, Tanzania: First Biennial National Forum on Early Childhood Development in Tanzania	2012	160	N/A	29	90%	5 national ministers
Zanzibar, Tanzania: Affordable, Quality Pre-primary Education for All	2014	c. 200	14+	All country delegations + invited speakers	Vast majority	14 delegations representing ECCE at country policy level

While the volume of ECE international research and scholarly literature has expanded dramatically since 2000, along with very significant increases in the number of SSA countries with ECE-related policies, SSA-specific and SSA-led research remains, problematically, an insignificant contributor to the global literature. Most SSA countries (with the exception of South Africa) have a very restricted locally focused and locally led literature upon which to base policy, programme and practice guidelines. This chapter presents some of the findings from the *Tuwaendeleze Watoto Wetu (TWW)* project that was designed to address such evidence-based shortfalls at country (Tanzania) and regional (SSA) levels. This project also provided support for the development of the ECE international compendium led by the University of Victoria, Canada[11].

In what follows, we first provide an overview and details of the research design. This is followed by a summary of findings with specific reference to languages in ECE, and we then highlight some central discussion points arising from the TWW research.

Overview

Within a context in which quality ECE is increasingly recognised as an essential building block in an individual's educational trajectory, their capacity to participate productively at community or society level and enhance their overall wellbeing, a key question that needs answering focuses around what is known about ECE education provision in any given country. In other words, are the important foundation stones being provided for all young children? As we have seen above, there has been a surge of interest in recent years but while certain assumptions might be possible to make about ECE in north American or European contexts, much less is known in terms of a strong evidence base about ECE in Sub-Saharan Africa. In any case, knowledge and constructions of ECE from and about one context, while they have the potential to inform practice in another, are not directly applicable and a huge danger exists of importing wholesale perspectives and

---

[11] The Compendium project led by the ECDVU and supported through this research has been described in other publications (Pence and Ashton, in press; Ashton and Pence, 2014)

practices from elsewhere. The foundation for all school learning is what children bring from their home and community environments and it is essential to understand these particular life experiences *in their community languages* that children bring with them to school. There is, thus, a need to understand better the prevailing local landscapes. This study therefore aimed to strengthen the evidence base with respect to national capacity and approaches to interventions for the delivery of effective ECE interventions in Tanzania.

Design of the TWW ECE landscaping study

In a country as large as Tanzania with 28 different regions, including Zanzibar, it was not possible within the scope of the project to landscape the entire ECE provision countrywide. We therefore took a decision to do an in-depth mapping in half of the regions, covering regions as shown in Figure 1 below.

Figure 1: TWW coverage

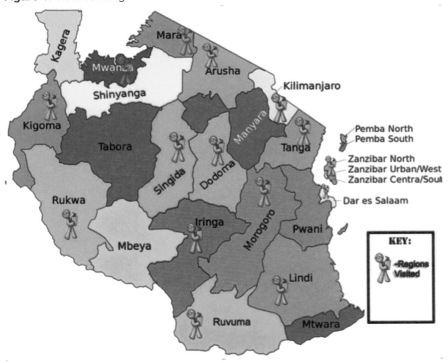

Factors that led to the identification of these regions included visiting each of the seven Teacher Training Colleges (TTCs) that had been nominated by the Ministry of Education to become the centres of excellence for ECE in Tanzania. We also gathered data in the private sector, including some private teacher training colleges (TTCs) and universities offering ECE programmes, given, as mentioned earlier, that the private sector plays a decisive role in the provision of ECE in Tanzania. In tracing the ECE landscape in Tanzania one cannot easily disentangle education institutions from the civil society and\or NGOs. Civil society collaborates and co-operates with educational institutions in a number of ways, such as in advocacy, and some NGOs support educational institutions financially to run ECE programmes. Similarly, educational institutions also offer instructional, technical and material support to civil society and we therefore included all these stakeholder groups within our sample. The achieved sample is summarised in Table 2.

Table 2: TWW achieved sample

Region	HEI[12]	Education centre	CSO[13]	Government
Mwanza	2	7	7	-
Mara	1	-	-	-
Kilimanjaro	4	1	2	-
Tanga	2	2	5	-
Singida	1	-	2	-
Morogoro	2	1	3	-
Iringa	5	1	4	-
Rukwa	1	-	2	-
Zanzibar	2	2	-	2
Dar es Salaam	5	-	3	3
Lindi	2	4	4	-
Dodoma	2	-	2	-
Arusha	2	1	3	-
Kigoma	1	-	-	-

As observed in Table 2, we also gathered data from three main ministries in the forefront of supporting ECE, namely the Ministry of Education and Vocational Training (MoEVT), the Ministry of Community Development Gender and Children (MCDGC) and the Ministry of Health and Social Welfare (MoHSW).

---

[12] Higher Education Institution: universities, teacher training colleges, vocational educational colleges
[13] Civil Society Organisations

Approach

We adopted an interactive and stakeholder engagement approach to the TWW research design. An initial workshop was conducted with diverse ECE stakeholders – government, learning institutions and civil society – where participants engaged in a series of questions such as:

a. What ECE curricula, materials and resources do you provide to trainers and practitioners?

b. What funding (and by whom) does your sector provide or receive for ECE activities?

c. How is your sector involved in monitoring and assessing ECE?

d. What does "Early Childhood Education" mean to your sector – how do you define it and how does your sector agree or disagree on the definition?

e. What is your sector's current role in ECE? Future roles and responsibilities?

f. What are the objectives of ECE?

ECE stakeholders also supported the identification of key themes (see Table 3) and perceived gaps in ECE in Tanzania and the development and validation of the interview protocols. Subsequently, working in collaboration with the national Tanzanian Early Childhood Development Network (TECDEN[14]), two data collection, archiving and analysis workshops were conducted, the interview protocols were piloted, revised, and Kiswahili and English versions developed. Interview data was collected in the period April to September 2014 around the following major focal areas, as summarised in Table 3.

Table 3: Guiding themes for data collection

Themes	Themes
Programming and Training	Inclusion and Equity
Leadership	Quality Assurance
Resources	Standards
Assessment	Advocacy
Community Engagement	Conceptualisations of ECE
Attitudes	Policy
Renewed Interest in ECE	Policy Implementation

As noted from the above listing of identified research themes, this study did not set out to research issues of language in ECE specifically, nor was 'language' flagged as major in any way during the research start-up phase. However, as we collected and analysed the data it became clear that language issues raise significant challenges for quality ECE provision. In the next section, we present some of our findings focusing on the language of ECE training, conceptualisations of ECE and instructional implications, and attitudes to language and quality.

---

[14] TECDEN is a national network with 18 chapters in each of the regions in Tanzania. Four of these TECDEN chapter members supported the data collection in the regions.

Selected findings

Language for training ECE teachers and caregivers

In this study we observed that pre-school teacher training in the government TTCs visited was conducted in Swahili, as per policy. The private TTCs on the other hand undertook their training in English. The explanation for this observed difference is based on the rationale that the government-trained pre-school teachers are sent to teach in government pre-schools where the medium of instruction is Swahili. The government, however, is not responsible for the job placement of pre-school teachers trained in private institutions who, thus, seek employment independently and usually end up in employment in the private ECE sector; that is, private pre-schools where the medium of instruction is English. It can therefore be argued that the use of English or Swahili in educational institutions that train teachers to teach in early years classes is shaped by the prevailing circumstances such as the demands of the job market.

However, while some may argue that the use of two different languages to train pre-school teachers might not necessarily be a cause for concern, this situation does raise some critical issues for those tutors training future ECE teachers in the public sector TTCs. These tutors will normally be graduates and have studied through the medium of English at university. This means that tutors will have received their university education through English only to be expected to conduct their training for pre-primary and primary teachers in state-run TTCs through Swahili. Our data strongly suggests that the assumption that there can be a smooth transition between language use across the sectors – university and TTC – is misguided, as the following quotation highlights:

> We were taught all the jargons and concepts in English, and here we are teaching in Swahili, it's difficult. (12\A\3\NM\20.5.14)[15]

But such concerns are not restricted to the tensions arising from the use of two different languages at different times and for different purposes. A second issue that has emerged from our data has to do with the levels of English proficiency of the teacher trainers, even for those who studied ECE through the medium of English:

> It is a problem, as you have seen yourself, our students [teacher trainees] can't comfortably express themselves in English and yet they are expected to teaching[16] pupils in English medium schools after graduating ... it's not their fault, it's the education system, It's the language policy in the country ... we shift from one language to the other just like that. (6\A\6\NM\20.3.14)

What we observe here therefore is a dual problem: one of transitioning from one language to the other and another concerning poor English proficiency levels of future ECE teachers.

---

[15] Our coding is as follows: 12 refers to region; A–D refers to the type of institution sampled; 3 denotes the informant; initials refer to the individual interviewers, followed by the date that the data were collected

[16] These are verbatim transcriptions and some contain syntactic infelicities

Compounding the issues above were factors around the lack of ECE resources, such as books and other print and learning materials, to allow for or support an effective shift from one language to the other. Our informants told us that they lacked Swahili teaching resources and materials such as books, and that they depended on online resources available through the internet. However, those that they could locate online were unfortunately resources in English and thus there was a need for them to be translated into Kiswahili before using them, and it was reported that they struggled in this translation process.

The lack of resources does not only affect the state-run TTCs which use Swahili as the language for training ECE practitioners, and a challenge of a different kind was evidenced in the private TTCs. The private sector TTCs reported that they depended to a considerable extent on the available online resources in English. However, although their college trainers will have gained their undergraduate degrees through English-medium instruction, the private TTCs reported a lack of sufficient tutors with a good enough command of the English language, noting that many of their tutors struggled with the material in English and that they were also challenged in providing the ECE training through the medium of English. In other words, there is a situation in which college tutors struggle to both comprehend the resources available in English and to instruct the ECE trainee teachers through the medium of English. This finding therefore raises issues of quality in the implementation of the ECE training at the college tutor level and the impact that inadequate English language skills on the part of the tutors may have on those trainees who, in turn, will be expected to provide quality English language-mediated ECE for young children in the private sector.

A third challenge linked to training for ECE is also related to resources. Not only did our respondents report a significant lack of materials in Swahili or in the ethnic community languages[17], when contrasted with the wealth of materials available in English, they also commented that materials accessed by and large via the internet are by default not grounded in the ECE realities of Sub-Saharan Africa, let alone the specific contexts found across Tanzania. For example:

> However, we lack resources like teaching materials, we depend much on searching online on the internet and see how the West are doing it. The thing is we see how they do it, but in most cases they are kind of things which we can't get hold of them here in Morogoro, and the way they teach is far beyond our capability, so in most cases we end up printing out only some articles. (4\A\5\NM\19.3.14)

Our findings are compounded by the very significant difficult circumstances in which ECE trainers find themselves, with the complexity of the issues, language and others, explained as follows:

> We use the government curriculum but since ECE is still quite new course, we spend a lot of time planning for a lesson, searching for references, for learning materials. We try our best searching for books but we end up getting very old books from the

---

[17] There is the expectation that in government-run primary and pre-schools the medium is Swahili

library, and no books at all in our books stores here in Singida, we do not even have modern technology like projectors and other modern technology. Our classes are crowded as you have seen, we now have 184 students, but we are only three ECE teachers, we don't even have enough chairs and tables for our students. (6\A\3\ NM\20.3.14)

I visited a school called X Primary School[18] in Dodoma; it had 140 students and one teacher. (Informant L, 19.3.14)

Taken together, these findings, we suggest, point to issues of quality in the implementation of ECE training and the impact that inadequate English language skills and a paucity of resources for ECE in an appropriate language may have on the teacher trainees who, in turn, will be expected to provide quality ECE for young children mediated through either English or Swahili.

Conceptualisations of ECE

Unsurprisingly in our research, what constitutes good practice in ECE was articulated and explicitly defined in several different ways. We were also able to capture understandings and operationalisations of ECE through, for example, the focus of the advocacy activities of the educational institutions visited. Interestingly, in this study all participants engaged in advocacy initiatives, describing advocacy as (i) enabling – providing ECE basic needs and training teachers appropriately; (ii) education/engagement – educating and engaging parents and communities about the importance of ECE; and (iii) collaboration – working with different stakeholders.

Participants who understood advocacy as enabling, embraced broad conceptualisations of ECE, encompassing issues such as the protection of child rights, development of basic social and emotional needs, good parenting skills, physical, cognitive and linguistic development, and the welfare of vulnerable groups. We heard about many programmes providing competently trained teachers by addressing children's holistic development. Of particular relevance to this chapter is the finding that a number of informants in this study noted that the renewed interest in the provision of ECE services in Tanzania is a reaction to the poor primary school learning outcomes where a significant number of primary school leavers cannot read or write, in English or Swahili (www.twaweza.org/uploads/files/Uwezo_EA_Report-EN-FINAL.pdf; UWEZO 2010). Without ignoring the connection between pre-primary school attendance and primary school learning outcomes, we highlight the possibility and indeed the narrowness of the view of pre-primary schools being seen as an opportunity to teach reading and writing formally. The danger here obviously being that an exclusive or narrow focus on teaching students to read and write ignores the development of other important skills and capacities, such as the passing to the next generation knowledge about plants used for the preparation of herbal medicine.

---

[18] The observation was undertaken in a Standard 1 class (first year of primary) with children aged approximately seven years old

Fortidas Bakuza

Figure 2
The example above was taken from a caregiving context in a Masai community and illustrates how indigenous knowledge is developed in community contexts. Also observed in the same community is a locally produced play area, where children are playing in a construction that inside resembles a maze – they are having fun interacting in a 'safe play' environment with their peers.

Fortidas Bakuza

Figure 3
This contrasts starkly with the quotation below from one of the TTC tutors as he explained the advocacy initiatives that his institution was engaged in, highlighting the perceived importance of ECE as providing opportunities for formal literacy and numeracy development:

> We have a group made up of ten people, some from the TTC and others from N. primary school. Together we have formed an advocacy committee to inform teachers on three main things which are essential skills for pre-school children, and these are counting, reading and writing. We inform them on how to train kids to acquire these essential skills, the 3K's – Kuhesabu-Kusoma-Kuandika[19] (TTC Tutor 12\A\3\NM \12.05.2014)

What seem to be missing from such explanations or accounts are the processes through which the foundations for formal learning are established and capacities

---

[19] Translated from Kiswahili as: Arithmetic-Reading-Writing

acquired, through, for example, play, games and structured talk. There was a perspective coming through some of our data that ECE is an opportunity to bring formal classroom learning into the pre-school with a focus on formal learning and outcomes, as a means to ensure better learning outcomes at the end of the primary phase. In other words, there is a disconnect in some quarters where pre-primary is viewed as 'primary for younger children', as opposed to being a phase that focuses on the whole child and understanding the role, for example, of play in developing both linguistic and narrative skills as a preparatory phase which helps children be prepared for primary school.

Attitudes: language and quality ECE

Not unrelated to the findings above are certain attitudes we found in our data in relation to English-medium and Swahili-medium ECE provision. We have evidence that supports a view that English-medium schools offer a better quality early childhood education, as opposed to schools which use Swahili, in areas such as teacher–pupil ratios, and conducive and colourful learning environments with more teaching aids in the private sector. However, 'language' also emerged as a valuable tool that defines quality in ECE:

> We thought that it is important to use English as a medium of instruction in this TTC to meet the employment demand, you know, for example, the way we are moving with the East African community, soon or later we will be required to work in other East African countries. (4\A\5\NM\19.3.14)

> These days if you start an educational institution and you do not use English as a medium of instruction you won't get clients. Parents want their children to learn English even if they can't speak English themselves. They want their children to be able to compete in the employment market. (1\A\4\NM\13.6.14)

It is revealing, and in some senses disturbing, that within the context of ECE the concern – as evidenced in the two comments above – is about employment demand when it should perhaps be about helping develop happy, socialised, well adjusted and socially minded citizens! Given the advocacy strengths within Tanzania and across the different ECE sectors and players, there should be a goal that focuses more on the salience and need for quality ECE for quality citizenship and wellbeing rather than benefits that derive from economic productivity and the labour market.

The private education sector has been active for the last 20 years, since 1995 when the educational policy allowed for the establishment of private schools, marking a major transformation in the education system in the country that, among other things, entrenched the prevailing language policy. Additionally, within this relatively short time period it has shaped and had a significant impact on attitudes towards quality education. From 1995, Tanzania witnessed a mushrooming of private schools, most of which used English language as a medium of instruction. Private schools also required tuition fees to enrol, usually substantial, rendering them inaccessible to the majority. In consequence, private schools symbolised a good quality of education, – out of reach for low income families – and a manufacturer of elites on account of the medium of instruction, namely English.

Schools that use English as a medium of instruction are seen or perceived to be raising elites, and most of these schools are privately owned. It is these privately owned schools that have learning materials, better teacher–student ratios and so forth. In addition, state-funded programmes run through Swahili only introduce English as a subject in Standard 3; thus in this respect children in the private sector have a distinct advantage at one level as far as English language skills development is concerned. These private schools are also mostly located in the cities, are expensive and so accessible to the privileged few, thus evidencing some of the injustices within the system: children go to different schools but are assessed the same way (i.e. national examinations), and at the end of the day they compete in the job market, in an unfair competition. You would not pit a heavyweight and a featherweight boxer against each other in a boxing match.

Further, it is not the case that all English-medium ECE is of a high quality and, as seen above, there are challenges to achieving quality and high standards on account of language issues. Nonetheless, the view that English medium is 'best' is fairly widespread. Reasons for this perception are varied. One is that since the 'elite' referred to above do well, there is the assumption that this achievement will be universally available to all if ECE is through the medium of English. There are then attitudes that have been, perhaps, entrenched since earlier decades in Tanzania's history, a legacy that prevails from colonial times (albeit over 50 years ago) where professional occupations required English and minor administrative positions required only Swahili. Whilst the current generation of parents will not have experienced colonial Tanzania, it is their parents who may have perpetuated this attitude towards English. Thus English for this and other reasons is seen as a 'prestige' language, and a corollary of this is that English medium means that the quality is higher.

There is little if any objective evidence that these private English programmes are actually providing a higher quality at the ECE level, an area we suggest needs further focused research. We can say, therefore, that there is an in-built bias towards 'English as quality'. However, it is the case that many – not all – English-medium schools (mostly owned by the private sector) are indeed better resourced, in terms of human resources and learning materials, and in the primary and secondary school leaving examinations rank higher in the national exams. An example of one such well-resourced English-medium primary class in the capital city is seen in the photo below.

Figure 4
This privileged environment can be contrasted with the situation that is unfortunately somewhat typical in rural Sub-Saharan African pre-schools.

Figure 5
In summary, a complexity of factors contributes to the view of 'English is better'. It is clear from our data that these assumptions do not always hold.

Discussion

As stated earlier, language was not identified at the outset of this research as a major issue for the analysis of the ECE landscape in Tanzania. In reality, the data we have gathered and the findings pertaining to language issues are just the tip of the iceberg, with a whole host of related issues remaining to be investigated. Below, we discuss three possible implications for language use in ECE within a context that is essentially multilingual.

Firstly, while Tanzania has 120 ethnic communities, many with their own languages albeit unscripted, Swahili, the national language, is culturally used as the common language of communication among communities and is the medium of instruction at pre-primary and primary school (Bakuza, 2014). As revealed in our sample findings, data from the TWW project indicates that civil society relates language of instruction to quality of education, in particular the superiority of English as the medium for 'quality' ECE. However, while the general impression of public early childhood centres and pre-schools may be that of 'poor quality' due to the use of

Kiswahili as the language of instruction, Howard (2001[20]) asserts that culturally relevant teaching empowers students socially, emotionally, intellectually and politically. Similarly, the use of language that is part of the learners' culture, Kiswahili in the case of Tanzania, can empower learners to relate to their lived experiences and build conceptual knowledge, which may be difficult to do in English considering the minimal use of it in many children's lives. Further, the use of community ethnic languages in ECE rather than English, it is argued, affords teachers and learners to contribute their funds of knowledge towards their classroom experiences (Gonzales et al., 2006). In our data, therefore, counter to those who view ECE mediated through English as superior in some respects, it can be argued that those pre-schools that use Kiswahili as their medium of instruction could be seen to be contributing towards more relevant and culturally appropriate learning experiences. There is additional evidence, not widely reported in Tanzania, to suggest that there is a significant and widespread use of community languages, i.e. language other than Kiswahili, in particular in rural households (SIL: Studies in Linguistics, personal communication) and there is certainly predominantly more Kiswahili than English use within communities nationwide. Given the richness and diversity of language use across Tanzanian households, it is argued here that the use of English – the dominant language of a small minority – can be seen as a tool that introduces discord in children's transition from home to pre-school, militating against the potential benefits from home-school knowledge exchange. In terms of community language use in ECE, we have little data to contribute but one NGO centre sampled had a programme that trained members from the Maasai community to teach young children in pre-schools using their mother tongue, i.e. Maasai, as the medium of instruction; being nomadic, the community was mobile and hence the school needed to be as well. We observe in Figure 3, a locally constructed 'maze' in which young Maasai children are encouraged to play but in a manner within their community.

Notwithstanding, there are significant language acquisition and conceptual development issues that arise for young children not only in Tanzania but also in the many other multilingual countries worldwide. One of the themes emerging from this volume is the need for the support of the L1 in ECE. If the children participating in these programmes in Tanzania have Kiswahili as their L1 but do not get supported in their L1, this creates problems not only for their L1 development and their L2 (English) acquisition, but also for their early conceptual formation for that matter. A second issue relates to the issue of community languages. Given that 'private is English' and 'state is Kiswahili', there is the added complexity that for many children Kiswahili is not their mother tongue and they speak a community language in the home. Very little, if any, research has been done on integrating these other (minority) languages into ECE provision. Some organisations are beginning to develop early literacy resources in community languages (personal communications). This is clearly an area crying out for further research.

---

[20] In the context of African-American students

A further layer of complexity relates to the teaching and exposure to Kiswahili in private sector ECE pre-schools and centres. Some, albeit private, are primarily Kiswahili medium (e.g. Montessori). Others, the majority, use very little Kiswahili, with possibly the introduction of a few Kiswahili songs from time to time. There are also instances reported (personal communications) where parents threaten to remove their children from the English-medium EC facility if Kiswahili is used. These findings within a multilingual ECE context point to the urgent need for research to untangle some of the critical linguistic issues.

Secondly, in respect of ECE trainers, Christ and Wang (2013: 352) argue:

> ...Early childhood teachers possess a wealth of instructional, practical, institutional and personal knowledge that can (and should) be used to make choices about their practices...

As we have seen, in Tanzanian state schools and teacher training colleges as well as in the private ECE sector, the trainers, the teacher trainees and the ECE teachers are predominantly indigenous Tanzanians with lived experiences in, and surrounded by, Kiswahili. As such, one may wish to argue the high value of using Kiswahili in ECE contexts as the language that enables these trainers and teachers to use their funds of knowledge to enhance both the classroom experiences of young children[21] and their early development in informal home and community settings (see Figures 1 & 3). However, the use of personal and community funds of knowledge according to the interview data collected from college tutors, teachers and our other informants did not emerge as a significant finding nor was seen as a crucial issue. This would in fact require a conceptual change for the EC trainers and practitioners who currently tend to follow the curriculum/syllabus rigidly. According to Hardman et al. (2011) comparative research shows that education reform is most effective when what is culturally or nationally unique about a context is combined with universal knowledge in classroom pedagogy (p. 827). Therefore, using the advantage of Kiswahili as the language of culture, there is potential to enhance the current practice. And this point, allowing for inclusion of funds of knowledge in the ECE learning environment would probably require some kind of educational reform. Thus, in addition to conceptual change for the use of funds of knowledge, enhancing skills, knowledge and attributes for being an ECE practitioner become crucial elements of professional development for teachers in Tanzania. The use of a familiar language, Kiswahili in this case, could be considered a tool to support conceptual dialogue and engagements among learners and with the teachers. Bearing in mind that the state teacher preparation colleges also use Kiswahili as the medium of instruction, including the practicum experience, creating learning experiences in the same language would seem a natural progression into practice.

Thirdly, in this chapter we have looked at the language transitions and tensions for ECE teacher trainers, but we have not addressed key challenges for the young children themselves. For example, what are the implications and impact of a

---

[21] It is to be noted that Kiswahili medium primary schools will teach English as a subject but this is usually from Standard 3, i.e. the third year of primary school

linguistic fissure in the continuum for children who move from the home where an ethnic community language is spoken to pre-school where the medium is for the majority to be Swahili (in the case of Tanzania) and for a minority English? To what extent are we actually limiting a child's potential right at the start of their lives through language policies that work for the elite few? As persuasively summarised by Shaeffer (2013: ix):

(1) hundreds of millions of children around the world are forced to study in a language they barely understand; and (2) children become most easily literate in their mother tongue, their language of daily use, and the skills they gain in this process can be applied subsequently to gain literacy in national and international languages. Bringing their languages and cultures into the classroom is thus an important way to make education more inclusive and equitable.

What we have observed however in our research, this particular study and others (e.g. Rea-Dickins et al., 2008, 2013), is the allure of English and the promises it brings in terms of a better life and bright economic futures, resulting in a situation where English-medium instruction even in pre-primary ECE represents a strong pull for parents. While there is agreement among many ECE practitioners and researchers on the importance of interaction, whether it be child-child, parent-child, or teacher-child interaction, for the holistic development of the children, we run the risk of promoting inequity through policies and practice that limit through various means opportunities for children to access quality ECE in their own languages.

It is interesting to reflect, from an historical perspective, that in 1953 UNESCO stated:

We take it as axiomatic ... that the best medium for teaching is the mother tongue of the pupil. (p.6)

Further, in 2006, ADEA reported the following encounter between a government minister and a parent in a rural village who told the minister:

It's not skill in his mother tongue which makes a child succeed in life, but how much English he knows. Is it going to be one type of school for the rich and another for the poor? At the end of the day we are expected to pass examinations in English! (ADEA, 2006: 6)

Does current policy that elevates proficiency in English as the gateway to quality ECE and, more generally, future economic opportunities do so in the knowledge that this will reinforce the already privileged positions of the middle classes who are much more likely to have increased exposure to books, to spoken English and in the knowledge that this policy will further perpetuate the economic and social divide?

Conclusion

This chapter has highlighted some of the problems, disparities and inequalities that exist in the provision of ECE in Tanzania. The issue of language medium, of mother tongue instruction in ECE, has been found to be a key issue and a challenge for quality early years provision in Tanzania. And the situation would not be expected to be much different in similar multilingual education contexts. These language issues have become a key topic in recent years internationally. UNESCO, for example, launched in 2014 a consultation on mother-tongue instruction in accordance with UNESCO General Conference Resolution 12:

> ... the requirements of global and national participation, and the specific needs of particular, culturally and linguistically distinct communities can only be addressed by multilingual education. (www.unesco.org/new/en/education/ themes/strengthening-education-systems/languages-in-education/single-view/ news/ongoing_consultation_measuring_mother_tongue_instruction_in_early_ childhood/)

We can see from the data from our TWW ECE research that Tanzania has a long way to go in addressing such needs.

In conclusion, ECE has become a major focus for international development globally, and that focus is evident in Africa as much as in other parts of the Global South. A concern expressed by some authors is that such development is being led by donors from the Global North, utilising child development and ECD research that is largely from the North. The project described in this chapter represents an effort to 'give voice to' and attempt to better understand key dynamics regarding ECE in one country in the Global South – Tanzania. It is believed that such enhanced understandings can support a generative process wherein Tanzania can avail itself not only of recent research and priorities of the Global North, but research and priorities identified from within Tanzania itself.

The promise, it seems to us, lies in the hands of policy makers to develop language polices and strategies that will minimise disadvantage and ensure that all learners and teachers have a more equal share of resources and opportunities that are available. Recognising and celebrating the linguistic diversity and resources that students and teachers have through the formulation of a linguistically inclusive ECE policy would be one suggestion. Parents and guardians, too, will need to be mobilised, as they represent an extremely powerful force in wanting 'more English and the earlier the better'. The use of media such as radio and newspapers in particular, as well as television in areas where this is available, prove to be very effective ways of communicating with the wider public.

References

Alidou, A, Boly, A, Brick-Utne, B, Diallo, YS, Heugh, K and Wolff, H (2006) *Optimizing Learning and Education in Africa – The Language Factor: a stock-taking research on mother tongue and bilingual education in Sub-Saharan Africa.* Working Document, ADEA. Biennial Meeting, Gabon, March 27th – 31st.

Ashton, E and Pence, A (2014) 'Early childhood education, care and development in sub-Saharan Africa: A glimpse at the published literature', in Pence, A (ed) *Africa ECD Voice,* 3, 12-26.

Bakuza, FR (2014) Educating Tanzanian Children in the New Millennium: Progress and Challenges. *Childhood Education,* 90:6, 407-413, DOI: 10.1080/00094056.2014.982970.

Christ, T and Wang, XC (2013) Exploring a community of practice model for professional development to address challenges to classroom practices in early childhood. *Journal of Early Childhood Teacher Education,* 34(4), 350-373.

Engle, P, Fernald, LCH, Alderman, H, Behrman, J, O'Gara, C, Yousafzai, A, de Mello, M, Hidrobo, M, Ulkuer, N, Ertem, I, Iltus, S and the Global Child Development Steering Group (2011) Strategies for reducing inequalities and improving developmental outcomes for young children in low-income and middle-income countries. *The Lancet,* 378(9799), 1339-1353.

Gonzalez, N, Moll, LC and Amanti, C (2006) *Funds of knowledge: Theorizing practices in households, communities, and classrooms.* Hoboken: Taylor and Francis.

Hardman, F, Ackers, J, Abrishamian, N and O'Sullivan, M (2011) Developing a systemic approach to teacher education in sub-Saharan Africa: Emerging lessons from Kenya, Tanzania and Uganda. *Compare: A Journal of Comparative and International Education,* 41(5), 669-683.

Heckman, JJ, Stixrud, J and Urzua, S (2006) The effects of cognitive and noncognitive abilities on labor market outcomes and social behavior. *Journal of Labor Economics* 24(3), 411-482.

Heckman, J (2006) Skill formation and the economics of investing in disadvantaged children. *Science,* 312/57820, 1900-1902.

Howard, TC (2001) Telling their side of the story: African-American students' perceptions of culturally relevant teaching. *The Urban Review,* 33(2), 131-149.

Pence, A and Ashton, E (in press) 'Early childhood research in Africa: The need for a chorus of voices', in Farrell, A. Kagan, SL and Tisadall, EKM (eds) *The SAGE Handbook of Early Childhood Research (Ch. 23).* London: Sage.

Pence, A and Benner, A (2015) *Complexities, capacities, communities: Changing development narratives in early childhood education, care and development.* Victoria, BC: University of Victoria.

Rea-Dickins, P, Khamis, Z and Olivero, F (2013) 'Does English-medium instruction and examining lead to social and economic advantage? Promises and threats: a Sub-Saharan case study', in Erling, E and Seargeant, P (eds) *English and International Development*. Bristol: Multilingual Matters Ltd: 111-138.

Rea-Dickins, P and Yu, G (2013) 'English medium instruction and examining in Zanzibar: Ambition, pipe dreams and realities', in Benson, C and Kosonen, K (eds) *Language Issues in Comparative Education*. Sense Publishers: 189-207.

Rea-Dickins, P, Rubagumya, C and Clegg, J (2008) *Evaluation of the Orientation Secondary Class*. Zanzibar: Ministry of Education & Vocational Training.

Shaeffer, S (2013) 'Foreword', in Benson, C and Kosonen, K (eds) *Language Issues in Comparative Education*. Sense Publishers: ix-x.

UNESCO BREDA (2012) *World Inequality Database on Education (WIDE). The State of Education in Developing Countries*. Data set prepared for EFA Global Monitoring Report 2012. Paris, 2012.

UNESCO (1953) *The Use of Vernacular Languages in Education: Monographs of Fundamental Education*. United Nations, Educational, Scientific and Cultural Organization, I.F.M.R.P Paris, France.

UNESCO (1990) *World Declaration on Education for All*. Adopted by the World Conference on Education for All. Meeting Basic Learning Needs, Jomtien. Published by UNESCO for the Secretariat of the International Consultative Forum on Education for ALL. Paris.

United Nations (1989) UN General Assembly, *Convention on the Rights of the Child*, 20 November 1989, United Nations, Treaty Series, vol. 1577, p. 3, available at: www.refworld.org/docid/3ae6b38f0.html [accessed 05 June 2015]

UWEZO (2010) *Are Our Children Learning?* (Annual Learning Assessment Report Tanzania 2010). Dar es Salaam: UWEZO.

1.6

Australia

Making the ESL classroom visible: indigenous Australian children's early education

Lauren Gawne, Gillian Wigglesworth, Gemma Morales,
University of Melbourne

Susan Poetsch, Sally Dixon, Australian National University

Introduction

The Indigenous population of Australia makes up approximately three per cent of the overall Australian population, with the majority living in New South Wales. However, the Northern Territory, with a total population of under 250,000, has the highest percentage of Indigenous residents at 30 per cent. In this chapter, we focus on the education and language of Indigenous children living in the Northern Territory who are attending schools classified as remote or very remote[22] rather than those attending schools situated in urban localities.

Indigenous children in Australia grow up in a variety of contexts, but those growing up in remote communities are often raised in complex linguistic environments with a great deal of variation in terms of their access to amenities and services. The data that we will be drawing on for this chapter comes from a series of studies of children living in different remote communities in the Northern Territory.

Indigenous Australian children's linguistic ecology

Of the original 250+ languages spoken in Australia at the time of European settlement in 1788, only about 20 continue to be learned as a first language by Indigenous children and it is predicted that there will be none in 50 years' time (McConvell and Thieberger, 2001). However, linguistic work in Australia has tended to focus on the documentation of these endangered languages, and there are few studies of the first language acquisition of these children. Descriptive work looking at child language has focused on the acquisition of some of the more cross-

---

[22] Remote areas have "very restricted accessibility of goods, services and opportunities for social interaction", while very remote areas have "very little accessibility of goods, services and opportunities for social interaction". (Australian Government, 2001: 22)

linguistically interesting aspects of the grammar of Aboriginal languages such as case systems (e.g. see Bavin and Shopen, 1991, for an overview of research into children's Warlpiri), as well as child language as evidence for nascent change in the language (e.g. Dalton et al., 1995). A third strand of work on children's use of traditional languages has focused on acquisition in the context of emergent bilingualism with English in the schooling system. For example, Hill (2008) explored how school-aged Yolŋu children were learning Yolŋu Matha (their first language) at apparently 'age appropriate' levels, and were more gradually and systematically acquiring English as a second language.

In some communities, languages are undergoing, or have undergone, rapid shift away from the traditional language to mixed languages or creoles. O'Shannessy's (2005, 2008, 2011, 2012, 2013) extensive study of Warlpiri children suggests that as a result of being exposed to code-mixed Warlpiri and Aboriginal English/Kriol children have developed a new mixed language, which shows both elements of conventionalisation and innovation, and has become a way to demonstrate Warlpiri identity specific to the Lajamanu community. Meakins (2008) discusses the complexity of the linguistic situation in Kalkaringi where children are exposed to the traditional language, Gurindji, as well as a creole (known as Kriol in Australia) and a new mixed language, Gurindji Kriol, as well as Warlpiri and English. These languages are used by different groups, and in different domains, and reflect the default multilingualism traditionally found in many Indigenous communities. As McConvell (2008) argues, there is a natural predisposition towards multilingualism in Australian Indigenous communities and a long history of code switching between different traditional languages as well as varieties of English and contact languages such as Kriol.

Schultze-Berndt et al. (2013) point out that Kriol is the first language of approximately 20,000 Aboriginal people, spoken as a chain of dialects across northern Australia with differences in the Kriol spoken in different places, probably as a result of different substrate influences. English is the lexifier language and Kriol itself is often referred to as "English" despite the fact that it is a separate language for both speakers, and those who come in contact with it. Kriol is generally unacknowledged in public contexts, the media or service delivery and this lack of visibility is compounded by the fact that Kriol is most often used in oral form, and restricted to domestic domains. This is partly associated with its low social status, which fosters the view that the language should be restricted to specific domains such as oral communication (Wigglesworth and Billington, 2013: 236). The invisibility of Kriol, despite its widespread use in Indigenous communities, means it tends to be unrecognised in the Census (Angelo and McIntosh, 2014), and even the recent *Our Land Our Languages* (Australian Parliament, 2012) report referred almost exclusively to Traditional Indigenous Languages and concern about Indigenous people having adequate access to Standard Australian Languages (Sellwood and Angelo, 2013).

Standard Australian English (SAE) is the language of education, media and official spaces. Indigenous children's access to SAE prior to their entry in the school system, at least in remote areas, tends to be mainly through television and radio, and in interactions with non-Indigenous people. In many cases children would rarely be required to produce SAE until they enter the classroom. Therefore, if they enter a 'mainstream' English school instead of one of the small number of bilingual schools, then they will be required to produce a variety of English to which they have had limited exposure.

In sum, by school age Indigenous children living in remote communities are generally speaking one or more of the languages of their community – which may be traditional languages, or contact languages such as the new mixed languages or varieties of Kriol – and are beginning to incorporate SAE into their already complex repertoires.

Indigenous Australian children's education

Indigenous children who come from non-English-speaking (Standard Australian) backgrounds face multiple challenges in finding schooling in remote communities in Australia that adequately caters for their language repertoires.

In the following sections we explore why this is the case with reference to the attitudes towards school language and home language, the support for teachers and students, the use of testing programmes like the National Assessment Programme – Literacy and Numeracy (NAPLAN), and the broader educational policy and research environment. We will see that while each strand illustrates a different component relevant to understanding the inadequacy of the educational options afforded Indigenous children, a key thread runs throughout each section: the dominance of SAE and the general invisibility of languages other than English in the education system.

Home language and school language

For those Indigenous children in remote communities who are educated in English-only schools, without a dedicated bilingual programme, the difference between home and school language is significant. Generally speaking, home languages are not used as a medium of instruction and SAE is not explicitly taught. Students are then left in the precarious position of acquiring the medium of instruction 'on the run' while also trying to learn lesson content.

This situation results from a confluence of related reasons. Firstly, the lack of attention to home languages inside of the classroom stems from Australia's focus on English as the dominant language of education and public life. This 'monolingual mindset' (Clyne, 2005) creates such a single-minded focus on SAE that it often results in negative attitudes towards other languages that children speak. Hill (2008: 271) observes that in situations where children acquire traditional languages as their L1, this is seen as a problem for English language acquisition. This 'problem' exists within the narrow worldview of an English-centric population in Australia, which fails to recognise that the majority of the world's population live in bilingual or multilingual situations. Instead of focusing on the existing language experience of students, the focus tends to be on a 'deficit' model – students' lack of SAE language skills is the overriding concern, rather than the acknowledgement of their own (often complex) linguistic skills and experience (Ciborowski, 1976: 120-121; Hill, 2008; Kral and Ellis, 2008; Angelo, 2013a).

When a student's first language is a contact variety with a strong English influence, such as Kriol or Aboriginal English, negative attitudes may result from the erroneous view that these languages are inferior or 'deviant' versions of the standard (Siegel, 2006; Wigglesworth and Billington, 2013). The effects of these attitudes may be compounded when there is little understanding of the differences (and similarities) between (SAE) learner and L1 language features. Children's non-standard output is seen through the SAE lens, potentially resulting in assessments of language as being delayed (Gould, 2008). To demonstrate the effect of the SAE lens, Dixon (2013) examined the language produced by one seven-year-old child, Tiffany, who speaks the contact language, Alyawarr English (discussed in more detail below) as her mother tongue. She attends an English-medium school and has begun her acquisition of SAE in this context. Dixon examined Tiffany's speech from the perspective of a traditional 'error analysis' and then re-examined the data from a perspective incorporating an understanding of her L1. Dixon demonstrated that features of Tiffany's language considered 'errors' in an L1 context are in fact features of her own L1 variety. The analysis was able to provide a more nuanced picture of Tiffany's language development, which included demonstrating her movement toward acquisition of SAE.

Not only do children's existing language competencies tend to be ignored (or seen only through the SAE lens), but their existing linguistic knowledge and literacies are generally likewise unrecognised. Recent years have seen increasing recognition of the variety of traditional practices in which children engage. For example, Kral and Ellis (2008: 160) note that our tendency is to conflate literacy with printed materials, but while Indigenous communities may not be print rich, they have their own culturally acquired literacies. They may learn sand drawing narratives (Eickelkamp, 2008; Kral and Ellis, 2008) as well as gestural sign systems (Capell, 1963; Kral and Ellis, 2008; O'Shannessy, 2011). Authors who talk about these practices also note the high value that communities place on strong oral narrative competency (Eickelkamp, 2008: 85; O'Shannessy, 2011: 148). As Kral and Ellis (2008) argue, we should not assume that Indigenous communities are devoid of literacy, an approach which plays into the 'deficit' model of Indigenous language and literacy competencies. Instead, we need to remember that the types of literacy that we expect from Indigenous students in remote communities has been experienced by only a few generations, and at a time during which there has been profound language shift and cultural change.

Teacher training and support

There is a lack of attention to language in general, and multilingual educational contexts in particular, in pre-service teacher training in Australia, and commensurately ESL qualifications are not enforced as essential requirements for teaching in remote contexts. Teachers trained in urban university contexts who move to work in remote communities often receive little if any training in Indigenous languages and cultures, and few attempts are made to mediate the cultural experiences of Indigenous children for the classroom in ways that could also assist in facilitating student comprehension of teaching material (Hill, 2008: 295; Malcolm, 2013; Angelo and Carter, 2015). Instead, there is a tendency for teachers to enter the remote classroom with the cultural attitudes towards learning of their mainstream peers, assuming that the students have the English competency necessary to engage with the class in the same way as their monolingual peers, which, as we will demonstrate below, is clearly not always the case. Teachers may then erroneously attribute 'poor' SAE skills to other factors such as socio-economic disadvantage, poor hearing, inattentiveness or cultural differences (Angelo and Carter, 2015). One important caveat to this is the many Indigenous teachers and assistant teachers who are employed throughout the remote north, and who usually speak the same first language(s) as the students and permanently reside in the community.

So while the implementation of 'best practice' models is repeatedly observed as vital for teaching literacy, there is currently no consistent implementation of training for teachers to deal with the challenges of working in an 'English-medium' classroom where none of the children are English L1 speakers of SAE (Moses and Wigglesworth, 2008; Hill, 2008: 295). This is also true for speakers of contact language varieties such as Kriol and Aboriginal English varieties, where the creole-lexifier relationship blurs the L2 target for children to varying extents, and often makes L2 errors invisible to teachers not trained to deal with the EFL (or ESL) context (Sellwood and Angelo, 2013; Angelo, 2013a).

This puts a heavy load on the school to provide in-service support and training for teachers in remote contexts, and as a result practices vary greatly from classroom to classroom. In schools that have operated as bilingual schools there may be greater residual awareness of the language needs of students, and one of the legacies of this approach to schooling has been the development of co-teaching strategies that utilise the strengths of both Indigenous and non-Indigenous teachers (Disbray, 2014). For example, in Poetsch's research context, the school is supported by a languages and literacy curriculum consultant who works with both teachers and students in five remote schools. The consultant has ESL qualifications and extensive experience in remote communities. This support helps teachers and draws attention to the complex linguistic environment these English-medium schools are situated in. In this school context, staff, both Indigenous and non-Indigenous, have worked together to try various ways to incorporate the children's L1 into teaching and learning. Arrernte is used as a support for learning (referred to as 'getting the meaning across') in all classes, right through to the upper grades even though the children in the upper grades have stronger English than the children in the lower grades.

However, in general the teaching context in the Northern Territory is characterised by very high staff turnover: the average length of time a teacher spends in a remote school in this jurisdiction has been as short as nine months (Milburn, 2010). In addition to the effect it has on morale and motivation (Hill, 2008), it severely compromises the efficacy of the current model, which relies so heavily on in-service training to give teachers the skills to meet the multilingual language needs of their students.

NAPLAN and metrics

The National Assessment Programme – Literacy and Numeracy (NAPLAN) is designed to assess the literacy and numeracy of all Australian school children in years 3, 5, 7 and 9, and to act as a diagnostic as to whether children are meeting intended educational outcomes. Introduced in 2008, NAPLAN is administered annually in May. There are a number of problems with the use of NAPLAN for its intended purposes. The use of such norm-referenced tests is internationally recognised as being problematic for assessing children who are circumstantially bilingual (Genishi and Brainard, 1995; Thomas and Collier, 2002) and similar issues have been thoroughly explored with reference to the Australian context (Ciborowski, 1976; Harkins, 1994; Simpson et al., 2009; Wigglesworth et al., 2011, Angelo, 2012, 2013a, 2013b). Similar to issues in speech pathology, where tests normed to SAE-speaking L1 children result in Indigenous children being categorised as 'disordered' (Gould, 2008), standardised testing of English for Indigenous children often results in scores that fall short of the mainstream population and are subsequently interpreted as a generalised failure at schooling rather than as the natural pathway travelled by students learning English as a second language.

At the remote school level the direct emphasis on NAPLAN may in fact be quite minimal (as observed at several of our host sites), contrary to the response observed in more urban classrooms where NAPLAN results in a narrowing of teaching 'to the test' (Angelo, 2012, 2013b). Rather, the 'wash back' of NAPLAN in remote classrooms occurs via its impact on government policy.

For example, when the results from the first NAPLAN tests were released in September 2008, the scores for Indigenous children in remote communities were so alarming that the knee-jerk reaction of politicians in the Northern Territory was the decision to mandate that the first four hours of schooling should be in English. The consequence was the dismantling of almost all the last remaining bilingual education programmes (apart from those in non-government schools), without replacing them with a coherent plan to improve the children's acquisition of SAE (Simpson et al., 2009, 2011; Disbray, 2014).

A second way in which the NAPLAN regime has perpetuated the invisibility of children's language repertoires and language learning needs stems from the way data regarding Indigenous students' language skills is collected and interpreted. The NAPLAN language data category 'Language Background Other Than English' (LBOTE) includes all students who are exposed, to any degree, to a language other than English via their parents. It has been described as 'a form of recognition that results in misrecognition' (Lingard et al., 2012: 320). Firstly, there is good evidence that it is applied inconsistently to Indigenous students across jurisdictions, (Dixon and Angelo, 2014; Simpson and Wigglesworth, 2012), with interpretations seeing 'Indigenous' and 'LBOTE' as mutually exclusive categories. Secondly, while this category does not in any way capture English proficiency (it is not an 'ESL' category) it is often interpreted that way, with the result that since LBOTE status does not correlate negatively with NAPLAN performance, a major operative variable in student achievement is obscured (Angelo, 2013b; Dixon and Angelo,

2014). This is in addition to the fact that Indigenous students are the only ethno-cultural group disaggregated (and negatively correlated with NAPLAN results), making their performance highly visible and subject to policy scrutiny, and with the result that poor NAPLAN performance is more likely to be attributed to 'being Indigenous' than being a learner of English as a second or foreign language.

Policy environment

Educational policy documents rarely acknowledge the linguistic contexts that disadvantage Indigenous students in their learning, and often fail to mention their EFL status. Language policy aspirations regarding proficiency are assumed to refer only to SAE, and do not acknowledge explicitly students different L1s (McIntosh et al., 2012). Angelo and Carter (2015) examined two national policies that influence Indigenous education: the National Indigenous Reform Agenda (NIRA) and the National Aboriginal and Torres Strait Islander Education Action Plan (NATSIEAP), both of which have targets relating to NAPLAN results. The NIRA does not acknowledge students' language backgrounds at all, while the NATSIEAP does so in the contextualising information at the start of the report, but not in the quantifiable responses and targets for improving students' educational outcomes. Such policy foci, and the data that drives them, contribute to making the linguistic challenges Indigenous students face invisible (Dixon and Angelo, 2014).

McIntosh et al., (2012) note a particular silence in policy documents regarding the complexity of Indigenous language situations, including a lack of recognition of contact languages. Even widely recognised creole varieties, and the well-attested use of Aboriginal English, remain unacknowledged at State and Federal level. Indeed, the documents even fail to acknowledge children who speak traditional Indigenous languages who are the most visible of these groups. While the focus in many of these documents is 'literacy', children will struggle in an education setting without proper acknowledgement of the basic L2 language competency needed to develop literacy in a second language.

Angelo and Carter (2015) argue that without making language(s) a central feature of educational policy, schools face a challenge in educating their Indigenous students. In general, the education system does not acknowledge that children arrive at school with fully-fledged competence in their first language(s). Yet this awareness is the first step in understanding that schools operating in these contexts are multilingual learning environments in which students are moving towards Standard English proficiency. Although researchers consistently advocate for bi- or multilingual programmes (Hill, 2008; Simpson et al., 2009) this rarely appears to impact on policy.

Indigenous children in the classroom in remote Australia

In this section we look at how the invisibility of Indigenous children's language repertoires and language learning needs can play out in classroom interactions. Specifically, we explore the communicative challenges faced by students and teachers in the early years of schooling in 'English-medium' contexts where the students begin their acquisition of SAE.

Data

The data in this chapter is drawn from three corpora of classroom interactions between primary school children aged between four and eight, and their teachers. The corpora come from a variety of linguistic and educational contexts, but they all centre on Indigenous Australian children beginning their formal education. In all of these contexts the children speak a contact language variety, or local traditional languages (or a combination of the two) as their first languages and are learning SAE, the language of the classroom, as a second language. All of the recordings were made as part of the Aboriginal Child Language Acquisition 2 (ACLA2) project.[23]

The Dixon corpus consists of over 50 hours of naturalistic video recordings made between September 2009 and April 2011. The recordings focus on six children aged four to eight, plus their relatives, classmates and teachers at six-monthly intervals over a two-year period in a small remote community south of Tennant Creek. Recordings used here were made in the school context. Children in this community speak a contact variety called Alyawarr English (AlyE) as their mother tongue. AlyE includes influences from a number of sources including English, Kriol (Munro, 2000; Schultze-Berndt et al., 2013), Aboriginal English varieties (Koch, 2000), and Alyawarr, a Pama-Nyungan language from the Arandic sub-group (Yallop, 1977). The lexicon of AlyE is mainly derived from English and/or Kriol with some Alyawarr words in common usage. Alyawarr, the traditional language, is commonly heard in the home, and children will frequently respond (in AlyE) to conversation in that language. The teachers in this corpus received quite variable pre- and in-service training or support for working in English as a Foreign or Second Language classrooms.

The second corpus (Morales corpus) is a collection of recordings of children, their teachers and caregivers in a small and very remote community on the North East coast of the Northern Territory. This corpus includes recordings at school in formal classroom situations and unstructured, less supervised, play. This corpus was collected in October and November 2014. Unlike the children from the Dixon corpus who speak an English-based contact variety, the children in this community grow up primarily speaking Dhuwaya, a dialect of Yolŋu Matha. Yolŋu Matha is the Indigenous language of the area, which has over a dozen clanlects. We have included these children in the discussion to show that as English as a Foreign Language speakers – because they live in a non-English-speaking community – they face similar classroom challenges and difficulties to the students in the Dixon corpus who speak a contact language and have greater exposure to SAE. The teachers in this corpus received no additional pre-service training or support for working in English as a Foreign or Second Language classrooms.

The Poetsch corpus is a collection of recordings of six- to seven-year-old children in a remote Aboriginal community in Central Australia. In this corpus the children

---

[23] This project, *A longitudinal study of the interaction of home and school language in two Aboriginal communities*, is the second phase of a longitudinal study funded by the ARC. We refer to the project as ACLA2 (the Aboriginal Child Language Acquisition project, phase 2). This project is funded by the ARC Discovery Grant (2008–12) DP0877762.

are engaged in conversations with their teachers and peers during maths and science lessons in an English-medium Year 1–2 classroom (composite-level classrooms are common in Australia, particularly in remote communities where school populations may be small). The children in this community grow up with Arrernte as their first language, which is the traditional language of the area (Wilkins, 1989; Henderson and Dobson, 1994). Unlike the children in the Morales corpus, the children do not come to school speaking a koine variety of their language, but a traditional form. The teacher is usually the only person in the classroom who is a native speaker of English, but the school has a number of Arrernte teaching assistants to facilitate communication, and access to a languages and literacy curriculum consultant who periodically visits the school, as described above. Of the three schools in our discussion this is the one in which the language situation is rendered most visible and both teachers and students are offered the most support.

While some of the children in these corpora, particularly in the Poetsch and Dixon corpora, have access to pre-school, this is not always a norm for remote communities, although it is increasingly being implemented in the Northern Territory. Attending school (or sometimes pre-school) is often the first encounter children have with SAE, although they may have some limited exposure through media or older members of their family interacting with non-Indigenous members of the community. The start of schooling is also the first time they are required to use SAE themselves. By drawing on corpora that include children who are native speakers of English-based contact varieties (Dixon corpus), as well as children who speak traditional languages (Morales and Poetsch corpora), we explore some of the children's encounters with the SAE classroom environment.

Classroom discourse patterns

Classroom discourse is a particular interactional style and people often assume that children who are able to follow directives and basic conversations can follow classroom discourse. However, as Cummins (1981, 1991, 2001) has argued, the language of the classroom is far more cognitively demanding and "context reduced" than is the language of everyday conversation, and the ability of students to follow simple instructions in a second language is no indication that they can yet understand explanations or hypothetical propositions in that language. Children require time and support to become familiar with the routines of the classroom (or what has been called the 'hidden curriculum') and, in an ESL context, to develop their second language proficiency to participate in those routines.

In Example 1, the teacher attempts to engage a student in a question–answer discussion to elicit knowledge. The most striking feature of this episode, familiar to those who have observed these classroom contexts, is the silence of the student who consistently does not respond to the elicitations – interrogative forms followed by a pause of at least one-second duration.

Example 1

MT	Which one do you think goes next? [1.1 seconds]
	People buying them,
	or people eating them?
	[name] [1.4 seconds]
	Do you think they eat it,
	or do you think they go to the shop
	and the markets and buy it? [1.2 seconds]
	Which one do you think? [0.7 second]
	This one,
	or this one?
MC1	[gestures towards image]
MT	You think this one?
	Okay.

(age 6;7 Morales corpus 7:18.2-7:48.3)

The teacher adheres to an obviously unsuccessful exchange pattern, in this and subsequent interactions, as she tries to engage the student. This example is representative of the one-sided exchange discussed elsewhere in the literature (see also Moses and Wigglesworth, 2008, for a more extreme example of this, where the teacher also provides the expected responses to fulfil the discourse pattern), where often the accompanying analysis focuses solely on the child, and speculates about specific Aboriginal 'learning styles' that preclude the use of direct questioning or the impact of differences in general interactional styles (such as preference for longer between-turn silences, concepts of 'shame' at being singled out (see Harris, 1984, as an example of this approach)). However, more recent corpus-driven work has shown Aboriginal children engaging in very similar question–answer routines with caregivers at home in their first languages (see Moses and Yallop, 2008), and using direct questions as part of information-seeking activities (Reeders, 2008), suggesting that the reticence of the children in the classroom is as or more likely to stem from unfamiliarity with SAE, rather than unfamiliarity with the question–answer routine itself. In that vein, we suggest that this interaction speaks more explicitly to the student's developing proficiency in SAE: a (non-verbal) response is eventually forthcoming once the teacher reformulates her complex questions into the more simple: 'This one or this one?' The interaction as a whole is representative of the lack of teacher training in working in non-English-speaking classroom contexts. As a primary-trained teacher, she had received very limited language teaching training, and only minimal additional training and support for working in remote communities.

Sensitivity to how the ESL/EFL classroom may differ in terms of discourse patterns is essential. And given that it is good practice to give second language learners more 'wait time' for them to formulate a response, this is a useful practice to recommend to teachers regardless of whether longer silences also conform to more L1 discourse styles. However, in our experience teachers are more likely to receive this (sound) advice than they are expected to teach the L2 explicitly. In the ESL/EFL context, any differences in interactional style or unfamiliarity with classroom routines may exacerbate communicative disfluency, but they are not the primary drivers of it.

A focus on content, not language

In the schools and classrooms in the corpora under examination here, the focus on the explicit teaching of SAE varies greatly, but generally is never on par with the focus on teaching of content. Of course, lessons in which the teacher may be focused on content are still also language lessons by virtue of the students' still-developing competencies in SAE. We will now examine some extracts to explore how this dynamic plays out in the classroom.

In Example 2 the teacher is primarily focused on the elicitation of knowledge and not on practising a particular structure of SAE: there has been no introductory modelling, for example, focusing the students on some feature of SAE. The teacher's initial question is formulated as an open question in the past tense, and the formally 'fitted' response would also be in the past tense ("I fed the baby"). The teacher then provides a kind of candidate response ("Were you feeding the baby?"), though its continuous form is not formally fitted to the previous question. Instead it is matched with the quickly following open question ("What were you doing?"). The student can then mine the candidate answer and provide a fitted, though brief, response ("feeding"), which the teacher confirms is acceptable by repeating it.

While it is clear that the simple past tense is not the object of practice here (since the teacher abandons it quite quickly), it may have been a factor in the student's lack of response (perhaps in addition to the 'openness' of the initial question). Teachers trained to work in ESL/EFL contexts monitor their formal use of language even when content is the focus for precisely this reason. This example highlights the difficulty in being purely 'content focused' in the ESL/EFL classroom.

Example 2

MT	What did she do with the babies?
	What did you do with the babies?
	[3.1 seconds]
	Were you feeding the baby? [.]
	What were you doing?
MC1	Feeding.
MT	Feeding.
	Were you doing anything else with your baby?
	She was feeding her baby.
	What else were you doing [name]?
	[10.0 seconds]
	[name],
	I saw you
	When you went to sit at the table.
	What were you doing at the table today?
	[7.6 seconds]
MCC	Colouring.
MC1	Colouring.
MT	Colouring.
	What was your picture,
	That you were colouring?

(age 6;7 Morales corpus 2:28.5-5:26.8)

In Example 3, the teacher is more successful in maintaining control over her own use of questions, thus reducing the language load for her student. In Example 3 the teacher is talking one-on-one with a child about what she has been learning in science. The conversation occurs at the end of a set of lessons on the topic of gravity and force. It is based on a poster that each child has made to summarise findings from a set of class experiments. The summary posters consist of the children's pictures and captions. Although the teacher has no ESL/EFL training, she has used concrete materials in a series of structured activities to explore the weight and movement of toys and other objects and how and why they yield to or resist air, water, push, pull and other forces. These provided a shared context for developing the children's understanding of concepts and English vocabulary related to the topic, thus supporting learning in the more cognitively demanding and "context reduced" language of the classroom highlighted by Cummins (1981,

1991, 2001). An Arrernte teaching assistant was also present in the classroom to support the children's learning.

There are lengthy silences and delays in the child's responses to the teacher's questions but it is also evident that the child has learned key concepts and can use English vocabulary related to the topic taught. The silences and delays may be a sign of the cognitive load involved for the children in explaining the concepts in English rather than her L1, which is consistent with Moses and Yallop's (2008) findings that children are more likely to respond to questions in their L1, and that the reticence of children in the classroom may stem from unfamiliarity with English rather than unfamiliarity with classroom question–answer routines.

Example 3

PT	what's that a picture of?
	[3.4 seconds]
PC1	pushing the ball
PT	what's p- what's pushing the ball?
	[8.0 seconds]
PC1	air
PT	[.]in this one? is that air that's pushing the ball?
PC1	[shakes head and smiles]
PT	[smiles]
	no what is it?
PC1	[1.1 seconds]
	umm
	[1.3 seconds]
PT	something is pushing the ball you're right
	something is stopping the ball from going all the way down
PC1	gravity
PT	gravity is trying to pull it down
	what's pushing it up? what's holding it up?
	[6.2 seconds]
PC1	water
	[2.5 seconds]
PT	very good, the water, and so what does this say?

(age 7;4 Poetsch 2014.11.27 LA: LA 0:36-1:25)

In response to the teacher's question, "What's that a picture of?", the student responds "pushing the ball". The teacher then tries to elicit the missing subject, using a what-question that incorporates the student's prior answer. She adheres quite tightly to this format in subsequent turns: 'something is pushing the ball', 'something is stopping the ball...', 'what's pushing it up?' 'what's holding it up?' allowing the student to offer a variety of fitted responses to fill the subject slot ('air', 'gravity', 'water'). In this way she can pursue a focus on the concept of gravity in a way that is less likely to be derailed by use of more complex or haphazard questioning.

However, this is still clearly a content-focused lesson, since the student is not supported to produce more than a one-word response in each case. In fact, the one-word or partial clause is an overwhelming SAE utterance type for the children across the corpora. When there is little focus on explicit language instruction, students are often given few opportunities to practise larger chunks of SAE.

As in these examples, in many of the classroom interactions recorded, the discourse is focused on content, and not language instruction, entirely understandable given the teachers' lack of training in language instruction, and the lack of focus on language teaching generally in teacher training.

Inconsistent responses to non-standard SAE

So far we have examined examples in which student responses, when they appear and however minimal, are grammatically fitted to the previous utterance. We will now look at what happens when students produce utterances that are non-standard from the perspective of SAE. In language learning classrooms, teachers will often correct their students' errors when the focus is on formal correctness. Such correction is essential for students to progress their understanding of and fluency in the target language. However, it is only against a backdrop of explicit and focused learning of specific language structures that 'in the moment' corrections of errors become useful to the student. It is equally as important for there to be opportunities for students to practise expressing themselves without constant interjection, and competent foreign language teachers will structure their class activities to explicitly move students from one type of interaction to another (Seedhouse, 2004).

Pre-service teachers generally receive limited training in developing and delivering teaching programmes for English-medium classrooms in which the learners are not speakers of English. In schools in cities and regional areas children with ESL needs receive additional classroom support from trained ESL specialists and are more likely to be learning in classroom contexts in which some/many of their peers are L1 English speakers; this contrasts starkly with the EFL context of Indigenous students in remote locations. ESL/EFL pre-service training and/or in-service ESL/EFL professional development opportunities can assist teachers in the transition to this classroom environment.

Example 4 is part of a sustained discussion of a poster project between the teacher and a single student. Note that although throughout the 16-minute interaction the child frequently uses the Kriol past tense marker, *bin* (widely used in varieties of Aboriginal English and Kriol), the teacher does not comment on the non-Standard English, focusing rather on the content of the student's speech.

Example 4

PT	do you remember when we [.] had a big bucket of water?
	[.] and what did we do?
PC1	um we bin touch
	Um we touched
	[.] we bin get that ball big ball and we bin put it down but the-
	we got that ball big ball and we put it down but the -
	[3.4 seconds]
	um and then when you bin let it go and then he bin go um up
	um and then when you let it go and he went TR up
PT	it you could feel it couldn't you?
	you could feel it pushing up, yeah?

(age 7;4 Poetsch 2014.11.27 LA: LA 1:38-2:02)

Passive acceptance of non-standard English in examples such as 4 can be an educationally sound decision in particular interactions, and indeed an absence of correction on the part of the teacher is characteristic of activities in other language learning classrooms in which the focus is on developing fluency (Seedhouse, 2004). In this example the child is demonstrating their understanding of complex ideas in their second language. The fact that the teacher is trying to assess whether the child has acquired the concepts may be more important in this moment than correcting use of past tense. However, it is important that both teacher and student are consciously aware that English fluency or lesson content is the object of this exercise. And, crucially, that the teacher has the capacity to monitor mistakes in order to plan further explicit English language instruction.

We see similar examples of passive acceptance of non-standard English from the other corpora. Example 5 from the Dixon corpus illustrates this where the teacher is asking a student the meaning of a word.

Example 5

DT	illustrations by Ben Spilby	
	[.]	
DT	What does illustrations mean_	
	[1.3 seconds]	
DC1	um that mean [.] when he draw the picture	
DT	yeah beautiful alright next page_	

(age 7;8 Dixon corpus B1.1-6)

The student conveys the correct meaning, but there are errors in the grammar: verbs 'mean' and 'draw' are missing the agreement marker 's', and the subordinating conjunction 'when' is used (perhaps because it is phonologically equivalent to the AlyE subordinating conjunction wen) instead of the SAE 'that', and 'picture' should possibly be plural. However, unlike in the previous example, the student is not presenting a complex argument, which could be negatively impacted if correction were to intercede. In fact, students in this classroom are routinely asked to identify the illustrator and author of each book they read, and are periodically questioned about what an 'author' or 'illustrator' does. So this would be a good opportunity to model and practise standard usage.

Example 6 comes from a spur of the moment 'let's make up some question sentences' interaction that happened while the teacher and student were waiting for another student to finish copying from the board. As such, it was a (rare) exercise in formal structure.

Example 6

1	DC1	when (1.0) we going shopping
2		(.)
3	DT	when are we going shopping
4		gee you're good
		(0.2)
5	DT	fantastic
		(0.2)
6	DT	another one

(Age 7;2 Dixon corpus A1.1-21)

In Line 1, the child makes a question that is formally complete in AlyE (which does not have a present tense auxiliary), but is incomplete in SAE, which requires the auxiliary 'are'. Since the interrogative pronoun 'when' is common to both SAE and AlyE, the one element that the teacher should focus on in terms of question formation is auxiliary existence, agreement and movement in interrogative clauses. In response the teacher recasts the question with the auxiliary included, but does not stress this point of difference between her sentence and the student's – she appears to be impressed that the student has used the word 'when' and praises her. The teacher's focus on the question words results in overt praise of an already-known item, which consequently overshadows the passive correction of 'are'. This example illustrates the challenge in teaching SAE in a context where the L1 is a contact variety, and where, in addition to no formal ESL/EFL training, the teacher has no knowledge of how the structures of the L1 overlap and diverge from the L2. In this way the language repertoires and learning needs of students who speak contact varieties can be more invisible in the classroom as the communicative imperative can more easily override the need to address grammatical differences (Angelo, 2013a: 78).

However, there are some occurrences of overt correction, as in Example 7:

Example 7

DC2	the roots WHAT
	(0.5)
DC3	is growing
DC2	[is growing,
	(.)
DT	yep
	(0.2)
DT	not is not is
	(.)
DC2	are
DT	are thank you

(Ages C3 10;10 C2 10;11 Dixon corpus F4.1-11)

In this example the students have been practising (orally) whole complex sentences before writing them in their books, so there is some prior teaching to contextualise this correction for the student. However, this prior teaching has not specifically focused on auxiliary agreement and so while the teacher appears to assume that the students should know this structure, she has no evidence at hand that they have ever been explicitly taught it (since they haven't been taught it by her).

While direct feedback on formal correctness is important for children developing their SAE skills, in the examples shown here we see that unlike a structured ESL class, the remote classroom is a place that is largely absent of the explicit teaching of English structures that ultimately makes explicit correction meaningful and profitable for students. Because of this it is often unclear for the students when content is being corrected, or when language is being corrected. Examples 5-7 show the teacher giving no language feedback (5), passive language feedback (6) or direct language feedback (7). This can be challenging for children who need to work out what the focus is, but we reiterate again that this is really an issue of training for the teacher. In today's climate, all teachers need language training because there are few teachers who will not encounter a child who does not speak English as an L1 in their classroom.

Children's language competency

If everything we knew about the spoken language skills of the children in these corpora was what is revealed by their participation in these observed discussions with their teacher, we would have little understanding of what the children could do with language. Yet teachers of Indigenous children are required to make judgements about the communicative abilities of their students based on the performances they witness and record in the English-medium classroom. These judgements are about their communicative abilities in English.

The irony here is that judgements of Aboriginal children's communicative abilities are often being made by monolingual educators, who have, at best, limited access to the animated and fluent conversations that the children engage in when talking with each other. Frequently, this talk is closed off to non-Indigenous teachers because of their own limited linguistic repertoire. Consequently they often tend to view this talk as 'chatter', which fills the interstices of 'important' classroom discourse.

When the children in the Morales corpus are playing unsupervised during an unstructured part of the day they show much more creative and extended language use. Here two children are playing and using Dhuwaya, the variety of Yolŋu Matha used when people of different tribes gather together, including at the school. C1 is the same child we encountered in examples 1 and 2, and demonstrates a remarkable difference in linguistics competence:

Example 8

MC2	*Mayawa*	*dhuwa*	*ŋarra*	*cents-tja*
	Shandi	this	I	cents-FOC[24]
	djuduparama		*malany*	
	put.into		groups	

'Shandi, I'm putting these coins in groups.'

MC1	*yow'*	*cents-tja*
	yes	coins-EMPH

'Yes coins.'

	Dhuwa	*nhä*	*yuwalk-dja?*
	this	what	truly-EMPH

---

[24] FOC=focus marker; EMPH=emphatic marker; PART=particle

'what is this really?'

Dhaŋaŋ   ŋi?

lots.of   right

'there are many (coins) right?'

nhä   *dhuwa*   *Gamandjan?*

what   this   skin.name

'what is this Gamandjan?'

Wukirray

excitement.PART

'how exciting!'

Makarrp   *ŋatha*   *mala-ny*

Nice.to.see   food   group-EMPH

'I'm so excited to see all this food.'

(C1 age 6;6; C2 7;0 Morales corpus)

Example 9 is an excerpt from a recording of two children from the Poetsch corpus. PC1 and PC2 are sitting together on the floor, working on a maths activity. At this point in the lesson the children are in pairs, cutting out a set of 12 images, which they then have to categorise in terms of the probability that the events depicted will occur (e.g. snow being less likely in their community than football training). PC1 is aged 7;4 (and is the child in examples 3 and 4) and PC2 is 8;3. Arrernte is the children's L1 and they have also developed some English proficiency. Throughout the lesson they move between Arrernte and English as they talk with each other, their classmates and their teacher. In the excerpt below, PC1 and PC2 are working as a pair, discussing the content of one of the images, and negotiating the tasks of cutting and arranging.

Example 9

PC1   *ante*   *yanhe*   *anteme*   *ake-ø*

and   that(mid)   now   cut-IMP

'and now cut that.' (pointing to page of images still to be cut)

PC2   *nhenhe*   *ampere*   *arrule-ipenhe-nge-ntyele*

this   place   long.ago-AFTER-ABL-ONWARDS

'this is from a long time ago.' (image of football oval and players)

PC2   *train-irre-ke*   *itne-areye*   *mape*   *eh?*

      train-INCH-PST   3PL-GRP   PL   eh

      '(when) they all used to train eh?'

PC1   *mhm*   *there*   *ingkerrinyeke*

      mhm   there   all/every

      anthurre anteme

      INTENS   now

      'mhm, all of them there now.'

PC1   *oi*   *ayenge*   *anthe-ø-aye*

      oi   1SGO   give-IMP-EMPH

      'oi give me (this one).'

PC1   *(squeal) wareyaye*

               just.kidding

      '(squeal) just kidding.'

PC1   *I'll*   *nhenhe*   *ake-rle [.]*   *or*   *kele*

      I'll   this   cut-GENEVT   or   ok

      unte   *ake-rlane-eye*

      2SGS/A   cut-CONT-PERM

      'I'll cut it, or ok you can keep on cutting.'

PC2   *the*   *arle*   *ake-rlane-me*   *[.]*

      1SGA   FOC   cut-CONT-PRES

      unte   *glue-eme-ile-me*

      2SGS/A   glue-E.TR-CAUS-PRES

      'I'm cutting, you're gluing.'

(PC1 age 7;4, PC2 age 8;3 Poetsch 2014.11.19-2: 1:01-1:17)

These examples demonstrate clearly that being unable to respond in Standard Australian English in the classroom does not mean they are unable to use complex and engaging language in contexts in which they are familiar both with the language and with cultural expectations. The fact that the children may not be able to interact fluently in SAE, especially in the first few years of school, is hardly surprising given that it is neither their L1, nor the language of the community. However, the current approach to teacher training means that many of these children carry this disadvantage throughout their school years because few of them will be lucky enough to encounter a teacher qualified in the teaching and learning of English as a Second or Foreign Language.

Conclusion

This chapter has explored how the invisibility of Indigenous students' language repertoires, and their language learning needs, pervades the schooling system in remote Australia. As we have shown, this plays out in several directions, from teacher training, to interpretation of standardised testing results. Against this backdrop, classroom interactions reflect and compound this state of affairs.

In laying out the ways in which language invisibility plays out, we hope to have clarified the multiple paths forward. Teachers allocated to remote community schools need pre-service training in ESL/EFL methodologies and experience in implementing these skills in a context where the curriculum focus will still largely be on content. Part of this training must include an understanding of the range of language ecologies and, in particular, the nature of Australia's various contact languages so that children speaking these are not misidentified as native SAE speakers. In-service training should likewise be targeted at helping teachers manage the complex task of integrating explicit language instruction across the curriculum. Bilingual schooling models remain international best practice when it comes to the education of children who speak a first language that is different from the language of wider schooling. Bilingual models build on existing language and literacy competencies of children, whereas, as we have seen, monolingual models tend to ignore them. For this reason, the development and improvement of such models is consistently the conclusion of reviews into both Indigenous education and languages in Australia (e.g. Australian Parliament, 2012).

Outside of the classroom, the broader policy environment needs to explicitly frame language and languages as central to any curriculum or pedagogical approach it is supporting. In particular, NAPLAN results need to be interpreted as indicative of progress in a second language only, and this will only be made possible if the LBOTE category is re-worked to be specifically an ESL/EFL category.

Australia's urban classrooms are increasingly linguistically rich environments through the immigration of families with complex language repertoires, which may or may not include English. The situation described in this chapter is therefore not necessarily isolated to Indigenous communities. This also means that bringing language and languages into central focus within the classroom and education system has the potential to benefit a large number of students (for example, foreign language background students now constitute 25 per cent of the Victorian schooling population (DEECD, 2012)). Teachers too, whether of migrant students, Indigenous students or any other student, want to be able to provide students with the best possible instruction. This will allow them to help their students build on the knowledge they already have, and consequently equip them to fully participate in their futures in Australia and beyond.

References

Angelo, D (2012) 'Sad Stories. A preliminary study of NAPLAN practice texts analysing students' second language linguistic resources and the effects of these on their written narratives', in Ponsonnet, M, Dao, L and Bowler, M (eds) *Proceedings of the 42nd Australian Linguistic Society Conference – 2011*. Canberra: Australian Linguistic Society, 27-57.

Angelo, D (2013a) Identification and assessment contexts of Aboriginal and Torres Strait Islander learners of Standard Australian English: Challenges for the language testing community. *Papers in Language Testing and Assessment, 2*(2): 67-102.

Angelo, D (2013b) NAPLAN implementation: implications for classroom learning and teaching with recommendations for improvement. *TESOL in Context, 23* (1 and 2): 53-73.

Angelo, D and Carter N (2015) 'Schooling within shifting langscapes: Educational responses in complex language contact ecologies', in Yiakoumetti, A (ed) *Multilingualism and Language in Education: Sociolinguistic and Pedagogical Perspectives from Commonwealth Countries*. Cambridge: Cambridge University Press, 114-192.

Angelo, D and McIntosh, S (2014) 'Anomalous data about Aboriginal and Torres Strait Islander language ecologies in Queensland', in Stracke, E (ed) *Intersections: Applied linguistics as a meeting place*. Newcastle on Tyne: Cambridge Scholars Publishing, 270-293.

Australian Government (2001) *Measuring Remoteness: Accessibility/Remoteness Index of Australia (ARIA) Revised Edition. Occasional Papers: New Series No. 14.* Canberra, Australia: Department of Health.

Australian Parliament. House of Representatives. Standing Committee on Aboriginal and Torres Strait Islander Affairs (2012) *Our land our languages: language learning in Indigenous communities.* Canberra: Parliament of the Commonwealth of Australia. http://www.aph.gov.au/Parliamentary_Business/Committees/House_of_ Representatives_Committees?url=/atsia/languages/report/index.htm

Bavin, EL and Shopen, T (1991) 'Warlpiri in the 80s: an overview of research into language variation and child language', in Romaine, S (ed) *Language in Australia*. Cambridge: Cambridge University Press, 104-117.

Capell, A (1963) 'Discussion on languages', in Stanner, WEH and Sheils, H (eds) *Australian Aboriginal Studies. A Symposium of Papers presented at the 1961 Research Conference*. Melbourne: Oxford University Press, 166-168.

Ciborowski, T (1976) 'Cultural and cognitive discontinuities of school and home: Remedialism revisited', in Kearney, GE and McElwain, DW (eds) *Aboriginal cognition: Retrospect and prospect*. New Jersey: Humanities Press.

Clyne, M (2005) *Australia's language potential.* Sydney: UNSW Press.

Cummins, J (1981) 'The role of primary language development in promoting educational success for language minority students', in California State Department of Education (ed) *Schooling and language minority students: A theoretical framework.* Los Angeles: California State University, Evaluation, Dissemination and Assessment Center, 3-49.

Cummins, J (1991) 'Interdependence of first- and second-language proficiency in bilingual children', in Bialystok, E (ed) *Language processing in bilingual children.* Cambridge: Cambridge University Press, 70-89.

Cummins, J (2001) *Negotiating identities: Education for empowerment in a diverse society.* Los Angeles: California Association for Bilingual Education.

Dalton, L, Edwards S, Farquharson R, Oscar S and McConvell, P (1995) Gurindji children's language and language maintenance. *International Journal of the Sociology of Language,* 113: 83-96.

Department of Education and Early Childhood Development (DEECD) (2012) *English as an Additional Language in Victorian Government Schools 2012.* State Government of Victoria. www.education.vic.gov.au/school/teachers/teachingresources/ diversity/eal/Pages/ealonlin ereports.aspx

Disbray, S (2014) 'At a benchmark? Evaluating the Northern Territory bilingual education programme', in Gawne, L and Vaughan, J (eds) *Selected Papers from the 44th Conference of the Australian Linguistic Society, 2013.* Melbourne: The University of Melbourne, 103-120.

Dixon, S (2013) Educational failure or success: Aboriginal Children's Non-standard English Utterances. *Annual Review of Applied Linguistics, 36*(3): 302-315.

Dixon, S and Angelo, D (2014) Dodgy data, language invisibility and the implications for social inclusion: a critical analysis of Indigenous student language data in Queensland schools. *Annual Review of Applied Linguistics, Vol. 37, No. 3.*

Eickelkamp, U (2008) '"I don't talk stories like that': On the social meaning of children's stories at Ernabella', in Simpson, J and Wigglesworth, G (eds) *Children's language and multilingualism.* London: Continuum, 79-99.

Genishi, C and Brainard, M (1995) 'Assessment of bilingual children: A dilemma seeking solutions', in Garcia, E and O'Laughlin, B (eds) *Meeting the challenge of linguistic and cultural diversity in early childhood education.* New York: Teachers College Press, 49-63.

Gould, J (2008) 'Language difference or language disorder: Discourse sampling in speech pathology assessments for Indigenous children', in Simpson, J and Wigglesworth, G (eds) *Children's language and multilingualism.* London: Continuum, 194-215.

Harkins, J (1994) *Bridging Two Worlds: Aboriginal English and Cross-cultural Understanding.* St. Lucia: University of Queensland Press.

Harris, S (1984) 'Aboriginal learning styles and formal schooling', in Christie, M, Harris, S and McLay, D (eds) *Teaching Aboriginal Children: Milingimbi and Beyond.* Mount Lawley: Institute of Applied Aboriginal Studies, 3-23.

Henderson, J and Dobson, V (1994) *Eastern and Central Arrernte to English Dictionary.* Alice Springs, Northern Territory: Institute for Aboriginal Development Press.

Hill, S (2008) *Yolŋu Matha and English learning at Galiwin'ku, an Indigenous community in North-east Arnhem Land.* [unpublished PhD thesis], University of New England, NSW.

Koch, H (2000) Central Australian Aboriginal English: In comparison with the morphosyntactic categories of Kaytetye. *Asian Englishes: An International Journal of the Sociolinguistics of English in Asia/Pacific,* 3: 32-58.

Kral, I and Ellis, E (2008) 'Children, language and literacy in the Ngaanyatjarra lands', in Simpson, J and Wigglesworth, G (eds) *Children's language and multilingualism.* London: Continuum, 154-172.

Lingard, B, Creagh, S and Vass, G (2012) Education policy as numbers: data categories and two Australian cases of misrecognition. *Journal of Education Policy,* 27(3), 315-333.

Malcolm, IG (2013) Aboriginal English: Some grammatical features and their implications. *Australian Review of Applied Linguistics,* 36(3): 267-284.

McConvell, P (2008) 'Children's production of their heritage language and a new mixed language', in Simpson, J and Wigglesworth, G (eds) *Children's language and multilingualism.* London: Continuum, 237-260.

McConvell, P and Thieberger, N (2001) *State of indigenous languages in Australia: 2001. Australia State of the Environment Technical Paper Series (Natural and Cultural Heritage), Series 2.* Canberra, Australia: Department of the Environment and Heritage.

McIntosh, S, O'Hanlon, R and Angelo, D (2012) 'The (In)visibility of "language" within Australian educational documentation: Differentiating language from literacy and exploring particular ramifications for a group of "hidden" ESL/D Learners', in Baldauf, R (ed) *Future directions in Applied Linguistics: Local and global perspectives – 35th Applied Linguistics Association Australia (ALAA) Congress.* Brisbane: The University of Queensland Press, 447-468.

Meakins, F (2008) 'Unravelling languages: Multilingualism and language contact in Kalkaringi', in Simpson, J and Wigglesworth, G (eds) *Children's language and multilingualism.* London: Continuum, 283-302.

Milburn, C (2010) Wanted: teachers to go the distance. *The Age*, Melbourne, 23 August.

Moses, K and Wigglesworth, G (2008) 'Silence of the frogs: Dysfunctional discourse in the 'English-only' Aboriginal classroom', in Simpson, J and Wigglesworth, G (eds) *Children's language and multilingualism.* London: Continuum, 129-153.

Moses, K and Yallop, C (2008) 'Questions about questions', in Simpson, J and Wigglesworth, G (eds) *Children's language and multilingualism.* London: Continuum, 30-55.

Munro, JM (2000) 'Kriol on the move: a case of language spread and shift in Northern Australia', in Siegel, J (ed) *Processes of language contact: studies from Australia and the South Pacific.* Saint–Laurent, Quebec: Fides, 245-270.

O'Shannessy, C (2005) Light Warlpiri: A new language. *Australian Journal of Linguistics,* 25(1): 31-57.

O'Shannessy, C (2008) 'Children's production of their heritage language and a new mixed language', in Simpson, J and Wigglesworth, G (eds) *Children's language and multilingualism.* London: Continuum, 261-282.

O'Shannessy, C (2011) 'Young children's social meaning making in a new mixed language', in Eickelkamp, U (ed) *Growing up in Central Australia: New anthropological studies of Aboriginal childhood and adolescence.* New York: Berghahn Books, 131-155.

O'Shannessy, C (2012) The role of code-switched input to children in the origin of a new mixed language. *Linguistics,* 50(2): 305-340.

O'Shannessy, C (2013) The role of multiple sources in the formation of an innovative auxiliary category in Light Warlpiri, a new Australian mixed language. *Language,* 89(2): 328-353.

Reeders, E (2008) 'The collaborative construction of knowledge in a traditional context', in Simpson, J and Wigglesworth, G (eds) *Children's language and multilingualism.* London: Continuum, 103-128.

Schultze-Berndt, E, Meakins, F and Angelo, D (2013) 'Kriol', in Michaelis, S, Maurer, P, Haspelmath, M and Huber, M (eds) *The survey of pidgin and creole languages* (Vol. 1). Oxford: Oxford University Press, 241-251.

Seedhouse, P (2004) *The Interactional Architecture of the Language Classroom: A Conversation Analysis Perspective.* Malden, MA: Blackwell.

Sellwood, J and Angelo, D (2013) Everywhere and nowhere: invisibility of Aboriginal and Torres Strait Islander contact languages in education and Indigenous language contexts. *Australian Review of Applied Linguistics,* 36(3): 250-266.

Siegel, J (2006) 'Keeping creoles and dialects out of the classroom: is it justified?', in Nero, S (ed) *Dialects, Englishes, Creoles, and Education*. Mahwah, NJ: Lawrence Erlbaum, 39-67.

Simpson, J and Wigglesworth, G (2012) *Ecology, Equity and Ethics in Education in Aboriginal Australia*. Keynote presentation at the Australian Council of TESOL Associations, Cairns, Australia, 2-5 July.

Simpson, J, McConvell, P and Caffery, J (2009) *Gaps in Australia's Indigenous Language Policy: Dismantling bilingual education in the Northern Territory (AIATSIS Discussion Paper no. 24)*. Canberra: Aboriginal Studies Press.

Simpson, J, McConvell, P and Caffery, J (2011) 'Maintaining languages, maintaining identities: what bilingual education offers', in Baker, B, Mushin, I, Harvey, M and Gardener, R (eds) *Indigenous language and social identity: papers in honour of Michael Walsh*, 408-428.

Thomas, W and Collier, V (2002) *A national study of school effectiveness for language minority students in long-term academic achievement*. Final Report. Washington DC: Centre for Research on Education, Diversity and Excellence.

Wigglesworth, G and Billington, R (2013) Teaching creole-speaking children: Issues, concerns and resolutions for the classroom. *Australian Review of Applied Linguistics,* 36(3): 234-249.

Wigglesworth, G, Simpson, J and Loakes, D (2011) NAPLAN language assessment for Indigenous children in remote communities: Issues and problems. *Australian Journal of Linguistics,* 34(3): 320-343.

Wilkins, D (1989) *Mparntwe Arrernte (Aranda): studies in the structure and semantics of grammar.* [unpublished PhD thesis], Australian National University, Canberra.

Yallop, C (1977) *Alyawarra: An Aboriginal language of Central Australia*. Canberra: Australian Institute of Aboriginal Studies.

1.7

Eastern Asia

English as a foreign language (EFL) and English medium instruction (EMI) for three- to seven-year-old children in East Asian contexts

Yanling Zhou and Mei Lee Ng, The Hong Kong Institute of Education, Hong Kong

Increased globalisation has promoted the English language as one of the most widely used around the world. Being able to speak English as a second language is therefore becoming an important aspect of social status. Learning English is accordingly an important issue for parents to consider when planning their children's education in East Asian societies such as China, Hong Kong Special Administrative Region (HKSAR), Taiwan, Korea and Japan. The educational systems in these countries are also renowned for their academically oriented practice and results. For example, Shanghai, HKSAR, Taipei, Korea and Japan were all in the top five per cent for literacy and mathematics in the world-ranking Programme of International Student Assessment (PISA) study (OECD, 2010; 2013). Parents in these societies have come to believe in the idea that their children need to have the best start in life and they aim to offer learning opportunities to their children as young as the age of pre-school or even earlier (Scheider and Lee, 1990). As a result, English learning is being introduced to children in these societies at younger and younger ages, despite the fact that English does not have daily significance in the lives of the majority of people in these contexts.

Despite the rapid growth in the numbers of children starting to learn English through pre-school or primary school at young ages, there is a lack of sufficient provision for quality assurance (see, for example, Baldauf et al., 2011; Cameron, 2003; Ng, 2013; Nunan, 2003) and a dearth of solid research evidence for either its immediate or long-term effectiveness. English is a foreign language (FL) for the majority of people in East Asia, hence the majority of very young (aged three to six) and young (aged six and above) children are therefore learning English as a foreign language (EFL). At the same time, a number of young children are learning English through a form of immersion education where English is the Medium of Instruction

(EMI). In this chapter, we examine how EFL and EMI education works in these East Asian societies and identify the challenges of different modes of English learning in these contexts. While the focus of this volume is on children's English pre-school educational experiences and learning (aged up to seven years old), there is relatively little research on EFL and EMI in East Asia. Consequently, our discussion also extrapolates from existing research findings targeted on primary school English learners, with relevant discussions of kindergarten children where appropriate. We emphasise that the crucial factors lie within the teaching pedagogies and curricula appropriate to these children's social, cultural and linguistic backgrounds. We start by providing background information about the policy and curriculum of EFL education in China, Korea, Japan, HKSAR and Taiwan, before identifying several key issues for EFL in these contexts. We then shift focus to analyse some key aspects of EMI education in these contexts. By discussing both EFL and EMI, we hope to present a comprehensive picture of English language education in early childhood settings (including kindergarten and primary school English learning) in East Asian societies. We also draw attention to a few key issues that deserve the attention of policy makers and language teaching professionals.

EFL in East Asian contexts

Overview of EFL policy and curricula in East Asian contexts

Despite the popularity of English in Eastern Asia, English is a FL in that it is generally not spoken or encountered in most communities. In China, Korea, Japan and Taiwan, for example, English is not an official language and the majority of people use their native tongues for daily communication. English is an official language in HKSAR; however, Cantonese is the most frequently used language at home and work for the majority of people (Evans, 2010; Evans and Green, 2001; Peng, 2005; Poon, 2010). Despite the prestige of English as a colonial and official language, English in HKSAR has never become a language of the society at large, and even in the workplace it is more commonly used in writing than in spoken communication (in contrast to Singapore, for example). The educational systems in these contexts have clear structures within which English is taught and learned as a FL. The comparison tables presented by Nunan (2003) and Baldauf and colleagues (2011) demonstrate that for the majority of East Asian societies, the learning of English is not officially introduced until Grade 3 (age nine) (China, Taiwan and Korea) or Grade 5–6 (age 11–12) (Japan). The exception is HKSAR, where English is introduced at kindergarten level (age three). In China, Taiwan, Japan and Korea, English is taught as a FL from one to four times a week. In the majority of HKSAR kindergartens, English is also taught as a FL and offered once or twice a week (Ng, 2014). At most HKSAR primary schools, English is taught for four to six hours per week from Grade 1 and onward; whereas at secondary school it is taught seven to nine hours per week as standard (Baldauf et al., 2011). A small number of primary schools in HKSAR are EMI schools and will be discussed in the latter part of this chapter.

As indicated above, from an educational policy point of view (with the exception of HKSAR), most East Asian societies adopt a policy where English is learned as a FL from eight/nine years of age onward. It is felt that at this time children's first language (L1) knowledge and development is well established, and hence it is appropriate to introduce a foreign language at this time – the implication being that introducing a FL/L2 at this time will not impede development of the L1. However, while HKSAR is the only society where English is (officially) learned from the age of three, unofficially, in the rest of these East Asian cultures, parents and kindergartens are also pushing for English to be learned from increasingly younger ages (see, for example, Chen, 2011; Jeong, 2004; Zhou, 2004). Even in HKSAR the proliferation of English in pre-school settings (to be discussed below) is based on a general concern in media discourse about declining language standards (Li and Lee, 2004). In HKSAR, as with other countries in East Asia, parental pressure has been an enormous force in driving the development of pre-primary educational contexts in which children are educated in English. In HKSAR, this pressure has stemmed from the government's 'streaming' policy where secondary schools were required to offer Chinese-medium instruction unless the school could meet the government requirements regarding teachers' English standards (Lai and Byram, 2003). The reasons for this pressure are characterised in the quote from Li and Lee (2004) below:

> *Chinese parents whose children are allocated to Chinese-medium schools are concerned about their children not getting enough exposure to English. Many students, upon being allocated to a Chinese-medium school against their will, felt depressed about being seen as "second best". As for school principals and teachers, their main worry is the school's inability to attract academically competent students, which in turn has implications for the school's public image and overall teaching performance.* (Li and Lee, 2004: 757)

This parental pressure in HKSAR has trickled down to pre-primary levels where, despite contrary policy recommendations, early partial immersion programmes have been on the rise (in other countries in East Asia as well). This is a potential concern because comparatively little is known about how very young learners learn EFL in these contexts and the quality of provision for very young learners can vary greatly. Hence it is not yet clear from a research point of view whether the consequences of starting at such a young age are entirely advantageous.

Central issues of EFL education in East Asian societies

Despite a comparative lack of research, there has nonetheless been some investigation of primary school EFL education and how it has been implemented. However, the effects across East Asian regions have not always been wholly positive (see, for example, Cameron, 2003; Copland et al., 2013; Hu and McKay, 2012; Kaplan et al., 2011; Spolsky et al., 2012) despite the growing popularity of English learning in this region (Chang, 2011; Sung and Zhang, 2013). For example, Kaplan et al., (2011) outline 12 issues that in their view highlight the problems of implementing primary EFL in these contexts:

1. Inadequate time dedicated to language learning
2. Inappropriate or insufficient local teacher training
3. Native English speakers cannot fill the proficiency and availability gap
4. Insufficient and inappropriate educational materials

5. Inappropriate teaching methodology for desired outcomes

6. Inadequate resources for the needs of the student population

7. Discontinuity of provision for English teaching

8. Problem with language norms

9. International assistance programmes may not be useful

10. Primary school children may not be prepared for early language instruction

11. Instruction may not actually meet community and/or national objectives

12. Children's local or first language may be at risk of attrition.

The teacher factor in primary school settings

Among these 12 problems, those relating to teachers and pedagogy are regarded as the most central issues in this region (see, for example, Cameron, 2003; Copland, et al., 2013; Hu and McKay, 2012; Kaplan, et al., 2011; Spolsky and Moon, 2012). English teachers of young learners are reported to generally lack training, specialist knowledge and resources (see, for example, Butler, 2004; Chen and Tsai, 2012; Copland et al., 2013; Jeong, 2004; Machida and Walsh, 2014; Wang and Gao, 2008; Leung et al., 2013). For example, Butler (2004) surveyed primary school English teachers in Korea, Japan and Taiwan on their current and desired English oral language proficiency levels, showing that across all three cultures over 80 per cent of teachers believed that their current levels did not meet the minimum levels for teaching primary school English effectively. This indicates not only that these teachers perceived themselves as having limited English proficiency, but also reflects their lack of confidence and training in teaching EFL. Low levels of language proficiency among local primary English teachers, especially in a productive language domain, have an impact not only on their confidence, but also on their pedagogical skills, the content of their teaching, and student motivation. This viewpoint is further illustrated by Wang (2008) in an investigation of issues relating to teaching and teacher education in primary school English in Taiwan. Wang shows that only 27 per cent of the primary school English teachers in her study reported having a qualification in teaching English and 25 per cent held neither an English nor a general primary school teaching qualification. All the teachers interviewed in the study were dissatisfied with the in-service training they had received, as the trainer was regarded as having low competence in teaching English to young learners. Indeed, as Hu (2007) also points out, one of the major challenges for primary English teaching in China is a teacher shortage and insufficient training. Given these difficulties at the primary level, it would not be surprising to find similar difficulties at the pre-primary level as well, though more research is needed in early years settings.

There are no clear policy guidelines for English proficiency levels in EFL teaching at primary or pre-primary school level across East Asian cultures. Even in HKSAR, which is a wealthy city with an historical background of English-language education, there is a general lack of appropriately trained primary and pre-primary English teachers (Nunan, 2003). For example, in HKSAR, kindergartens usually provide three-year programmes (K1-K3) mostly half-day (i.e. 9am–12 noon) sessions, but also offer some whole-day services as well as after-school childcare.

All these kindergartens are privately run, either by non-profit-making organisations or private enterprises, which in turn results in much variation and little regulation, particularly with respect to the specific curricula that are followed in these early years settings. From a young learners' point of view, Butler (2007) noted a positive association between teachers' level of English proficiency and young children's English learning. Indeed, several studies have demonstrated a 'Peter Effect' (see, for example, Applegate and Applegate, 2004; Binks-Cantrell, et al., 2012) in that one cannot expect a teacher to teach what he or she does not possess. Applegate and Applegate (2004) and Binks-Cantrell et al. (2012) illustrated that teachers who themselves were not interested in reading proved to be less effective teachers of reading themselves. Analogous with these studies, non-native speakers with low levels of English proficiency are less equipped to provide students with the content, knowledge and skills that are essential for English learning. In HKSAR, Lim and Li (2005) identified through their survey that some kindergartens employ local teachers who lack appropriate training and have relatively low levels of English proficiency. Therefore, even though more research needs to be carried out in this area, one of the main issues which consistently emerges from examining EFL in pre-primary educational settings concerns the extent to which teachers have received appropriate training and support, and whether they have appropriate levels of English language proficiency.

EFL teaching pedagogy for primary school

In addition to the concern about English language proficiency, the question of adopting the most appropriate pedagogical approaches is also an issue under investigation. In many countries in East Asia, governments have spent less attention on pre-primary educational services. Pre-school education is not mandatory in countries in East Asia; however, it is virtually universal in many. For example, in HKSAR, it is estimated that over 95 per cent of children between the ages of two and six attend either kindergartens or day nurseries (Ho, 2008; Rao and Li, 2009). However, as indicated above, there is wide variability in terms of whether and to what extent these different institutions adopt the 'child-centred' and 'developmentally appropriate' guidelines laid down by the HKSAR Education Bureau. There is often a divide between aspirations of educators and expectations of parents, where in the past in HKSAR parents viewed pre-primary education as a downward extension of primary school and, therefore, expecting three-year-olds to spend long periods of time copying complex Chinese characters was viewed as educationally appropriate (Rao and Li, 2009). Childhood educators in HKSAR and elsewhere do not believe children benefit from this practice.

In many countries in East Asia, efforts are being made to shift English teaching pedagogy from traditional rote memorisation or grammar-focused approaches to more communicative or task-based approaches, as these are considered to tap into learners' communication skills rather than merely memorised literacy skills (Deng, 2011; Kam, 2002; Jeong, 2004; Machida and Walsh, 2014). However, there are real challenges in terms of how teachers apply such approaches in what are typically large classrooms where there may be more than 35 pupils per class in primary school, and 20 to 35 or more in kindergarten classrooms in this region. A task-based teaching approach, which is more learner than teacher centred, is a process of meaning making that allows students to use the target language freely in activities with a clear communicative goal. Such activities are typically evaluated in terms of communication outcomes (Deng, 2011; Willis, 1996). The problems of implementing task-based teaching approaches was raised in Deng (2011) who observed four primary school English teachers in Grade 2 (age seven) to Grade 5 (age 11) in their implementation of task-based teaching in China and suggests that not only do contextual factors such as local examinations and restricted time for teaching influence the effectiveness of task-based teaching, but, more importantly, teachers' understanding, beliefs and perceptions have a powerful influence on their practice. She observes that teachers with inadequate understanding of, and negative beliefs about, task-based teaching tended to apply more teacher-centred approaches and often encountered discipline issues. However, teachers with adequate understanding and positive beliefs about task-based teaching sought to apply this approach in their pedagogy. A lack of knowledge of task-based teaching affected teachers in designing effective activities.

Butler (2005) compared primary school English teachers from Korea, Japan and Taiwan through their discussions over English classroom video clips from the different cultures. Their discussions revealed that their lack of understanding of communicative and task-based teaching approaches contributed to challenges in teaching EFL in primary schools across all three cultures. A similar phenomenon has also been identified in HKSAR, where teachers who lacked understanding of the task-based approach also held negative beliefs about it such as expecting it to involve additional preparation time, constrained textbook use, and so on (Carless, 2003). Similarly, Littlewood (2007) raises five concerns expressed by English teachers about task-based approaches: classroom management, avoidance of using English by students, minimal demands on language competence, incompatibility with public assessment demands, and conflict with educational values and traditions. These concerns touch upon various issues including individual differences in students' language ability; individual differences between teachers in terms of attitude, time and class management abilities; the curriculum; and the educational system as a whole. In Bronfenbrenner's ecological theory (1979), these factors within the microsystems as well as other cultural factors and external systems will all significantly affect children's English learning. In a case study, Carless (1998) demonstrates that a high standard of English proficiency, a positive attitude towards innovation and teaching, and a desire for improvement both personally and professionally are all associated with the successful implementation of task-based approaches. Some adaptive teachers may be more receptive to changes in teaching approaches, but it may be a significant challenge for many teachers to adopt such an approach, especially if they themselves did not learn English in such a way and are working within the same educational system they had experienced themselves as students. As some teachers put it, they may simply feel safer using methods with which they are familiar to help children learn, even if these are not the most effective.

A team teaching model of native and non-native English-speaking teachers in primary school

A team teaching model, where both native and non-native English-speaking teachers work together, might be one way of addressing some of these issues (Jeon and Lee, 2006; Machida and Walsh, 2014). Carless (2006) interviewed and observed team teaching in three different programmes: the Japan Exchange and Teaching Programme (JET), the English Programme in Korea (EPIK) and the Primary NET scheme in HKSAR (PNET). He concludes that successful team teaching in these contexts can be found if the following conditions apply (Carless, 2006; 350):

1. Sensitivity and goodwill of participants.
2. The development of relationships inside and outside the classroom.
3. Willingness to let minor points of tension subside for the sake of maintaining harmonious relationships.
4. Either some degree of shared philosophy or a willingness to compromise or make sacrifices.
5. Native English-speaking teachers exhibiting a respect for, or acquiescence in, culturally well-established classroom practices even when holding different views.
6. Continuity of personnel over time, which could be manifested either by a pair being given the time to develop a productive relationship or the practice of team teaching with multiple partners over time.

Jeon (2010) suggests that in Korea, non-native teachers' English proficiency also has a significant impact on co-teaching practice for young English learners, although in general both parties benefit from the experience. Oga-Baldwin and Nakata (2013) identify positive results from the JET programme, with local and native speaker English teachers serving as different role models in the classroom and positively contributing to students' EFL acquisition. They suggest that while native speakers can serve as a linguistic model, the local (non-native) English teacher can be seen as modelling the language learning process; he or she can demonstrate good language learning behaviours in the classroom, and will better understand the difficulties experienced by young Japanese learners. However, Machida and Walsh (2014) show that while positive changes in attitude and pedagogy were identified among Japanese local English teachers involved in team teaching, the majority of non-native English teachers voiced anxiety about speaking and instructing in English. They were also concerned that poorly trained native English speakers were being recruited, as they felt that these teachers could not cope with large classes in a foreign country. Similar views are expressed by Luo (2014) looking at the Taiwan Native English-Speaking Teacher (NEST) programme. Taiwanese local teachers involved in NEST reported improved English proficiency as well as better content knowledge of English teaching. However, the native English teachers recruited to the programme lacked teaching qualifications and commitment to the job, so neither the local teachers nor the students reported positive perceptions of the programme.

Typically, unqualified teachers are likely to lack the pedagogical context knowledge required for teaching English to young learners (Chen and Cheng, 2010). Even qualified teachers may find it a challenge to manage large classrooms (Chen and Cheng, 2010; Garton, 2014; Machida and Walsh, 2014) and groups of children with mixed abilities (Garton, 2014). Ng (2014) observed a problematic co-teaching practice in a HKSAR kindergarten. She attributes the failure of the partnership to the fact that the native English-speaking teacher had no professional qualifications and had not been trained to teach EFL to kindergarten children. The evidence suggests there is an urgent need to recruit qualified English teachers as well as providing in-service training for both native and non-native-speaking teachers in early childhood educational settings. In practice, unfortunately, due to the lack of qualified native English-speaking teachers, unqualified native English teachers are often employed in ESL jobs (Carless, 2006) especially at primary and pre-primary levels. Lack of qualifications and in-service training for both native and local non-native English-speaking teachers is an unresolved issue in primary English education in this region (Garton, 2014).

EFL in kindergartens

Despite some of the challenges in introducing EFL in kindergartens in East Asia over the last few decades, and the relative lack of research in this area, a growing number of studies have demonstrated the potential in very young children learning a FL. One such example is Kuhl et al (2003) who demonstrated that children even as young as a few months old can learn aspects of a FL. They ran a 12-session Mandarin teaching laboratory with native Mandarin speakers working with American monolingual children aged nine months, and found that the learning group outperformed the control group on a Mandarin speech perception task. Their second experiment also demonstrates that such a learning effect only occurred when the infants had social interactions with the native Mandarin teachers, but not in the condition of Mandarin exposure, only via audiovisual or audio recordings. Their study demonstrates the human capacity to learn another language at an early age and also stresses the importance of social interaction in very young children's FL acquisition.

Although limited in their extent, studies looking at various aspects of EFL in young children do suggest that while very young children are capable of learning a FL, this does not necessarily imply the 'earlier the better' (Marinova-Todd, et al 2000). Successful learning depends on the environment provided, teaching quality, sustainable learning motivation, and so on (see also Murphy, 2014). The Hong Kong Pre-school Guide (2006) explicitly states that English is learned through experience and play. However, Ng (2013) shows that kindergarten English learning is bounded by textbooks or pre-specified materials, and both native and local English teachers have insufficient training about how children at kindergarten learn language. Despite the guidance for learning through play, it is common to pair vocabulary and phonics learning with homework such as copying English words and sentences, as these are obviously measurable standards that parents and teachers can follow. In addition, a 20- or 30-minute class is usually dominated by the teacher talking and instructing. Lau and Rao (2013) also show that HKSAR kindergarten teachers, when teaching vocabulary, focus primarily on recognition and memorisation rather than understanding and use of vocabulary. Thus there appears to be a mismatch between guidance (stating young EFL learners should learn through play) and the reality, where teachers are adopting very specific and discrete exercises that in some respects limit the opportunities young children have to be exposed to and use their emerging knowledge of English.

Given the ecology of EFL in these contexts, with limited exposure to and use of the target language, most kindergarten children who learn EFL will have a maximum of one 20–30-minute daily exposure to it in a policy-supported context such as HKSAR (Lau and Rao, 2013). It is therefore important for parents, teachers and policy makers to manage their expectations of very young children's progress in EFL in East Asian contexts, which tend to place a strong emphasis on academic skills. In one of the only East Asian cultures to introduce English officially at kindergarten level, the *Guide to the Pre-primary Curriculum* in HKSAR suggests that English is a second language learned in context and that *"most of the principles of teaching the mother tongue are applicable to both the mother tongue and the second language"* (Curriculum Development Council, 2006: 30). While suggestions and recommendations are provided for pre-primary EFL education, they can be confusing for teachers and parents in terms of expectations about their children's development, given the children's first and second language develop at different rates. For example, children are expected to read and write already before they can even hold a simple conversation in English. Or in other cases, parents expect their children to speak English well despite only having 30 minutes a day or a week for learning English.

To sum up, the situation in EFL learning for young and very young learners in East Asian contexts is complex, and in many respects far from ideal. Several key issues deserve attention from parents, teachers and policy makers when making decisions about children's EFL learning, particularly in the context of early years settings. Research has consistently demonstrated that very young children have the ability to learn EFL, which can have positive long-term benefits, and this is equally true in East Asia. However, teacher education and in-service training for both local and native English-speaking teachers (Jeon and Lee, 2006) is one of the key factors having a direct impact on children's FL learning, given that the teacher may be the only resource for exposure to, and use of, English. Quality teacher training addresses the issues of applying appropriate teaching approaches and methods in EFL learning for young children in East Asia. The widespread practice of collaboration between local (non-native) and native English-speaking teachers in teaching is another aspect of teacher education that deserves much more attention in East Asia. These factors should be addressed at the policy level as well as in curriculum design. Furthermore, since many pre-primary settings in East Asia are either run by private institutions or fall outside the remit of educational regulation, there is wide variability in terms of which curriculum is followed, and whether and to what extent the teachers have either appropriate qualifications and/or appropriate levels of English language proficiency. Finally, very young children's language acquisition and general developmental characteristics should be taken into consideration when designing EFL curricula in East Asia to facilitate the establishment of age- and language-appropriate learning goals for them.

EMI tradition in Hong Kong SAR

Another important educational setting in which young learners are exposed to English in East Asia is in the form of English immersion. English immersion education in HKSAR has a long history given that it is a former British colony; where only in 1974 did Chinese gain equal status with English as an official language (Johnson, 1997), in 1960, the HKSAR education system included an elite early immersion (primary school) programme. Since then, the system has gradually been changed so that over 90 per cent of immersion programmes are found in secondary schools. However, as mentioned above, due to mounting parental pressure, English taught through pre-primary settings has been on the rise in HKSAR and throughout East Asia. In HKSAR, there has been a widespread proliferation of 'bilingual' kindergarten programmes, ranging from early to just short of total immersion. As indicated above, pre-primary education is mostly run by private organisations and typically only those in the middle class and above can afford to send their children to private (high tuition fee-paying) schools (from kindergarten to secondary school) which, almost without exception, offer some form of immersion education in English. In addition, international schools in HKSAR are mandated by the government to teach Mandarin Chinese instead of Cantonese as a FL.

It is worth noting that English is primarily taught by qualified native or native-level English-speaking teachers in international private schools in HKSAR, which is not always the case in state-funded educational settings. However, even less research has been carried out to look at the development of children's first and second languages in this context, despite the fact that many Cantonese-speaking children stop receiving mother-tongue support through education and start to acquire English as their main language in school, and for whom Mandarin becomes a FL. It is, therefore, an important and complex context to investigate more thoroughly in terms of L1 and English outcomes and development. Mandarin is different from Cantonese but is closely related. Even local Cantonese-speaking children, when they learn to read and write, actually acquire written Cantonese through Mandarin grammar and vocabulary. This means they receive comparatively little formal instruction in Cantonese. In a recent study, Zhou and McBride (2015) examined native and non-native Chinese-speaking children studying at one of the very few bilingual (Mandarin–English) international schools in HKSAR. The results show that even though these children acquire both languages starting at the age of four, by Grade 3, groups of native and non-native Chinese-speaking children both performed equally well on English reading and writing, although the non-native children's Chinese was significantly less developed than their native-speaking peers in Mandarin reading and writing. Interestingly, members of both groups expressed a preference for learning English over Chinese. These results suggest that native Chinese-speaking children can achieve native levels of English proficiency, like their English-speaking peers, through bilingual immersion programmes, even though English is not their first language. The same does not seem to be true for Chinese proficiency among non-native Chinese-speaking children.

In state schools, before 1997 when Hong Kong became a special administrative region of China, many schools adopted an EMI policy since English was (and remains) a high-status language. However, in 1997 (after the handover to China), many schools adopted a compulsory mother-tongue (Cantonese) policy as part of the 'language-in-education' reform. Cantonese was the medium of instruction up until senior forms of secondary school, unless schools applied for and received specific exemption to remain EMI (Lai and Byram, 2003). Primary schools could remain EMI if they were able to identify that the children were academically capable and that teachers had the necessary experience and expertise (which relates to the issues of appropriate levels of English proficiency as described in the EFL section above). EMI education for young learners in Hong Kong is largely characterised as an 'elite' model since they are more prevalent at independent (i.e. fee-paying) primary schools and tend to be reserved for only the most academically able pupils. Some researchers have suggested that EMI practices for very young learners are inappropriate because young children are still developing their first language (Poon, 2010), though, as indicated above, there is a significant lack of research investigating this issue. What we do know is that research throughout the world has continually demonstrated that immersion programmes can be highly effective educational programmes in promoting both first and second language proficiency and literacy (e.g. Genesee, 2004), hence there is no reason to assume immersion programmes in state schools in HKSAR would be detrimental in any way to young language learners, assuming that the balance of L1 and L2 support was appropriate. This balance, however, may not be being struck in EMI programmes in HKSAR.

EMI in other East Asian contexts

EMI in Korea and China is a much more recent trend. It is growing in popularity among parents and students (Copland and Garton, 2014; Dearden, 2015). However, in most of these cultures, EMI is more widely implemented at secondary and university level than at primary or pre-primary school level. Korea's *Teach English through English* (TEE) certification scheme (in place since 2009) is one of the few attempts to improve local English teachers' teaching quality in both primary and secondary schools (Choi, 2014). In Korea, it is officially recommended that EMI constitutes at least 80 per cent of classroom instruction (Ministry of Education and Human Resources Development, 2006). Policy here also dictates that both pre- and in-service teachers undergo English proficiency training. Choi (2014) found that despite moderately positive feedback from parents and other teachers, Korean English teachers reportedly hold rather negative views on EMI instruction at both primary and secondary school, and some have even expressed strong opposition to the policy. Despite government policy, the reality is that very few primary school teachers can conduct an English class in English (Park, 2009). In addition, Choi (2014) shows that teachers' opposition to the policy is mainly derived from misconceptions and inadequate teacher training, coupled with the contextual constraint of local examinations, which focused on grammar, reading comprehension, translation and writing. A few teachers in the study raised the concerns that EMI would not be sufficient for examination preparation.

In mainland China, EMI is also being experimentally implemented (see, for example, Cheng et al., 2010; Knell et al., 2007). Qiang and Kang (2011: 14) comment that *"the impulses of English immersion in China originated from political imperatives, the need of economic growth, the demand of information technology and internal dissatisfaction with English language education".* Such education has traditionally emphasised rote memorisation and grammar drills. These experimental implementations of immersion adopt two models: firstly, the Canadian model (Lambert, 1992) and, secondly, a partial immersion programme with almost half the school day spent using each of Chinese and English. English is normally the medium of instruction for language-related subjects as well as music, art, mathematics and science. Most English immersion programmes start at kindergarten and onward (that is, early immersion). A range of published studies report positive effects of a partial bilingual programme (Cheng, 2012; Cheng et al., 2010; Knell et al., 2007). Children in immersion programmes perform significantly better than children in non-immersion programmes on English language skills including oral language and literacy. In addition, they do not fall behind on Chinese and mathematics (Cheng et al., 2010; Knell et al., 2007); in other words, there is no 'cost' to their Chinese development or their academic skills in mathematics, but real benefits to their English language skills. The teachers in this context had a positive attitude towards EMI (Kong et al., 2011). Primary school English teachers in this study received various forms of in-service training provided by the specific projects. This training included not just professional qualification training, but also frequent short courses, inter-school lesson observations and discussions. They demonstrated strong commitment to EMI despite a comparative lack of teaching resources. This study reinforces the importance of supporting teachers in EMI programmes, since when they are well supported, higher academic and linguistic outcomes for young learners are attained.

While there are clear positive effects of adopting EMI programmes for young learners in East Asian contexts, concerns and doubts have also been raised. Hu (2009) questions the socio-economic consequences of EMI in general in China. So far, EMI has taken place on a small scale in primary schools. Hu fears that larger-scale promotion of Chinese–English bilingual education may entail tremendous public spending on teacher training, employment, facilities and learning materials. On a practical level, teacher development is seen as a critical issue for China's immersion programme (Song and Cheng, 2011). English classes of the immersion programmes reported in these studies were all conducted by local English teachers who were not close to being native speakers (see, for example, Cheng et al., 2010; Knell et al., 2007). The majority were female teachers aged under 30 who did not have extensive educational backgrounds but nonetheless adopted a communicative, interactive and learner-centred teaching approach (Song and Cheng, 2011). They reported that they taught English in a way that would help students derive meaning from the context, but when they taught subjects, they adopted an inquiry-based approach in which English was regarded as a cognitive tool. The greatest challenge for these teachers was that as the students developed, they struggled for subject and linguistic knowledge as well as teaching competence. Therefore, Song and Cheng (2011) advocate a more comprehensive, maybe even lifelong, in-service professional development culture for Chinese teachers using EMI. While these findings relate mostly to primary students and above, the concern about appropriate support for teachers is equally (if not more) relevant for pre-primary contexts for which there is a serious lack of research in mainland China.

In addition, although it appears EMI has enjoyed some short-term success in China, the long-term effect is not yet clear. Based on the successfully regarded Singapore model of English language education (Pakir, 2008), where total immersion starts from primary school and English is the second language of the majority of Singapore children, early immersion is thought to benefit students' long-term academic skills. In studies of international student achievement (e.g. PISA), Singapore is in the top league across the literacy, mathematics and science tables. However, in China, unlike in Singapore, English is not an official language that is widely spoken. The English immersion policy in Singapore was put in place to promote inter-ethnic (i.e. Chinese, Malay and Indian) communication as well as to connect Singapore with the Western world socially, economically and culturally (Dixon, 2005). While the success of English immersion in Singapore has also produced bilingual or multilingual students, the social and cultural impact has been significant. Dixon (2005) analyses the socio-historical roots of English immersion in Singapore, particularly in relation to students' academic outcomes. The results of her analysis show that despite most Singaporean students having English as a second language, they nonetheless developed their literacy and concepts through English, even when they tried to write in their home language, and while maintaining their mother tongue as an oral language at home. The implication of Singapore language policy is that Singapore has become a place shifting from *"a diverse multilingualism to a more uniform bilingualism in English and other official language"* (Dixon, 2009: 133). The question is whether this is the direction in which China, Korea, Japan, HKSAR and Taiwan would also like to go. It is important to recognise as well that just because a policy was deemed successful in one country, it does not mean it will be equally successful in all other countries.

Looking at EMI in East Asia overall, it appears that EMI provision is being adopted across the different cultural contexts in the region. In HKSAR some form of English immersion provision seems to be the norm at pre-primary levels, and in Korea government policy mandates the use of EMI in primary as well as secondary English FL classrooms. In China very small numbers of experimental immersion programmes at kindergarten and primary levels have shown some success in terms of bilingual literacy and mathematical achievement. However, sustainable and high-quality teacher training for local teachers is essential and critical in these different contexts. The educational and socio-cultural consequences of EMI practice are yet to become clear and more research is needed to address these issues.

Conclusion

There is a clear demand for EFL and/or EMI to start at an earlier and earlier age in the East Asian context as a whole. Although there is evidence that very young children, even babies, have the ability to acquire a FL, it is not guaranteed that learning English from very early on will produce good results. As articulated in Murphy (2014), the quality of English outcomes depends largely on the quality of teaching and teachers, and the quality of the programme. To the extent that teachers have adequate training and proficiency in English, that the curriculum is well designed and supported, and that the resources are appropriate, children in East Asia can make good progress in learning English in early years settings. Despite the efforts and investment of governments across different cultures in the East Asian region, the effect of EFL is not yet fully understood at primary or pre-primary levels due to the very significant lack of research examining these issues, as well as the lack of attention directed to early years settings by respective governments. Indeed, governments in East Asian countries tend to have adopted a more relaxed approach to provision offered in English (either EFL or EMI) in early years settings. From the brief (and selective) review provided in this chapter, it is clear that the main issues surrounding English language learning in early childhood settings concern the training and qualifications of teachers, their English language proficiency and the particular curricula and methodologies being followed.

With the growing popularity of English learning for very young children (three to six, or even younger) in this region, the possible educational, socio-economic and cultural consequences (Hu and McKay, 2012) need to be adequately recognised and addressed by policy makers. Furthermore, there must be a concern over whether there are sufficient resources to provide children with quality EFL or EMI programmes. As suggested by Marinova-Todd, et al (2000: 28–29):

> ... investment in elementary foreign language instruction may well be worth it, but only if the teachers are themselves native or native-like speakers and well trained in the needs of young learners; if the early learning opportunities are built upon with consistent, well-planned, ongoing instruction in the higher grades, and if the learners are given some opportunities for authentic communicative experiences in the target language. Decisions to introduce foreign language instruction in elementary grades should be weighed against the costs to other components of the school curriculum.

Although these comments from Marinova-Todd et al. (2000) were made in the context of primary school foreign language teaching, these concerns equally extend to English learning at kindergarten and early years levels. Similarly, EFL education in kindergartens should also take into consideration the ecology and context of young children's holistic development. Kindergarten children are at a stage of developing into a whole social person. While the foreign language programme can be treated as merely an additional subject to their kindergarten life, the policy maker and curriculum designer should nonetheless take a holistic approach, considering teacher factors, parental factors, as well as the child factor when integrating English into the early years curriculum.

Pedagogical concern for English language learning among young and very young learners deserves the attention of parents, teachers and policy makers. As the example of Chinese immersion learning shows, when a learner-centred and task-based approach is applied appropriately, it can have a significant and beneficial effect on learning and academic performance (Song and Cheng, 2011). However, these methods may not always be appropriately implemented by the majority of teachers in these East Asian nations due to a lack of training and development. Investment in systematic and sustainable teacher training and resources is required to underpin high-quality English education in both EFL and EMI programmes for young learners in East Asia.

References

Applegate, AJ and Applegate, MD (2004) The Peter effect: Reading habits and attitudes of preservice teachers. *Reading Teacher, 57*(6), 554-563. Retrieved from http://search.ebscohost.com/login.aspx?direct=trueanddb=aphandAN=12420583a ndsite=ehost-live

Baldauf, RB, Kaplan, RB, Kamwangamalu, N and Bryant, P (2011) Success or failure of primary second/foreign language programmes in Asia: What do the data tell us? *Current Issues in Language Planning, 12*, 309-323. doi:10.1080/14664208.2011.6097 15

Binks-Cantrell, E, Washburn, EK, Joshi, RM, and Hougen, M (2012) Peter effect in the preparation of reading teachers. *Scientific Studies of Reading, 16*(6), 526-536. doi:10 .1080/10888438.2011.601434

Bronfenbrenner, U (1979) *Ecology of human development: Experiments by nature and design.* Cambridge, MA: Harvard University Press.

Butler, YG (2004) What level of English proficiency do elementary school teachers need to attain to teach EFL? Case studies from Korea, Taiwan and Japan. *TESOL Quarterly, 38*(2), 245-278. doi:10.2307/3588380

Butler, YG (2007) How are non-native English-speaking teachers perceived by young learners? *TESOL Quarterly, 41*(4), 731-755. doi:10.1002/j.1545-7249.2007. tb00101.x

Cameron, L. (2003). Challenges for ELT from the expansion in teaching children. *ELT Journal, 57*(April), 105-112. Retrieved from http://eltj.oxfordjournals.org/ content/57/2/105.short

Carless, DR (1998) A case study of curriculum implementation in Hong Kong. *System, 26*(3), 353-368. doi:10.1016/S0346-251X(98)00023-2

Carless, DR (2003) Factors in the implementation of task-based teaching in primary schools. *System, 31*(4), 485-500. doi:10.1016/j.system.2003.03.002

Carless, DR (2006) Good practices in team teaching in Japan, South Korea and Hong Kong. *System, 34*(3), 341-351. doi:10.1016/j.system.2006.02.001

Chang, B (2011) The roles of English language education in Asian context. *Pan-Pacific Association of Applied Linguistics, 15*(1), 191-206.

Chen, A (2011) Parents' perspectives on the effects of the primary EFL education policy in Taiwan. *Current Issues in Language Planning, 12*(2), 205-224. doi:10.1080/14664208.2011.606783

Chen, CW and Cheng, Y (2010) A case study on foreign English teachers' challenges in Taiwanese elementary schools. *System, 38*(1), 41-49. doi:10.1016/j.system.2009.12.004

Chen, S, and Tsai, Y (2012) Research on English teaching and learning: Taiwan (2004-2009). *Language Teaching, 45*(02), 180-201. doi:10.1017/S0261444811000577

Cheng, L, Li, M, Kirby, JR, Qiang, H and Wade-Woolley, L (2010) English language immersion and students' academic achievement in English, Chinese and mathematics. *Evaluation and Research in Education,* 1-19.

Cheng, L (2012) English immersion schools in China: Evidence from students and teachers. *Journal of Multilingual and Multicultural Development, 33*(4), 379-391. doi:10.1080/01434632.2012.661436

Choi, T-H (2014) The impact of the "Teaching English through English" policy on teachers and teaching in South Korea. *Current Issues in Language Planning.* 1-20. doi:10.1080/14664208.2015.970727

Copland, F and Garton, S (2014) Key themes and future directions in teaching English to young learners: introduction to the Special Issue. *ELT Journal, 68*(3), 223-230.

Copland, F, Garton, S, and Burns, A (2013) Challenges in teaching English to young learners: Global perspectives and local realities. *TESOL Quarterly, 48*(4), 738-762.

Curriculum Development Council (2006) *Guide to the Pre-Primary Curriculum.* http://www.edb.gov.hk/attachment/en/edu-system/preprimary-kindergarten/overview/pre-primaryguide-net_en_928.pdf

Dearden, J (2015) *English as a medium of instruction - A growing phenomenon.* London: The British Council.

Deng, C (2011) *Communicativeness of activities in EFL primary school classrooms in Nanhai Guangdong, China: Teachers' interpretations of task-based language teaching.* Hong Kong: The University of Hong Kong. Retrieved from http://hdl.handle.net/10722/146131

Dixon, LQ (2005) Bilingual education policy in Singapore: An analysis of its socio-historical roots and current academic outcomes. *International Journal of Bilingual Education and Bilingualism, 8*(1), 25-47. doi:10.1080/jBEB.v8.i1.pg25

Dixon, LQ (2009) Assumptions behind Singapore's language-in-education policy: Implications for language planning and second language acquisition. *Language Policy, 8*(2), 117-137. doi:10.1007/s10993-009-9124-0

Evans, S (2010) Language in transitional Hong Kong: Perspectives from the public and private sectors. *Journal of Multilingual and Multicultural Development, 31*(4), 347-363. doi:10.1080/01434632.2010.497218

Evans, S and Green, C (2001) Language in post-colonial Hong Kong: The roles of English and Chinese in the public and private sectors. *English World-Wide, 22*(2), 247-268. doi:10.1075/eww.22.2.04eva

Garton, S (2014) Unresolved issues and new challenges in teaching English to young learners: The case of South Korea. *Current Issues in Language Planning, 15*(2), 1-19. doi:10.1080/14664208.2014.858657

Genesee, F (2004) 'What do we know about bilingual education for majority language students?', in Bhatia, TK and Ritchie, W (eds) *Handbook of bilingualism and multilingualism*. Malden MA: Blackwell.

Ho, CWD (2008) Exploring the definitions of quality early childhood programmes in a market-driven context: Case studies of two Hong Kong pre-schools. *International Journal of Early Years Education, 16,* 223-236.

Hu, G (2009) The craze for English-medium education in China: Driving forces and looming consequences. *English Today, 25*(04), 47. doi:10.1017/S0266078409990472

Hu, G and McKay, SL (2012) English language education in East Asia: Some recent developments. *Journal of Multilingual and Multicultural Development, 33*(4), 345-362. doi:10.1080/01434632.2012.661434

Hu, Y (2007) China's foreign language policy on primary English education: What's behind it? *Language Policy, 6*(3-4), 359-376. doi:10.1007/s10993-007-9052-9

Jeon, I (2010) Exploring the co-teaching practice of native and non-native English teachers in Korea. *English Teaching, 65*(3), 43-68.

Jeon, M and Lee, J (2006) Hiring native-speaking English teachers in East Asian countries. *English Today, 22*(04), 53. doi:10.1017/S0266078406004093

Jeong, Y-K (2004) A chapter of English teaching in Korea. *English Today.* 20(2), 40-46. doi:10.1017/S026607840400207X

Johnson, RK (1997) 'The Hong Kong education system: Late immersion under stress', in Johnson, R and Swain, M (eds) *Immersion Education: International Perspectives,* 71-189.

Kam, HW (2002) English language teaching in East Asia today: An overview. *Asia Pacific Journal of Education, 22*(2), 1-22. doi:10.1080/0218879020220203

Kaplan, RB, Baldauf, RB, Jr, and Kamwangamalu, N (2011) Why educational language plans sometimes fail. *Current Issues in Language Planning, 12(2).* doi:10.1080/14664208.2011.591716.

Knell, E, Haiyan, Q, Miao, P, Yanping, C, Siegel, LS, Lin, Z, and Wei, Z (2007) Early English immersion and literacy in Xi'an, China. *The Modern Language Journal, 91*(3), 395-417. doi:10.1111/j.1540-4781.2007.00586.x

Kong, S, Hoare, P and Chi, Y (2011) Immersion education in China: Teachers' perspectives. *Frontiers of Education in China, 6*(1), 68-91. doi:10.1007/s11516-011-0122-6

Kuhl, PK, Tsao, FM and Liu, HM (2003) Foreign-language experience in infancy: Effects of short-term exposure and social interaction on phonetic learning. *Proceedings of the National Academy of Sciences of the United States of America, 100(15),* 9096-9101.

Lai, PS and Byram, M (2003) The politics of bilingualism: A reproduction analysis of the policy of mother-tongue education in Hong Kong after 1997. *Compare: A Journal of Comparative and International Education,* 33, 315-334.

Lambert, WE (1992) Challenging established views on social issues: The power and limitations of research. *American Psychologist, 47*(4), 533.

Lau, C and Rao, N (2013) English vocabulary instruction in six early childhood classrooms in Hong Kong. *Early Child Development and Care, 183*(10), 1363-1380. doi:10.1080/03004430.2013.788815

Leung, C-SS, Lim, SEA and Li, YL (2013) Implementation of the Hong Kong language policy in pre-school settings. *Early Child Development and Care, 183*(10), 1381-1396. doi:10.1080/03004430.2013.788816

Li, DCS and Lee, S (2004) 'Bilingualism in East Asia', in Bhatia, TK and Ritchie, WC (eds) *The Handbook of Bilingualism.* Oxford: Blackwell Publishing Ltd.

Lim SWA and Li, YL (2005) Hong Kong pre-school provisions for early English language experiences: A case for redesigning pedagogy. *First International Conference on Educational Research on Redesigning Pedagogy: Research, Policy, Practice.* Singapore.

Littlewood, W (2007) Communicative and task-based language teaching in East Asian classrooms. *Language Teaching*, 40 (June), 243. doi:10.1017/S0261444807004363.

Luo, W-H (2014) An inquiry into the NEST programme in relation to English teaching and learning in Taiwanese primary schools. *English Language Teaching, 7*(1), 149-158. doi:10.5539/elt.v7n1p149

Machida, T and Walsh, DJ (2014) Implementing EFL policy reform in elementary schools in Japan: A case study. *Current Issues in Language Planning,* 1-17. doi:10.1080/14664208.2015.970728

Marinova-Todd, SH, Marshall, DB and Snow, CE (2000) Three misconceptions about age and L2 learning. *TESOL Quarterly,* 34(1), 9. doi:10.2307/3588095

Murphy, VA (2014) *Second language learning in the early school years: Trends and contexts.* Oxford: Oxford University Press.

Ng, ML (2013) Pedagogical conditions for the teaching and learning of English as a foreign language in Hong Kong kindergartens. *English Teaching and Learning,* 37(3), 1-35. doi:10.6330/ETL.2013.37.3.01

Ng, ML (2014) Difficulties with team teaching in Hong Kong kindergartens. *ELT Journal,* 69(2), 188-197. doi:10.1093/elt/ccu057

Nunan, D (2003) The impact of English as a global language on educational policies and practices in the Asia-Pacific region. *TESOL Quarterly,* 37(4), 589. doi:10.2307/3588214

OECD (2010) PISA 2009 results: What students know and can do: Student performance in reading, mathematics and science. *OECD Education and Skills,* 1. doi:10.1787/9789264091450-en

OECD (2013) *PISA 2012 assessment and analytical framework: Mathematics, reading, science, problem solving and financial literacy.* doi:10.1787/9789264190511-en

Pakir, A (2008) 'Bilingual education in Singapore', in Cummins, H and Hornberger, NH (eds) *Encyclopedia of language and education* (2nd ed, pp. 1,642-1,654). Springer US.

Park, JK (2009) 'English fever' in South Korea: Its history and symptoms. *English Today,* 25(1), 50-57.

Peng, L (2005) The English language in Hong Kong: Review and prospect. *US-China Education Review,* 2(9), 76-81.

Poon, AYK (2010) Language use, and language policy and planning in Hong Kong. *Current Issues in Language Planning,* 11(1), 1-66. doi:10.1080/14664201003682327

Qiang, H and Kang, Y (2011) English immersion in China as a case of educational transfer. *Frontiers of Education in China,* 6, 8-36.

Quint Oga-Baldwin, WL and Nakata, Y (2013) Native vs. non-native teachers: Who is the real model for Japanese elementary school pupils? *Journal of Asia TEFL,* 10(2), 91-113.

Rao, N and Li, H (2009) Quality matters: Early childhood education policy in Hong Kong. *Early Child Development and Care,* 179, 233-245.

Scheider, B and Lee, Y (1990) A model for academic success : The school and home environment of East Asian students. *Anthropology and Education Quarterly,* 21(4), 358-377. doi:10.1525/aeq.1990.21.4.04x0596x

Song, X and Cheng, L (2011) Investigating primary English immersion teachers in

China: Background, instructional contexts, professional development, and perceptions. *Asia-Pacific Journal of Teacher Education, 39*(2), 97-112. doi:10.1080/13 59866X.2011.560647

Spolsky, B, Moon, Y, Korea, S and Ho, S (2012) *Primary school English-language education in Asia: From policy to practice (Vol.1).* Routledge.

Sung, C and Zhang, K (2013) English as an international language in Asia: Implications for language education. *Language and Education, 27*(6), 585-586. doi:1 0.1080/09500782.2013.798129

Wang, W and Gao, X (2008) English language education in China: A review of selected research. *Journal of Multilingual and Multicultural Development, 29*(5), 380-399. doi:10.1080/01434630802147908

Wang, W-P (2008) *Copyright statement: Teaching English to young learners in Taiwan: Issues relating to teaching, teacher education, teaching materials and teacher perspectives.* The University of Waikato, New Zealand.

Willis, J (1996) *A Framework for Task-Based Learning.* Harlow, UK: Longman Addison-Wesley.

Zhou, J (2004) Pre-school English education in Mainland China: Problems and trends. *Hong Kong Journal of Early Childhood, 3*(2), 14-19.

Zhou, Y-L and McBride, C (2015) An investigation of cognitive, linguistic and reading correlates in children learning Chinese and English as a first and second language. *Bilingualism: Language and Cognition.* Available on CJO 2015 doi: 10.1017/S1366728915000279

2

Case studies in immersion / English Medium Instruction contexts

2.1

Supporting the home language of EAL children with developmental disorders

Johanne Paradis, University of Alberta, Canada

Children learning English as an additional language (EAL) from immigrant families typically speak a minority language at home, and learn the majority language, English, mainly through childcare centres, pre-schools or schools. This chapter is concerned with what early childhood educators, school teachers, special educators and clinicians often believe to be the best language choices for EAL children, especially those with developmental disorders. These professionals design interventions and give parental advice based on these beliefs that are, however well intentioned, not always in the best interests of the child or the family long term. For example, parents of EAL children are often advised to use English at home with their children instead of the home language because it is believed that EAL children would benefit from greater exposure to English to enable them to 'catch up' more quickly to their English native-speaker peers and, in so doing, strengthen their educational experiences. This advice to parents is given even more frequently for EAL children who have been diagnosed with developmental disorders that impact language, such as specific/primary language impairment (SLI), Down Syndrome (DS) or autism spectrum disorder (ASD) (Kay-Raining Bird et al., 2012; Jegatheesan, 2011; Kremer-Sadlik, 2005; Yu, 2013). Parents of EAL children with development disorders are given this advice because it is commonly believed that such children might be incapable of bilingual learning, and since the design of interventions is taking place in English, matching the home language with the language of intervention would cause less "confusion" and enhance the child's rate of language development and outcomes overall. This chapter brings forward evidence from Canadian and American research indicating that, contrary to these commonly held beliefs, supporting the home language and continued bilingual development of EAL children with developmental disorders is the more effective practice and is in the best interests of the child and family. In so doing, the aim is to help professionals working with young EALs with developmental disorders to reflect upon and possibly re-shape their assumptions about these children's language development, their teaching and clinical practices, and the advice they give parents about language use at home.

Benefits of bilingualism for all EAL children

Much research over the past 50 years has shown that maintaining continued development of the home language in EAL children is advantageous for their cognitive, academic and social-emotional development. Here we examine the central findings from this research, and evaluate how it may or may not apply to EALs with developmental disorders. The extent to which bilingualism could be advantageous is an important reason why educators and clinicians should support bilingualism in children with developmental disorders.

First, learning two languages can confer positive cognitive consequences on children, among them enhanced metalinguistic awareness, which is a skill underlying early literacy development (Bialystok, 2001). A second advantage has to do with the ability of bilingual children to share or transfer knowledge from one language to the other in the domain of academic linguistic, literacy and cognitive skills, which means they do not have to learn everything twice (Geva and Wang, 2001; Riches and Genesee, 2006). Regarding the first advantage, on one hand, bilingualism might benefit children with developmental disorders such as SLI by mitigating mild cognitive deficits present as part of the disorder (e.g. Peets and Bialystok, 2010), while on the other hand, depending on the severity and type of disorder, limitations in affected children's cognitive outcomes would be expected regardless of bilingualism. With respect to cross-language associations, a study comparing EALs with and without SLI showed that children with SLI were much less able to transfer grammatical knowledge from their native language to English than their typically developing peers (Blom and Paradis, 2014). In addition, studies investigating outcomes for EAL children with SLI in English-only and bilingual intervention programmes found limited evidence for cross-language effects, from English to the native language in particular (Ebert et al., 2014; Simon-Cereijido et al., 2013). It is possible, therefore, that bilingual children with developmental disorders show reduced cross-language sharing and transfer than their typically developing peers, but further research is needed on this topic.

A third advantage of bilingualism for EAL children lies in the domain of social-emotional development, and this advantage is likely to be even more important for EALs with developmental disorders. Maintenance of the home language in children from immigrant and/or bilingual families, regardless of the presence of disability, can have positive effects on children's sense of identity and belonging in their linguistic-cultural community of origin (Jegatheesan, 2011; Kremer-Sadlik, 2005; Wong Fillmore, 1991, 2000), on their relationships with their parents, extended family and community members (Jegatheesan, 2011; Kremer-Sadlik, 2005; Tseng and Fuligni, 2000; Wong Fillmore, 1991, 2000; Yu, 2013) and, additionally, could lead to education and employment opportunities in the future (Kay-Raining Bird et al., 2012; Yu, 2013). In-depth interviews with parents of EAL children with ASD from Chinese and South Asian backgrounds revealed that parents believed speaking the home language was crucial for transmission of cultural and religious values, and for communication with extended family members, especially elders (Jegatheesan, 2011; Yu, 2013). Furthermore, if immigrant parents never achieve high levels of proficiency in English, the more complex communicative needs of older children and adolescents can create communication barriers between parents and children (Wong Fillmore, 1991, 2000). In a study with 620 adolescents from East Asian, Filipino and Latino backgrounds, Tseng and Fuligni (2000) found that when youth and parents communicated more in the native language, there was greater cohesion within the family, more discussions of present and future concerns, greater closeness with mothers and fewer conflicts with fathers. Thus, continued bilingual development for all EAL children might be necessary for ease of communication between parent and child in the long term. Maintaining continued development of the home language in the case of EAL children with severe developmental disorders is vitally important because their parents and extended families are likely to be long-term caregivers and close companions.

In a nutshell, the current evidence suggests that there is slimmer support for the cognitive and academic advantages of bilingualism for EALs with developmental disorders than for EALs with typical development. But, crucially, there is no evidence that bilingualism causes disadvantages in these areas. Moreover, there is compelling evidence for the advantages of continued bilingualism for children's social-emotional development. What do these findings imply for educational and clinical practice? One implication is that special educators and clinicians could include a focus on helping EALs with developmental disorders to learn how to make use of cross-language associations as part of their intervention techniques. A second implication is that educators and clinicians should be aware of how bilingualism for EALs with developmental disorders will benefit the child and family's wellbeing long-term. This awareness should trickle down into education/ clinical planning and, importantly, advice given to parents. It is particularly crucial to think about long-term outcomes for the "whole child", and not just putative short-term gains in the child's English language abilities.

Successful bilingual development in children with developmental disorders

In this section, we shatter the number one, commonly held belief: bilingualism is too burdensome for children with developmental disorders. Children with developmental disorders actually can and do become bilingual, and there is no evidence that bilingualism exacerbates their impaired language development. French–English and Spanish–English children with SLI aged four to seven years old display similar grammatical abilities as their monolingual age peers with SLI in both languages (Paradis et al., 2003) or at least in English (Gutiérrez-Clellen et al., 2008). A longitudinal case study of a Chinese EAL boy with SLI showed he caught up to his monolingual peers with SLI in English after three years of English-language schooling (Paradis, 2010). Similarly, Kay-Raining Bird et al. (2005) compared the language abilities of bilingual and English monolingual children with DS who were matched for mental age and found no differences between bilinguals and monolinguals on comprehensive tests of English expressive and receptive language skills. Regarding bilingual children with ASD, several recent studies have found that children with this disorder have parallel language levels to their monolingual age peers with ASD (Hambly and Fombonne, 2012; Kay-Raining Bird et al., 2012; Ohashi et al., 2012; Petersen et al., 2011). For example, Ohashi et al. (2012)

compared comprehensive language and communication measures in three-and-a-half-year-old monolingual and bilingual children just diagnosed with ASD and found that the bilingual children were not delayed with respect to their monolingual peers. Chinese–English-speaking children with ASD, aged three-and-a-half to six years old, who had undergone English-language intervention, also showed English abilities parallel to same-aged monolingual peers with ASD and, moreover, their English and Chinese vocabularies were roughly equivalent, demonstrating that they were balanced bilinguals (Petersen et al., 2011). This research stands as evidence against the popular belief that learning two languages would be too burdensome for children with developmental disorders. This evidence, therefore, should shape how educators and clinicians working with these children design intervention and individualised education programming for these children; such programming can and should include support for continued bilingual development.

Use of English at home by first generation immigrant parents

It is well known that all children, especially those with developmental disorders that cause language-learning difficulties, need rich linguistic input in order to develop their full linguistic and literacy potential. This fact is at the root of many campaigns to promote home literacy activities with young children – activities that include both oral and written language. However, if parents are speaking a language they are not proficient in, then they might not be able to provide rich linguistic input. Numerous studies have shown that when English is used at home by parents who are non-proficient speakers of English, this has no demonstrable positive impact on EAL children's English development (Hammer et al., 2009; Hammer et al., 2012; Paradis, 2011; Paradis and Kirova, 2014; Place and Hoff, 2011), and can have a negative impact on their development of the home language (Hammer et al., 2009; Hammer et al., 2012). In a study of 169 EALs aged five to seven years old, Paradis (2011) found that the quality of children's English environment outside school (i.e. contact with native-speaker input through media, extra-curricular activities and playmates) was positively associated with children's vocabulary and grammar outcomes in English, but the amount of English spoken at home among family members was not. Furthermore, proficiency in English can be context-dependent. Yu (2013) found that the majority of Chinese-speaking mothers that she interviewed were professionals who used English in the workplace. Nevertheless, some mothers reported not being comfortable speaking English at home with their children because their knowledge of English vocabulary and topics of conversation was limited to their professional lives. For instance, one mother said she did not know how to say "itchy" in English when speaking with her child (Yu, 2013: 19). Taken together, this research indicates that shifting the language at home to English might not be a choice that immigrant families can or should make. Therefore, when promoting home literacy activities for EAL children, educators should broaden their suggestions to include activities that take place in the home language. This is no less true for EAL children with developmental disorders.

Home language use in families of EAL children with developmental disorders

Home language maintenance can be a challenge for families of EAL children with developmental disorders because continued learning of two languages is very often discouraged by professionals such as speech-language pathologists/speech therapists, physicians, teachers and psychologists, with only a minority of parents receiving support for their child's bilingualism (Kay-Raining Bird et al., 2012; Jegatheesan, 2011; Kremer-Sadlik, 2005; Yu, 2013). For EAL children with ASD in particular, the child undergoes numerous hours of intervention programming in English, and parents are usually given language-based therapy activities to do at home with their child in English (Jegatheesan, 2011; Kremer-Sadlik, 2005; Yu, 2013), thus increasing their exposure to the majority language compared with their typically developing EAL peers. First generation immigrant parents who have heeded the advice of professionals to switch to English at home reported that there were barriers in their communication with their (now) English monolingual child (Kremer-Sadlik, 2005), or that they simply could not sustain speaking only English with their child for any length of time because they did not feel they could fully express themselves in English (Yu, 2013). In some families studied by Kremer-Sadlik (2005), the child with ASD was often left out of family conversations in the home language, was uninterested in cultural, religious or community activities in that language, and even showed rejection of ethnic identity. By contrast, parents who have continued to raise their child with ASD bi- or multi-lingually in spite of advice from professionals report more positive experiences about their child's communicative development (Jegatheesan, 2011; Kay-Raining Bird et al., 2012). Jegatheesan (2011) discusses how switching to just one language in the South Asian families she studied would have been impossible anyway, since these were large extended families where multilingualism was the way of life. The three children with ASD in her study nevertheless developed from being essentially non-verbal to using words and sentences in two or three languages over the course of one-and-a-half years. Regarding therapy activities at home, Kremer-Sadlik (2005) found that parents were less likely to engage in these activities if their English was not proficient, and if parents could have done the activities in their native language, compliance might have been higher.

Hearing from parents first hand will serve to anchor these research findings. What follows below are quotes from parents (mainly mothers) of children with ASD from diverse linguistic-cultural backgrounds on: 1) advice from professionals about language use at home, and 2) their experiences with English-only or bi- and multi-lingual language use with their children:

He was like age four. In order to help him move forward a little faster to make her – to make him speech can catching up as same age kids I-she [the clinician] suggested we need to use English more often. (Kremer-Sadlik, 2005: 1,225)

Learning two totally different languages at the same time and understand them properly and use them properly at the same time, she [the clinician] mentioned about that would be extremely difficult with the kids who have speech problem. (ibid: 1,231)

The family doctor, speech therapist and teacher from the school district, they all told me not to speak Chinese with [Shane] any more. His family doctor said that because Shane had a language delay, he recommended that I speak only one language with him to keep him from being confused. (Yu, 2013: 18)

She said that English was going to be of utmost importance to him because all of the language therapy and ABA sessions were going to be in English ... [She] recommended that we designate a certain room in the house to speak English. But I don't think that's very practical ... (ibid: 18)

He said we know now that speaking the mother tongue, like Chinese or Spanish, is very important. Children should be encouraged to learn their mother tongues and their culture. After I heard him say that, I thought it made a lot of sense. (ibid: 18)

He has grandparents, and they cannot speak English. So how our child can communicate with his grandmother if he knows only English? What they [professionals] are asking is unreasonable. So, it is best we don't tell them anything. They don't need to know what we speak at home because it's a headache for us to make them understand. They just don't. (Jegatheesan, 2011: 196)

Note. Quotes in italics are fully or partially translated.

Interviewer: And so do you think he understands you when you speak?

Mother: No. He doesn't pick up any Chinese that time. He doesn't pay attention. And even later on the age, and he still if – if we talk Chinese he'll shut up. He'll, he'll not talking at all. He'll not interact. (Kremer-Sadlik, 2005: 1,229)

They all asked us to speak English with our child. The problem was my English was not very good. How can they expect me to speak English with him? I failed at it. Then I thought if I could not help him in English, then I will do it in Chinese. That is how I felt. I also felt really inadequate. (Yu, 2013: 18)

...Raqib understands what she [grandmother] says when she speaks to him using any one of her languages. He responds to her in her language. Even if it is a few words, he responds and it makes my mother-in-law happy. Being able to talk to one another has allowed them to have their own special relationship ... (Jegatheesan, 2011: 193)

... And he communicates with whatever language he has, like he will talk mixing Bangla, English and some nonsensical words. Sometimes he tries to annoy Bibi [maternal aunt] by responding to her using rhyming words from Dr. Seuss ... (ibid:1 94)

... If I was to start over again, I would speak in the language [French, minority language]. With time, your child will speak the majority language [English] anyway ... (Kay-Raining Bird et al., 2012: 59)

Note. Quotes in italics are fully or partially translated.

Summary of recommendations for clinicians and educators

There is no evidence to support the advice to parents of EAL children to stop speaking the home language with their child once that child has been diagnosed with a developmental disorder. In light of this evidence, clinicians and educators should encourage parents of EAL children to speak to them in the language(s) they are most proficient in, usually their native language, and to engage in meaningful and diverse activities in their native language with their child in and outside the home, including literacy activities. If the native language is not a written language, parents should be encouraged to tell stories in their native language following the pictures in English books. Insofar as possible, teachers should demonstrate support and encouragement for both the home language and English within the classroom environment as well. Regarding specialised programming, special educators and clinicians should work with parents directly or through cultural brokers and interpreters to devise means for conducting language therapy activities and language use strategies at home in the native language, or in both English and the native language. Above all, parents of EAL children should be advised that, for their child's wellbeing within the family and community long term, bilingualism is the best choice and that their child has the potential for this even if they have a developmental disorder.

References

Bialystok, E (2001) *Bilingualism in development. Language, literacy and cognition.* Cambridge: Cambridge University Press.

Blom, E and Paradis, J (2014) Sources of individual differences in the acquisition of tense inflection by English second language learners with and without specific language impairment. *Applied Psycholinguistics*: 1-24. DOI: 10.1017/S014271641300057X.

Ebert, KD, Kohnert, K, Pham, G, Rentmeester Disher, J and Payesteh, B (2014) Three treatments of bilingual children with primary language impairment: Examining cross-linguistic and cross-domain effects. *Journal of Speech, Language and Hearing Research* 57: 172-186.

Geva, E and Wang, M (2001) The development of basic reading skills in children: A cross-language perspective. *Annual Review of Applied Linguistics, 21,* 182 -204.

Gutiérrez-Clellen, V, Simon-Cereijido, G and Wagner, C (2008) Bilingual children with language impairment: A comparison with monolinguals and second language learners. *Applied Psycholinguistics* 29: 3-20.

Hambly, C and Fombonne, E (2012) The impact of bilingual environments on language development in children with autism spectrum disorders. *Journal of Autism and Developmental Disorders*, 42: 1342-1352.

Hammer, CS, Komaroff, E, Rodriguez, B, Lopez, L, Scarpino, S and Goldstein, BG (2012) Predicting Spanish–English bilingual children's language abilities. *Journal of Speech, Language, and Hearing Research* 55: 1251-1264.

Hammer, CS, Davison, MD, Lawrence, FR and Miccio, AW (2009) The effect of maternal language on bilingual children's vocabulary and emergent literacy development during Head Start and kindergarten. *Scientific Studies of Reading* 13: 99-121.

Jegatheesan, B (2011) Multilingual development in children with autism: Perspectives of South Asian Muslim immigrant parents on raising a child with communicative disorder in multilingual contexts. *Bilingual Research Journal* 34/2: 185-200.

Kay-Raining Bird, E, Cleave, P, Trudeau, N, Thodardottir, E, Sutton, A and Thorpe, A (2005) The language abilities of bilingual children with Down Syndrome. *American Journal of Speech-Language Pathology* 14: 187-199.

Kay-Raining Bird, E, Lamond, E and Holden, J (2012) Research Report: Survey of bilingualism in autism spectrum disorders. *International Journal of Language and Communication Disorders*, 47/1: 52-64.

Kremer-Sadlik, T (2005) 'To be or not to be bilingual: Autistic children from multilingual families', in Cohen, J, McAlister, KT, Rolstad, K and MacSwan J (eds) *Proceedings of the 4th International Symposium on Bilingualism*. Somerville, MA: Cascadilla Press, 1225-1234.

Ohashi, JK, Mirenda, P, Marinova-Todd, S, Hambly, C, Fombonne, E, Szatmari, P, Bryson, S, Roberts, W, Smith, I, Vaillancourt, T, Volden, J, Waddell, C, Zwaigenbaum, L, Georgiades, S, Duku, E, and Thompson, A (2012) Comparing early language development in monolingual- and bilingual-exposed children with autism spectrum disorders. *Research in Autism Spectrum Disorders* 6: 890-897.

Paradis, J (2010) Keynote Article: The interface between bilingual development and specific language impairment. *Applied Psycholinguistics* 31: 3-28.

Paradis, J (2011) Individual differences in child English second language acquisition: Comparing child-internal and child-external factors. *Linguistic Approaches to Bilingualism.* 1/3: 213-237.

Paradis, J and Kirova, A (2014) English second language learners in pre-school: Profile effects in their English abilities and the role of home language environment. *International Journal of Behavioral Development* 38/4: 342-349.

Paradis, J, Crago, M, Genesee, F and Rice, M (2003) Bilingual children with specific language impairment: How do they compare with their monolingual peers? *Journal of Speech, Language and Hearing Research* 46: 1-15.

Peets, KF and Bialystok, E (2010) An Integrated approach to the study of SLI and bilingualism [Peer Commentary on Keynote Article 'The interface between bilingual development and specific language impairment']. *Applied Psycholinguistics* 31/2: 314-319.

Petersen, JM, Marinova-Todd, SH and Mirenda, P (2011) Brief Report: An exploratory study of lexical skills in bilingual children with autism spectrum disorder. *Journal of Autism and Developmental Disorders*. DOI 10.1007/s10803-011-1366-y.

Place, S and Hoff, E (2011) Properties of dual language exposure that influence two-year-olds' bilingual proficiency. *Child Development* 82: 1834-1849.

Riches, C, and Genesee, F (2006) 'Crosslinguistic and crossmodal issues', in Genesee, F, Lindholm-Leary, K, Saunders, WM and Christian D (eds) *Educating English language learners* (pp. 64-108). New York, NY: Cambridge University Press.

Simon-Cereijido, G, Gutiérrez-Clellen, V and Sweet, M (2013) Predictors of growth or attrition in Latino children with specific language impairment. *Applied Psycholinguistics*, 34: 1219-1243.

Tseng, V and Fuligni, A (2000) Parent-adolescent language use and relationships among immigrant families with East Asian, Filipino and Latin American backgrounds. *Journal of Marriage and Family*, 62: 465-476.

Wong Fillmore, L (1991) When learning a second language means losing the first. *Early Childhood Research Quarterly* 6/3: 323-346.

Wong Fillmore, L (2000) Loss of family languages: Should educators be concerned? *Theory into Practice* 39/4: 203-210.

Yu, B (2013) Issues in bilingualism and heritage language maintenance: Perspectives of minority-language mothers of children with autism spectrum disorders. *American Journal of Speech-Language Pathology* 22: 10-24.

2.2

A setting-based oral language intervention for nursery-aged children with English as an additional language

Silke Fricke and Gill Millard, University of Sheffield, England

Introduction

Oral language (OL) provides a critical foundation for children's readiness to learn and successful school participation (Law et al., 2013; Roulstone et al., 2011), and children entering school with poor OL are at risk of educational and social underachievement (Clegg et al., 2005; Muter et al., 2004). There is an increasing emphasis on the importance of OL in literacy instruction (Rose, 2006, 2009; Tickell, 2011) while concern has grown about the number of children entering school with poor OL (Bercow, 2008). Early interventions are high on government agendas (Allen, 2011) as high quality provision and 'rich and engaging language environments' (Castro et al., 2011) are needed to address these skills before difficulties become established and start to impact on learning. However, many intervention programmes are published and available to schools without sufficient evidence of their effectiveness. In light of this, recent reviews (e.g. Allen, 2011) highlight the need for more rigorous research to provide evidence of beneficial effects of intervention approaches implemented in schools – over and above gains expected from routine classroom provision. This information is essential to enable schools to make wise decisions about the investment of time and resources in their aim to boost OL skills and provide children with important foundations for literacy development and educational attainment.

A growing number of children entering UK primary schools are identified as speaking English as an Additional Language (EAL), which is the most widely used term in the UK to refer to children for whom English is not the dominant language at home and who are therefore learning English in addition to their home language(s). Statistics suggest around 18.1 per cent of the primary school population nationally speak EAL, and as much as 98.8 per cent in some schools (DfE, 2013). A large proportion of this population enter school with lower language skills than their monolingual peers, facing the dual challenge of learning English and accessing the curriculum. As they progress through school the gap with their monolingual peers often widens (Castro et al., 2011) and they tend to underperform in national assessments in primary school (DfE, 2010). In the UK context, particular difficulties have been identified in the areas of vocabulary knowledge and comprehension (Burgoyne et al., 2009; Burgoyne et al., 2011). Explanations for this underachievement are likely to be complex, and include factors such as too little exposure to and insufficiently developed competence in English, while many families of children with EAL live in areas of socio-economic disadvantage (Baker, 2006).

An additional challenge to UK schools is the vast number of first languages present in some classrooms, making it difficult to support children's home language. The majority of literature concerning support for children with EAL comes from the US, and often focuses specifically on Spanish-speaking children learning English (Farver et al., 2009; Kohnert and Medina, 2009). Findings can therefore not be simply transferred to the UK population and education system. Likewise, although research investigating effective early interventions for monolingual children with language weaknesses has produced encouraging results (Bowyer-Crane et al., 2008; Fricke et al., 2013), these findings offer little evidence-based guidance as to whether and how these interventions work for children with EAL.

From the international intervention studies available, most focus on enhancing phonological and early literacy skills (Farver et al., 2009; Vadasy and Sanders, 2010), while others target older age groups (Lesaux et al., 2010; Proctor et al., 2011), or evaluate interventions in language contexts other than English (Chlapana and Tafa, 2014; Ennemoser et al., 2013; Segers et al., 2001).

From the handful of intervention studies focusing on OL in the Early Years (EY) and children with EAL, most target vocabulary (for an exception see Dockrell et al., 2010). Storybook reading as a method of vocabulary instruction is widely researched (Collins, 2010; Lugo-Neris et al., 2010; Silverman, 2007). Alternative approaches include 'comprehensive curriculum' (Wilson et al., 2013) or small group OL instruction (Dockrell et al., 2010; Riley et al., 2004). Although such intervention studies have demonstrated gains in taught vocabulary (e.g. Collins, 2010; Crevecoeur et al., 2014; Nelson et al., 2011), they tend not to find any generalised effects on standardised language tests. Furthermore, limitations such as small sample sizes or lack of a control group limit the conclusions that can be drawn from many of these studies.

For example, Silverman (2007) evaluated a teacher-delivered 'Multidimensional Vocabulary Programme' in five American kindergarten classrooms. Both native English speakers (n=44) and children with EAL (n=28) showed significant gains in taught vocabulary following the intervention; the latter group showing the greatest benefit. However, results must be interpreted cautiously as the sample size was relatively small and unbalanced, participants were not matched for ability at the outset, and there was no control group.

Dockrell et al. (2010) compared a 15-week, small group intervention targeting vocabulary, inferencing and narrative (*Talking Time*; n=46) with storybook reading (n=40) and no intervention (n=20). Three pre-school settings, one per intervention group, were involved in the study. *Talking Time* improved children's verbal comprehension, vocabulary naming (BASII, Elliot et al., 1996) and sentence repetition (GAPS, Gardner et al., 2006) significantly more than storybook reading or no intervention. However, despite direct and indirect work on narrative in *Talking Time*, no significant advantage was found in narrative skills in the intervention group. As before, study limitations such as unequal group sizes and potential setting effects limit the generalisability of the findings.

Thus, although there is some emerging evidence for setting-based interventions having a positive impact on language, in particular vocabulary skills, in children with EAL, questions remain regarding the effectiveness and feasibility of such interventions (Law et al., 2012; Snowling and Hulme, 2011). More research into early OL interventions focusing on and beyond vocabulary for children with EAL is clearly needed.

The current study

The current intervention study aimed to extend previous research carried out with monolingual children with language weaknesses in UK nursery and Reception (Carroll et al., 2011; Fricke et al., 2013) to children with EAL. More specifically, it investigated whether an OL programme targeting active listening, vocabulary and narrative skills could be shown to improve the OL skills in nursery-aged children with EAL.

Method

We conducted a randomised controlled trial (RCT) to evaluate the effectiveness of the intervention. Ethical permission was granted by the Ethics Review Panel of the Department of Human Communication Sciences, University of Sheffield. A project timeline is presented in Figure 1.

Figure 1: Timeline of nursery intervention project

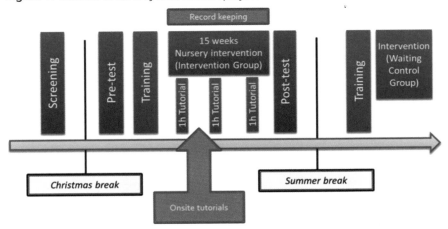

Participants

Twelve EY settings (nine nursery schools; three children centres) with a relatively high proportion of children with EAL from South Yorkshire were involved in the project. At the beginning of the study we screened all children with EAL in these nurseries (N=299 with 49 different languages spoken at home) excluding children who had not yet acquired any English language skills. From this initial sample, we identified eight children per nursery (N=96 with 25 different languages spoken at home; M_{age} =3;7) with the lowest vocabulary and grammar skills to take part in the project. These children (50 boys; 46 girls) were given additional language and early literacy tests (pre-test) before being randomly allocated to either an intervention group (n=4/nursery) or a waiting control group (n=4/nursery). Children were reassessed immediately following the intervention (post-test; M_{age} =4;3) at which point seven children were no longer present due to moving settings or countries (intervention n=2; waiting control n=5).

Assessments

The assessments tapped skills directly targeted by the intervention and standardised measures of speech, language and early literacy measures in English. Here, we focus only on language measures. Given the variety of languages spoken by the participants, and the time and resource constraints for the project, it was not possible to include assessments in children's home languages.

Screening (t0)

To identify children with EAL who showed the weakest English vocabulary and grammar skills in comparison to their peers, children with EAL in participating settings were assessed on two sub-tests of the *Child Evaluation of Language Fundamentals-Pre-school UK* (CELF-Pre; Semel et al., 2006) and four sub-tests of the *New Reynell Developmental Language Scales* (NRDLS; Edwards et al., 2011): NRDLS Production – Object Naming; NRDLS Comprehension – Selecting Objects/A1, Relating Two Items/B1, and Verbs/C1; CELF-Pre Expressive Vocabulary and Sentence Structure.

Pre-test (t1)

Children identified to take part in the project were assessed on the following standardised language measures: NRDLS Production – Relating 2 Objects/B1, Relating 2 Objects-Prepositions/B2, Verbs/C1, and Sentence Building/D1; NRDLS Comprehension – Relating 2 Objects-Prepositions/B2 and Sentence Building/D1; and the *Renfrew Action Picture Test* (APT; Renfrew, 2003).

A three-picture-story retelling task to assess children's narrative production was developed. Verbatim transcriptions allowed the analysis of a variety of narrative skills using CHAT/CLAN (MacWhinney, 2012) such as mean length of utterance in morphemes (MLUm) and number of words used (Narrative Words). A random selection of the 42 words taught in the intervention was assessed using Expressive Picture Naming and Receptive Picture Selection.

All children were re-assessed on all screening and pre-test measures presented here immediately following the intervention (post-test; t2).

Intervention programme

The intervention group received a 15-week OL intervention in nursery (3x20mins group sessions/week) aimed at improving children's vocabulary, narrative skills, active listening and confidence in independent speaking. The intervention was delivered by a Teaching Assistant (TA)/Early Years Practitioner (EYP) selected by each nursery who received one day of training prior to the intervention covering the theoretical foundations of the intervention and delivery of the programme. To ensure treatment fidelity and provide support for the TAs/EYPs, they were provided with a comprehensive intervention manual and accompanying resources, attended regular group tutorials and completed records of delivered sessions. Furthermore, the research team observed each TA/EYP delivering an intervention session and provided immediate feedback and advice.

The content of the intervention programme was based on findings from earlier research (Bowyer-Crane et al., 2008; Clarke et al., 2010; Fricke et al., 2013) and adapted to reflect needs of children with EAL (e.g. Paradis et al., 2011). It was also designed a) with reference to Statutory Frameworks for the Early Years Foundation Stage (EYFS) and Primary Years (e.g. DCSF, 2008; DfES, 2006), b) literature specific to effective interventions for children with EAL (e.g. August and Shanahan, 2006; Baker, 2006; Castro et al., 2011; Lesaux, 2006; Stow and Dodd, 2003), and c) in consultation with EYPs, speech and language therapists and local authorities.

Children were taught using multi-contextual techniques within a repetitive framework that followed established principles for teaching listening, vocabulary and narrative (e.g. Beck et al., 2013; Carroll et al., 2011; Locke, 1985, 2006). Activities were designed to be enjoyable and to encourage the children to actively engage with each other and with the TA/EYP. Table 1 provides an overview of the sessions' content and structure.

Table 1: Breakdown of content and structure of an intervention session (20min)

Activity	Purpose	Time (min)
Introduction	Greet and settle children into session, revise the days of the week and the listening rules	2
Listening Game	Improve listening skills through interactive games and encourage active listening	3
Vocabulary	Introduce new vocabulary or consolidate vocabulary from previous session using a multi-contextual method	6
Narrative	Improve storytelling skills such as sequencing and knowledge of story elements	6
Plenary	Revise overall session to foster sequencing skills, reinforce taught vocabulary and award 'Best Listener'	3

Results

The 15-week intervention consisted of 45 intervention sessions, of which the TAs/EYPs delivered on average 34.82 (Range: 30-45) sessions. The number of sessions each child attended also varied considerably (M=27.50; Range: 2-41).

Table 2 shows the means and standard deviations for the language measures for the two groups at t0, t1 and t2. They did not differ significantly on any measure before the intervention, as expected given random allocation. To assess the impact of the intervention on children's language skills, group differences at t2 were analysed using regression models in STATA 12 (StataCorp, 2011), controlling for the covariates performance at t0/t1 (baseline), age and gender; and using robust standard errors to allow for the non-independence of observations from children nested within the 12 settings.

Table 2: Means (SD and range) on all measures at screening (t0), pre-intervention (t1), and post-intervention (t2) for intervention and waiting control groups

Measures (max. score)	Test Point	Intervention			Waiting Control		
		M	SD	Range	M	SD	Range
Taught vocabulary: Expressive Naming (15)	t1	3.43	3.06	0-11	3.91	2.89	0-9
	t2	6.76	3.68	0-14	5.79	3.25	0-11
Taught vocabulary: Receptive Selection (10)	t1	4.49	2.15	0-9	4.83	2.51	0-10
	t2	7.97	2.02	3-10	6.33	2.48	1-10
CELF Expressive Vocabulary (40)	t0	2.17	3.10	0-13	2.71	3.94	0-15
	t2	5.50	5.67	0-20	6.13	5.46	0-18
CELF Sentence Structure (22)	t0	2.67	3.39	0-12	2.28	2.88	0-9
	t2	6.81	4.72	0-14	5.95	3.98	0-15
APT Information (40)	t1	7.03	5.87	0-22.5	8.42	7.18	0-27.5
	t2	10.77	7.35	0-26.5	11.68	6.06	0-24.5
APT Grammar (37)	t1	4.00	4.57	0-17	4.99	5.17	0-18
	t2	7.64	6.26	0-26.5	8.78	6.07	0-24
Narrative MLUm	t1	3.25	1.65	0-7.9	3.47	2.48	0-9.5
	t2	4.69	2.99	1-16.7	4.27	2.24	0-8.3
Narrative Words	t1	14.63	12.95	0-63	11.53	9.55	0-33
	t2	21.50	16.84	0-66	20.11	13.95	0-63
NRDLS Production							
NRDLS Naming Objects (A; 10)	t0	3.60	3.28	0-10	3.27	3.51	0-10
	t2	7.00	3.47	0-10	6.88	3.32	0-10
NRDLS Relating 2 Objects (B1; 5)	t1	1.06	1.46	0-5	1.11	1.62	0-5
	t2	2.30	1.82	0-5	2.26	1.87	0-5
NRDLS Relating 2 Objects (B2; 5)	t1	.29	.85	0-4	.21	.41	0-1
	t2	.61	1.04	0-4	.57	.83	0-3
NRDLS Verbs (C1; 5)	t1	1.74	1.61	0-5	1.70	1.73	0-5
	t2	2.83	1.67	0-5	2.83	1.69	0-5
NRDLS Sentence Building (D1; 5)	t1	.28	.77	0-4	.47	1.14	0-5
	t2	.79	1.42	0-5	.90	1.31	0-5
NRDLS Production Composite (30)	t0/t1	6.94	6.72	0-24	6.54	6.99	0-24
	t2	13.22	7.19	0-27	13.24	7.29	0-25

NRDLS Comprehension							
NRDLS Selecting Objects (A1; 5)	t0	3.02	1.94	0-5	2.65	1.95	0-5
	t2	4.61	.91	1-5	4.31	1.24	1-5
NRDLS Relating 2 Objects (B1; 5)	t0	1.15	1.53	0-5	1.19	1.61	0-5
	t2	3.50	1.59	0-5	3.38	1.79	0-5
NRDLS Relating 2 Objects (B2; 5)	t1	1.21	1.46	0-5	.92	.92	0-3
	t2	2.22	1.71	0-5	1.98	1.47	0-5
NRDLS Verbs (C1; 5)	t0	2.07	1.73	0-5	1.58	1.61	0-5
	t2	3.81	1.47	0-5	3.70	1.60	0-5
NRDLS Sentence Building (D1; 5)	t1	2.34	1.87	0-5	2.74	1.80	0-5
	t2	3.40	1.75	0-5	3.33	1.63	0-5
NRDLS Comprehension Composite (25)	t0/t1	9.65	7.12	0-25	8.79	6.64	0-21
	t2	16.91	6.43	2-25	16.29	6.65	1-25

The analyses revealed significant group differences in favour of the intervention group on measures of taught vocabulary; Expressive Naming (p=.024) and Receptive Picture Selection (p<.001). No significant difference between groups was found on any of the other measures. The results presented in Figure 2 show the difference between the groups' adjusted means (t2 performances controlling for covariates), with 95 per cent confidence intervals (CIs) and effect sizes. Any positive group differences represent more progress in the intervention group compared to the waiting control group. A statistically significant effect (p<.05) is evident where the 95 per cent CIs do not cross the x-axis. Effect sizes were small/medium to large on the significant bespoke measures (d=0.49 and.85 respectively; Cohen, 1992). All other effect sizes were negligible with the exception of Narrative MLUm, which had a small effect size (d=0.30).

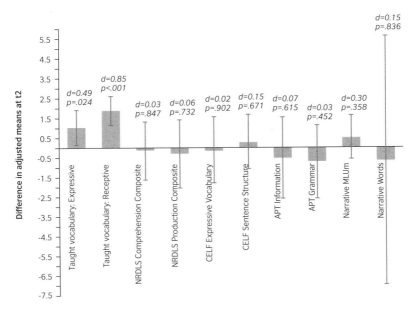

Figure 2: Comparison of the intervention and waiting control groups at t2 (controlling for covariates) on language outcome measures [with 95 per cent CIs, effect sizes (d, difference in progress between the groups divided by pooled SD at t1)] and significance levels.

Discussion

This RCT evaluated the effectiveness of a 15-week intervention programme designed to support the active listening, vocabulary and narrative skills of children with EAL in nursery settings. Immediately following the intervention, the programme showed significant beneficial effects for the intervention group over the waiting control group on taught vocabulary measures, suggesting that the intervention led to gains in vocabulary knowledge. However, such significant effects of the intervention were not found for standardised language assessments or narrative skills.

The significant intervention effects for taught vocabulary are encouraging, as the target vocabulary was selected with reference to EYFS and Primary School curricula and, therefore, represent vocabulary the children need as foundations for future schooling. Furthermore, the finding also provides evidence that rich and robust vocabulary instruction providing multiple encounters and practice with the target words in a variety of contexts (Beck et al., 2013) can be used successfully with children with EAL.

The lack of generalisation to standardised language assessments is disappointing but not uncommon (Burgoyne et al., 2012; Duff et al., 2014; Pollard-Durodola et al., 2011). One explanation for this might be that standardised language measures are designed to distinguish between typical development and difficulties (not to detect changes following intervention) and are suggested to often be insensitive to language growth (Elleman et al., 2009). The finding that the intervention did not impact on children's narrative skills despite being addressed in the programme seems also discouraging but in line with Dockrell et al. (2010). They argued that improvements resulting from their intervention were not sufficiently large to impact on narrative re-telling skills because narrative tasks pose a particular challenge for children, requiring a certain level of linguistic competence. Given that we selected children with EAL who showed the weakest English skills in comparison to their peers, their general English language skills at post-test might still have been too restricted and improvements in taught vocabulary not sufficient to support their narrative performance.

Another explanation for the missing effects on standardised and narrative assessments might be that the programme was too short or lacking in intensity (Beck and McKeown, 2007; Justice et al., 2008; Pollard-Durodola et al., 2011). Transfer to some standardised language assessments has been shown, for example, in RCTs with monolingual children after longer (20 or 30 weeks) and more intense periods (3x/week small groups sessions combined with 2x/week individual sessions) of language intervention in Reception only (Bowyer-Crane et al., 2008) or in nursery and Reception (Fricke et al., 2013). Indeed, as in the current study, the nursery part of the intervention designed by Fricke and colleagues included three small group sessions per week over a period of ten weeks. Looking at the results immediately following this initial phase of the programme, the intervention group did not significantly outperform the waiting control group on taught vocabulary measures. Evidence of effective vocabulary instruction was only found following the entire 30-week programme. This poses the question whether it is feasible to deliver interventions in nursery settings for a sufficient duration and intensity to result in reliable effects. A daily intervention schedule, for example, seems unrealistic as children's attendance patterns vary from half a day to five full days per week. Moreover, many pre-school settings may not have the resources to ensure regular and consistent intervention implementation. In the present study many TAs/EYPs fulfilled multiple roles in their settings, which often impacted on their availability to deliver the intervention and resulted in fewer sessions being delivered than anticipated by the programme. Settings with the most regular and frequent intervention delivery seem to be those where intervention sessions were time-tabled for the TA/EYP, with appropriate cover put in place and dedicated space provided (for similar influential factors see Dockrell and Stuart, 2007). A possible solution that could be explored in future studies might be combining a nursery-based intervention with parent involvement (Roberts, 2008) or using community volunteers instead of setting staff to deliver the intervention (Riley et al., 2004).

Intervention effects might also be enhanced if intervention content was reinforced in the wider setting context (Beck et al., 2013). This was unfortunately not possible in the present study, as the waiting control group attended the same settings as the intervention group. Moreover, it is worth noting that the waiting control group received treatment as usual in their settings, which might not have been an actual 'no intervention' comparison. Questionnaire data revealed that ten out of the 12 settings were already using other intervention and support programmes. In line with suggestions by Duff et al. (2014) the missing generalised intervention effects might therefore be a reflection of positive changes to educational practices aiming to offer high-quality provision for all and at-risk children (Allen, 2011; Rose, 2006; Tickell, 2011).

One might also argue that OL interventions are more effective for children who show weaknesses in their language skills for whatever reason but have reached a certain threshold needed for benefiting from the support. Thus, selecting children with the poorest language skills within each setting might not be the best approach for identifying children that are likely to benefit the most from the kind of intervention provided. However, the literature regarding this aspect is inconclusive (Allen et al., 2012; Crevecoeur et al., 2014; Lugo-Neris et al., 2010; Ruston and Schwanenflugel, 2010; Silverman, 2007) and evaluating it was not an aim of the study.

Finally, it may be that broader outcome measures are needed to pick up changes resulting from the programme. For example, qualitative feedback collected from TAs/EYPs and other setting staff suggests improvements in 'softer skills' (e.g. "The children have improved their vocabulary but their language and confidence has been an even bigger improvement," and "The children have become more confident and willing to talk. They initiate more with the adults in the setting,") highlighting the need to pay attention to such skills in future projects.

Conclusion

Designing and implementing interventions that are successful in boosting the OL skills of young children, and are feasible and viable in real-life educational settings, is a challenging task. Nonetheless it is a crucial one, when teachers are under pressure to support their pupils to make substantial progress in OL skills before they begin to have a wider impact on learning. Having conducted an RCT, we have provided robust evidence that vocabulary skills can be promoted as early as pre-school in children with EAL. The study also contributes further evidence that setting-based OL interventions can be successfully delivered by trained and supported TAs/EYPs who are likely to use their enhanced skills to benefit all children in their settings (Collins, 2010; Dockrell et al., 2010). The study is therefore an important step towards developing evidence-based and effective interventions for children with EAL that can be applied successfully in pre-school settings. More longitudinal research with larger samples, however, is clearly needed to investigate what intervention approaches are most effective in improving OL skills and to shed light on the various factors influencing their outcomes. Such research findings must then be disseminated to practitioners and teachers who are advised to keep abreast of new developments to ensure they base their decisions regarding interventions on the most recent and relevant findings, and to only implement interventions with the best evidence base available.

Acknowledgements

The research was funded by an Early Career Researcher/EPSRC Knowledge Transfer Grant from the University of Sheffield. We thank many colleagues for their valuable contributions to this work and the TAs/EYPs, nurseries, children and parents for their participation.

References

Allen, G (2011) *Early Intervention: The Next Steps – An Independent Report to Her Majesty's Government*. London: DfE.

Allen, MM, Ukrainetz, TA and Carswell, AL (2012) The Narrative Language Performance of Three Types of At-Risk First-Grade Readers. *Language, Speech and Hearing Services in Schools* 43/2: 205-221A.

August, D and Shanahan, T (2006) *Developing literacy in second-language learners: Report of the National Literacy Panel on Language Minority Children and Youth*. Mahwah, NJ: Erlbaum.

Baker, CR (2006) *Foundations of Bilingual Education and Bilingualism*. Ontario: Multilingual Matters.

Beck, I and McKeown, MG (2007) Increasing young low-income children's oral vocabulary repertoires through rich and focused instruction. *The Elementary School Journal* 107/3: 251-271.

Beck, IL, McKeown, MG and Kucan, L (2013) *Bringing words to life: Robust vocabulary instruction*. NY: Guilford Press.

Bercow, J (2008) *The Bercow Report: A Review of Services for Children and Young People (0–19) with Speech, Language and Communication Needs*. Nottingham: DCSF.

Bowyer-Crane, C, Snowling, MJ, Duff, FJ, Fieldsend, E, Carroll, JM, Miles, J and Hulme, C (2008) Improving early language and literacy skills: differential effects of an oral language versus a phonology with reading intervention. *Journal of Child Psychology and Psychiatry* 49/4: 422-432.

Burgoyne, K, Duff, FJ, Clarke, PJ, Buckley, S, Snowling, MJ and Hulme, C (2012) Efficacy of a reading and language intervention for children with Down syndrome: a randomised controlled trial. *Journal of Child Psychology and Psychiatry* 53/10: 1044-1053.

Burgoyne, K, Kelly, JM, Whiteley, HE and Spooner, A (2009) The comprehension skills of children learning English as an additional language. *British Journal of Educational Psychology* 79/4: 735-747.

Burgoyne, K, Whiteley, HE and Hutchinson, JM (2011) The development of comprehension and reading-related skills in children learning English as an additional language and their monolingual, English-speaking peers. *British Journal of Educational Psychology* 81/2: 344-354.

Carroll, JM, Bowyer-Crane, C, Duff, FJ, Hulme, CJ and Snowling, MJ (2011) *Developing Language and Literacy: Effective Intervention in the Early Years*. Oxford: Wiley-Blackwell.

Castro, DC, Páez, MM, Dickinson, DK and Frede, E (2011) Promoting Language and Literacy in Young Dual Language Learners: Research, Practice, and Policy. *Child Development Perspectives* 5/1: 15-21.

Chlapana, E and Tafa, E (2014) Effective practices to enhance immigrant kindergarteners' second language vocabulary learning through storybook reading. *Reading and Writing* 1-22.

Clarke, PJ, Snowling, MJ, Truelove, E and Hulme, C (2010) Ameliorating Children's Reading-Comprehension Difficulties: A Randomised Controlled Trial. *Psychological Science* 21/8: 1106-1116.

Clegg, J, Hollis, C, Mawhood, L and Rutter, M (2005) Developmental language disorders – a follow-up in later adult life. Cognitive, language and psychosocial outcomes. *Journal of Child Psychology and Psychiatry* 46/2: 128-149.

Cohen, J (1992) A power primer. *Psychological Bulletin* 112/1: 155-159.

Collins, MF (2010) ELL pre-schoolers' English vocabulary acquisition from storybook reading. *Early Childhood Research Quarterly* 25/1: 84-97.

Crevecoeur, YC, Coyne, MD and McCoach, DB (2014) English Language Learners and English-Only Learners' Response to Direct Vocabulary Instruction. *Reading and Writing Quarterly* 30/1: 51-78.

DCSF (2008) *Statutory Framework for the Early Years Foundation Stage*. Nottingham: DCSF.

DfE (2010) *Statistical First Release: Key Stage 2 Attainment by Pupil Characteristics, in England 2009/10*. London: DfE.

DfE (2013) *Statistical First Release: School Census 2013*. London: DfE.

DfES (2006) *Primary framework for literacy and mathematics*. Norwich: DfES.

Dockrell, JE and Stuart, M (2007) *Talking Time*. London: Institute of Education.

Dockrell, JE, Stuart, M and King, D (2010) Supporting early oral language skills for English language learners in inner city pre-school provision. *British Journal of Educational Psychology* 80/4: 497-515.

Duff, FJ, Hulme, C, Grainger, K, Hardwick, SJ, Miles, JNV and Snowling, MJ (2014) Reading and language intervention for children at risk of dyslexia: a randomised controlled trial. *Journal of Child Psychology and Psychiatry* Online First.

Edwards, S, Letts, C and Sinka, I (2011) *New Reynell Developmental Language Scales (NRDLS; 4 ed).* London: GL Assessment.

Elleman, AM, Lindo, EJ, Morphy, P and Compton, D L (2009) The Impact of Vocabulary Instruction on Passage-Level Comprehension of School-Age Children: A Meta-Analysis. *Journal of Research on Educational Effectiveness* 2/1: 1-44.

Elliot, C, Smith, P and McCulloch, K (1996) *The British Ability Scales II (BAS II).* Windsor: NFER-NELSON Publishing Company.

Ennemoser, M, Kuhl, J and Pepouna, S (2013) Evaluation des Dialogischen Lesens zur Sprachförderung bei Kindern mit Migrationshintergrund. *Zeitschrift für Pädagogische Psychologie* 27/4: 229-239.

Farver, JAM, Lonigan, CJ and Eppe, S (2009) Effective Early Literacy Skill Development for Young Spanish-Speaking English Language Learners: An Experimental Study of Two Methods. *Child Development* 80/3: 703-719.

Fricke, S, Bowyer-Crane, C, Haley, AJ, Hulme, C and Snowling, MJ (2013) Efficacy of language intervention in the early years. *Journal of Child Psychology and Psychiatry* 54/3: 280-290.

Gardner, H, Froud, K, McClelland, A and van der Lely, HK (2006) Development of the Grammar and Phonology Screening (GAPS) test to assess key markers of specific language and literacy difficulties in young children. *International Journal of Language and Communication Disorders* 41/5: 513-540.

Justice, LM, Mashburn, AJ, Hamre, BK, and Pianta, RC (2008) Quality of language and literacy instruction in pre-school classrooms serving at-risk pupils. *Early Childhood Research Quarterly* 23/1: 51-68.

Kohnert, K and Medina, A (2009) Bilingual Children and Communication Disorders: A 30-Year Research Retrospective. *Seminars in Speech and Language* 30/4: 219,233.

Law, J, Lee, W, Roulstone, S, Wren, Y, Zeng, B and Lindsay, G (2012) *What works: Interventions for children and young people with speech, language and communication needs.* London: DfE.

Law, J, Todd, L, Clark, J, Mroz, M and Carr, J (2013) *Early Language Delays in the UK.* London: Save the Children.

Lesaux, NK (2006) Building consensus: Future directions for research on English language learners at risk for learning difficulties. *Teachers College Record* 108/11: 2406-2438.

Lesaux, NK, Kieffer, MJ, Faller, SE and Kelley, JG (2010) The effectiveness and ease of implementation of an academic vocabulary intervention for linguistically diverse students in urban middle schools. *Reading Research Quarterly* 45/2: 196-228.

Locke, A (1985) *Living Language*. Windsor: NFER-Nelson.

Locke, A (2006) *One Step at a Time*. London: Network Continuum Education.

Lugo-Neris, MJ, Jackson, CW and Goldstein, H (2010) Facilitating Vocabulary Acquisition of Young English Language Learners. *Language Speech and Hearing Services in Schools* 41/3: 314-327.

MacWhinney, B (2012) *The CHILDES Project: Tools for Analysing Talk. Electronic Edition. Part 1: The CHAT Transcription Format. Part 2: The CLAN Programmes*. Available online at http://childes.psy.cmu.edu/

Muter, V, Hulme, C, Snowling, MJ, and Stevenson, J (2004) Phonemes, rimes, vocabulary, and grammatical skills as foundations of early reading development: Evidence from a longitudinal study. *Developmental Psychology* 40/5: 665-681.

Nelson, JR, Vadasy, PF and Sanders, EA (2011) Efficacy of a Tier 2 Supplemental Root Word Vocabulary and Decoding Intervention With Kindergarten Spanish-Speaking English Learners. *Journal of Literacy Research* 43/2: 184-211.

Pollard-Durodola, S, Gonzalez, J, Simmons, D, Kwok, O, Taylor, A, Davis, M, Kim, M, Simmons, L (2011) The Effects of an Intensive Shared Book-Reading Intervention for Pre-school Children at Risk for Vocabulary Delay. *Exceptional Children* 77/2: 161-183.

Proctor, CP, Dalton, B, Uccelli, P, Biancarosa, G, Mo, E, Snow, C and Neugebauer, S (2011) Improving comprehension online: effects of deep vocabulary instruction with bilingual and monolingual fifth graders. *Reading and Writing* 24/5: 517-544.

Renfrew, C (2003) *Action Picture Test*. Milton Keynes: Speechmark Publishing Ltd.

Riley, J, Burrell, A and McCallum, B (2004) Developing the spoken language skills of reception class children in two multicultural, inner-city primary schools. *British Educational Research Journal* 30/5: 657-672.

Roberts, TA (2008) Home storybook reading in primary or second language with pre-school children: Evidence of equal effectiveness for second-language vocabulary acquisition. *Reading Research Quarterly* 43/2: 103-130.

Rose, J (2006) *Independent review of the teaching of early reading: Final Report*. Nottingham: DfES.

Rose, J (2009) *Independent Review of the Primary Curriculum: Final Report*. Nottingham: DfES.

Roulstone, S, Law, J, Rush, R, Clegg, J and Peters, T (2011) *Investigating the role of language in children's early educational outcomes (Project Report)*. Bristol: DfE.

Ruston, HP, and Schwanenflugel, PJ (2010) Effects of a Conversation Intervention on the Expressive Vocabulary Development of Pre-kindergarten Children. *Language, Speech, and Hearing Services in Schools* 41/3: 303-313.

Segers, E, Verhoeven, L, Boot, I, Berkers, I and Vermeer, A (2001) Effectiviteit van een software programma ter bevordering van de woordenschat van allochtone kleuters. *Pedagogische Studiën* 78/5: 287-297.

Semel, E, Wiig, E and Secord, W (2006) *Child Evaluation of Language Fundamentals-Pre-school UK* (2nd ed). Oxford: Pearson Assessment.

Silverman, RD (2007) Vocabulary development of English-language and English-only learners in kindergarten. *Elementary School Journal* 107/4: 365-383.

Snowling, MJ and Hulme, C (2011) Evidence-based interventions for reading and language difficulties: Creating a virtuous circle. *British Journal of Educational Psychology* 81/1: 1-23.

Stow, C and Dodd, B (2003) Providing an equitable service to bilingual children in the UK: a review. *International Journal of Language and Communication Disorders* 38/4: 351-377.

Tickell, DC (2011) *The Early Years: Foundations for life, health and learning – An Independent Report on the Early Years Foundation Stage to Her Majesty's Government Dame Clare Tickell.* London: DfE.

Vadasy, PF and Sanders, EA (2010) Efficacy of supplemental phonics-based instruction for low-skilled kindergarteners in the context of language minority status and classroom phonics instruction. *Journal of Educational Psychology* 102/4: 786-803.

Wilson, SJ, Dickinson, DK and Rowe, DW (2013) Impact of an Early Reading First programme on the language and literacy achievement of children from diverse language backgrounds. *Early Childhood Research Quarterly* 28/3: 578-592.

2.3

Language of instruction and the development of biliteracy skills in children: a case study of a pre-school in the Maldives

Naashia Mohamed, Maldives National University, Maldives

Language in education

It has been argued that the most important policy decisions in language in education are those related to the choice of languages as the medium of instruction (MOI) in schools (Tollefson and Tsui, 2004). Despite the key role of the mother tongue in a child's education, one major impact of globalisation is symbolised by the increasing trend to use English, the global lingua franca, as the MOI in education systems across the world (Hamid, Nguyen and Baldauf, 2013). This has been the case not only in the English-dominant parts of the world, but also in the Outer and Expanding Circle contexts (Doiz, Lasagabaster and Sierra, 2012). While some have claimed that English as an MOI policies are an extension of imperialism and explicitly seek to exclude other languages, and with them the children who speak them (Arnold, Bartlett, Gowani, and Merali, 2006), others have taken a more liberal view that it is an unavoidable by-product of globalisation.

In terms of the impact of immersion models in education, research evidence has favoured mother tongue-based education. Some studies (e.g. Benson, 2004) have shown that when the MOI is a language other than the child's mother tongue, it causes pedagogical and linguistic problems. Others (e.g. Salili and Tsui, 2005) indicate that it can be a motivational barrier for students. Kosonen (2005) has argued that a mother tongue-based education system will have higher enrolments and corresponding success rates. This may be because when children are encouraged to use their mother tongue in the education context, they have better thinking skills (Bialystok, 2001; Cummins, 2000) and higher levels of understanding (King and Mackey, 2007).

Despite the growing body of research that has shown that children's first language (L1) is the optimal language for literacy and learning throughout the early years and primary schooling (UNESCO, 2008), some studies (e.g. Turnbull, Hart and Lapkin, 2003) do point to the positive impact of foreign language immersion on not just the academic achievement of students but also their language development in both their L1 and other languages used in education.

Early literacy

The importance of the early years, particularly the pre-school period, in developing the foundations for future literacy has been emphasised in the research from the field of emergent literacy (Morrow and Tracey, 2007). Studies have shown that establishing the groundwork of literacy skills in the early years not only facilitates and accelerates children's acquisition of formal reading skills at school (Dickinson and Neuman, 2006), but that successful attainment of those skills is a predictor of children's future success at school. Where children receive pre-school education in an immersion or dual language context, it seems imperative that the pre-school pedagogy focuses on developing children's biliteracy skills so as to give them the best chance of success in language acquisition in both the L1 as well as other languages involved.

Whatever the role that students' L1 and L2 take in the school setting, for optimal language acquisition, Baker (2008) recommends that there be a balance in the use of language in the classroom. This includes balancing the relative amounts of use of the two (or more) languages on walls, in announcements, in non-curriculum activities such as school assemblies, and in the language of the playground, as well as the language of the classroom. Similarly, Baker (2008) advocates balance in the use of language by educators as well as in the allocation of languages in the curriculum. He argues that if one language is allocated fewer literacy-based areas (such as sports, craft and design) and the other language is allocated subject areas such as science and mathematics, it may send signals to the children that the majority language has more functional and prestigious value and will be associated with modernity and progression.

Context of the present study

Regardless of what the research evidence shows, and what prescribed curricula may state, what actually happens in the classroom is largely dependent on individual schools and teachers. As the school environment plays a key role in the development of language and literacy skills in the early years, it is important to identify how it affects the process of language learning and the ways in which it helps or hinders the learning process. The study reported here aimed to identify the factors that contributed to the development of language and literacy skills in children's L1 and L2.

The study was based in the Maldives. The Maldives is a unique context where, although the inhabitants share the same L1 (Dhivehi) and English is a second language in the community, English is the dominant MOI throughout the education system. Although only a small minority of the population use English exclusively in everyday communication, code mixing of English and Dhivehi has become common in recent years, especially in urban communities (Mohamed, 2013).

In most other Asian contexts multilingualism thrives. However, options for gaining an education through the medium of the local languages exist in those contexts. In the case of the Maldives, although there is only one local language, there are no schools that offer formal education through the medium of Dhivehi. Educational history of the Maldives shows that although schooling was provided initially in Arabic and/or Dhivehi, with the introduction of schools that offered English medium of instruction (EMI) in the early 1960s, all other forms of education were relegated to a second class status. EMI spread from secondary to primary schools and finally to pre-schools, with the result that since the early 2000s, there have been no schools that offer formal education in the L1. Despite recent attempts to encourage the use of Dhivehi as the MOI in pre-schools, this has not been popular either among educators or parents.

It is also noteworthy that, as the Maldives is a Muslim country, and Arabic is the language of the Qur'an, all Maldivian children learn to read and write the Arabic script from a young age. The focus of such learning is not on comprehension or communication; but simply to enable individuals to read the holy text of Islam. The pre-school curriculum introduces children to three languages: Dhivehi, the mother tongue; English, the language of instruction; and Arabic, the language of the Qur'an. Although Arabic is not taught as a language per se, children do have to learn three completely different scripts and sound systems.

The school reported here was situated in the capital island of Malé, and is one of the longest serving pre-schools in the country. It was selected for the study through simple random sampling. Catering to children between the ages of two-and-a-half and six, the school had an enrolment of around 800 students at the time of data collection. Classes were held in three sessions, with the oldest children attending school in the first session, the second age group attending school in the second session and the youngest group attending school in the afternoon session. Each session lasted two to three hours, with the first session starting at 7am and the last session ending at 5.30pm. As physical space was very limited, children spent most of their session time in the confines of a classroom. Class sizes were between 28 and 33 students. Each class had a teacher and an assistant teacher.

During each school session, when children arrived in class they usually marked attendance by placing their name card on the designated wall space and sat down for sharing time. The teacher began each day by identifying the day of the week, the date and by talking about the weather. She would then read the class a story related to the theme of the week, and/or sing songs together with the children. Next, she would explain the different activities set up at the different stations in the classroom and allocate the children to each station. Every class usually had a literacy station, an art station, a play area and a reading corner. For the large part of the school session, children would rotate among the different stations and the teacher would ensure that all children had completed all allocated work for the day. Each class would have about half an hour of music, computer skills or outdoor play every day. There was also a short break for snacks and drinks, followed by clean up before going home.

Following an ethnolinguistic case study model, data was collected over a period of six months, beginning during the first month of the academic year, so as to be able to record the linguistic and literacy progress achieved by children over a period of time. The data included 25 hours of video recordings of classrooms, field notes from school visits, interviews with two teachers and the head teacher as well as photographic evidence of student work. The recorded and transcribed data underwent a process of coding and categorising, to arrive at qualitative themes. The four dominant themes that arose from the analysis are detailed below.

Visible language

Upon first entry to the school, the first thing visitors would notice were the large banners around the school compound heralding the pride and importance of the mother tongue. These banners, written in the Dhivehi script, included statements such as "I can express everything I want in Dhivehi" and "We are proud to have our own unique language". Inside the classrooms, however, the picture was a little different. All the classroom walls were decorated beautifully. At the entrance to each classroom, the attendance area showed the names of the students present that day. In the majority of the classrooms, these names were only written in English. One part of each classroom was dedicated to exhibiting student work, with cellophane pockets for each student. In all classrooms, students' names on these were written only in English. In each classroom, there were wall displays of the daily routine, the days of the week, the months of the year, the three alphabets children learned (Dhivehi, English and Arabic), a number chart and a section headed "Things we are learning this week". This section contained information on the key learning areas of the curriculum: Islam, Dhivehi, English, Mathematics and Environmental Studies. Of these, information about the weekly learning for the first two areas was displayed in Dhivehi and was observed to change very infrequently. In fact, on many occasions, there was nothing displayed for Dhivehi. For English, Mathematics and Environmental Studies, however, all the weekly learning displays were in English and changed each week.

Language in the curriculum

According to the head teacher and classroom teachers, the school supported the current national policy of making Dhivehi the MOI at pre-school level. They recognised, however, that after "many years of teaching everything in English and focusing on developing children's English language," it was hard to make the shift back to Dhivehi. They claimed that they consciously "tried to put Dhivehi first" and aimed to interact with children mostly in Dhivehi while teaching them the key vocabulary in both Dhivehi and English. The head teacher felt that by placing the large banners around the school compound this emphasised the importance of the L1 and was one of the key strategies of the school to show how they were putting the L1 first.

However, the classroom evidence contradicted this importance given to the L1, with at least 70 per cent of all interaction taking place in English in every observed session. Furthermore, the language of the majority of curriculum resources was in English. All material relating to Mathematics and Environmental Studies was provided in English. The amount of curriculum time dedicated to teaching in English far outweighed the amount of time used for teaching in Dhivehi. This was evident in the amount of work completed in English and Dhivehi. In most classes observed, the amount of work done in English was more than double the amount of work completed in Dhivehi.

Educators' language use

All three of the educators interviewed identified that one of their greatest challenges was to consistently use the same language when interacting with the children. They recognised that they mixed a lot of English words into their interactions in Dhivehi, but rarely needed to code mix when interacting in English. This was observed to be true in all cases. A high dependence on English content words interfered with any communication meant to be conducted in Dhivehi. In one instance, the teacher was preparing the children to go downstairs to play outdoors. Her instructions to the class were as follows:

Kudhin slowly downstairs ah gos, play kuraanee. Play kuraanee sand akaa noon. Play kuraanee water akaa noon. Play kuraanee games. And running.

[Translation: You will slowly go downstairs to play. You will not play with sand. You will not play with water. You will play games. And running.]

As can be seen, much of the utterance was composed of English content words, joined together with Dhivehi grammar to make meaning. In another instance, a teacher was telling a story about a little girl who loved to play with water:

Dhen e girl jump kuramun jump kuramun dhiyaee hurihaa puddle thaku thereygaa splash kuramun. Varah happily run kuramun home ah dhiyaee.

[Translation: Then the girl jumped and jumped and splashed through all the puddles. She ran home very happily.]

When asked why teachers so frequently code mix between English and Dhivehi, two reasons were put forward. Two of the teachers explained that this practice had started as a means of teaching English vocabulary to students, but admitted that such habitual code mixing was now so ingrained that they were able to recall commonly used words in English easier than they could in Dhivehi. Using a mix of English and Dhivehi was, for these teachers, easy and automatic. The second reason indicated their perceptions regarding the lower status of Dhivehi in comparison to English. The teachers interviewed felt that the children were being given a "better quality of education when they learn everything in English" and that "it is just not possible to say some things in Dhivehi."

Emergent literacy skills

The children's developing literacy skills were evaluated from observations, from their completed work and from individual interactions with them during their class times.

Vocabulary

While all children were observed to have a very good knowledge of English vocabulary, this knowledge did not extend to Dhivehi. At five years of age, almost all children observed and evaluated knew the English words for colours, parts of the body, numbers, names of classroom objects, common food items and days of the week. Of these children, only a very small fraction could name the same things in Dhivehi. Even those who did know the Dhivehi words, their first preference was to offer the names in English, regardless of whether the question was asked in Dhivehi or English. To elicit the Dhivehi words, the children had to be asked what it was called in Dhivehi. In most cases, children took longer to recall the words in Dhivehi than they did to recall a word in English. Using the Dhivehi alphabet chart as a prompt, individual children were asked to name the things pictured (e.g. rooster, tree, nose). Children always opted to name them in English even though they were labelled in Dhivehi.

When doing artwork, the teacher often asked the children what their picture depicted. Their response was then written on the illustration. In a large number of cases, these descriptions would include at least one English word and, sometimes, the descriptions would be entirely in English.

Phonological awareness

In most of the lessons observed, the focus was more on developing children's letter recognition and writing. Very little emphasis was given to relating symbols with sounds. As a result, children were observed to have difficulty sounding out words and making connections between letter combinations and sounds. This was the case for both English and Dhivehi.

Print awareness and alphabetical knowledge

Print awareness begins with a child understanding how to hold a book and turn the pages and often extends to a child trying to make out the individual letters in each word. It must be noted here that while English is written from left to right, the Dhivehi script is written from right to left. The reading corners in each of the classrooms observed had a number of books in English and a few options in Dhivehi. Most frequently, children were observed to be looking through English books, and even when they were using ones written in Dhivehi, often, they flipped the pages and 'read' the book as if it was written in a left to right script.

Children's knowledge of the different alphabetical letters was observed to gradually develop over time, with the most development evident with English letters. At three years of age, almost every day, the children were expected to write or trace or colour in a letter of the English alphabet. By the time the children were five years, they were writing words, their own name and short sentences in English every day. Although the same activities were conducted for Dhivehi too, the frequency with which they took place was much less and the children's progress was recognisably slower.

Conclusion

This chapter has reported on the development of children's pre-literacy skills in one pre-school in the Maldives, highlighting the imbalance between the children's L1 and L2. While this study was largely descriptive and, further, more robust evidence would be ideal, this imbalance was nonetheless evident in the time and resources allocated to the languages in the curriculum as well as the use of language in the classroom. As a result, it was seen to have been transferred into the children's literacy achievements in the two languages. Despite the prescribed and declared policy regarding use of the child's L1 at pre-school, failure to implement it and bring the children's L1 to prominence in the classroom resulted in children achieving literacy skills in English but failing to match that in their own mother tongue. Contrary to the displays in the school compound, the proclaimed pride in the mother tongue was sadly absent in both the classroom environment and in practice. Similarly, teachers' claims that it was easier to resort to English vocabulary indicated their beliefs that it was easier and more prestigious to express themselves in what was essentially their L2.

It is possible to conclude that this disparity between the two languages will affect individual children's linguistic futures as well as the status and use of these languages in the community as a whole. Without adequate development of a child's L1, their L2 and their learning of other subjects at school might be negatively affected. Additionally, if a child's pre-school years place such heavy emphasis on the L2 and reduce the L1 to a status of lesser prominence, questions arise as to how such children will regard their mother tongue later in life and opt to use it in regular communication. It is also possible to predict that this trend in code mixing is likely to result in a major language shift in the community when this generation of pre-schoolers grow older.

References

Arnold, C, Bartlett, K, Gowani, S, and Merali, R (2006) *Is everybody ready? Readiness, transition and continuity: Reflections and moving forward.* Background paper for EFA Global Monitoring Report 2007.

Baker, C (2008) Postlude. *AILA Review*, 21(1),104 –110. DOI: 10.1075/aila.21.08bak

Benson, (2004) *The importance of mother tongue-based schooling for educational quality.* Paper commissioned for the EFA Global Monitoring Report 2005, The Quality Imperative, UNESCO, Paris.

Bialystok, E (2001) *Bilingualism in development: Language, literacy, and cognition.* Cambridge: Cambridge University Press.

Cummins, J (2000) *Language, power and pedagogy.* Clevedon, UK: Multilingual Matters.

Dickinson, D and Neuman, SB (2006) *Handbook of Early Literacy Research*: Volume II. New York, NY: Guilford Press.

Doiz, A, Lasagabaster, D and Sierra, JM (eds) (2012) *English-medium instruction at universities: Global challenges*. Bristol; Buffalo; Toronto, Multilingual Matters.

Hamid, MO, Nguyen, HTM and Baldauf, R (2013) Introduction. *Current Issues in Language Planning*, 14(1).

King, K and Mackey, A (2007) *The bilingual edge: Why, when, and how to teach your child a second language*. New York: Collins.

Kosonen, K (2005) Education in local languages: Policy and practice in Southeast Asia. *First languages first: Community-based literacy programmes for minority language contexts in Asia.* Bangkok: UNESCO Bangkok.

Mohamed, N (2013) The challenge of medium of instruction: a view from Maldivian schools, *Current Issues in Language Planning.* DOI:10.1080/14664208.2013.789557

Morrow, LM and Tracey, DH (2007) 'Best practices in early literacy development in pre-school, kindergarten, and first grade', in Gambrell, LB, Morrow, LM and Pressley, M (eds) *Best Practices in Literacy Education* (3rd ed.), 57–82. New York: Guilford Press.

Salili, F and Tsui, A (2005) 'The effects of medium of instruction on students' motivation and learning', in Hoosain, R and Salili, F (eds) *Language in multicultural education* (Series: Research in Multicultural Education and International Perspectives) 135-156. Greenwich, CT: Information Age Publishing.

Tollefson, J and Tsui, A (2004) *Medium of instruction policies: Which agenda? Whose agenda?* Mahwah, NJ: Lawrence Erlbaum Associates.

Turnbull, MD Hart, D and Lapkin, S (2003) Grade 6 French immersion students' performance on large-scale reading, writing, and mathematics tests: Building explanations. *Alberta Journal of Educational Research* 49, no. 1, 6 -23.

UNESCO (2008a) *Mother Tongue Matters: Local Language as a Key to Effective Learning.* Paris: UNESCO.

2.4

Do Hong Kong pre-school teachers of English engage in learning and teaching activities conducive to young children's vocabulary development?

Richard Wong Kwok Shing, Hong Kong Institute of Education, Hong Kong

Introduction

Despite the emergence of major economic powers in Asia such as China, Japan and South Korea, English remains the international language of commerce, education, science and technology (Wong, 2009), and its importance is unlikely to diminish in the decades to come. According to Crystal (2008), the number of non-native speakers of English in the world far exceeds the number of native speakers in the ratio of 3:1. Because of this perceived status of English as a global language, it is not atypical for children in East Asian cultures to receive early exposure to the English language through their early years education because of their parents' belief that an earlier exposure will lead to a greater proficiency. In the case of Hong Kong, where pre-school education is completely private and there is no statutory pre-school syllabus, it is uncertain whether young children are learning English in a way that can be regarded as effective. Quality education can be defined in numerous ways, such as whether teachers have made use of specific learning strategies that support children's learning (such as scaffolding) or whether the strategies used are known to foster specific aspects of child development.

This chapter will explore this quality issue by examining how Hong Kong pre-school teachers of English support young children to learn English. Hong Kong was chosen as the site for this study for a number of reasons. First, it has a unique history. The city was a British colony for over 150 years until 1997, when sovereignty was resumed by the People's Republic of China. Historically, the city was seen as the gateway between East and West, and new ideas from the West (e.g. the constructivist approach to learning) were more likely to be experimented with in Hong Kong schools than in schools in China.

Second, curriculum planning and assessment is largely driven by market forces. All pre-schools in Hong Kong are privately run and their curricula are only loosely bound by the Guide to Pre-primary Curriculum issued by the Hong Kong Education Bureau (2006). As parents have high expectations of their children's language proficiency in English (e.g. a recent survey conducted by Wong (2014) found that 49.5 per cent of Hong Kong parents would not mind if their pre-school-aged children had acquired English rather than Cantonese as their first language!), all pre-schools in Hong Kong are currently 'bilingual', supplementing lessons conducted in Cantonese with lessons that use English as the medium of instruction. Since the majority of Hong Kong parents do not use English as the home language (Hong Kong Census and Statistics Department, 2011), Hong Kong children's primary exposure to English largely resides in the school environment, thus the way in which the schools approach this issue is likely to be significant.

Third, there is a mismatch between the demand for native-speaking English teachers and the number of such teachers who hold an appropriate qualification residing in Hong Kong. To survive in a very competitive pre-school market, schools might have no choice but to hire native English speakers who do not possess relevant teaching qualifications or teaching experience in order to lower their operation costs.

Fourth, instruction time in English is generally limited in schools using mainly Cantonese as the medium of instruction (English exposure time probably averages 25 minutes per day, five days a week) (See Wong et al., 2013).

All these conditions have made Hong Kong a prime site for study: does what teachers of English do in their classroom conform to the best practices as recommended by academics, despite the privatised nature of early years education, loose guidelines from the government and unrealistic expectations from parents? There are three specific questions to be explored:

1. How much time do pre-school teachers of English actually spend on various language and literacy activities conducive to young children's English language development?

2. What types of shared reading strategies do teachers use when they use a picture book in their classrooms?

3. Are teachers' modes of teaching (e.g. relative time spent in various activities, shared reading strategies) related to their academic qualifications, children's proficiencies in English and the time available for the teaching of English?

Question 1 is important because the data obtained will allow us to evaluate whether pre-school teachers are usefully spending time on activities that are known to promote young children's oral language development. Accumulated findings from developmental studies have revealed that the focus of early language learning should rest primarily on oral language development, especially in the area of vocabulary development (Graves et al., 2013; Snow et al., 2007; Wong, 2009; Wong et al., 2013). Vocabulary knowledge in early childhood is one of the indicators of verbal abilities (Graves et al., 2013; Sternberg, 1987) and a significant predictor of reading comprehension in the school years (Baumann, 2005; Beck et al., 1982; Cunningham and Stanovich, 1998; Scarborough, 1998; Snow et al., 2007). Activities involving storybooks (such as story-telling and read-aloud) and story-related discussions are known to be effective strategies for improving children's vocabulary knowledge (Graves et al., 2013; Roberts and Neal, 2004; Wasik and Bond, 2001). In addition, vocabulary is crucial for triggering children's development in phonological awareness (PA) (see Goswami, 2001; Nagy, 2005), which refers to the ability to attend to and manipulate sound units smaller than a word (McBride-Chang et al., 2005). Research shows that PA is a pre-requisite to phonics instruction and children with PA deficits are likely to develop reading difficulties in the school years (Ehri et al., 2001). Intervention programmes with a focus on PA can effectively reduce children's risk of developing reading difficulties in the future (Byrne et al., 1992; Nancollis et al., 2005; Siegel, 2009).

With respect to Question 2, reading research has revealed that shared reading and read-aloud are effective strategies for promoting young children's oral and literacy development (Bus et al., 1995; De Temple and Snow, 2003; Graves et al., 2013; Lonigan and Whitehurst, 1998). In shared reading, an adult interacts with young children with the use of a picture book. Every now and then the adult will pause and ask the children to think about the meaning of a word, what is special about the story, and how the story might be relevant to their lives (Adams, 1990; Graves et al., 2013). However, when it comes to the components within shared reading that are predictive of children's language and literacy development, researchers have found that it is not the reading itself that triggers children's vocabulary development (see Snow et al., 2007, for a review). Rather it is the ensuing discussion that is critical: the discussion directs children's attention to words, encouraging them to reflect on the usage of words (Beck and McKeown, 2006; Snow et al., 2007). The implication for teaching is that, apart from talking about pictures and texts from a picture book, it is essential for teachers to make use of strategies such as encouraging the children to predict the plot of a story and discuss the ending in order to engage learners in a deeper level of language processing.

Finally, with regards to Question 3, teachers' observed behaviours in (1) and (2) may be a result of a multiplicity of factors, including the age levels and perceived abilities of the children, time available for the teaching of English and their own qualifications. Examining the effects of each of these factors will help us decide what influences teachers' decisions in the classrooms.

Methods

Participants

One-hundred-and-eighty-one teachers of English from 148 pre-schools (circa 15 per cent of the total number of pre-schools in Hong Kong) participated in the survey. The schools were evenly distributed across the different parts of the city in approximate proportion to the population size of each region (Hong Kong: 19.3 per cent; Kowloon: 21 per cent; New Territories: 55.1 per cent; Outlying islands: 4.5 per cent). All respondents were participants in professional development workshops delivered by the author. Table 1 shows their demographics: the vast majority of the respondents were female, and 78.1 per cent had attained the minimum entry qualifications (i.e. a diploma in ECE/BEd in ECE/PGDE in ECE) for pre-school teachers in Hong Kong. The proportion of male teachers in our survey was slightly larger than the reported figure of 1.2 per cent for the whole of Hong Kong (Ho and Lam, 2014). Almost half of the teachers had less than three years of teaching experience in a pre-school, and around 70 per cent of them were born in Hong Kong, schooled in Hong Kong and speak Cantonese as their first language.

Table 1: Demographics of the survey respondents (n = 181)

Particulars	Number (per cent)
Gender	
Female	175 (97.2)
Male	5 (2.8)
Academic Qualifications	
Diploma in ECE	68 (39.1)
BEd in ECE	47 (27)
PGDE	21 (12.1)
Master's degree	13 (7.5)
TESOL or others	49 (27.1)
Aspiration beyond minimum entry qualifications	83 (62.4)
Years of experience	
Less than 3 years	87 (48.1)
Between 3 and 5 years	21 (11.6)
Between 5 and 10 years	31 (17.1)
Above 10 years	42 (23.2)
Place of Birth	
Hong Kong	131 (73.6)
Non-Hong Kong	47 (26.4)

Particulars	Number (per cent)
Place of Schooling	
Hong Kong	122 (70.5)
Non-Hong Kong	51 (29.5)
First Language	
English	15 (8.5)
Cantonese	134 (75.7)
Others	28 (15.8)
Major language of communication (Outside school)	
English	34 (19)
Non-English	145 (81)

Survey tool

A purpose-designed questionnaire consisted of three sections seeking information on the participants' demographic details (e.g. their academic qualifications, years of teaching experience), their learners' characteristics (e.g. the age level and English proficiencies of the learners) and the characteristics of their teaching practice (e.g. the relative frequency of various types of learning and teaching activities, how often they use particular shared reading techniques). The questions in the teaching practice section came from several sources: existing questionnaires (e.g. Pressley et al., 1996), surveys that target home literacy practice (e.g. Roberts at al, 2005) and recommendations made by literacy experts (e.g. Graves et al., 2013; Lonigan and Whitehurst, 1998; Snow et al., 2007). The draft questionnaire was first reviewed by a panel of three experts in the field of early literacy development, and then piloted on five teachers of English. The items were subsequently revised and clarified. The questionnaire was readministered to the same teachers two weeks after the first administration. Only one teacher changed her responses to the questionnaire because she had taken over another class whose teacher was on maternity leave.

Statistical analyses

All analyses were conducted using SPSS version 19.0 (SPSS Inc., Chicago IL, 2011).

Results

Initially, we looked for extreme values in the dataset. We noticed that in the variable 'instruction time for English', there were a number of impossible values: the time indicated exceeded the maximum amount of time possible in a school day. Six values (3.31 per cent) were thus removed from the analysis.

Since teachers' strategies may be affected by the amount of instruction time available for each class in the school, we were, first of all, interested in how often the teachers see their children per week. Among those who responded (106 out of 181), the total amount of instruction time ranged from 15 minutes to 20 hours (i.e. four hours per day in a whole-day school) per week, with a median of 100 minutes per week (or 20 minutes per day) and a standard deviation of 5.69 hours. The data suggests that children's exposure time to English varies greatly across the schools in the current sample.

Next, we were interested in what teachers of English reported that they had done in their classrooms in order to engage their children to learn English. In particular, how often did the teachers engage in various types of language and literacy activities? Did they make use of strategies that afford a deeper level of language processing during their shared reading? The results (Table 2) showed that on a scale of 1 to 4 (1: never; 2: seldom; 3: some lessons; 4: every lesson), oral conversations, read-aloud and nursery rhyme singing are among the most typical English learning activities. On the other hand, the teaching of literacy-related skills (phonological awareness = 2.6; phonics = 2.97) and writing-related skills (letter and word writing) were somewhat less frequent. An unexpected finding was that teachers seldom use non-fiction books in their lessons, probably reflecting the fact that these books are rarely used in shared reading compared to typical storybooks. For extension activities, teachers were more likely to use show-and-tell rather than pair work.

Table 2: Frequency of different types of activities in the English lessons

Strategies	Mean*	SD
Oral conversations	3.14	.88
Story-telling	2.89	.73
Read-aloud	3.19	.76
Non-fiction	1.97	.80
Teach rare words	2.84	.81
Nursery rhymes	3.28	.70
Phonological awareness: teaching of beginning sounds	2.6	.88
Phonics	2.97	.79
Write letters	2.65	.97
Write words	2.56	1.04

Extension activity: show-and-tell	3.02	.83
Extension activity: pair work	2.56	.87

*1: never; 2: seldom; 3: some lessons; 4: every lesson

With respect to the use of shared reading strategies (Table 3), the results showed that on a five-point scale, teachers were more likely to spend time on the pictures and words in a picture book than on tasks that demand a deeper level of language processing, such as predicting the story content, discussing the story ending or conducting role play. The overall patterns suggest that the learners were more likely to be engaged in receptive learning than in the expressive use of language in their English lessons.

Table 3: The use of various shared reading techniques

Techniques	Mean*	SD
Talk about pictures	4.03	1.04
Point to words	4.16	.96
Predict content	3.62	1.09
Discuss ending	3.26	1.21
Role play	3.07	1.18

* 1: never; 2: seldom; 3: sometimes; 4: often; 5: always

Table 4: Vocabulary-building activities and shared reading strategies by qualifications and by children's proficiencies in English

	Vocabulary-building activities [scale: 1 to 4]	Shared reading strategies [scale: 1 to 5]
Qualifications		
Diploma in ECE	2.72 (.64)	3.44 (.87)
BEd in ECE	2.56 (.55)	3.52 (.91)
PGDE	2.99 (.44)	3.8 (.82)
Master's	3.28 (.42)	3.96 (.75)
Perceived abilities of the learners		
Minimal English	2.51 (.59)	3.25 (.77)
Single words	2.67 (.62)	3.45 (.86)
Phrases	2.84 (.52)	3.67 (.72)
Sentences	2.94 (.57)	3.89 (.97)
Stories	3.35 (.46)	4.07 (.80)

Note: SD values are inside brackets

Our next step of investigation was to examine whether teachers' choice of activities and their use of specific shared reading strategies were sensitive to factors such as the amount of teaching time available, age and English proficiencies of the learners, and the teachers' academic qualifications. Since we were primarily interested in whether teachers engaged in vocabulary-building activities and made use of shared reading strategies, we first created a composite variable called 'vocabulary-building activities' by averaging the following variables: oral conversation, storytelling, read-aloud, use of non-fiction and teaching rare words. Likewise, we recoded the variables of talk about pictures, point to words, predict the plot, discuss the ending and role play into a single variable called 'shared reading strategies'.

To examine the effect of teaching time on teachers' behaviour, we recoded the variable of instruction time into a new variable with two categories: teachers whose instruction time was 125 minutes per week or less vs. those whose instruction time was above 125 minutes per week. 125 minutes was used as the cut-off because it has been reported in previous literature that pre-schools in Hong Kong typically offer 20–25 minutes of daily English lessons (Wong et al., 2013). The results revealed that amount of exposure time was neither related to teachers' vocabulary-building activities ($F(1,95) < 1$) nor to their use of shared reading strategies ($F(1,94) = < 1$).

With respect to the effects of academic qualifications, our results showed that teachers with different academic qualifications differed significantly in their use of vocabulary-building strategies ($F(3,134) = 5.595$, $p < .001$). Generally speaking, the higher the academic qualification attained, the more likely the teacher concerned will engage in vocabulary-building activities. A Tukey post-hoc test revealed that teachers with a master's degree did not differ from their peers who hold a PGDE in ECE ($p > .05$); however, they spent significantly more time in vocabulary-building activities than those holding a diploma in ECE ($2.56 \pm .55$, $p < .05$) or a BEd in ECE ($2.72 \pm .64$, $p < .01$). In terms of the relationship between the use of shared-reading strategies and academic qualifications, there was no difference between the groups ($F(3,134) = 1.599$, $p > .05$).

Next, we examined the effects of learners' English proficiencies on teachers' behaviour. The results showed that in the area of vocabulary building, teachers were sensitive to the English proficiencies of the learners ($F(4,154) = 5.75$, $p < .001$). A Tukey post-hoc test revealed that teachers used fewer vocabulary-building strategies when working with learners with minimal English than with those who were able to speak sentences ($p = .05$) or tell stories ($p < .001$). With respect to the use of shared reading strategies, the observed patterns were similar: there was a statistically significant difference between groups ($F(4,154) = 3.53$, $p = .01$). Teachers used fewer shared reading strategies with learners whose English was minimal than with learners who could speak sentences ($p = .04$) or tell stories ($p = .04$).

Finally, we investigated the effects of children's age levels on teachers' behaviour. No statistically significant effects on teachers' vocabulary-building activities

(F(4,156) = 1.446, p > .05) or on their use of shared reading strategies (F(4,156) = 2.04, p > .05) were found.

Discussion

We began our study with the concerns of whether pre-school teachers of English in Hong Kong were focusing on activities conducive to children's vocabulary development and whether they were making use of recommended shared reading strategies, given the fact that Hong Kong pre-schools are all privately run and that they are only loosely controlled by the government. The overall news is positive: based on self-reporting, teachers stated that they spent relatively more time on oral conversations, storytelling and read-aloud than on letter- or word-writing activities. Their choice of activities was generally consistent with the guidelines issued by the Hong Kong Education Bureau (2006), which stated that the informal learning of English through stories and songs was preferable to the formal teaching of skills and writing.

Nevertheless, the survey identified a number of areas in which teachers could make improvements: first, phonological awareness (PA) activities were less frequent than phonics teaching. Since the success of phonics instruction depends on whether learners have adequate levels of vocabulary knowledge and phonological awareness, it is imperative that teachers of English should check whether their learners can segment the first sound and last sound in a word before they proceed to phonics instruction. Teachers' current emphasis on phonics rather than on PA might explain why Hong Kong pre-schoolers performed poorly in phonological awareness measures in developmental studies (Huang and Hanley, 1995; McBride-Chang et al., 2005). Second, with respect to shared reading strategies, it appears that teachers do recognise that young children derive meaning from a picture book through reference to both pictures and texts. However, to further enhance young children's vocabulary development, it is important for teachers to plan more activities which afford multiple exposures to the target words (e.g. role play) and challenge the children to think about the meaning of words and how these words are relevant to their lives through predictions and discussions in shared reading activities. Third, the infrequent use of non-fiction implies that the children had somewhat restricted exposure to vocabularies that may be unique to particular text types (e.g. scientific vocabularies in non-fiction).

With respect to the effects of instruction time, teachers' qualifications, age levels and the English proficiencies of learners on teachers' behaviour, our results showed that more teaching time does not translate into more frequent vocabulary-building activities or a greater use of shared reading strategies. However, teachers' academic qualifications do matter. Teachers with postgraduate qualifications (i.e. those who possess a PGDE in ECE and those with a master's degree) were more likely to engage in these vocabulary-building activities than their peers who possess a degree or a sub-degree level of qualification. On a positive note, the teachers' choice of activities and their use of shared reading strategies were more sensitive to children's English proficiency level than to their chronological age, suggesting that the teachers did take into account the developmental needs of individual children rather than simply basing their teaching on the age of the children.

Conclusion and future direction

Given the current conditions (such as the lack of direction from the Government, a strong incentive to lower costs in private schools, and the limited time available for the teaching of English), Hong Kong teachers of English are not doing a bad job in the sense that they respond to the developmental needs of learners by focusing more on oral language than on written language, and they do base their teaching on the perceived abilities of their learners rather than simply reacting to the age of the children. In addition, our data suggested that further professional training is beneficial because higher academic qualifications were found to be related to teachers' better use of strategies conducive to children's vocabulary development. Despite these findings, the current study has two main limitations. First, the sample is biased: although the pre-schools concerned covered all geographical areas in Hong Kong, the participants were all sent by their pre-schools to participate in the professional development seminars. It is uncertain whether those who do not receive any off-site or on-site professional training would respond differently. Secondly, self-reporting is different from direct observation of classroom teaching. Ideally, future research should observe the teaching practice of a sample of teachers in order to verify how reliable self-reported results are.

Acknowledgements

This research was supported by the Hong Kong Research Grant Council #845113 and the conference grant #ECE/CG14014 provided by the Hong Kong Institute of Education, both awarded to Richard Wong Kwok Shing. I thank all participating teachers and schools.

References

Adams, MJ (1990) *Beginning to read: Thinking and learning about print*. Cambridge, MA: MIT Press.

Baumann, JF (2005) 'Vocabulary-comprehension relationships', in Maloch, B, Hoffman, JV, Schallert, DL, Fairbanks, CM and Worthy, J (eds) *Fifty-fourth yearbook of the National Reading Conference*. Oak Creek, WI: National Reading Conference, 117-131.

Beck, IL, Perfetti, CA and McKeown, MG (1982) The effects of long-term vocabulary instruction on lexical access and reading comprehension. *Journal of Educational Psychology*, 74, 506-521.

Beck, IL and McKeown, MG (2006) *Improving comprehension with questioning the author: A fresh and expanded view of a powerful approach*. New York: Scholastic.

Bus, AG, van IJzendoorn, MH and Pellegrini, AD (1995) Joint book reading makes for success in learning to read: A meta-analysis on intergenerational transmission of literacy. *Review of Educational Research*, 65, 1-21.

Byrne, B, Freebody, P and Gates, A (1992) Longitudinal data on the relations of word-reading strategies to comprehension, reading time, and phonemic awareness. *Reading Research Quarterly*, 27/2, 140-151.

Crystal, D (2008) 'Into the Twenty-First Century', in Mugglestone, L (ed) *The Oxford History of English*. Oxford: Oxford University Press. 394-413.

Cunningham, AE and Stanovich, KE (1998) What reading does for the mind? *American Educator*, 22/1-2, 8-15.

De Temple, J and Snow CE (2003) 'Learning words from books', in van Kleeck, A, Stahl, SA and Bauer, EB (eds) *On reading books to children*. Mahwah, NJ: Erlbaum, 16-36.

Ehri, LC, Nunes, SN, Stahl, SA and Willows, DM (2001) Systematic phonics instruction helps students learn to read: Evidence from the national reading panel's meta-analysis. *Review of Educational Research*, 71/3, 393-447.

Goswami, U (2001) 'Early phonological development and the acquisition of literacy', in Neuman S and Dickinson D (eds) *Handbook of Research in Early Literacy for the 21st Century*, 111-125.

Graves, MF, August, D and Mancilla-Martinez, J (2013) *Teaching Vocabulary to English Language Learners*. New York: Teachers College Press.

Ho, D and Lam, H (2014) A study of male participation in early childhood education: Perspectives of school stakeholders. *International Journal of Educational Management*, 28/5, 498-509.

Hong Kong Education Bureau (2006) *Guide to the Preprimary Curriculum*. Hong Kong: Hong Kong Government Printer.

Hong Kong Census and Statistics Department (2012) *2011 Population Census*. Hong Kong: Hong Kong Government Printer.

Huang, HS and Hanley, RJ (1995) Phonological awareness and visual skills in learning to read Chinese and English. *Cognition*, 54/1, 73–98.

Lonigan, CJ and Whitehurst, GJ (1998) Relative efficacy of parent and teacher involvement in a shared-reading intervention for pre-school children from low-income backgrounds. *Early Childhood Research Quarterly*, 13, 263-290.

McBride-Chang, C, Cho, JR, Liu, H, Wagner, RK, Shu, H, Zhou, A, Muse, A (2005) Changing models across cultures: Associations of phonological awareness and morphological structure awareness with vocabulary and word recognition in second graders from Beijing, Hong Kong, Korea, and the United States. *Journal of Experimental Child Psychology*, 92, 140-160.

Nagy, WE (2005) 'Why vocabulary instruction needs to be long-term and comprehensive', in Hiebert, E and Kamil, M (eds) *Teaching and learning vocabulary*. Mahwah, NJ: Erlbaum, 27-44.

Nancollis, A, Lawrie, BA, and Dodd, B. (2005) Phonological awareness intervention and the acquisition of literacy skills in children from deprived social backgrounds. *Language, Speech, and Hearing Services in Schools*, 36, 325-335.

Pressley, M, Rankin, J and Yokoi, L (1996) A Survey of Instructional Practices of Primary Teachers Nominated as Effective in Promoting Literacy. *The Elementary School Journal*, 96/4, 363-384.

Roberts, J, Jergens, J and Burchinal, M (2005) The Role of Home Literacy Practices in Pre-school Children's Language and Emergent Literacy Skills. *Journal of Speech, Language, and Hearing Research*, 48, 345-359.

Roberts, T, and Neal, H (2004) Relationships among pre-school English language learners' oral proficiency in English, instructional experience and literacy development. *Contemporary Educational Psychology*, 29, 283-311.

Scarborough, HS (1998) 'Early identification of children at risk for reading disabilities: Phonological awareness and some other promising predictors', in Shapiro, BK, Accardo, PJ and Capute, AJ (eds) *Specific reading disabilities: A review of the spectrum*. Timonium, MD: York Press, 75-119.

Siegel, L (2009) 'Remediation of reading difficulties among English language learners', in Pugh, K and McCardle, M (eds) *How children learn to read: Current issues and new directions in the integration of cognition, neurobiology and genetics of reading and dyslexia research and practice*. New York: Psychology Press, 275-286.

Snow, CE, Porche, MV, Tabors, PO and Harris, SR (2007) *Is literacy enough? Pathways to academic success for adolescents*. Baltimore, MD: Paul H. Brookes Publishing.

Sternberg, RJ (1987) 'Most vocabulary is learnt from context', in McKeown, MG and Curtis, ME (eds) *The nature of vocabulary acquisition*. Hillsdale, NJ: Erlbaum, 89-105.

Wasik, BA and Bond, MA (2001) Beyond the pages of a book: Interactive book reading and language development in pre-school classrooms. *Journal of Education Psychology*, 93/2, 243-250.

Wong, KSR (2009) *Challenges in Early English Learning*. Hong Kong: Pearson Longman.

Wong, KSR, Perry, C, MacWhinney, B and Wong, OLI (2013) Relationships between receptive vocabulary in English and Cantonese proficiency among 5-year-old Hong Kong kindergarten children. *Early Child Development and Care*, 183/10, 1407-1419.

Wong, KSR (April, 2014) Press release: *Survey of over 3,000 parents on children's English learning environment*. Hong Kong: Oxford University Press.

2.5

A case study of early childhood education and the pre-school curriculum in Singapore

Lynn Ang, Institute of Education (IOE), University College London

Introduction: Early childhood education in Singapore

This chapter presents a case study of early childhood education delivered in a pre-school setting in Singapore for children aged three to six years who are bilingual speakers of English and Mandarin. It presents the findings of an ethnographic study, undertaken through the methodology of sustained narrative observations. With reference to examples of practice, the discussion explores how early years education is delivered through the pre-school curriculum to support children's learning, and the work of the pre-school teachers who play an integral role in constructing the curriculum. The case study discusses the approach and philosophy to early childhood education and the curriculum as espoused by the setting, and critically examines some of the issues and debates that arise from the setting's practices, more specifically in relation to the children's experiences as both native and non-native speakers of English.

Singapore is a Commonwealth nation in South East Asia with a population of approximately 5.4 million. The country is multicultural with three main ethnic groups – Chinese, Malay and Indian, with Chinese as the largest community. With a high Gross Domestic Product (GDP) per capita, low unemployment rate at less than two per cent, and a literacy rate at more than 96 per cent, the country is recognised globally as a well developed and affluent nation (Singapore Department of Statistics, 2014). Education in Singapore is highly valued, accounting for more than 20 per cent of government expenditure, equivalent to approximately 3.1 per cent of the country's GDP (Ministry of Education 2013a).

A cornerstone of Singapore's education system is its compulsory bilingual policy, introduced in 1966, which stipulates English as a first language alongside a mother tongue – Mandarin, Malay or Tamil – as a second taught language (Gopinathan, 1996; Cheah and Lim, 1996). The majority of pre-schools offer a bilingual education in English and Mandarin, while a few are bilingual in English and either Malay or Tamil. Pakir (1998) makes an early observation: *'[n]o other country in the world has the ambitious aim of making its entire population bi-literate in English and one other official language'*. Inevitably, the national bilingual policy has led to raising expectations among parents and teachers for children to learn two languages at an early age, in order to achieve a level of competency before they begin formal education (Cheah and Lim, 1996; Lee, 2012). Indeed, bilingual literary is widely regarded as a necessary pre-requisite for children's long-term academic attainment in a highly competitive education system. The government has consistently pushed for a results-driven education environment and maintaining a strong international standing in academic attainment globally, for instance, through the Programme for International Student Assessment (PISA) scores (Ministry of Education, 2013b). This drive towards excellence in education has implications for the way early childhood education (ECE) in Singapore is shaped, where young children's learning and development, even at pre-school age, are perceived as fundamental to lifelong learning and the future development of society (Ministry of Education, 'Opening address', 2012a).

Against this wider educational landscape, improving the pre-school sector has become a national priority in Singapore, especially in the context of international research and advocacy, with governments around the world recognising the crucial need to ensure quality pre-school services (OECD, 2006; UNESCO, 2012). Pre-schools in Singapore generally fall under two categories: kindergartens and childcare centres. Kindergartens are largely perceived as educational settings that support the academic development of young children, while childcare centres assume a broader function of full or partial day care for children aged two months and above. The compulsory school age for children is seven years, with pre-schools catering for children aged seven years and below. Kindergartens generally provide a three-year educational-based provision for children aged four to six years consisting of nursery, kindergarten one and kindergarten two. Childcare centres offer a provision of full-time care from 7am to 7pm with a number of centres providing infant and toddler care for children aged two to eighteen months (Ang, 2012).

In recent years, the Singapore government has put in place cumulative measures to regulate the pre-school sector to raise the quality and accessibility of services. In 2011, the national accreditation framework, the Singapore Pre-school Accreditation Framework, was introduced by the Ministry of Education (MOE) for pre-school providers as a quality assurance self-evaluation tool to evaluate areas of provision such as leadership, curriculum and administration. In 2012, a new development framework, the Early Years Development Framework (EYDF) was introduced by the Ministry of Community Development, Youth and Sports (MCYS), now known as the Ministry of Social and Family Development (MSF), to provide a programme of care for children from two months to three years of age (MCYS, 2011), and a new statutory board, the Early Childhood and Development Agency (ECDA), was established in April 2013 to oversee all issues pertaining to early years services.

Early Childhood Education (ECE) is therefore an important part of Singapore's public policy. National statistics estimate that "more than 99 per cent" of primary one-going children at six years of age attend "at least one year of pre-school in either a childcare centre or a kindergarten" (MCYS, 2012; MOE Press Release, 2012a, 1). This increase in participation rate is paralleled by a significant expansion of childcare centres in recent years, driven partly by burgeoning government initiatives and partly by socio-economic demands. Changing demographic patterns such as the rising participation rate of women in employment has driven a demand for services (Singapore Department of Statistics, 'Labour Force Participation Rate', 2011), with an increase in the number of childcare centres from 785 in 2009 to 982 centres in 2012 (MCYS, 2012).

Yet, significantly, in the process of accelerating developments, issues and debates around ECE prevail. In an international review of pre-school provision conducted by the Economic Intelligence Unit (EIU) across 45 countries, Singapore was ranked 29th in a league table of indicators relating to the availability, affordability and quality of services. The report noted that an effective early childhood national strategy needs to be addressed (Economist Intelligence Unit (EIU), 2012). Underlying issues such as a high turnover in the workforce and inequalities in terms of the affordability and quality of pre-school services continue to be a focus of debate, especially in such a diverse sector where ECE provision varies considerably and caters for children from diverse backgrounds in different socio-economic, cultural and linguistic contexts (Ang, 2012; Khoo, 2010).

The study

This short case study narrative is derived from a larger ethnographic study of pre-schools in Singapore undertaken through a qualitative methodology of sustained narrative observations and semi-structured interviews. The fieldwork was conducted over two years, for a period of three to eight weeks each time as a close working relationship was established between the researcher and the pre-schools. The ethnographic study explores the everyday life of the pre-schools, their characteristics and the way ECE is delivered. It offers an insight into the integrated curriculum of the pre-school and its ECE provision in English and Mandarin. The ethnographer, Michael Agar, defines ethnographic research as essentially 'collaborative' as people in the community help co-author the study. He contends: *"[y]ou need those people – not just, or even mainly, to answer questions – but to teach you, to work with you, to help you figure out what's going on in their world. It's always been that way"* (Agar, 1996). This ethnographic approach recognises precisely this – that the participants are paramount to the research as knowers and creators of their own knowledge and experience.

The discussion that follows presents an excerpt from research conducted on a particular model of ECE and bilingual education, drawn from field notes, interview transcripts and observations of the daily routines of a pre-school in Singapore. In reviewing the literature around bilingual education, there is extant research that shows the diverse pedagogical and curricular approaches to language acquisition and the implications on children's learning and development (De Jong, 2006; DePalma, 2010; Drury, 2007; Lee, Hill-Bonnet and Gillispie, 2008; Howard, Sugarman and Christian, 2003). A model of bilingual education delivered in two distinct languages through children's participation in an integrated curriculum has given rise to an expansion of language programmes sometimes referred to as a two-way immersion approach (Baker, 2006; DePalma, 2010; Drury, 2007; Howard,

Sugarman and Christian, 2003). Howard et al (2003) argue that while such a model of bilingual education provides learners with the opportunity to develop their oral and written language competence in their first and second language acquisition, the long-term outcomes for children's development are difficult to ascertain given the inherent differences among learners and the variables that affect learning. Indeed, it is widely recognised that the process of language acquisition is a complex issue with ongoing debates around 'how best' children acquire language and the appropriate curricular and pedagogical approach. The phrase 'bilingual education' in itself, generally describing an educational programme which involves the teaching and learning of two languages in a shared educational context, can also hold different connotations across cultures and countries (Brisk, 2006; Drury, 2007; Howard et al 2003; Lee et al 2008). The question of what it means to be 'a bilingual' is influenced by children's cultural and socio-economic backgrounds and diverse linguistic abilities. It is also shaped as much by the nature of the learning experience as the social and cultural context of the educational environment; all of which play a major role in influencing children's learning and development.

A snapshot of an ECE programme: Linton Kindergarten[26]

Founded in 1980, Linton is a pre-school that caters for children aged eighteen months to six years. It is located in an exclusive private neighbourhood in the western part of Singapore, in a prime residential district well known for its high cost of properties. As a childcare centre, Linton offers full- and part-day care from 7am to 7pm, Mondays to Fridays, and 7am to 2pm on Saturdays. The setting employs 20 teachers, with two teachers allocated for every class: an English and Mandarin teacher. The setting's fee structure at S$1,312.50 per month for full-day care and S$829.50 per month for half-day care is almost 50 per cent more than the national average cost of childcare. The high cost of fees marks out the setting's clientele at the higher end of the market. By reputation, this is a pre-school with parents who seek a quality ECE provision for their children, and who are willing and have the means to pay for such a provision. Arguably, the setting is not representative of the 'average' pre-school in Singapore, but was nonetheless recruited to the study for offering a useful insight into a particular socio-economic milieu and distinct approach to ECE.

The curriculum at Linton is best described as an 'integrated thematic approach', organised around six main areas of learning: language and literacy, mathematics, knowledge and understanding of the world, creative development, personal, social and emotional development, and physical development. The daily routine is planned across the six learning areas according to the weekly themes. Given the competitive nature of education in Singapore, enrichment activities such as computer studies, cooking, and speech and drama are also included in the curriculum. As described in the handbook for parents, a typical schedule for the day is as follows:

---

[26] The name of the setting has been changed for ethical reasons.

7:00	Educational play activities
8:00	Breakfast
9:00	Circle time/group reading/English language activities
9:20–9:50	Creative Development
9:50–10:15	Physical Education/Outdoor activities
11:15–11.30	Snack Time
11:30–12:30	Mathematics and Understanding of the World
12:30–1:00	Lunchtime (AM students)
1:00–1:30	Shower Time/Rest Time
1:30–2:30	Circle Time
2:30–3:00	Creative Development (music and movement/speech and drama/imaginative play)
3:00–3:15	Snack Time
3:15–4:00	Chinese language
4:00–5:00	Mathematics and Knowledge
5:00–5:25	Physical Education
5:25–6:00	Free Play

The timetable seems somewhat structured, but in reality the day is rather seamless as the activities overlap and run into each other. Most of the children arrive at 8am, in time for breakfast, following which the school day formally begins. The teachers would usually begin the day with circle time, led by either the Chinese or English teacher, or sometimes both. This is followed by an English or Mandarin language session revolving around the theme for the week.

The afternoon schedule seems somewhat less structured, as the children move around different activities depending on their interests. At 12.30pm the children have lunch, after which some parents would arrive to pick up the half-day children while the full-time children return to their classroom for a nap or rest from 1.30pm until 2.30pm. After their rest, the children are engaged in play or creative activities, reading stories, or art and craft, followed by an afternoon snack. This is followed by free play at 5.25pm until 6pm when parents begin to arrive to collect their children for home.

An integrated curriculum: The bilingual child

A distinct aspect of Linton's provision is its bilingual curriculum, where the children simultaneously learn two languages: English and Mandarin. In the first paragraph of the orientation handbook sent out to parents, Linton is described as a pre-school which offers an 'integrated curriculum' with 'both an English-speaking teacher and a Chinese-speaking teacher present in each class, ensuring that the children are completely immersed in both languages and therefore have a strong chance of developing a high level of proficiency in both English and Mandarin'. Most pre-schools in Singapore offer a bilingual provision, which entails a second language or 'mother tongue' being taught as a separate language lesson at a specified time during the curriculum (usually half an hour to an hour) and usually conducted in a separate classroom. Lee (2012) contends that this can be traced to the 1980s where the government's policy with its emphasis on English as the main medium of instruction for formal education has relegated the teaching of Mandarin to discrete 'mother tongue' language classes, as opposed to a more holistic language provision. As such, what is distinctive about Linton is its teaching of Mandarin as an 'equal medium of education' alongside the English language, with its practice of having two language teachers simultaneously in the classroom at all times, assuming joint ownership in planning the curriculum, and conducting all activities in both English and Mandarin simultaneously.

An integrated, bilingual approach to ECE is embedded in all aspects of Linton's provision, from the curriculum to the physical environment. Each classroom is adorned with a myriad of posters and charts in both English and Mandarin. Charts and pictures of the alphabet, Chinese strokes and short poems are displayed prominently around the white board and on the walls of each classroom. There is an English and Mandarin teacher in each class at all times, where both languages are used interchangeably throughout the day. An illustration of this was during an observation of a lesson with the English teacher, Shannon, and the Chinese teacher, He Lao shi, in their Casuarina kindergarten class of four to five year olds. This bilingual dialogue begins as soon as the children step into the setting:

Abstract taken from observation notes

7.30am: The children begin to arrive. Teacher Shannon is standing by the classroom door greeting the children and sharing exchanges with the parents as they stream in. He Lao shi is in the classroom arranging the chairs and equipment, setting up the classroom for the day. She greets the children in.

8.30am: Most of the children have arrived by now. Lao shi directs the children to gather on the floor rug at the front of the classroom.

Lao Shi: 'xiao peng you zhao an' (children, good morning). The children return the greeting to Lao shi in Mandarin.

Shannon [standing next to lao shi]: 'Good morning children'. The children response to Shannon's greeting in English: 'good morning Ms. Shannon'.

Lao Shi: Xiao peng you, jin tian xin qi ji? (children, does anyone know what day it is today?) Lao shi looks around the room for an answer.

Shannon: 'remember, yesterday was Tuesday, so today must be...'? Shannon and Lao shi pauses for an answer. Several children call out the right answer 'Wednesday'.

Shannon praises the children for answering correctly.

Lao shi reinforces the response: tui, jin tian shi xin qi san (yes, today is Wednesday!).

Shannon: 'Does anyone know what date it is?'

Lao shi reinforces the question in Mandarin.

Shannon: 'put up your hands if you know the date'. A few hands go up and there is a chorus of 'January'. Shannon smiles and says: 'yes the date today is 15 January". She writes the date on the white board.

What is striking about the lesson was the double-act that both Shannon and the Chinese teacher Lao shi seemed to carry out so effortlessly in their interactions with the children. At times, Lao shi took the lead as she explained to the children a particular activity that she wanted them to do, and at other times Shannon led the class. It seemed so natural in the way both Lao shi and Shannon worked in tandem, interacting with the children in both English and Mandarin; supporting and reinforcing what the other was saying and doing. The children seemed attuned with both teachers as they code switched fluently in English and Mandarin between Shannon and He Lao shi. On several occasions, the children were observed relaying a message to one teacher in one language and simultaneously passing it to the other in another language. During the observations of the classroom activities over time, it was apparent that this bilingual practice is the cornerstone of Linton's curriculum, where code switching between the two languages occurred naturally throughout the day. Another interesting episode is presented below. The observation extract is based on a lesson on symmetrical shapes, the theme for that week:

11.30am: Shannon gathers the children at the front of the class on the rug. She sits on a chair in front of the children and Lao shi is sat next to her.

Shannon [enthusiastically], 'Children, we are going to do something very interesting today. We are going to look for something special and we are going to learn something new today [Shannon says this slowly and expressively, as if to build up the excitement]. We are going to learn a new word "symmetrical". Shannon stands up to draw on the white board three different shapes of leaves that are symmetrical.

Lao shi [pointing to Shannon's drawing]: 'xiao peng you, ni kan Shannon lao shi zai hua se mo?' (children, look at what teacher Shannon is drawing?)'.

Shannon completes her diagram and explains to the children that she has drawn the shapes of three leaves, with the same contour on either side, which indicates that they are symmetrical.

Lao shi [pointing to the shape that Shannon has drawn]: 'ni men chai zhe shi se mo xing fang? (children, guess, what shape do you think it is?)'

Children: A few raise their hands immediately to answer. Lao shi calls out to one of them who responds in Mandarin.

Shannon [points to the next shape she has drawn and asks the children again if they knew what shape it is.] Children [respond in a chorus]: "heart shape".

Both Shannon and Lao shi praise the children for knowing their shapes.

Shannon [enthusiastically]: 'Let's go to the garden to find leaves which are symmetrical in shape.'

Lao shi: stands up and ushers the children to line up to get ready to go outside.

What is clear from the observation excerpt is that both Shannon and He Lao shi share a belief in the benefits of a bilingual curriculum and language acquisition as a crucial tool in the children's overall development. However, both teachers also shared that while they espoused the benefits of having a bilingual provision, they are often faced with difficult questions from parents. As Lao shi said: '... *some parents get worried, and will ask us 'will my child get confused when there are two teachers in class and they hear two languages at the same time?' but as you can see, the children know when to use Mandarin and when to use English. They use both languages at the same time. I don't think they are confused ... [Shannon nodded to indicate her agreement with Lao shi].* It is evident from the study that both teachers' conviction about the curriculum they offer is very much influenced by their own perceptions and beliefs about the children's learning; that the children are competent and confident learners, and therefore capable of actively participating in a bilingual educational environment.

Closing remarks: A blend of East and West

This chapter has provided a brief glimpse of a case study of ECE in Singapore, which supports children who are speakers of other languages apart from English. Throughout the study, the children were observed not only using two distinct languages in different contexts, but also actively engaging with and participating in various social and cultural activities. Importantly, what is also interesting about Linton is its approach and philosophy of ECE, which appears to be a blend of both Western and local influences, as shaped by the teaching of English and Mandarin. While the children are encouraged to express and appreciate themselves as individuals (a generally Western concept based on the notion of the 'individual self'), they are also encouraged to respect and value one another, and in particular their relationship with parents and elders (a concept rooted in the Chinese, Confucian culture of respecting one's elders and filial piety). One could argue that what emerges from Linton, therefore, is a curriculum that can be described as mixed or hybrid, with different cultural elements, and where different educational philosophies and pedagogical styles come together. In many ways, the bilingual and ECE provision at Linton is the product of a cultural juxtaposition, and underpinned by what Caren, the principal, describes as a shared experience of ECE that is *"familiar to [the children], which is in their local context and which makes learning both meaningful and fun"*.

References

Agar, M (1996) *The Professional Stranger.* USA: Academic Press.

Ang, L (2012) *Vital Voices for Vital Years. A Study of Leaders' Perspectives on Improving the Early Childhood Sector in Singapore.* Lien Foundation: Singapore.

Baker, C (2006) *Foundations of Bilingual Education and Bilingualism* (4th ed). Clevedon: Multilingual Matters.

Brisk, M (2006) *Bilingual Education: from Compensatory to Quality Schooling* (2nd ed). London: Lawrence Erlbaum Associates Publishers.

Cheah, YM and Lim, SE (1996) 'Literacy and biliteracy issues in Singapore', in Lai, EFK, (ed) *Reading Research Symposium 1996: Asian perspectives on biliteracy research: facts, issues and action* (Hong Kong, Hong Kong Reading Association), 23–40.

De Jong, E (2006) Integrated Bilingual Education: An Alternative Approach. *Bilingual Research Journal: The Journal of the National Association for Bilingual Education,* 30, (1), 23-44.

DePalma, R (2010) *Language Use in the Two-Way Classroom, Lessons from a Spanish- English Bilingual Kindergarten.* New York: Multilingual Matters.

Drury, R (2007) *Young Bilingual Learners at Home and School: Researching multilingual voices.* Stoke-on-Trent: Trentham Books.

Gopinathan, S (1996) Globalisation, the State and Education Policy in Singapore. *Asia Pacific Journal of Education,* 16:1 pp74-87.

Howard, ER, Sugarman, J and Christian, D (2003) *Trends in two-way immersion education: A review of the research.* Report 63. Baltimore, MD: Center for Research on the Education of Students Placed At Risk.

Khoo, KC (2010) The Shaping of Childcare and Pre-school Education in Singapore: From Separatism to Collaboration. *International Journal of Child Care and Education Policy* 4, no.1: 23-34.

Lee, CL (2012) Saving Chinese-language education in Singapore. *Current Issues in Language Planning,* 13/4: 285–304.

Lee, JS, Hill-Bonnet, L and Gillispie, J (2008) Learning in Two Languages: Interactional Spaces for Becoming Bilingual Speakers. *International Journal of Bilingual Education and Bilingualism,* 11 (1), 75-84.

Ministry of Community Development, Youth and Sports (MCYS) (2011) *Early Years Development Framework, Singapore:* MCYS https://www.ecda.gov.sg/PressReleases/Pages/Early-Years-Development-Framework-(EYDF).aspx

Ministry of Community Development, Youth and Sports (MCYS) (2012) *Statistics on Child Care Services*. http://app.msf.gov.sg/Portals/0/Files/Early%20Childhood%20Development%20Agency%20Statistics.pdf

Ministry of Education (MOE) (2013a) *Government expenditure on education. Parliamentary Replies.* www.moe.gov.sg/media/parliamentary-replies/2013/10/government-expenditure-on-education.php

Ministry of Education (MOE) (2013b) International OECD Study Shows That Singapore Students Are Ready to Thrive in the 21st Century. www.moe.gov.sg/media/press/2013/12/international-oecd-study-shows-that-singapore-students-are-ready-to-thrive-in-the-21st-century.php

Ministry of Education (MOE) (2012b) *'List of MOE-Registered Kindergartens'.* Singapore: MOE. www.moe.gov.sg/education/pre-school/find-a-kindergarten/

Ministry of Education (MOE) (2012a) *Opening Address by Mr Lawrence Wong, Minister of State, Ministry of Defence and Ministry of Education,* at PECERA 13th Conference on Friday, 20 July 2012, at the National Institute of Education. www.moe.gov.sg/media/speeches/2012/07/20/opening-address-by-mr-lawrence-at-pecera-conference.php

Organization for Economic Co-operation and Development (OECD) (2006) *Starting Strong II: Early Childhood Education and Care.* Paris: OECD. http://www.unicef.org/lac/spbarbados/Implementation/ECD/StartingStrongII_OECD_2006.pdf

Pakir, A (1998) 'Innovative Second Language Education in Southeast Asia', in Corson, D and Tucker, R (eds) *Second Language Education, Vol. 4, Encyclopaedia of Language and Education,* 221-230. The Netherlands: Kluwer Academic Publishers.

Singapore Department of Statistics (2014) *Latest Key Indicators.* Singapore. www.singstat.gov.sg/

United Nations Educational, Scientific and Cultural Organisation (UNESCO) (2012) *Early Childhood Care and Education EFA Goal 1. Asia-Pacific End of Decade Notes on Education for All.* Bangkok: UNESCO and UNICEF. http://unesdoc.unesco.org/images/0021/002171/217145e.pdf

2.6

Nursery rhymes for cognitive development: from listening comprehension to maths skills

Kalyani Samantray, Utkal University, Odisha, India

Introduction

Nursery rhymes are regularly used for young learners (YL) of English due to several obvious advantages such as exposure to natural language, usage and rhythm, and for practice in producing natural English. However, while rhymes are regularly used in YL English classes, teaching remains restricted to listening, rote memorisation and reproduction, and less on making it meaningful (Brown, 2001; Morley, 2001; Arnold, 2005). However, many rhymes can be used for other aspects of the cognitive development of YLs (Davanellos, 1999; Linse, 2006), including listening comprehension skills and maths knowledge, the focus of this chapter.

For YLs, both listening (Shin, 2011; Vandergrift, 2002) to nursery rhymes for comprehension and learning basic mathematical operations are complex cognitive achievements. Rhymes can be used to develop the two in tandem. However, in formal teaching contexts, as in India, rhymes are used largely for the rote purposes mentioned earlier (Mackay, 2013), and without any explicit methodology. For example, repetition for memorisation has been observed as the primary purpose of using rhymes with YLs in an Indian case study by Piller and Skillings (2005).

In the case study reported in this chapter, we attempted to make rhymes more functional for young learners of English by using them for two objectives: development of listening comprehension, and development of mathematical processes and concepts that arise out of listening comprehension.

Listening comprehension is not a conscious procedure in the routine of teaching nursery rhymes to YLs (Kenney, 2005; Lee, 2012). Furthermore, syllabus planners and teachers (in India) tend not to associate maths skills with nursery rhymes despite the fact that many rhymes are replete with maths connections that can serve as a natural motivator for YLs to develop maths skills and concepts. These two specific advantages of nursery rhymes were exploited in this exploratory and descriptive case study to evaluate how rhymes might be used for such a meaningful extension. The study reports the use of rhymes with YLs of English for developing listening comprehension skills in English at the same time as inculcating age-appropriate mathematical skills and concepts.

The context

The study was carried out with ten six-year-old YLs of English whose mother tongue was Odia, and who attend a school where English is the medium of instruction from the second year of school. The study was carried out for three hours a week for six months (resulting in a total of 72 hours). This six-month period was divided into three blocks of two months each, to gradually introduce the maths concepts.

Teaching listening comprehension in English helps to develop young learners' cognitive, academic and social abilities. A listening focus was used since listening forms the basis of most classroom activities (Florit, Roch, and Levorato, 2011; Florit, Roch, Altoè and Levorato, 2009) in which learners cannot perform correctly unless they have heard and understood the relevant instructions/information. The purposes of teaching numbers and basic mathematical concepts to YLs are to help develop the concepts of number, operations, patterns and other mathematical operations that form the foundation of higher-level maths, and lay the foundation for learning later abstract maths subjects they will eventually encounter. Given the importance of early development of these listening and maths skills, too narrow a scope is allowed in the Indian school system to develop these for functional purposes. With an understanding of the gaps, the case study addressed two important issues: i) considered use of listening comprehension of English nursery rhymes, and ii) developing mathematical skills through nursery rhymes.

Materials

It was planned to promote the use of nursery rhymes in developing listening comprehension and to extend listening comprehension to a variety of maths connections, such as numbers, patterns, shapes and sequences available in the rhymes to function as natural motivators for teaching maths skills and concepts. Several rhymes also explore maths-related concept words that YLs of English need to learn, such as words of shape, size, sequence (e.g. *any, many, none, a few, plenty, after, before,* and so on). Learning beyond numbers and operations contributes to YLs' basic maths foundation, which later helps in maths abstractions. For example, early instruction in shapes lays the groundwork for future learning in geometry. Rhymes and related activities were used in this case study to help YLs understand maths concepts, and practise the basic functions. Table 1 presents the rhymes used in the study and the listening and maths activities generated from each rhyme:

Table 1: Rhymes and the listening and maths activities for each

Rhymes / Activities	Listening to story frames	Numbers and counting	Addition and subtraction	Shapes and geometry	Sequences and patterns	Maths concepts
One, two, buckle my shoe		√		√	√	
Baa, baa, black sheep	√		√			√
One and one are two		√	√		√	
One for me and one for you		√	√		√	
Rub-a-dub-dub, Three men in a tub	√		√	√		
Good morning, Mrs Hen	√	√	√	√	√	√
Five little snowmen	√	√	√		√	
Ten little sparrows cheeping at the door	√		√	√	√	
Old Mother Hubbard	√			√		√
The Queen of Hearts	√			√		√
Sing a song of six pence	√	√		√		√

Extra rhymes related to mathematical operations and notions were used for practice activities and consolidation of the skills (see Appendix).

Procedure to enhance listening comprehension

The procedure used to encourage the YLs of English to interact with the rhymes to enhance their listening comprehension skills involved the following:

- Listening to and responding to rhymes and story frameworks generated from the rhymes.
- Reproducing rhymes and stories with action.
- Responding to the events and characters through discussions.
- Discussing numbers, concepts and maths operations occurring in the rhymes.
- Using rhyme-related games and activities for practice.

The listening activities continued for the entire duration of the study. The procedure is presented in Table 2.

Table 2: Procedure adopted in case study

Listening comprehension	Characters and their actions	Events and sequences	Numbers, concepts, shapes and operations	Maths vocabulary
Miming/pointing at pictures	Miming actions of characters	_____	Miming numbers and shapes using fingers and hand gestures, and pointing at pictures	Miming words like big/small, many/none, empty/full/ more/less using gestures, and pointing at pictures
Answering/ discussing key questions	Who are there in the rhyme? What is X doing/ asking? Where is X going?	What happened to ___? What happened after that?	Count up to 5/10/20. What comes after/before 5/8...? What shape is a pie/coin/window ...? Add 1+1, 2+2... up to 10/15/20. Take away ½/... birds from 5/10.... birds.	Which one/ group is bigger/ smaller? How many chickens does Mrs. Hen have?
Using rhyme-related games and activities	Reciting with action	Sequencing events using pictures	Using objects and pictures to work out numbers, shapes and maths operations	Discussing maths vocabulary using objects and pictures

From listening to maths skills

The development of understanding of number, patterns, shapes and sequence were encouraged by investigating and communicating about:

- Quantities, their representations and the basic operations using quantity.
- Physical features of objects and collections, e.g. shape, size.
- Sequence and pattern.

Table 3 presents the progression of learning mathematical concepts and operations in the six-month period of the study, which was divided into three two-month blocks, as there was incremental addition of maths competencies in each block. For listening comprehension, the period was not divided into blocks since the aims in listening comprehension remained constant (Table 2) for the duration of the study.

Table 3: Progression of learning maths concepts throughout the study

Mathematical concepts and operations	Sept–Oct	Nov–Dec	Jan–Feb
Recognising and counting numbers	Naming and using number names up to 10 forward and backward through number rhymes, stories Counting games and activities	Naming and using number names up to 20 forward and backward through number rhymes, stories Counting games and activities	Naming and using number names: 30, 40 …100 Counting games and activities to identify quantities in small collections of the same and different objects
Adding and subtracting	Adding up to 10 in various combinations, e.g. 1+1 is 2; 2+2, 4; … 5+5, 10 through rhymes, fingers, drawings, and using objects and geometric figures	Adding up to 20 in various combinations using the activities as for numbers 1–10	Subtracting from 10 down to zero in 1's, 2's and 5's using rhymes, fingers, drawings, objects and geometric figures Subtracting from 20 down to zero using the same activities
Identifying numbers in small quantities: grouping and comparing	Identifying numbers in groups of objects as used in rhymes Drawing pictures that represent two groups of objects; for example: 5 fish and 10 fish/ 10 snowmen and no snowmen	Identifying which group has more/less	Creating smaller groups larger, and larger groups smaller

Mathematical concepts and operations	Sept–Oct	Nov–Dec	Jan–Feb
Identifying and creating sequences	Identifying if numbers (1-10) are in sequence Sequencing random numbers between 1–10	Identifying if numbers (1–20) are in sequence Sequencing random numbers between 1–20	Sequencing 10, 20, 30…100 Revision activities for numbers 1-20
Recognising shapes, sizes and patterns	Identifying circles and squares Putting the shapes in separate groups according to size and shape	Identifying triangles and rectangles Distinguishing the shapes, particularly, squares and rectangles	Classifying objects by 1, 2 or 3 attribute/s: shape, size and number Activities to identify collections of the same and different objects and in different arrangements in various representations
Describing what has been done while identifying/ patterning/ sequencing/ classifying	Teacher models 'maths talk' and elicits responses using patterns: What did I/we do? I/we counted forward or backward/ grouped … Which number comes after/ before …	Teacher models 'maths talk' and elicits responses using patterns: What did I/we do? I/we counted forward or backward/ grouped/put in order or sequence … This group is smaller than that group. I made this group larger/smaller. This tray has more toys. That has none. These toys/pictures belong to this group.	Activities to use and practise maths vocabulary: a. quantifiers: none, any, some, many, a few… b. comparatives: big/ small, long/short/ more/less… c. terms for sequencing: before/after/ between… d. terms for shapes and patterns: circle/ square…
Eliciting responses from YLs	Your turn to say which number comes after/ before…	Your turn to say which group is larger/ smaller. How did you find that out?	Which group has more/fewer apples? Which number comes between – and –? Name these shapes.

Since there was no formal assessment in this exploratory study, whether the children were able to complete the task acted as an informal check that the YLs had indeed listened to and interacted with the rhymes together with the associate story frames, and were able to complete the maths tasks that followed. Comprehension was checked through Total Physical Response (TPR), miming, comprehension questions and discussion. The next level of discussion and activities with the children focused on numbers, mathematical operations and concepts available in the rhymes. The researcher (as teacher) described concepts and discussed processes as she demonstrated each maths operation. The YLs imitated the same process to describe maths concepts and operations after they completed the maths activities. They used fingers for numbers and other gestures, (e.g. hand movements, for maths vocabulary like 'none/some/any', and pictures/ toys/objects to identify shape and size, to group, to sequence and for other such operations). Data was collected from the group rather than from individual YLs (Anderson, 2005). All of these activities were carried out in English.

The 'Number' activities required the following tasks to be completed:

- Counting forward and backward
- Sequencing
- Knowing the position of a number relative to other numbers
- Identifying quantities of collections
- Representing the same quantities using different objects and drawings
- Investigating the attributes of collections using maths vocabulary, e. g, more/less
- Performing addition and subtraction.

The children started with counting up to five, since the number corresponds to the fingers and toes in a hand or a foot. This counting skill was boosted by using everyday objects such as a bowl of apples or toys. The children developed their counting in small increments. Activities and objects were used for addition and subtraction. They kept adding one more elephant/child to the group as they recited and counted *One elephant went out to play* …. A similar procedure introduced subtraction with the rhyme: *Five little monkeys jumping on the bed, One fell off and bumped his head* … The forward and backward counting in these rhymes helped establish the early operations of addition and subtraction. The operations extended through adding or subtracting apples from a bowl and then counting the enhanced or the reduced number (O'Neill et al, 2004; Monroe, 2010).

Next, the children learned to apply sequence, one number at a time, to items being counted, and developed the awareness of addition and the final number of items in a set. Knowing 'how many' items were in a set depended, first, on the ability to count, and then knowing that the last number counted was the quantity of the set (Aunio and Niemivirta, 2010; Muldoon et al, 2010). To assess the child's ability to do this, we asked them to identify the next number or a number that occurs after another in a natural counting sequence. In counting backwards, children were asked to identify numbers that come before a given number.

Children learnt to identify the shapes of objects as each object was displayed matching with the ones in the rhymes (see the Appendix). They named mathematical terms for the shapes as they listened to and responded to rhymes and stories. The next task was to recognise and identify shapes in their surrounding environment; for example, the shape of a table, a classroom window or door, a whole pizza and a section of a pizza. Comparison with similar objects they were familiar with (e.g. a circle 'is like a pizza' or a square 'is like my sandwich') reinforced the concept of the basic shapes: circle, triangle, square and rectangle.

To assess the children's knowledge of shapes, we asked them to identify different shapes, create shapes in crafts, and use shape names in answering rhyme-related questions. They described the shapes, and compared the similarities and the differences using features such as 'a triangle has three sides' and 'a circle goes round and has no sides'. They repeated the rhymes and matched shapes using objects for each description. Then, they took turns to describe a shape of their choice as the class displayed the matching shape, and named each shape.

When learning about sequence and pattern, the learners engaged with these fundamental mathematical ideas. They:

- Identified, understood and used the significant components and sequences of a rhyme
- Learnt and used the language of order and sequence: *after, next, between, before ...*
- Became familiar with the language related to sequence and pattern: *match, same, different ...*
- Matched the order of objects and numbers in sequence
- Created patterns using objects and materials.

In order to gauge how much the children had learned they were asked to create the sequence of events based on the rhymes/story frames using pictures that depicted the significant events. They classified objects by what matched with what, and by sorting objects into big and small, more and less, same and different (Kirova and Bhargava, 2002).

Table 4 presents the assessment rubric and observations on learner achievements in task completion and verbalisation of the concepts and the processes. Task completion has been categorised under 'behavioural knowledge', and verbalisation under 'tacit knowledge'.

Table 4 : Assessment of listening comprehension, maths concepts and operations

Main skills focus with inputs: rhymes, frames, questions, pictures, objects	Expected response	Observations on achievements
Listening to rhymes and storyline for overall text comprehension	Correlating text and action through gestures and TPR to demonstrate text meaning	Demonstrated tacit and behavioural knowledge of overall text comprehension, e.g. they executed standalone TPR requirements even when not listening to any particular rhyme: Tr: Pick up the pencil. YL: (completes the action)
Listening for details (who, what, how, where, when ...)	Answering text-based questions on characters, events, actions using expressions from the text	Demonstrated behavioural knowledge of details: Tr: Where were the birds? YLs: On the wall Demonstrated partial tacit knowledge of details, e.g. they answered questions without miming or imitating teacher action; failed initially in answering *how* questions
Listening to match and group expressions with objects/ numbers/shapes/size	Matching and grouping activities	Demonstrated tacit and behavioural knowledge by matching words with objects/ numbers/shapes, and by grouping similar objects/ shapes
Working out maths operations	Using fingers, pictures, objects in activities to indicate, identify, respond to and complete maths operations: sequencing, adding, subtracting	Demonstrated behavioural knowledge of the operations Demonstrated tacit knowledge of the operations, e.g. they described how they formed sequences with ascending/ descending order of numbers/ events in the rhymes; used after/next/ ...; worked out addition/subtraction independently using rhymes
Using maths-related vocabulary	Articulating and using such vocabulary supported by pictures and objects	Demonstrated tacit and behavioural knowledge of the concepts, e.g. in counting, sequencing, grouping, identifying shapes, adding and subtracting, they used terms, such as after, before, matches, same, different, plus and take away

Discussion

Rhymes with maths elements bring together the two important early skills of listening comprehension and maths competency for YLs of English. In this case study, listening skills and early numeracy development were facilitated by using rhymes for text comprehension, counting, elementary mathematical operations, and sequences and patterns present in the rhymes. Activities were planned that were close to the experiences of the YLs, in which they used and described:

- Attributes and representations for numbers, sequences, patterns and collections
- Classified objects, and described a characteristic of the collection, such as number, shape or size
- Maths-related language, e.g. comparatives and positionals
- Early mathematical operations using objects, pictures and drawings.

Listening comprehension focused on the overall theme and the important details of the rhymes (e.g. characters, actions, events and sequences). Numbers and maths concepts and operations were focused on in subsequent sessions, to facilitate composite development of listening and maths competencies. As this was largely a descriptive and exploratory study, no formal assessment of learner achievements was utilised; however, task completion and verbalisation of maths processes and concepts were employed to record learning accomplishments (Table 4). Task completion demonstrated both behavioural and tacit knowledge of concepts and their application, while verbalisation confirmed the tacit knowledge of operations and concepts. The YLs were asked to do maths tasks and to describe how they recognised quantity, shapes of objects, sequenced or grouped objects and shapes, and used numbers for mathematical operations. Thus, task completion and description determined the nature and level of learning accomplished.

The children's ability to listen to rhymes and storylines for overall text comprehension and for details (Table 2) was their highest achievement, except for answering *how* questions early in the comprehension stage. This could be due to the non-factual nature of the *how* questions that required an advanced understanding of the text. They were able to answer this type of question in the second and the third blocks of this study (e.g. in months three through to six of the study, see Table 3), showing development in this regard. As expected, the development of tacit knowledge in maths concepts and operations was somewhat slow, although progress in tacit understanding was evident overall from the initial to the final stages of the study. The learners attempted to describe the processes and the concepts in the initial stage, even though they were not always accurate. Accuracy in verbalising concepts and operations appeared in the second and the third two-month block periods. The highest levels of achievement consistently remained with listening for overall text comprehension, and the lowest was for addition and subtraction (Table 4). The lowest achievements can be ascribed to the fact that the learners were being initiated into logical and deductive numeracy activities for the first time in English. They could complete matching and grouping tasks satisfactorily in 'listening and doing' activities and, later, could do similar activities by carrying out teacher instruction. Initially, they had problems with shape and size names, which were gradually overcome with practice, and they could identify, name and categorise similar shapes. Not surprisingly, they used maths-related vocabulary (e.g. before, after, next, same, different, smaller, bigger...) early on the basis of their occurrence in the rhymes and the stories.

Conclusion

This case study was designed and conducted to investigate the use of rhymes for purposeful language and the learning of maths by YLs of English. Since this was the earliest opportunity for these YLs to build up their listening comprehension and maths activities in English, attempts were made not to pressurise them in any manner but to develop these early skills in a stress-free and fun context. The full extent of what the children were able to achieve, therefore, could not be succinctly recorded owing to these facts. However, the first major accomplishment of this study was to introduce and execute appropriate listening comprehension activities to develop the YLs' English listening skills, which is not currently being carried out systematically in the Indian context. The other major achievement was allocating a broader scope than normally associated with teaching rhymes to YLs, by deliberately associating text comprehension skills with maths skills available in the rhymes. Listening thus engaged the thematic as well as the numerical aspects present in the rhymes. It was observed that activities related to numbers and operations seemed to help the children develop an awareness of early number knowledge, and helped them to move from listening comprehension to number skills and basic mathematical operations.

The study findings are consistent with our initial belief that rhymes can be profitably used to enhance various English listening comprehension skills in YLs and, at the same time, develop their behavioural and conceptual knowledge of maths operations. Further research, both quantitative and qualitative, needs to be conducted to further the investigation on the co-developmental and potentially reciprocal aspects of listening and early numeracy skills. For now, however, the findings of this study are suggestive that developing listening comprehension skills in English in YLs can have more benefits than just the learning of English, and might also potentially help young children develop basic mathematical skills.

References

Anderson, NJ (2005) 'L2 strategy research', in Hinkel, E (ed) *Handbook of Research in Second Language Teaching and Learning* (pp. 757-772). NJ: Lawrence Earlbaum Associates.

Arnold, W (2005) Listening for young learners. *Teaching English*. Retrieved 10 Feb 2012 from www.teachingenglish.org.uk/think/articles/listening-young-learners.

Aunio, P and Niemivirta, M (2010) Predicting children's mathematical performance in grade one by early numeracy. *Learning and Individual Differences*, 20; 427-435.

Brown, D (2001) *Teaching by principles: An interactive approach to language pedagogy*. New York: Longman.

Davanellos, A (1999) Songs. *English Teaching Professional*, 13, 13-15. 1999.

Florit, E, Roch, M and Levorato, C (2011) Listening Text Comprehension of Explicit and Implicit Information in Pre-schoolers: The Role of Verbal and Inferential Skills. *Discourse Processes,* 48 (02), 119-138.

Florit, E, Roch, M, Altoè, G and Levorato, C (2009) Listening comprehension in pre-schoolers: The role of memory. *British Journal of Developmental Psychology*, 27, (4), 935-951.

Kenney, S (2005) Nursery rhymes: Foundations for learning. *General Music Today*, 19 (1), 28-31.

Kirova, A and Bhargava, A (2002) Learning to Guide Pre-school Children's Mathematical Understanding: A Teacher's Professional Growth. *Early Childhood Research and Practice,* 4:1.

Lee, SJ (2012) 'Philosophy in mathematics education (Ch 2)', in Lee, JK (ed) *An Introduction to Mathematics Education for College Students*, (pp 21-45), Seoul, Korea: Kyo-Woo.

Linse, C (2006) Using favorite songs and poems with young learners. *English Teaching Forum*, 44(2), 38-42.

Mackay, R (2013) *Teaching Rhymes and Poems to Young Learners*. Retrieved October, 2014 from https://www.youtube.com/watch?v=I3LWGFguPjE

Monroe, F (2010) *Nursery rhymes, songs and early language development*. Interior Health Authority. KBYU Eleven. Doa 1.08.2014 http://webcache.googleusercontent.com/search?q=cache:c-aPVJAdWjMJ:www.kbyutv.org/kidsandfamily/readytolearn/file.axd%3Ffile%3D2011%252F3%252F2%2BRhymers%2Bare%2BReaders.pdf+&cd=2&hl=en&ct=clnk&gl=in

Morley, J (2001) 'Aural comprehension instruction: Principles and practices', in Celce-Murcia, M (ed) *Teaching English as a second or foreign language*. Boston: Heinle and Heinle.

Muldoon, K, Lewis, C and Freeman, NH (2010) Putting Counting to Work: Pre-schoolers' Understanding of Cardinal Extension. *International Journal of Educational Research, 39,* 695-718.

O'Neill, DK, Pearce, MJ and Pick, J (2004) Pre-school children's narratives and performance on the Peabody Individualized Achievement Test – Revised: Evidence of a relation between early narrative and later mathematical ability. *First Language, 24,* 149-183.

Piller, B and Skillings, MJ (2005) English Language Teaching Strategies Used by Primary Teachers in One New Delhi, India School. *TESL-EJ,* December 2005, *9(3).* Retrieved October 2014 from www.tesl-ej.org/ej35/cf.pdf

Shin, JK (2011) *Teaching Listening.* Retrieved 10 Feb, 2012 from http://blackboard.umbc.edu

Vandergrift, L (2002) Developing metacognition in L2 listening comprehension. *The Canadian Modern Language Review,* 58, (pp 555-575).

Appendix

Extra rhymes are used from the following sources:

Brown, Ron. *What Number Comes First?* Retrieved from www.songsforteaching.com/math/kindergarten-firstgrade/whatnumbercomesfirst.php (March 2012)

Brown, Ron. *Sorting (colour, shape, size).* Retrieved from www.songsforteaching.com/math/kindergarten-firstgrade/sorting.php (March 2012)

CanTeach. Retrieved from: www.canteach.ca/elementary/songspoems82.html (March 2012)

3

Case studies in EFL contexts

3.1

Just singing, role playing and reading: a case study in education for bilingualism

Claudia Lucía Ordóñez, Universidad Nacional de Colombia, Bogotá, Colombia

Introduction

The school experience is one of the main contexts supporting the development of language after four or five years of age (e.g. Barriga-Villanueva, 2002; 2003). This is because school creates for the child the need to communicate with new people, in new situations, about new topics and within new discourse types. Furthermore, children begin reading and writing, one of the most important sources of linguistic expansion. But even though in Colombia socio-linguistic contexts are mostly monolingual in Spanish, with just a few areas of the country bilingual Spanish plus an indigenous or creole language, formal Colombian public education has been quite unsuccessful in supporting Spanish language development. According to the last published results of the state standardised language test taken at Grade 5 by a sample of 102,000 primary students throughout the country, 43 per cent of the fifth graders were at the minimum level of performance in reading and writing and 21 per cent at the insufficient level. Only 26 per cent showed a satisfactory level of performance (Instituto Colombiano para la Evaluación de la Educación, ICFES, 2009).

Given the fact that educational provision is not adequately developing L1, learning a foreign language from a very young age is probably not desirable in Colombia; it has no immediate relevance for learners and it takes precious instruction time from Spanish (Ordóñez, 2004; 2005; 2008). Nevertheless, early bilingualism in English is imposed in Colombia both by policy and common belief.

Bilingualism in English has been state policy since 2006 (Ministerio de Educación de Colombia, 2006). To achieve it, public and private schools are trying to implement the only practices known in Colombia to be effective for producing bilinguals: those of traditionally bilingual, semi-immersion elite schools. They include teaching the foreign language and using it as a medium of instruction from pre-school (five years of age) and using the foreign language during at least half of school time. Many monolingual public and private schools are, then, in the process of becoming bilingual in English.

In monolingual contexts such as most of Colombia, schools committing to the goal of Spanish–English bilingualism need to be careful not to overlook the need to support continued development in the first language as well as the second/foreign one. However, the Colombian reality is that concern for the lack of use of English in the immediate social context causes bilingual schools to focus on it at the expense of Spanish (the L1), the development of which they take for granted (De Mejía, Ordóñez and Fonseca, 2006). Schools also often ban Spanish from classes in English, convinced that this would prevent interference and promote greater proficiency in English. Formal arguments against the necessity to start early are not widely known (e.g. Marinova-Todd et al, 2000) in the educational context in Colombia and the evidence of very successful users of a second language acquired later in life is not readily visible.

Unfortunately, it is exceedingly difficult to argue against entire school administrations and communities of parents who share the popular belief that good development of a foreign language needs to begin in early childhood and take up a half or more of school time. It was definitely impossible to argue against the bilingual education policies in the specific school in the case I report in this chapter, where I was hired as a consultant to improve the English programme. The school is located in a medium-sized city far from big capitals, where English is even more foreign and less relevant for young children than in larger, more urban, cosmopolitan cities. Even though it had defined itself as bilingual for 15 years, it served a socio-economic elite, and it had teachers with good English who had acquired it from undergraduate teaching or foreign relations programmes, the students were not actually interested in using English effectively and their English was not considered good enough.

I was only able to convince the school that in order to improve English it was necessary to implement a genuinely bilingual curriculum, stimulating the development of Spanish and connecting it to the development of skills in English. The programme I created followed three rules: specific work on Spanish skills came before the same type of work done in English; reading and writing in English were not to be introduced before third grade, when reading and writing in Spanish were already advanced; and Spanish could be used in the English class as needed. The rest was built on trust in the ability of young children to learn anything they are interested and able to participate in.

I worked with both English and Spanish teachers and the co-ordinators of the two areas in designing a curriculum for the entire K-to-12 school, connecting developments in both languages. We used as its bases the concept of *authentic communicative performances,* originating in constructivist principles of human learning and communicative language analysis (Ordóñez, 2010). As authentic communicative activities for young children, we made the students participate in deciding what was going to be done to communicate and how it was going to be done, and mostly used singing songs, reading books and role play in both languages. From the beginning of the project it was important for the school and for me as a university researcher to be able to answer two main questions: Did working simultaneously with Spanish and English in making language learning more meaningful for students improve their motivation for learning English? And did it improve their level of English proficiency? We, then, complemented the intervention with a research study to answer these two questions. Here I only report on a specific case study of the youngest learners in the school.

The study

As a result of the intervention, both the Spanish and the English teachers were learning how to do things quite differently from the very traditional, formal way in which they used to conduct language activities; I, then, collected only qualitative data of what was happening in both language classes, in order to find evidence for the efficacy of the curriculum (Ordóñez, 2011; Guevara and Ordóñez, 2012; Ordóñez, 2012). The data for this case study comes from in-depth, semi-structured teacher interviews and class videos taken on four separate occasions during an academic year. They come from the Spanish class of a Kindergarten 1 group of 25 five-year-olds and the English classes of two Kindergarten 2 groups of 25 six to seven-year-olds each, and their three teachers. In what follows I compose related vignettes from parts of teacher interviews and parts of our class observations, which characterise the children learning both languages in authentic oral activities.

Vignette 1: Bilingual use and motivation

The Kinder 1 Spanish teacher acknowledges the benefits of working collaboratively with the English teacher: *"I never worked with the English teachers before … but now … I really understand the importance of working with them, because the children learn English on the basis of their first language … Now we do meet … we have improved in teamwork … We identify the language [to teach]; we plan each activity together … This has made it easier for the children to understand many more things in English."* She saw her students change their attitudes toward their language classes: *"The children [now] have the opportunity to learn what they want to, because we're working with their interests, not strictly with what we have determined we will teach."*

The Kinder 2 English teachers saw the same big changes in their students' attitude towards their class and in their learning. One of them stated that *"… the children are very motivated … going to the English class is something fun, something they like …. And because they like it … I am pushing them to speak in English and they're doing it … and so they like it even more…!"*

And she continued: *"Finishing this second [school] period, my children are speaking more than all my previous students at the end of the year … Today we had a festival at another school … all pre-school children; and all presented songs and other things. My children spoke … and their pronunciation, their fluency, everything was incredibly better … for me … this shows that what we're doing has really had good results."*

"… [Before]", says the other English teacher, *"there used to be a lot of desk work … Everything was focused on listening. You told the children something and they understood, but they couldn't express anything … Maybe in the third or fourth year … [they uttered] very simple things. But now I realise that children can … interact in a situation in English and handle it, obviously in appropriate terms for their age."* "Yes,"

says the first teacher, *"it has been a vast change from last year to the present ... because [before] there were many worksheets and no fun."*

As in the Spanish class, now in English *"... students are the ones who do the class themselves; they are the ones who speak, propose and demand. This motivates them; they participate totally in the activities, and most of the things they propose are carried out, because we are looking for what they like."*

Motivation in both language classes and the development of oral skills in English were, then, results that teachers could see from early on in the implementation of the new teaching programme. These results were attributed to the fact that the Spanish and English classes were connected and that the children were engaged in communication activities that they participated in choosing from their own interests.

Vignette 2: Role play and the use of Spanish

But what was it that students did in Spanish and English? Both in Kinder 1 Spanish and Kinder 2 English the children worked on the topic of people's professions, for example. The Spanish teacher describes how *"... we have talked about the people who work at the school in 'What's my school like?' We use topics they want to know about."* Here is a Spanish class on professions: *"... I gave them the opportunity to choose what they wanted to be when they grew up ... but not a [common] profession, because we had already done that ... I gave them the example of magicians ... So who are dancers? ... singers?... guitarists?... scientists? The children dressed up and presented their songs, their magic tricks, their scientific experiments ..."*

After this, professions also became wonderful sources of language production in role play in Kinder 2 English. *"We have worked with professions [all the time]. [The children] play with them ... The first time [we did it,] we talked about their parents' professions [in Spanish and then in English] ... They brought clothing to represent them ..."* Teachers and children worked, for example on being doctors: *"... they already knew what their experiences at the doctor's had been, [so they asked us how to say] 'The doctor gives me injections; sometimes I only go for a check up'... They learned all the vocabulary, [talked in Spanish and then English and role played] how to tend to the patient; how to diagnose him; something simple, at their level ... and the kids enjoyed it a lot,"* explained one of the English teachers.

Watching the children in their English class, we described the activity as follows: *"The students are playing doctors ... They play different roles: doctors, receptionists, nurses, and patients. They are divided into groups and use toys to simulate the situation of somebody going to the doctor. They say things like 'How can I help you?' 'I need a doctor!' 'What's your name?' 'What's your telephone number' 'What's your profession?' 'My baby is ill!' 'Let me see his/her stomach, eyes, etc.'"*

Playing chefs was another role play. *"An international chef came to the school, so the kids were super motivated ... She cooked and showed a video of her TV show [in Spanish], so we decided to take advantage of that ..."* said one of the English teachers. *"We saw cooking shows, brought recipe books, talked about cooking ware, food ... recipes and steps ... very simple ones like cutting, putting things in the oven ..."*

The class was described like this in our observations: *"The students are presenting recipes ... They're in groups of three ... One first presents their group and the recipe they're going to prepare ... Another student presents the ingredients and kitchenware to be used, and the last student prepares the recipe ... each student dressed according to their role, and they took to class the ingredients and materials ..."* And then we saw the children:

"St1: This is a good way to start the morning. Now is the opportunity for a wonderful chef to cook something for us...

St2: Good morning, my name is XXX. I am six years old. My recipe is 'Mickey Mouse eggs.' The ingredients are ketchup, salt, and four eggs. The materials are a plate, a knife, and a spoon. Now, the chef.

St3: Good morning, my name is XXX. I am six years old. [For] 'Mickey Mouse eggs' ... step number one, put the eggs in water; step number two, cut the eggs in small pieces; step number three, decorate the Mickey Mouse eggs with the ketchup; step number four, eat the Mickey Mouse eggs and enjoy them ..."

Role play was a great way to the children's hearts. Allowing them to work on it in Spanish first helped a lot in really using what they wanted to do, and then changing to English.

Vignette 3: Book reading as a surprise
Oddly, the Spanish teacher had never worked much with books, but the connected curriculum asked her to do so, in order for books to be later introduced to the children in English. She discovered a mine of interest in the children: *"I'm amazed! ... The children are hungry for reading this year! They have asked for stories all the time ... When we were reading about dinosaurs, all the books were gone [from the library] in a week; they asked for them both in Spanish and English. They 'read' the pictures, and they do it as if they are really reading. They are fascinated by books, and when we use computers, they say 'Oh, yeah, I already know that; I looked it up [in a book] at home. They are motivated to continue looking for information in other sources, not only at school but also in books, on the TV and asking their parents ... The motivation is the best ... and ... they have increased their vocabulary..."*. Our observations showed classes such as the following one: "In this class the teacher reads a story and, as she reads, she asks the students to repeat the information in it. Sometimes she lets the students suggest what's going to happen according to the illustrations in the book."

In English the same pleasure in reading was apparent: *"... they always ask for 'story time' ... and I always do it when they ask. At the beginning I didn't consider it a class activity but break time, but now we work 'story time' in class too"*. In a class observation *"... the teacher was reading a big book and working with the meaning of new words in the story by connecting the pictures, words in the book, and actions by the children"*:

"T: Today we are going to have storytelling time, OK? Storytelling! Don't you remember the books we are reading?

Sts: Ah, yes!

T: (Showing the book Quick as a Cricket, by Audrey Wood) Quick is fast, fast. It's a cricket; do you know what a cricket is?

Sts: Yes. Un saltamontes? [A cricket in Spanish]

T: Yes! It's fast, fast [mimics]. Fast is the same as quick, everybody. Quick, quick, quick. Fast, fast, fast [the teacher mimics and the students imitate].

T: OK … This is a boy. What do you see here? The boy is saying: 'I am as fast as a cricket' … This is a cricket. Everybody fast, fast, fast or quick; it's the same [the teacher mimics and the students imitate].

T: [Reading] 'I am as slow as a snail.' Slow, slow, slow like a snail [mimics] …"

Surprisingly, work with books was not a common class activity at this school. Classes were more formal and focused on learning specific material. Book reading was discovered by teachers and students as an authentic language activity, and it became the source of much learning both in Spanish and English.

Vignette 4: Songs and language games as sources of language
The Spanish teacher used a lot more music and children's games than before and was enthusiastic about the results: *"[They love] all riddles, playground songs, games, songs … They learn the songs, identify the main characters, describe them…"*. In a Spanish class based on a song *"the students are singing children's songs [they have learned], identifying them from pictures the teacher draws on the board. They sing, and then she asks information about the song, writing words from the song on the board to teach reading and writing."*

And in English, *"… the children love singing … At the beginning they took a longer time learning a song, and now I plan a song for 90 minutes, and before the first 30 minutes they already know it. We choose songs for which they already have a lot of previous knowledge, so it's easier for them [to learn them] and they acquire a lot more vocabulary."* In our class observations, songs the children already knew were often the beginning warm-up activities and new songs were great sources of new language: *"The students are singing songs while they mimic what they are singing. One of the songs contains 'slow' and 'fast.' The children move their hands according to the song."*

Singing songs and playing language games such as riddles and tongue twisters are very authentic language activities for children. Before the intervention was put into practice, they were never real learning material in Spanish or English, but they quickly became so. The children enjoyed them immensely and learned a lot in both languages from them.

Conclusion

The vignettes presented in this chapter reveal the activities the teachers designed, the way they connected Spanish and English, and the learning and motivation both the teachers and us, the researchers, observed in the young students. Changes were impressive for the teachers, as they expressed, for example, in relation to oral production, which was practically non-existent at these levels before. The changes came mostly from the fact that Spanish, prohibited in English classes before, was now being used freely for introducing language. Furthermore, the bilingual curriculum ensured that Spanish was given the importance it deserves; and, as the same strategies for making language activities authentic were used in both languages, the children's attitudes toward all their language classes improved and their learning was stimulated.

Also, the children's interests were taken into account when both Spanish and English teachers worked collaboratively in planning their classes and how to connect them. The children were even able to participate in deciding what role play they wanted to engage in and what they wanted to say, choosing the books they wanted to read and the songs they wanted to sing. The power of the first language and the empowerment of the students were key to the success depicted in these vignettes. They demonstrate that children can learn whatever they are interested and can participate in, even when they are learning a language which is not very relevant for them and is one they cannot really use outside of school. Maybe the future will show them that it may be good to be bilingual.

References

Barriga-Villanueva, R (2002) *Estudios sobre habla infantil en los años escolares: "... Un solecito calientote"*. Mexico: El Colegio de Mexico.

Barriga-Villanueva, R (2003) 'Construyendo realidades: El lenguaje infantil de los años escolares', in Matute, E and Leal, F (eds) *Introducción al Estudio del Español desde una perspectiva multidisciplinaria*. Guadalajara: Universidad de Guadalajara.

De Mejía, AM, Ordóñez, CL and Fonseca, L (2006) *Estudio investigativo sobre el estado actual de la educación bilingüe (inglés-español) en Colombia*. Available online at: www.colombiaaprende.edu.co/html/productos/1685/articles-266111_archivo_1.pdf

Guevara, DC and Ordóñez, CL (2012) Teaching English to very young learners through authentic communicative performances. *Colombian Applied Linguistics Journal* 14(2): 9-27.

Instituto Colombiano para la Evaluación de la Educación ICFES. Saber 5° y 9° 2009 – Resultados Nacionales Resumen Ejecutivo. Available online at: https://portal.icfes.s3.amazonaws.com/datos/Informe%20nacional%20de%20resultados%20de%20SABER%205o%20y%209o%202009%20Resumen%20Ejecutivo.pdf

Marinova-Todd, S, Marshall, B and Snow, C (2000) Three misconceptions about age and second language learning. *TESOL Quarterly* 1: 9-34.

Ministerio de Educación de Colombia (2006) *Formar en Lenguas Extranjeras: Inglés ¡el reto! Estándares Básicos de Competencias en Lenguas Extranjeras: Inglés.* Bogotá DC: Imprenta Nacional.

Ordóñez, CL (2004) EFL and Native Spanish in Elite Bilingual Schools in Colombia: A First Look at Bilingual Adolescent Frog Stories. *International Journal of Bilingual Education and Bilingualism, Special Issue: Bilingual Education in South America* 7(5): 449-474.

Ordóñez, CL (2005) 'Oral Bilingual Proficiency of Colombian Adolescents in an Elite Bilingual School', in Cohen, J, McAllister, K, Rolstad K and MacSwan, J (eds) *ISB4: Proceedings of the Fourth International Symposium on Bilingualism.* Somerville, MA: Cascadilla Press, 1765-1783.

Ordóñez, CL (2008) Education for Bilingualism in International Languages in a Monolingual Socio-Linguistic Context. *Lenguaje* 36 (2): 353-384.

Ordóñez, CL (2010) 'Desempeño auténtico en educación', in Ordóñez, CL and Castaño, C, *Pedagogía y didáctica: Texto del docente.* Quito: Ministerio de Educación de Ecuador, 151-160.

Ordóñez, CL (2011) Education for Bilingualism: Connecting Spanish and English from the Curriculum, into the Classroom, and Beyond. *PROFILE* 13(2): 147-161.

Ordóñez, CL (2012) Educación para el bilingüismo y aprendizaje de maestros: comprensión del desempeño auténtico en la acción de cambiar prácticas pedagógicas. *FOLIOS* Segunda época (36): 3-22.

3.2

Pre-school children's production of sibilant phonemes in English: developing phonemic awareness through multi-sensory teaching

Alberto Navarro Martinez, Yvette Coyle and Julio Roca de Larios, University of Murcia, Spain

Introduction

English has been part of the pre-school curriculum in Spain since 2004 when it was first introduced in schools to children at the age of five. Since then, the collective interest in early language learning by parents and educational authorities has led to English being extended to three- and four-year-old children, and it is now taught in state and private schools throughout the country. Current recommendations in the statutory pre-school curriculum suggest that teachers should promote positive attitudes to language learning and develop children's oral skills. Although no explicit reference is made to the teaching of phonics, in recent years multi-sensory methods such as Jolly Phonics (Lloyd and Wernham, 1994), which combine auditory, visual and kinaesthetic modalities, have become increasingly popular in young learner classrooms.

Yet despite the abundance of literature relating to children's phonemic awareness in their first language (L1), understood as their ability to segment and blend phonemes into words, with success in learning to read (Hulme et al, 2012; McGeown and Medford, 2014), very little is known to date about the potential advantages of phonics teaching with pre-school learners of English as a second language (L2). The case study we present in this chapter attempts to address this gap by exploring the effects of explicit instruction on Spanish children's pronunciation of sibilant phonemes in English. By doing so, we hope to provide some tentative support for the teaching of simple phonics in the pre-school classroom.

Traditionally, it is assumed that children are better at learning languages than older L2 learners. The alleged advantage of younger learners for acquiring native-like accents in an L2 was originally attributed to the existence of a Critical Period for language learning at around the age of six, after which it was considered impossible for older language learners to fully master the L2 phonological system (Lenneberg, 1967). However, the findings of more recent studies carried out in formal (rather than naturalistic) learning contexts with adults (Bongaerts et al, 1997), as well as with children and adolescents (Fullana, 2006; García-Lecumberri and Gallardo, 2003), have provided some evidence that older learners often outperform their younger counterparts in the perception and production of L2 vowels and consonants. These results are sustained by alternative theories of phonological development such as the Speech Learning Model (Flege, 1995) or the Native Language Magnet (Kuhl, 1993), which share the premise that phonological learning ability is strongly influenced by the learner's L1. In this sense, the phonetic categories of the L1, which are thought to be fully formed between the ages of five and seven (Flege, op cit), act as 'magnets' that attract the different or non-existent categories of the L2 so that, initially at least, learners may have difficulty in perceiving L2 phonemes. In this sense, raising children's phonemic awareness through explicit phonics teaching is held to be important in helping them to overcome this initial 'deafness' to new or dissimilar L2 sounds (Gayoso et al, 1999). This rationale underlies the study we describe below.

The study

The aim of this small piece of research was to analyse the pronunciation of sibilant phonemes by two groups of young learners in a school in south east Spain. We were interested in testing the children's ability to produce the sounds /s/, /z/, /ʃ/, /tʃ/ and /dʒ/ from the English phonemic system, since these are often a source of difficulty for learners whose mother tongue is Spanish. Specifically, we wanted to find out whether teaching English sibilant phonemes to children using a multi-sensory methodology could influence both their acquisition of these sounds and their motivation during the teaching sessions. In particular, we were curious as to the role of actions in helping the children learn, since these are a key feature of phonics teaching methods such as Jolly Phonics (Lloyd and Wernham, op cit) or Letterland (Carlisle and Wendon, 1995).

It is generally assumed that the combination of actions and sounds can help children develop multi-sensory clues for recognising and reproducing phonemes. This idea is theoretically grounded in the understanding that gestures (actions) and speech are two components of a single integrated system that work together to support and enhance the comprehension and production of language (Kelly et al, 2010). It is also believed that words learnt simultaneously with meaningful gestures are imprinted more deeply in memory (Kelly et al, 2009) and that this may be due to neural connections in the brain which link the areas responsible for language and gesture (Nishitani et al, 2005). With younger learners, empirical evidence in support of the positive effects of gestures on learning has been found for the comprehension of mathematical concepts by Spanish learners of English (Church et al, 2004) and for EFL vocabulary acquisition by five-year-old French-speaking children (Tellier, 2008). Whether these results might also extend to the pronunciation of specific English sounds was an area we hoped to shed light on.

Participants

A total of 32 children (20 boys and 12 girls) aged between four and five years from two intact classes in an infant school in a small rural town participated in the study. One class was assigned randomly as the experimental group (EG) and the other as the control group (CG), with 16 children in each. In the control group, there were children of diverse nationalities and linguistic backgrounds including Algerian, Ecuadorian, Lithuanian, Russian and Malian. In the experimental group, there was one child from Morocco. The rest of the pupils in both groups were Spanish native speakers. The children were in their second year of learning English at school, and so had only very basic, mostly receptive, knowledge of the language. English was taught in twice-weekly half-hour sessions. In their classes, the children generally carried out routines in English: practising the date and the weather every day, learning and reviewing key vocabulary with flashcards and action games, as well as using worksheets for colouring, matching and drawing activities. Emphasis was placed on the development of oral skills and positive attitudes towards language learning.

Teaching methodology

The study followed a pre-test, post-test experimental design with an instructional intervention carried out over a period of three weeks. Fifteen words were selected as language input (see Table 1) for a number of reasons. Firstly, the chosen words were new for the learners and could be easily represented by a visual image; secondly, the sibilant phonemes were mostly located in initial position, thus increasing their saliency; and finally, since the words were either monosyllabic or bisyllabic, longer words that could have been more difficult for the children to remember were avoided.

Table 1: Temporal distribution of the study

Week	Session	Sibilant	Words taught
1	Pre-test		
2	1	/s/ /z/	Sun, bus, socks; Sneeze, zero, zebra
	2	/ʃ/ /tʃ/ /dʒ/	Ship, shoe, shell Chocolate, sandwich, chicken Jump, soldier, jacket
3	3 and 4	Practise of all the phonemes	
4	5 and 6		
5	Post-test		

The children's English teacher, who was also one of the researchers, carried out the teaching sessions in both groups. A total of six 30-minute sessions, two per week, were carried out in each class (see Table 1) preceded and followed by productive pronunciation tests.

The methodology followed in both classes was oral and participative. In each session, the teacher introduced the corresponding sounds by showing pictures of the words containing the target phoneme. The children were then encouraged to practise each phoneme through a variety of whole-class and individual repetition drills and vocabulary recognition games, so that they could learn to discriminate each sound, notice differences between them and try to produce the sound accurately. The teacher's ongoing feedback was crucial in drawing the children's attention to the correct pronunciation of each phoneme. The principal difference between the groups was the use of actions in the experimental group by both the teacher and the children when producing the sibilant sounds (see Table 2). In the experimental class, the children were encouraged to learn each gesture and to use it when attempting to reproduce the corresponding phoneme. The control group children engaged in the same games and activities but were taught the sounds without actions.

Table 2: Sibilant phonemes and their associated actions

Sound	Actions taken from Jolly Phonics (jollylearning.co.uk)
/s/	Moving your arm and hand like a snake
/z/	Moving your hand and fingers imitating the flight of a bee
/ʃ/	Placing your index finger on your lips as when asking for silence
/tʃ/	Moving both arms in circles imitating train wheels
/dʒ/	Wobbling your whole body like jelly on a plate

Data collection and analysis

Before and after the teaching sessions, the children from both classes were tested to determine whether they could accurately produce the target phonemes. The tests consisted of researcher-made colourful pictures of the 15 words, three for each sound. The children were initially asked to state the words in Spanish to check that they were already familiar with them conceptually and then requested to name the word in English, which they were mostly unable to do. In the post-test, the children were required to say the words in English only. They repeated each word twice in order to ensure the researcher had heard and registered the sounds consistently. The pre- and post-tests were carried out individually in a quiet room to avoid any environmental noise that could have interfered with the researcher's perception of the children's oral production. Video recordings were also made of the tests to enable the researcher to score each child's performance as accurately as possible through repeated listening. The test results were scored by tallying the number of phonemes pronounced accurately by each child at both time periods. This process was meticulously carried out by the first researcher and any specific doubts were consulted in collaboration with the other two members of the research team. Given the small number of participants and non-normal distribution of the data, we computed the test scores using non-parametric statistics. A Mann Whitney test was run to check for differences between the groups and a Wilcoxon signed-rank checked for within-group differences.

In addition, the teaching sessions were video-recorded and written notes taken by the researcher were collected to allow us to analyse the degree of attention and motivation shown by each of the young learners in both classrooms. Two of the six sessions, the initial and final sessions in each group, were observed and coded by the researchers and any disagreements resolved by discussion. This was necessary as several parameters were observed simultaneously for each child. A scale scored from 0 to 5 was applied to the following categories: 'Looked at the teacher'; 'Listened attentively'; 'Imitated sounds'; 'Imitated facial movements'; and 'Participated in games'. It was assumed that by observing the extent to which the children engaged in the classroom activities, we could determine their degree of interest and motivation towards the phonics classes. This procedure is similar to Huang's (2011) study of young Taiwanese EFL learners' motivation towards content-based instruction, in which observable behaviours such as paying attention to the teacher or actively taking part in classroom tasks were taken as indicators of the children's motivation. In our study, each learner was rated individually and the sum of their individual scores tallied to give an average for all five criteria. This enabled us to establish comparisons between groups. Once again, a Mann Whitney test was performed on the data to check for significant differences between groups.

Results

As shown in Table 3, both groups of children were found to have improved their performance of sibilant phonemes after instruction. The mean score for the experimental group in the pre-test was descriptively slightly higher than that of the control group (1.13 and 0.75) and descriptively slightly lower in the post-test (5.56 and 5.94). These differences were not statistically significant.

Table 3: Mean scores for the production of sibilants before and after teaching

	Pre-test		Post-test		Gain Scores	
	Mean	SD	Mean	SD	Mean	SD
Experimental Group	1.13	1.360	5.56	3.224	4.43	1.864
Control Group	0.75	1.065	5.94	2.909	5.19	1.844

In spite of this lack of differences across groups, a closer look at the results indicated that, within each group, the learners were found to have significantly improved their production of the target phonemes (see Figure 1). A comparison of the mean ranks of the children's pronunciation scores immediately before and after instruction revealed significant differences both within the experimental group (Z=3.42; p <.001) and within the control group (Z=3.41; p <.001). Prior to the teaching sessions, the young learners in both groups produced on average between one to five sounds correctly (out of 15), although the most frequent scores were 0 and one. After the six teaching sessions at Time 2 (T2), all the children (with one exception from each group) were found to pronounce correctly an average of five sibilants. The phonemes most easily produced by the children were /s/ and /tʃ/, especially when they were in word-initial position. Both of these phonemes have corresponding L1 sounds in Spanish. On the contrary, those sounds which have no corresponding phoneme in the L1, that is /z /, /dʒ / and /ʃ/, were the most difficult for the children to master regardless of their position within the word.

A breakdown of the scores for individual learners revealed that three of the control group children (pupils 21, 26 and 30) had obtained excellent results in the post-test, producing from ten to 14 sounds correctly, while only one child from the experimental group (pupil 12) had managed to achieve a similarly high score (n=14). These individual results in the CG are likely to have contributed to this group's improved post-test score. In this respect, it is worth pointing out that two of the three high performers from the CG were immigrant children of Russian and Lithuanian origin for whom Spanish was a second and English a third language. This suggests that social and contextual factors may be an important influence on children's phonemic awareness, since it is possible that exposure to several languages from an early age may have enhanced the degree of receptiveness shown by these learners towards the sounds of new languages.

Taken together, these results suggest that specific instruction and repeated practice with the target sounds enabled the children in both groups to improve their performance of some of the sibilant phonemes over time. However, the results also raise some doubts regarding the influence of actions in helping to improve pronunciation, since the children who were specifically taught to perform an action when recalling and producing the phonemes in practice did no better than the control group children. This indicates a positive effect for pronunciation instruction but not for the use of actions.

Figure 1 : Change in pronunciation of sibilant phonemes over time

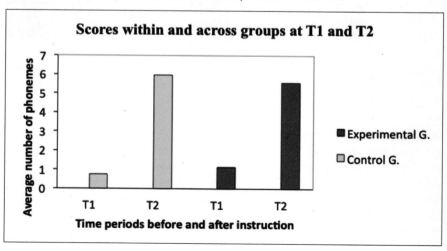

Regarding the children's behaviour while on task, the analysis of the classroom observation data in both groups gave us some indication of the degree of attention and motivation shown by the learners during the pronunciation teaching sessions (see Figure 2). Although there were differences between individual learners within each group, as a whole, the experimental group children were found to have scored higher on all five criteria than the children in the control group, particularly on looking at and listening to the teacher, actively repeating sounds and participating in the pronunciation games. A Mann Whitney test (z=2.33; p=.01) indicated that the overall scores obtained by the EG (M=3.58; SD=.09) were significantly better than those of the CG (M=2.87; SD=.68).

Figure 2 : Children's motivational behaviour during pronunciation instruction

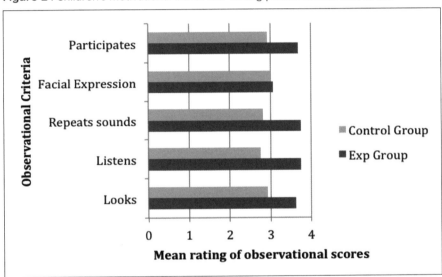

Discussion

The accurate identification and pronunciation of specific sounds is an essential component of phonemic awareness. When children are able to segment a word into its onset and rime, as in chi-cken, or discriminate the first sound in the word, as in / tʃ/, they are not only enhancing their listening skills, but also improving their ability to understand the sound-letter correspondences that are essential for reading and writing in the second language (Nicholson and Ng, 2004). The sounds of the L2, however, are not immediately transparent and children will always be more interested in the meaning of words rather than in their component parts (Durgunoglu et al, 1993). For this reason, directing learners' attention to pronunciation in the context of communicative activities would seem to be both theoretically and methodologically justified.

Although our study is only a small-scale exploratory piece of research, the results do provide tentative support for the idea that young learners can improve their pronunciation of English sibilant phonemes after only limited exposure to L2 input.

After three weeks, almost half of the children in both groups could pronounce correctly between one and five words (50 per cent in EG and 38 per cent in CG) while the remaining half were able to produce between six and nine of the words (44 per cent in EG and 44 per cent in the CG). A further four children, one from the EG (six per cent) and three from the CG (18 per cent) accurately produced between ten and 14 of the 15 sibilant sounds. Only one child from each class failed to make any improvement after instruction.

The children's varying ability to produce sibilant sounds coincides with the findings of earlier research with adult learners, which has highlighted the constraints of the phonological system of the learner's L1 on the acquisition of the L2 sound system (Suter, 1975; Avery and Ehrlich, 1992). For Suter (op cit), problems can arise when particular sounds are language specific. Thus, if learners do not possess specific phonemes in their own repertoire, they are likely to encounter increased difficulty in the production of those sounds in their second language. In a study carried out with young L1 Spanish speakers of English, You, Alwan, Kazemzade and Narayan (2005) found that their five-to-seven-year-old participants tended to mispronounce the L2 sibilants /dʒ/ and /z/, neither of which have an L1 equivalent. Similar errors were identified in our research for the phonemes /z/, /dʒ/ and /ʃ/. The children tended to produce /s/ instead of /z/ as in *sebra*; /s/ instead of /ʃ/ as in *sip*, and /tʃ/ instead of /dʒ/ as in *tʃaket*. Curiously, these errors were detected to a lesser extent in the children whose mother tongue was Malian, Russian, Arabic and Lithuanian. In comparison to the Spanish learners, the immigrant children's first language background, and their additional experience as language learners, may have heightened their awareness of English sibilant sounds.

The increased presence of children of nationalities other than Spanish in the CG (eight) in comparison with the EG (one) is a factor that was not taken into consideration on initiating the study. Given the school setting and the exploratory nature of the research, we decided to maintain the children's intact class groups. In hindsight, while this might have contributed to the ecological validity of the study, it has also highlighted the need for further research, which can explicitly account for the potential impact of linguistic diversity and previous language learning experience on children's pronunciation of specific L2 sounds.

Contrary to our initial expectations, the use of actions by the teacher and the EG children was not a determining factor for their successful production of the target phonemes. Rather, the repeated and varied oral practice of the sounds in the context of ludic activities and games, together with the teacher's input and feedback, were confirmed as relevant instructional techniques. This finding would appear to contradict theory and research that has advocated the usefulness of gestural support for language learning. A number of explanations can be suggested. Firstly, it is possible that the children were simply cognitively unable to establish successful associations between the various sources of multi-sensory input (visual, auditory and kinaesthetic) they were exposed to. Secondly, the mismatch between the actions (e.g. move your hands and fingers to fly like a bee) and the imagery (zero, zebra, sneeze) may have confused the children and reduced the positive impact of the non-verbal support on their encoding of the L2 sounds.

This finding is in line with research carried out by Kelly et al. (op cit) who found that the use of gestures helped English-speaking adults to learn Japanese words only when they conveyed meaningful information. Incongruent or meaningless hand movements were found to be less effective in facilitating word retention than the learners' repetition of the target words. Thirdly, the fun element involved in actively performing actions could actually have been a distraction from the language itself. In a study on lexical acquisition in young EFL learners, Coyle and Gómez Gracia (2014) found that copying the teacher's actions and onomatopoeias while singing a song seemed to divert the children's attention away from the target vocabulary rather than encouraging them to focus on it.

It would appear, then, that the effective use of kinaesthetic activities in increasing phonemic sensitivity in younger learners is not as straightforward as it may seem. From the results of the current study, it is evident that if actions are to act as a support for children's perception of specific L2 phonemes, they need to be unambiguously and explicitly linked to the sounds and letters they represent. This sound-letter connection is the defining feature of synthetic phonics methods such as Jolly Phonics, which were originally conceived to teach literacy to child native speakers of English. The multi-sensory element of synthetic phonics methods might, therefore, be more profitably employed for initiating young foreign language learners into sound and letter discrimination simultaneously, rather than focusing exclusively on pronunciation.

Regarding the children's attention and attitude during the phonics sessions, performing actions may be important in increasing children's motivation while on task, since the EG children displayed appropriate classroom behaviours such as listening to and looking at the teacher and actively participated in pronunciation games to a greater extent than the CG children. It would appear, then, that children whose attention is maintained with visual, auditory and kinaesthetic stimuli may become more emotionally engaged with learning. As a result, teachers might take full advantage of multi-sensory lessons to promote enthusiasm for language learning and cater for children with different learning styles and intelligences (Gardner, 1983). The promotion of positive attitudes towards phonics may, in the long term, lead to encouraging results. This is another area for future research to investigate.

Conclusion

The present case study examined the production of five sibilant phonemes by young learners of English and provides some evidence that pronunciation teaching can be useful for pre-school learners. At present, phonic teaching is not included as part of the pre-school curriculum in Spain, yet young learners have limited contact time with English per week, little or no access to English outside the classroom and use their mother tongue with their families. We suggest, therefore, that phonemic training should become an integral part of English teaching programmes from the early stages of foreign language learning. This evidently raises a number of further issues for policy makers and educational authorities to consider, including the need for linguistically competent teachers, and the development of child-friendly teaching materials and methodologies, together with effective assessment techniques, all of which would surely contribute to enriching English language learning in the early years.

References

Avery, P and Ehrlich, S (1992) *Teaching American English Pronunciation*. Oxford: Oxford University Press.

Bongaerts, T, Van Summeren, C, Planken, B and Schils, E (1997) Age and ultimate attainment in the pronunciation of a foreign language. *Studies in Second Language Acquisition*, 19/4: 447-465.

Carlisle, R and Wendon, L (1995) *Letterland ABC*. Letterland Direct.

Church RB, Ayman-Nolley, S and Mahootian, S (2004) The effects of gestural instruction on bilingual children. *International Journal of Bilingual Education and Bilingualism* 7/4: 303–319.

Coyle, Y and Gómez Gracia, R (2014) Using songs to enhance L2 vocabulary acquisition in pre-school children. *ELT Journal* 68/3: 276-285.

Durgunoglu, AY, Nagy, W and Hancin-Bhatt, BJ (1993) Cross-language transfer of phonological awareness. *Journal of Educational Psychology* 85/3: 453-465.

Flege, JE (1995) 'Second language speech learning: Theory, findings, and problems', in Strange, W (ed) *Speech perception and linguistic experience: Issues in cross-language research*. Timonium MD: York Press, 229-273.

Fullana, N (2006) 'The development of English (FL) perception and production skills: Starting age and exposure effects', in Muñoz, C (ed) *Age and the rate of foreign language learning*. Clevedon: Multilingual Matters, 41-64.

García-Lecumberri, ML and Gallardo, F (2003) 'English FL sounds in school learners of different ages', in García Mayo, MP and García-Lecumberri, ML (eds) *Age and the acquisition of English as a foreign language*. Clevedon: Multilingual Matters, 115-135.

Gardner, H (1983) *Frames of mind: The theory of multiple intelligences*. NY: Basics.

Gayoso, E, Blanco, M and Carrillo, M (1999) *Primary school learning of EFL through phono-metaphonological training*. Paper presented at the International Conference on Phonetics Teaching and Learning. University College London.

Huang, KM (2011) Motivating lessons: A classroom-oriented investigation of the effects of content-based instruction on EFL learners' motivated behaviours and classroom verbal interaction. *System* 39/2: 186-201.

Hulme, C, Bowyer-Crane, C, Carroll, JM, Duff, FJ and Snowling, MJ (2012) The causal role of phoneme awareness and letter-sound knowledge in learning to read combining intervention studies with mediation analyses. *Psychological Science* 23/6: 572-577.

Kelly, SD, McDevitt, T and Esch, M (2009) Brief training with co-speech gesture lends a hand to word learning in a foreign language. *Language and Cognitive Processes* 24/2: 313-334.

Kelly, SD, Özyürek, A and Maris, E (2010) Two Sides of the Same Coin: Speech and Gesture Mutually Interact to Enhance Comprehension. *Psychological Science* 21/2: 260-267.

Kuhl, PK (1993) Early linguistic experience and phonetic perception: Implications for theories of developmental speech perception. *Journal of Phonetics* 21: 125-139.

Lenneberg, E (1967) *Biological Foundations of Language*. New York: Wiley.

Lloyd, S and Wernham, S (1994) *The Phonics Handbook*. Essex: UK Jolly Learning Ltd.

McGeown, SP and Medford, E (2014) Using method of instruction to predict the skills supporting initial reading development: Insight from a synthetic phonics approach. *Reading and Writing: An Interdisciplinary Journal* 27: 591-608.

Nicholson, TW and Ng GL (2004) 'The case for teaching phonemic awareness and simple phonics to pre-schoolers', in Joshi RM and Aaron PG (eds) *Handbook of orthography and literacy*. Mahwah. NJ: Lawrence Erlbaum Associates.

Nishitani, N, Schürmann, M, Amunts, K and Hari, R (2005) Broca's region: from action to language. *Physiology* 20/1: 60-69.

Suter, RW (1975) Predictors of Pronunciation Accuracy in Second Language Learning. *Language Learning* 26/2: 233-253.

Tellier, M (2008) The effect of gestures on second language memorisation by young children. *Gesture* 8/2: 219-235.

You, H, Alwan, A, Kazemzade, A and Narayan, S (2005) Pronunciation variations of Spanish-accented English spoken by young children. *Proceedings of Interspeech*: 749-752.

3.3

Facilitating the learning of English through collaborative practice

Sandie Mourão, Independent Scholar, Portugal,
Penelope Robinson, University of Leeds, UK

This chapter describes collaborative practice in a school in central Portugal where school policy enables all children from age four to participate in English lessons. It begins with a brief overview of pre-primary education in Portugal, and then outlines the benefits of collaborative practices. It describes the school, the children and their teachers, and details an approach to facilitating the learning of English through play activities. Discussion highlights the roles of the two collaborating teachers and the importance of integrating English learning areas (ELAs), enabling child-initiated play and a positive home–school link.

Introduction

Pre-primary education in Portugal is considered to be an important foundation for successful schooling and the first step in the process of lifelong learning. Provision is made for children between the ages of three years and the school starting age of five or six years, but as attendance is not compulsory there is no official curriculum to support teaching in this sector. There are, however, government-produced guidelines providing principles for pre-primary educators (Ministério da Educação, 1997). These guidelines are influenced by socio-constructive approaches and favour active, child-led learning. As a result, a typical pre-primary classroom in Portugal is open plan and divided into different learning areas or activity centres, which aim to provide opportunities for children to benefit from teacher-initiated group work as well as have access to child-initiated 'potentially instructive play activities' (Siraj-Blatchford et al., 2002: 43). Effective educators create opportunities for children to learn by doing, in the belief that, by interacting with their environment, children develop as autonomous and responsible learners (Ministério da Educação, 1997; Oliveira-Formosinho, 2013).

There is no official early language learning strategy for pre-primary education in Portugal. According to a European Union publication (European Union, 2011, July) that summarised country contexts, the majority of state-run schools in Portugal do not provide language-learning opportunities, though some may offer extra-curricular language-learning activities. Private schools are said to offer either additional or optional foreign language lessons at an extra cost to parents. English is noted to be the most popular foreign language taught and teachers are recruited from outside the school to give the lessons. To note, no nationwide survey has been carried out to confirm this information. There is no information in the European documentation related to frequency of lessons, but anecdotal evidence points to lessons taking place once or twice a week for short periods of time (e.g. 30 to 45 minutes).

The information above indicates that foreign language learning in Portugal is often disassociated from other learning processes and is planned with a view to developing discrete language skills without consideration of how languages might contribute more widely to other aspects of classroom learning and development of the whole child. This practice does not seem to recognise the importance of providing a balance between teacher-initiated activities and child-initiated play, which is recommended practice in pre-primary education (European Commission, October 2014).

Collaborative practices

When the foreign language is given by a teacher who is a language specialist, and timetabled as an extra-curricular lesson at the end of the day, once the pre-primary educator has finished her schedule and is likely to be absent, it is doubtful that any connection is made between the children's learning contexts – that of their daily classroom learning and the foreign language. Fröhlich-Ward (1979) describes the attitude of a pre-primary educator affecting the success or failure of an early years language-learning project; however, the issue of collaboration between specialist and generalist teachers is a contentious subject in practice and in the main ignored in the research literature (Martin-Beltran and Peercy, 2014). Nonetheless, it is recognised that when teachers do have shared goals and both want to ensure quality teaching and learning, it has a positive effect on learning outcomes (Fullan, 2007). Sawyer and Rimm-Kaufman (2007: 213) describe collaboration as promoting an 'ethic of caring', and in the world of small children this seems particularly appropriate. Collaboration is essential in creating appropriate teaching/learning conditions for both learners and their teachers, yet in Portugal the way in which early language learning projects tend to be organised does not facilitate this kind of practice.

The study

The information shared in this chapter is part of a year-long study[27], the main objective of which was to research: 'What conditions or features in English learning areas are most effective at stimulating target language use?'. The practice reported is a snapshot of one classroom in the study. The focus is on the collaborative actions of two teachers, a pre-primary educator and an English teacher, committed to developing a language-learning methodology that reflects sound pre-primary practice and where the importance of English teaching and learning is recognised

---

[27] British Council ELT Research Partnership Scheme project entitled 'English learning areas (ELAs) in pre-primary classrooms: an investigation of their effectiveness' – led by the University of Leeds and involving investigators in Portugal and South Korea.

and supported by all stakeholders – the school director, the teaching and support staff, and the parents.

Data was collected from September 2013 to June 2014 and information for this chapter is taken from observation field notes, informal interviews and documentation analysis. For a complete description of the study see Robinson et al (2015).

The pre-primary institution in central Portugal

Centro Social Paroquial dos Pousos[28] (hereafter Centro) is a private institution, subsidised by both the Portuguese Ministry of Education and the Ministry of Work and Social Services (Private Institutions of Social Solidarity)[29] where parents pay an income-adjusted fee for their child to attend. The majority of children come from low to low-middle socio-economic backgrounds.

Children at the Centro are grouped according to their ages and are the responsibility of a qualified pre-primary educator, an educadora, and an auxiliary helper. Since 2001, all children in their last two years at the institution have learned English for one hour a week at the initiative of the school director. An English teacher is hired to give these English classes, which are divided into two 30-minute sessions and scheduled during the morning when the educadora is in the classroom with the children.

English at the Centro

The aims of the English programme are stated as being:

- To provide an enjoyable first encounter with another language
- To cater for the whole child – their physical, social, emotional, psychological and cognitive development
- To foster a positive attitude towards other languages, other peoples and other cultures
- To develop learning skills such as predicting, deducting and hypothesising
- To develop listening and speaking skills
- To build a solid foundation for continued language learning.

The English teacher and the educadoras plan together, ensuring that English is integrated into the short- and long-term planning of the children's learning programme. This involves the two teachers meeting at strategic times of the year to plan and reflect upon the learning programmes they are preparing for the children. These meetings, along with the ad-hoc conversations they have when they work together in the classrooms, ensure a consistent and coherent approach.

This chapter continues with a more detailed description of practice in one class in the Centro, Sala II. It first describes the children and their teachers and then explains and discusses collaborative approaches that prompt learning through play

---

[28] We have been given permission by the institution and the two teachers to use real names in this report.
[29] Around one-third of all pre-primary establishments in Portugal are Private Institutions of Social Solidarity (European Union, 2011: 104).

in English, focusing on the first four months of the children's language learning experience. The practice described is considered typical practice in this institution, though not necessarily representative of language learning practices in pre-primary institutions in Portugal.

The classroom
The classroom is approximately 75 m2, and characteristically open plan, with a circle time carpet area, groups of tables and chairs and clearly set up learning areas. At the beginning of September these learning areas included a house area for dramatic play; a book area for quiet reading; a game area for board games and puzzles; a construction and garage area for building blocks, LEGO® and toy transports; and a modelling table for clay and Plasticine®. By the end of September an area devoted to English (an English learning area) had also been set up.

The children
The group of children comprised 11 girls and 12 boys, aged between four and five years old. All children spoke Portuguese at home with the exception of two, one who spoke Ukrainian and the other Russian. One child had learning difficulties and was being supported by a speech therapist. They were typical of any group of four year olds: curious and keen to learn.

The teachers: Angela and Ana
Angela is a qualified pre-primary educator[30], who took the First Certificate of English when she was at university. She has been a teacher at the Centro since 2006 and has been responsible for the children since many of them began in the crèche in 2010. This was the first time Angela and the children in her care had experienced English lessons together.

Ana has a degree in French and English, specialising in language teaching for ten to 16 year olds. She has been an English and French teacher since 2001 and is typical of many English teachers in Portugal who have been working in primary education since English was introduced as a curricular enrichment activity in September 2005. She began working as a pre-primary English teacher in the Centro in October 2008.

Collaborative practices in action
English is scheduled as part of the children's curricular activities from the beginning of October to the end of June. However, preparation for English begins in September when the school opens for the new academic year. During their first meeting together in September 2013, Ana and Angela discussed how the following months would proceed and how they could collaborate. They talked through Ana's approach to teaching English using play activities and outlined a plan to incorporate into English the topics and activities Angela was preparing for that term. A major focus of this initial discussion was the setting up of an English learning area (ELA), which would become one of the many areas Angela planned to set up with the children in their classroom.

---

[30] A qualified pre-primary educator has a four-year university degree, which includes a teaching placement/practicum.

Incorporating an ELA in the classroom suits the approach to learning in Portugal, which incorporates learning areas and a balance of opportunities for teacher-initiated group work and child-initiated play, and so it was an initiative that Angela welcomed. An ELA serves to integrate English into the choice of free play activities available to the children at different times of the day, as it becomes one of several learning areas in the classroom. It increases the accessibility of English as a language that can be used in the classroom – it also contributes to making English evident as part of the children's learning, being permanently visible via the English signs, posters, books and related resources that are kept in the ELA.

Angela was especially excited about the ELA and decided to begin the year by involving the families in its creation. She believed that this would contribute to motivating both parents and children for their new learning experience. She chose a number of countries and allocated one to each child. At home, with their families, the children investigated these countries – where the country was in the world, which language was spoken there, what their flags were like and anything else they thought was interesting. Unbeknown to the children, Angela had asked them to investigate countries that had English as an official language.

During the last week of September children brought in their discoveries and shared them with Angela and their classmates. Angela described these discussions as being rich and animated. They also looked at a large globe, found Portugal and the other countries they had investigated, and placed miniature flags on each country. Children were quickly able to identify the countries and where they were in relation to Portugal.

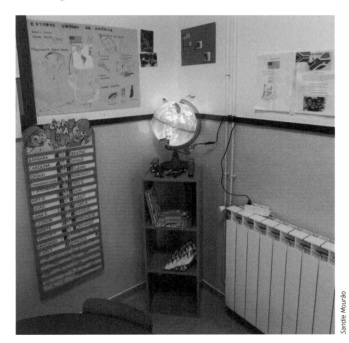

Figure 1: ELA with globe and shelf with objects brought in by the children

Some children brought in words and expressions they already knew or had learned in English, as well as objects and trinkets they had at home which came from English-speaking countries. Posters and objects are placed around a small shelf that Angela had prepared for the ELA (See Figure 1). These activities took place in Portuguese, and laid the foundations for future learning in and through English. Angela had successfully motivated her children and their parents, as well as setting up the class ELA. But, most importantly, she had set the scene for Ana. When Ana arrived on October 1, the children were both positive and enthusiastic. English was real and exciting and they knew lots about it. Ana was thus able to build on the foundation of knowledge, created through Angela's initiatives, to talk about colours and shapes in English, as well as develop the concept of nationality.

Formal instruction in English with Ana

Part of Ana's practice is to use a puppet called Hoola as her language assistant and the children's confidant. During the first lesson, Ana used some flags to encourage the children to share their recent discoveries and to guess where Hoola came from. In so doing she introduced simple greetings and skillfully rephrased their Portuguese chatter into English, saying things like, 'Yes, it's a flag from Australia'. Ana carefully modelled, 'I'm from Portugal, but Hoola is from Britain,' and encouraged the children to stand up and wave their hands around, and proudly say, 'I'm from Portugal,' (all children were born in Portugal, so this was appropriate).

As the lessons progressed, Ana set up routines to help children become confident at using greetings, saying their names, talking about the weather, responding to different instructions and answering the questions 'Where are you from?' and 'Where is Hoola from?'. These routines are pleasurable for children and provide a supportive, comfortable environment for learning to take place. Children also know what to expect when English starts, which avoids individual concerns and over-excitement.

As a means of illustrating meaning and strengthening of the link between the spoken form of the word and its meaning, it is common practice with small children to show a flashcard, say the word and perform an action associated with the meaning of the word. This procedure provides three forms of input to help the learning of new vocabulary. When demonstrating how to say things in English, Ana used flashcards and gestures adapted from American Sign Language (ASL). Thus, as Ana introduced any new language (e.g. 'I'm fine thank you'), she demonstrated the ASL gesture and asked, 'Can you do it? Can you say it?' When she first did this, she explained briefly in Portuguese that the gesture was part of a language for deaf people.

As Ana set up the routine activities with Hoola, she also focused on the topic language Angela had asked her to work with. She used the Portuguese and British flags to contextualise the colours (later in the term all the flags were used to look at shapes). Children were asked to identify colours (and later shapes) and Ana and Hoola rephrased their expressions into English, supported by the ASL gesture and flashcards. 'Yes, it's green. Look, green is like this. Green, green, green. Can you do it? Can you say it?' The children compared the flags; identified which had the same colours, which didn't, and which colours did not appear. In this way children were not only exposed to and encouraged to use the new English words, but they were also comparing, contrasting and looking for the odd one out – these are appropriate mathematical concepts for children of this age group according to the Portuguese *Metas de Aprendizagem* (Ministério da Educação, nd).

Over the following weeks, together with Ana and Hoola, the children sang songs, listened to stories and engaged in play-like activities, often with flashcards. These activities not only support the learning of the new language, but also give the children real reasons for using language in context. The activities were typical to EFL methodologies; however, Ana used a small battery of activities consistently, ensuring that children became familiar with the focus language as well as with the structure of the activity and its organisational language (see Mourão, 2014). These activities also support the development of cognitive skills, such as attention, memory, logic and reasoning, and audio and visual processing. As such, Ana provided what Vygotsky (1978) has referred to as 'formal' instruction during these 30-minute English sessions with the children – instruction that is teacher led or schooled (Gallimore and Tharp, 1990).

Informal instruction in the ELA

All the resources that Ana used during those moments of formal instruction were left with the children in their ELA. She left Hoola, as a constant reminder that they can speak English; she also left the country flags and flashcards, story cards, picturebooks and boxes with games inside (e.g. bingos and beetle games). Children also continued to bring in objects they associated with English – a bilingual picture dictionary, for example.

The ELA is a space that is resourced to deliberately stimulate memories of the teacher-led activities with Ana and to aid recall of the language associated with these activities. The actions and the target language become available to be used creatively during imaginative free play. As such, the ELA supports Ana's lessons, in the sense that it extends her formal instruction, providing opportunities for children to engage in child-initiated play in English, affording moments of informal instruction as children play together with no overt adult supervision. They learn from and with each other while playing, by exploring the materials and re-living situations for themselves. Thus, in this way an ELA helps to integrate English in a much more age-appropriate way, for it makes English available to the children to play in, with and through when they want to, during free play times. It also gives it an importance equal to other daily learning activities.

Angela as motivator, planner and bridge

Motivating children after formal instruction with Ana

As Ana's English lessons were in the morning, Angela was in the classroom, taking part or observing. So, once Ana had left the room, Angela reinforced some of the concepts: for example, the idea of ASL being a language in itself and used by deaf people, or the concept of having a nationality, as well as language the children had experienced with Ana and Hoola. Together, during circle time, Angela and the children remembered what Hoola and Ana had told and shown them, and the children were encouraged to share anything new with their families and carers. In this way Angela demonstrated her interest in their learning experience. With Angela the children reflected about what they knew, what they didn't know and often asked about other words and expressions, as such strengthening and extending what they had learned.

Planning for informal instruction through free play in the ELA

Angela was also responsible for ensuring the ELA was included in the children's free play choices. The ELA was part of the classroom set up, and thus included in the children's everyday choice for free play, so it was a natural part of Angela's planning and she was easily able to ensure that children played in the ELA.

It is common practice for Angela to set up free play in such a way as to allow her to monitor where each child plays to ensure they pass through all the learning areas. This, she believes, guarantees that children develop different skills and competencies. Through negotiation with the children it is decided how many can play at any one time in each learning area and if there are any particular rules (such as putting puzzle pieces back in boxes so they don't get lost, leaving the area tidy, or using English, etc.); this helps the children become both responsible and autonomous. As the year progresses these rules might change, but it is always a democratic decision. Angela prepares lanyards for each learning area, which the children wear when they play in an area. At the beginning of free play times the children decide where they want to play, put on their lanyards and go to the chosen areas. If a child wants to play somewhere else, after a while they can negotiate with their peers and swap. Angela keeps a record of their choices on a large board, so if a child chooses to play in an area he has played in the day previously, he is reminded by Angela or the other children that he should choose a different area.

A bridge between parents and English

Angela also acts as the link between English and the children's parents, for she sees many parents regularly. She is the first person they ask about the ASL gestures and the new English words and expressions to label or say things. Angela is able to tap into their interest and enthusiasm and feed this back to Ana. Because of their interest, an email was sent to all parents every two weeks, summarising the English lessons and sharing English words and expressions and song lyrics. Ana also provided a rationale for using ASL and the importance of playing in English.

Outcomes

The most important outcome of this collaborative practice using play activities was that children were motivated towards their English learning experience. This was evidenced in a number of ways:

1. The children's eagerness to play in the ELA – this was the greatest observable evidence: Angela noted that the ELA was the most popular learning area and was the first choice during free play for 18 of the 23 children in the group.

2. The children's enthusiasm and engagement during English lessons – Ana noted they were happy to see her, and used the ASL gestures and English words and expressions when they could. There were no signs of boredom or disinterest during the English lessons either.

3. The children's keenness to talk about English with Angela – Angela noted that children came to expect the reflection moments at circle time, were enthusiastic about demonstrating what they had remembered and helped each other if they couldn't remember (or recall) the language.

4. The ease with which the children used English in context when Ana was not present – Angela noted that many children were spontaneously inserting English words and expressions into Portuguese sentences, particularly the colour, shape and weather words. They also asked her regularly how to say words they had forgotten, often showing her instead the gesture they had remembered.

5. Anecdotal evidence from parents – parents shared with Angela examples of their child's use of English at home, but also wrote comments on the termly reports, e.g. 'Plays and speaks in English and uses gestures,' or 'Sings songs in English at home'. Parents also highlighted the children's enthusiasm to be at school on the days they had English.

The termly English reports that are sent home to parents included a section for the *educadora* to complete. Angela's involvement in the children's learning experience meant she was in an excellent position to comment on the children's behaviour towards English and their interest in using it during the day. Her comments were very positive, noting that the children played with the resources in the ELA, used Hoola as a speaking and singing partner, imitated the games they played with Ana and Hoola, and used both ASL gestures and English words and expressions in context.

Conclusion

English quickly became part of the children's classroom lives, and was certainly not restricted to the two 30-minute sessions that Ana gave every week. This is a direct outcome of two teachers collaborating. Both are responsible for English but in different ways. Ana was the formal English instructor, ensuring children were exposed to English in a systematic way through game-like activities. She was mediator between the language and the children. She was also responsible for ensuring that resources were available for the classroom ELA. Angela, on the other hand, was first and foremost a motivator, ensuring children saw English as part of their everyday lives. But she was also responsible for organising the space and planning time for English to be part of the classroom. Additionally, her role as bridge between parents and English was essential in ensuring that everyone was involved and understood what was happening.

Six *educadoras* have worked with an English teacher (not always Ana) since 2001 at the *Centro*, and each has approached the experience in a different way, but always with collaboration stemming from shared objectives and desired outcomes. Not all *educadoras* have had qualifications in English; two have spoken no English at all. Nevertheless, the attributes described in the cameo of Angela's classroom are evident in them all. English has successfully been integrated into the children's pre-primary lives as a result of the teachers' willingness to collaborate and create opportunities for the children to engage in play-like activities in English.

The practice described here shows that an intervention that enables a pre-primary educator to support the learning of another language by working with the English teacher can have very positive results – collaboration between teachers increases and enriches the opportunities for children to learn and use the English language in a manner which is appropriate to their stage of development.

References

European Commission (2014, October) *Proposal for key principles of a Quality Framework for Early Childhood Education and Care*. Report of the Working Group on Early Childhood Education and Care under the auspices of the European Commission. Retrieved from: http://ec.europa.eu/education/policy/strategic-framework/archive/documents/ecec-quality-framework_en.pdf

European Union (2011, July) *Country summaries based on contributions of the members of the thematic working group on early language learning* (ELL). Retrieved from http://ec.europa.eu/languages/orphans/ellp-summaries_en.htm

Fröhlich-Ward, L (1979) 'Environment and learning', in Freudenstein R (ed) *Teaching Foreign Languages to the Very Young*, Oxford: Pergamon Institute of English.

Fullan, M (2007) *The New Meaning of Educational Change* (4th edn). New York: Teacher's College Press.

Gallimore, R and Tharp, R (1990) 'Teaching mind in society: teaching, schooling and literate discourse', in Mol, LC (ed) *Vygotsky and Education*. Cambridge: Cambridge University Press.

Martin-Beltran, M and Peercy, MM (2014) Collaboration to teach English language learners: opportunities for shared teacher learning. *Teachers and Teaching: Theory and Practice*, 20/6, 721-737.

Ministério da Educação (1997) *Orientações Curriculares para a Educação Pré-Escolar,* Lisbon: Ministério da Educação.

Ministério da Educação (nd) *Metas de Aprendizagem: Educação Pré-Escolar.* Retrieved from http://metasdeaprendizagem.dge.mec.pt/educacao-pre-escolar/metas-de-aprendizagem/

Mourão, S (2014) Taking play seriously in the pre-primary English classroom. *ELT Journal Special Issue Teaching English to Young Learners*, July, 68/3, 254-264.

Oliveira-Formosinho, J (ed) (2013) *Modelos Curriculares para a Educação de Infância*. Porto: Porto Editora.

Robinson, P, Mourão, S and Kang, N-J (2015) *English Learning Areas in Pre-Primary Classrooms: an investigation of their effectiveness*. London: British Council. https://www.teachingenglish.org.uk/article/english-learning-areas-pre-primary-classrooms-investigation-their-effectiveness

Sawyer, LBE and Rimm-Kaufman, SE (2007) Collaboration in the context of the *Responsive Classroom* approach. *Teachers and Teaching: theory and practice,* 13/3, 211-247.

Siraj-Blatchford, I, Sylva, K, Muttock, S, Gilden, R and Bell, D (2002) *Researching Effective Pedagogy in the Early Years*. Research Report No. 356, London: Department of Education and Skills, HMSO.

Vygotsky, L (1978) *Mind in Society: The Development of Higher Mental Processes.* Cambridge, MA: Harvard University Press

3.4

A short, in-service training course for pre-school teachers in France

Gail Ellis, British Council, France

Countries vary widely in their provision and extent of initial teacher training and of continuing professional development for early childhood education teachers. As an essential element of teaching quality, training has recently received a good deal of attention. Nutbrown, in her 2012 review of early education and childcare qualifications in the UK, recommends a raising of standards and a clear, rigorous system of qualifications to equip practitioners with the knowledge, skills and understanding they need to give young children high-quality experiences. The proposal for key principles of a Quality Framework for Early Childhood Education and Care (European Commission, 2014) also provides evidence that better qualified staff are more likely to provide high-quality pedagogy. The ongoing professional development of teachers in relation to evolving societal needs, policy and curriculum changes is also essential in supporting them to manage change and meet current demands, as well as a key element in guaranteeing children's positive outcomes. This is more effective when it is based on identified training needs (European Commission, ibid).

This case study reports on a short in-service teacher training course for state pre-school teachers in France to equip them with the skills and confidence to introduce English into the pre-school curriculum. It also highlights the importance of a whole-school approach (Dobson et al., 2010) through effective leadership and management based on consultation and collaboration with teaching colleagues, and ensuring that all children in a school have the same opportunities, regardless of socio-economic or other circumstances.

Pre-school provision in France

In an Economist Intelligence Unit (2012) report, which assesses the extent to which 45 governments worldwide provide a good, inclusive early childhood education for children between the ages of three and six, France is ranked seventh overall and scores highly on the legal right to pre-school provision. State provision of early childhood education is available for all children from age three to six in France, when compulsory schooling begins. Although it is optional, nine out of ten children attend school from the age of three.

Political pressure or political will?

Early childhood education teachers in France enjoy the same status and receive the same length of training as primary school teachers. However, there is currently no national policy on early language learning in pre-schools in France, although a Ministry of Education document (2011) encourages the teaching of foreign languages, most often English, through the use of songs, rhymes and simple exchanges as a preparation for more structured learning at primary school. A national strategic review of language education (Halimi, 2012) further recommends the establishment of sensitising children to other languages at pre-school. Pending a national policy, any language learning programmes in early childhood education settings in France are based on individual initiatives.

In the light of the above and with English viewed as one of the most widely spoken languages in the world, the mayor of a multilingual and multicultural district in Paris decided that English should be introduced in the seven state pre-schools in her constituency. The British Council was invited to provide two short in-service training courses during the autumn terms of 2011 and 2012 for the teachers concerned. The time allocated for each course was only ten hours and participants attended each session after a working day when energy levels were not at their highest.

Training needs

The courses were attended by one, two or more teachers from each school in the district, making a total of 25 teachers on each course, and some attended both courses. Training needs were identified via a pre-course questionnaire, which provided information on participants' self-assessed level of English as per the Common European Framework for Reference (CEFR) descriptors, initial and in-service training in English language and methodology, classroom English language and teaching needs, motivation and attitudes towards early language learning (see Appendix 1).

Participants' needs were wide ranging and there was great variation in terms of self-assessed English competency, which ranged from A2–C2, career stage, previous training and experience of using English in the classroom with pre-school children. However, all expressed positive attitudes towards the benefits of an early introduction of English to children as reflected in the following comments:

It is motivating

It develops listening skills

Children discover another culture

It opens minds to a new culture

Studies show that the earlier foreign language learning begins, the better the chance children have of acquiring it

Participants were eager to improve their English and teaching techniques in order to implement the project. Their positive attitudes and motivation were also demonstrated by their enthusiasm and willingness to attend training at the end of a working day and participate actively in training activities. In addition, the pre-school inspector of the district and some headteachers also attended the course. As one headteacher explained:

> As head of school, it is important for me to understand how this teaching will take place, even though I will not be teaching it myself.

This demonstrated commitment to the project, showed support for the teachers and contributed towards a collaborative, whole-school approach.

Common priorities that emerged from the needs analysis were:

- How to create a natural English-speaking environment in class by using child-directed speech (Aitchison, 1997; Dunn, 2013)
- How to provide a good model of English pronunciation
- How to plan and link activities to the French pre-school curriculum (www.education.gouv.fr/cid33/la-presentation-des-programmes-a-l-ecole-maternelle.html)

The main aim of the courses was to build on teachers' existing expertise and experience as pre-school teachers and to demonstrate how the approaches they currently use could be transferred to integrating English into the curriculum.

The pre-school curriculum in France

As Raveaud (2005) explains, the republican ideals inherited from the Revolution still have a major influence on education in France, which means that the child's personal experience is not always tapped into in class in an attempt to erase any outside factors of inequality. Children leave all family and community ties behind once they enter school. Because of this, there is generally little recognition of the child's home language if different to French, as the appropriation and development of French is the cornerstone of the pre-school curriculum. The integration of English into the curriculum represented a new challenge for the teachers. For each child it represented an opportunity to encounter another language on an equal footing. However, the varied English language skills of the teachers would inevitably impact on the quality of the language learning experiences the children would receive. Rixon (2013), in her survey of policy and practice in primary English language teaching worldwide, also addresses the question of transition from early years to primary and the issues of coherence.

The other main areas of the pre-school curriculum in France include learning what it means to be a pupil in a school environment in preparation for primary school at age six, developing fine and gross motor skills, becoming aware of the world around them and developing curiosity, building self-confidence, learning how to control their emotions and developing autonomy.

Challenges

Three main challenges emerged in order to meet the diverse needs of the participants:

i. How to build on participants' existing knowledge of English and develop their confidence to use English naturally in the classroom.

ii. How to shift participants' views that English should be delivered as 'discrete English lessons' once or twice a week to an approach where it is integrated into the curriculum so language derives naturally from daily routines in order to increase opportunities for exposure in a limited exposure setting. Research has shown that traditional sequential and subject-specific approaches are not effective in promoting children's learning in the early years, whereas a holistic approach that sustains children's overall development across several domains is more effective, as it is supportive of children's learning strategies (van Kuyk, 2006) and is focused on meaning-making (Bennett, 2013).

iii. How to maximise time on these short courses and address the priority needs of the participants.

Shifting teachers' views from 'English as discrete lessons' to an integrated, holistic approach was considered to be the priority challenge due to the low level of English of some of the teachers and their lack of confidence.

Course design

The starting point was to focus on teachers' English language skills and build their confidence so they could naturally and spontaneously interact with and respond to children in English. The courses were broken down into five two-hour sessions and each session was divided into two parts:

Part 1 – Focus on teachers' English language improvement.

Part 2 – Focus on methodology.

Part 1 of each session developed participants' ability to create the conditions for using English effectively in the classroom in order to provide 'adequate exposure to and engaging interaction in the language' (Rixon, ibid). Teachers therefore experienced and participated in activities that they could transfer to their own classes, thereby incorporating a secondary focus on methodology and maximising the limited time.

Part 2 of each session, methodology, was conducted in English in order to provide further input and exposure to the language. However, each trainer spoke French and was able to support participants' understanding whenever necessary and the French language versions of published materials were used (Slattery and Willis, 2004; Ellis and Brewster, 2007).

Part 1 – focus on English language improvement

To begin, participants analysed a typical school day to identify the daily routines and the English required for these, as well as for classroom management and giving instructions. This was followed by listening and speaking activities via drilling, with a particular focus on pronunciation to meet participants' expressed needs, to build their confidence and to address concerns such as:

> My English is not fluent and I don't want the children to speak English with a strong French accent.

To develop strategies to manage situations such as:

> I find it difficult to use English because children want to understand everything immediately.

To set up conditions to use English naturally in an integrated and holistic approach throughout the school day:

> I think it is very difficult to use English in a 'not English' environment, especially if it lasts only an hour or two per week – total immersion is, I think, much better.

The first hour of each session also served as a transition from use of French throughout the participants' working day to use of English in preparation for part two, *Focus on methodology*. Participants were happy to become 'pupils' and joined in with playful drills, stories, songs and chants and craft activities. It was both relaxing and enjoyable at the end of a day's work and perceived as extremely useful, as they experienced the natural language learning experiences they were preparing to create in their own classrooms.

Allaying teacher anxieties

Teachers' anxieties about their linguistic ability to integrate English into daily routines, and their fear that children would not be able to understand, were allayed by demonstrating techniques that the teachers were already familiar with for supporting French language development, but were unsure how to transfer to supporting English language development. Input on how children acquire a foreign language helped teachers understand that it is natural for children to use the shared classroom language or their mother tongue as a resource and to mix languages, as this is part of the learning process and evidence of learning. In order to become aware of this aspect of learning, transcripts from classroom interactions and storytelling sessions from Slattery and Willis (ibid) and our own classes at the British Council in Paris for pre-school children were analysed to highlight how and when code switching takes place. These extracts also highlighted the additional visual, audio and linguistic support teachers can use in order to convey meaning and maintain interaction in English.

This support involves the setting up of a language environment in which teachers use child-directed speech *'to provide a good basis for learners' uptake'* (Aitchison, ibid). This involves using specific strategies that are similar to those used by parents in first language acquisition such as slow, well-articulated, exaggerated intonation; short, well-formed utterances; repetition of key words in context, using language which is directed to present circumstances; using gesture and facial expressions; recasting, elaborating and extending. These strategies give children the opportunity to derive meaning from more than one source of information. Teachers identified these strategies in further transcripts of classroom interactions (Slattery and Willis, ibid) and practised using them in role-play situations.

Part 2 – focus on methodology

Part two of each session focused on how to create conditions to integrate English into familiar daily routines such as:

- Arrival and welcome time – where children make the transition from home to school life – involving the usual types of routines such as greetings, coming together to plan the day, establishing the day of the week/date, weather, talking about a special occasion such as a birthday, a festival, etc.
- Morning activities time – revolving around the curriculum and involving children in a range of activities including whole class or smaller groups, workshops, games, stories, painting, crafts, construction, literacy, numeracy.
- Play time – usually outdoor recreation
- Lunch time
- Quiet/rest time
- Afternoon activities time
- Review time
- Home time.

The *plan, do, review* (Hohmann et al., 2008) learning cycle was presented as an overarching, consistent routine in which to embed the daily routines. This allows for flexibility of working and gives children a feeling of both empowerment and security. It also enables them to develop a sense of timing, as activities happen at regular intervals and in predictable ways. It ensures children get the most out of each routine and allows a smooth transition from one routine to the next. This organisational aspect of the classroom means that common phrases in English are repeated and recycled regularly through interaction in familiar routines, thus increasing exposure and so allowing children to acquire familiar expressions and develop their confidence. It also provides similar security for the teachers who are able to transfer the language 'rehearsed' during the course into familiar classroom situations and routines. The *plan, do, review* routine was also applied to each training session in order to involve participants in a cycle of reflection, experimentation and further reflection.

Content

Based on Goddard (1982), much of the content and classroom techniques demonstrated such as storytelling, using songs and rhymes, physical activities, craft activities, etc. were linked to the four seasons. The seasons in Europe are distinctly different and build on children's natural curiosity about the immediate world around them and provide an annual structure that introduces children to language related to the different features of each season. This also allows for regular recycling, consolidation and extension of language (e.g. summer, winter, wet weather clothes, etc.). In this way, the four seasons act as a springboard for developing language and communication around topic areas related to the weather, clothes, temperatures, colours, shapes, the senses, trees and flowers, growing things, water, food, zoo and farm animals, birds and insects, outings, special occasions and cultural events, all of which link to the French pre-school curriculum. This emphasises the holistic nature of children's learning and development (Whitebread, 2003) as distinct from learning separated out into subjects and where language is seen as central to learning. Participants were shown how these topics can be further reinforced by using carefully selected picturebooks and a story-based methodology (Ellis and Brewster, 2007). See Appendix 2 for a sample curriculum overview and suggested storybooks.

Maximising course time

Clearly, five, two-hour sessions is limited but nevertheless allows for valuable opportunities to heighten teachers' professional awareness and improve their teaching skills. It also allows teachers to come together to share a common experience, build their own learning community and provide each other with mutual support. As mentioned above, this was also reinforced by the attendance of the pre-school inspector and headteachers. This third challenge was addressed in four ways:

i.   By sending a pre-course letter and needs analysis (see Appendix 1) to inform participants about the course and help them form realistic expectations. It asked them to reflect on and identify their own needs, so that the course could be shaped to meet these, and prepared them psychologically by asking them to reflect on their own motivation and attitudes to early language learning.

ii.   By developing a spirit of enquiry amongst the teachers by applying the *plan, do, review* cycle to the training sessions. This involved teachers in a cycle of theoretical input, practice and reflection in order to understand the rationale behind different classroom techniques and how to use and evaluate them. Each session encouraged participants to reflect on themselves as language learners and as teachers in order to raise their awareness of their individual strengths, differences and areas to improve.

iii.   By identifying personal action points according to participants' individual priorities at the end of each session. As part of the pre-course letter, participants were also asked to state realistically how much time per week they felt they would be able to dedicate to their own English language improvement and lesson preparation. They were asked to re-evaluate this time according to their action points and re-adjust as necessary in order to maintain motivation and manage their expectations.

iv.   By sharing resource lists and suggestions for continuing professional development so that participants could continue their own development and research independently between sessions and after the courses.

Outcomes

Despite the short duration of the courses, varying profiles of the participants and the challenges faced, end-of-course feedback was positive and the courses met the diverse needs of the participants:

i. Participants felt they had improved their English language skills for the classroom and felt more confident, as reflected in the following comments:

I have gained confidence in teaching English

I'm less afraid to teach

ii. There had been a shift in views that English should be delivered as 'discrete English lessons' once or twice a week to a more integrated and holistic approach. Post-course school visits included attendance at one school's Christmas celebrations where they had spent several weeks preparing 'Christmas songs and breakfast' entirely in English for all children in the school, spanning the three to six age range and their parents. This event demonstrated a whole-school approach incorporating songs, craft activities and cooking embedded in familiar Christmas festivities with a cultural aspect. In addition, participants said they were now aware of how they could transfer their existing skills to the teaching of English:

I was able to transfer skills and techniques immediately to my classroom

School visits included class observations where we saw teachers integrating English into their daily routines to a lesser or greater extent.

iii. The limited time was maximised in the ways described above. However, all participants felt they needed more sessions:

There were not enough sessions!

It is clear that the teachers required ongoing post-course support, but this was not within our remit. It is hoped that the spirit of enquiry developed during the courses enabled participants to become more autonomous and reflective practitioners and equipped them with the knowledge and skills to pursue their own development.

The features of the courses that participants felt contributed to its success were:

- Focusing on language development in simulated classroom situations, to build their competence and confidence.
- Building on teachers' existing pre-school skills and competencies and demonstrating how these can be transferred to English.
- Analysing daily routines in a pre-school classroom and the language required in order to create conditions for integrating English naturally and maximise exposure to the language.
- Analysing child-directed speech, and rehearsing in simulated classroom activities in the supportive atmosphere of the training room.

- Combining theory and practice by providing theoretical input on children's language development and a strong participative and experiential focus on rehearsing classroom techniques such as songs, rhymes, storytelling, using flashcards, etc.
- Establishing a supportive group community via continuity of trainers and visible commitment of school management in a whole-school approach.

For the trainers, it enabled us to gain a deeper understanding of pre-school education in France and to build relationships with the pre-school inspector and teachers in our district. These still continue today and have opened doors to intercultural understanding and knowledge sharing.

It is hoped that the features above will provide useful guidelines for others wishing to design and deliver short in-service courses for pre-school teachers and for encouraging a whole-school approach.

Acknowledgements

Co-trainers Julia Diallo, Nicky Francis and Nayr Ibrahim.

References

Aitchison, J (1997) *The Language Web*. Cambridge University Press.

Bennett, J (2013) *Early childhood curriculum for children from low-income and immigrant backgrounds*. Paper presented at the second meeting of the Transatlantic Forum on Inclusive Early Years held in New York, 10-12 July 2013.

Dobson, A, Murillo, M and Johnstone, R (2010) *Bilingual Education Project Spain Evaluation Report*. British Council. https://www.britishcouncil.es/sites/default/files/bilingual-education-project-spain-evaluation-report-en.pdf

Dunn, O (2013) *Introducing English to Young Children: Spoken Language*. Collins.

Economist Intelligence Unit (2012) *Starting well – Benchmarking early education across the world*. http://www.economistinsights.com/sites/default/files/legacy/mgthink/downloads/Starting%20Well.pdf

Ellis, G and Brewster, J (2007) *Enseigner par le storytelling théorie et pratique. French edition*. Pearson Longman. *Tell it Again! The Storytelling Handbook for Primary English Language Teachers. English edition. 2014*. British Council. www.teachingenglish.org.uk/article/tell-it-again-storytelling-handbook-primary-english-language-teachers

European Commission (2014) *Key principles of a Quality Framework*. http://ec.europa.eu/education/policy/strategic-framework/archive/documents/ecec-quality-framework_en.pdf

Goddard, E. (1982) *See the Daisies. Feel the Rain*. Greater London Pre-school Playgroups Association, Kingswood Press.

Halimi, S (2012) *Apprendre les langues Apprendre le monde* http://media.education. gouv.fr/file/02_Fevrier/91/5/Apprendre-les-langues-Apprendre-le-monde_206915.pdf

Hohmann, M, Epstein, AS and Weikart, D (2008) *Educating Young Children: Active Learning Practices for Pre-school and Child Care Programmes*. 3rd Edition. High/ Scope Educational Research Foundation.

Ministère de l'Education Nationale (2011) *Dossier de rentrée année scolaire 2011–2012*. http://media.education.gouv.fr/file/Rentree_scolaire/59/5/Rentree-scolaire-2011_190595.pdf

Nutbrown, C (2012) *Foundations for Quality. The independent review of early education and childcare qualifications. Final Report*. https://www.gov.uk/government/uploads/system/uploads/attachment_data/file/175463/Nutbrown-Review.pdf

Raveaud, M (2005) Inside French and English infant schools. *Education 3–13: International Journal of Primary, Elementary and Early Years Education*. Vol. 33/1.

Rixon, S (2013) *British Council Survey of Policy and Practice in Primary English Language Teaching Worldwide*. British Council. www.teachingenglish.org.uk/article/british-council-survey-policy-practice-primary-english-language-teaching-worldwide

Slattery, M and Willis, J (2004) *L'anglais à l'école. French edition*. Oxford University Press. English for Primary Teachers. English edition: 2001.

Van Kuyk, J (2006) 'Holistic or sequential approach to curriculum: What works best for young children?', in van Kuyk, J (ed) *The quality of early childhood education*. Arnhem: CITO.

Whitebread, D (2003) *Teaching and Learning in the Early Years*. 2nd Edition. Routledge Falmer.

Appendix 1

Translated from French

Dear Participant,

We are delighted you will be participating on our training course for early years teachers this term. The aims of the course are:

- *To help you improve your spoken English and build your confidence in using English effectively in the classroom*
- *To broaden your range of English language teaching techniques and activities and know how to link these to the pre-school curriculum in France.*

The course consists of five two-hour sessions. We will dedicate the first hour of each session to language improvement and the second hour to language teaching techniques and activities.

The course will also help you discover ways of learning English that are best for you and to develop your own strategies for continuing to learn after the course.

Before we begin the course, we would like to find out about you. We would be grateful if you would please complete the form below.

With many thanks.

Course trainers

Your language background

How would you evaluate your level of English? Please circle. See over for the CEFR levels.

A1   A2   B1   B2   C1   C2

What qualifications do you have in English?

**Did your initial teacher training provide English language classes?
If yes, please provide details**

Have you benefitted from any in-service English language training or teaching methodology courses? If yes, please provide details

Your language needs

Which of the following classroom situations would you like to practise during the course? 1 = most important, 5 = least important	
Providing a natural English-speaking environment and using child-directed speech	
Giving instructions in English and organising classroom activities	
Setting up classroom routines	
Setting up play-based activities	
Managing and controlling the class in English	
Using flashcards	
Listening and doing activities, e.g. total physical response activities	
Listening and making (craft activities)	
Singing songs and chanting rhymes	
Reading and telling stories	
Playing games	
Other	

Your teaching techniques and activities needs

Planning and integrating English into a sequence of work	
Integrating English activities into the French curriculum	
Exploiting storybooks	
Introducing a song or rhyme	
Setting up natural opportunities for children to use English	
Knowing when and how to correct	
Providing a good model of English	
Knowing where to find resources	
Other	

Your motivation

What do you think are the benefits of introducing English to children in the early years?

How much time do you think you can realistically spend per week practising your English/ preparing lessons in English?

Thank you for completing this questionnaire.

Appendix 2

Sample curriculum overview with suggested storybooks

The Four Seasons			
Autumn 1 – September	**Autumn 2 – October**	**Autumn 3 – November/ December**	**Winter 1 – January**
All about me Family Daily routines Clothes we wear and dressing Numbers 1–10 Sounds	Where we live Weather Shapes Autumn colours	Specials occasions Birthdays Christmas Weather Shapes	People and communities Numbers Homes Music Dance Songs Languages
Storybooks Mr Wolf's Week How do I put it on? My green day	Storybooks A Halloween Mask for Monster Little Cloud A bit lost Little blue and little yellow	Storybooks Froggy gets dressed The Snowman The Snowy Day	Storybooks We all went on safari Bear about town Knuffle Bunny
Winter 2 – February/ March	**Spring 1 – April/May**	**Spring 2 – June**	**Summer 1 – July**
Food and mealtimes Vegetables Fruit Meat Fish Healthy eating Meals	Growing and nature Animals At the zoo At the farm In the garden Spring/Easter Planting and growing	Things I can do Abilities Interests Pastimes Similarities and differences	Holiday time In the park At the river At the seaside Weather Clothes we wear Water safety
Storybooks Today is Monday Ketchup on your cornflakes?	Storybooks Elizabeth Hen Rosie's walk Good Night, Gorilla Peas! The Tiny Seed Titch Monkey and Me	Storybooks I can do it! Monster can't sleep	Storybooks Having a picnic The Bears who went to the seaside

3.5

Rhythmic patterns in stories and word order production (adjective + noun) in four-year-old EFL learners

Sarah Hillyard, Florence Nightingale School,
Buenos Aires, Argentina

Introduction

This chapter reports on an Action Research project carried out in a kindergarten classroom in a private school in the city of Buenos Aires, Argentina, in October 2011. The project involved 25 native Spanish speakers of four years of age, learning English as a foreign language. These English lessons (with the language as the focus of instruction) covered 40 minutes of a three-hour school day, with the rest of the lessons in Spanish. Its aim was to explore whether rhythmic patterns in stories enhance word order production. To narrow the scope, this investigation focused on the oral production of adjective + noun word order, which, in this case, was the opposite to its use in the children's first language (e.g. "blue horse" would be translated as "caballo azul" ("horse blue") in Spanish, the modifier occurring after the noun). This linguistic feature was considered of interest due to its complexity in terms of language transfer occurrences, as the children's mother tongue interfered with their learning of such a feature in their acquisition of the English language.

Stories, rhythm and learning

Stories are a valuable tool in classrooms of young learners learning a foreign language; more so, some authors suggest, when they involve repeated rhythmic utterances that enable children to grasp the language in a natural way (Brewster et al., 2002). Cameron (2001) suggests that the built-in repetition of words and phrases is one of the aspects of stories that allow children to learn language in an "incidental" way, defined by Brown (1994: 66) as the *"acquisition of linguistic patterns without explicit attention or instruction"*. That is to say, as very young learners are not "aware" that they are acquiring a foreign language, through stories, the learning process becomes natural.

Some stories repeat a set phrase with different words added in particular places, which students can then internalise easily and quickly (Roth, 1998). It seems that these patterns, repeated rhythmically, serve as a basic framework of language structure in which lexical elements can be replaced, as in the case of word order (e.g. adjective + noun). When these rhythmic utterances are continually repeated in the context of a line of events, children can spontaneously interact with the telling of the story, using the language in oral production (Kolsawalla, 1999).

According to *the Macmillan English Dictionary* (2002) "rhythm" is not only "a regular pattern of sounds or movements" or "a regular pattern of syllables in poetry", but also "a pattern in an activity that makes it enjoyable to watch or easy to do". Many well-known stories used to teach English involve regular rhythmic patterns (like the ones chosen for this investigation), which children seem to naturally pick up (Kolsawalla, 1999). Clark and Clark (in Kolsawalla, 1999) state that "regular articulatory patterns are easier to pronounce than irregular ones". Not only are rhythmic patterns easier to pronounce, they also provide a predictable framework that can enhance linguistic processing (Kolsawalla, 1999). Kolsawalla (ibid) states that few systematic studies have been made to research this area. As such, this research study follows on from Kolsawalla's action research (ibid).

The context

The context for this research project was a private Catholic girls' school in the city of Buenos Aires, Argentina, composed mainly of upper-class families. The 25 female students of four years of age in this kindergarten classroom spoke Spanish as their mother tongue. The teacher was a native English speaker who was also fluent in Spanish. These children had 40-minute English lessons four times a week. Most of them began their English lessons at the same school at the age of three and their exposure to the foreign language was limited, mainly to the school environment.

The four stories

This project involved four lessons, with each lesson focusing on one story, and each story told using a different approach (see Appendix 1 for lesson plans). First, the teacher told a story once and then the children were engaged in a second retelling immediately after, which encouraged participation. The retelling consisted of the children either producing the exact words used in the story or providing their own suggestions to expand on the story, with the purpose of noting whether they were able to produce the correct adjective plus noun word order.

This research follows the assumption that in interactive storytelling, rhythmic utterances and the repetition of patterns aid learning (Kolsawalla, 1999). These rhythmic patterns involve the prose being written in rhyme. The rhyme and rhythm of poems, songs and stories provide regular beats, a certain uniform swing, when being read aloud or performed. As Kolsawalla (1999) states, rhythmic sections in stories are one of the most popular formats of stories and it seems that they lead to "spontaneous joining in" by young learners. Therefore, the four stories chosen contain a similar number of adjective + noun samples. Each was told in a different way so as to add four different variables: two with no rhythmic patterns and two with rhythmic patterns, some with the aid of pictures, acting out the story or using a puppet:

- *The Grouchy Ladybug* (by Eric Carle) told with no rhythmic patterns but showing the pictures.
- *Brown Bear, Brown Bear* (by Bill Martin Jr.) with rhythmic patterns and showing the children the pictures in the book.
- *I Went Walking* (by Sue Williams and Julie Rivas) with rhythmic patterns but without showing the children the pictures – by acting it out without a puppet or any visuals.
- *The Very Busy Spider* (by Eric Carle) with no rhythmic patterns and no pictures shown – by acting it out with a puppet.

These stories were chosen because they all include many examples of the structure of adjective-noun word order, which in all cases focus on "colour-animal" (e.g. "red bird"). Due to cross-linguistic transfer from Spanish (word order being the opposite in these children's mother tongue, e.g. "pájaro rojo" = "bird red"), this structure had been interfering with the children's acquisition of the linguistic feature in English, becoming explicit in their oral production of the target structure.

Most of the animals and colours in all stories were familiar to the children, to facilitate the production of the animal and colour, and to instead be able to focus on word order. For instance, the rhythmic pattern from "Brown Bear, Brown Bear" is "colour+animal, what do you see? I see a colour+animal looking at me":

> *"Brown bear, brown bear, what do you see?*
>
> *I see a red bird looking at me.*
>
> *Red bird, red bird what do you see?*
>
> *I see a yellow duck looking at me."*

After each story, the children were asked to help the teacher retell the story by providing a novel adjective + noun word order utterance, e.g. "yellow bee".

Data collection methods

For the collection of data, three methods were used:

- Video recordings of four lessons were carried out by the teacher-researcher. These lessons were delivered as part of the normal everyday class routine so that they did not interfere with the syllabus and were complementary to normal lessons. The whole lessons were transcribed (see Appendix 2 for a selected section of the transcription).
- Field notes were kept to record general impressionistic views on the students' language learning and any interesting comments based on her observations (see Appendix 3).
- A simple assessment tool was designed as an observation sheet in which each student's relevant responses was recorded and an analysis of whether the correct word order was used or not was made:

Response Number	Student	Type of response	Response	Use of adj + noun (Y/N)
Lesson _____ Story: "_____"				

Total responses:	
Total spontaneous responses:	
Responses with help or completions:	
No use of adj+noun (N):	
Use of adj+noun (Y):	
Use of adj+noun with help (Y with help):	

The research questions were: How many adjective-noun responses were produced for each story? How many of these responses were spontaneous and how many were produced with help or as completions of others' utterances or the teacher's utterance? How many unsuccessful word order utterances were produced for each story?

The data

The data was measured in percentages and the utterances fell into different categories:

- "Spontaneous" response: a student was able to produce the correct word order alone, with no help or clue given by other students or the teacher.
- "With help": a student read the teacher's lips (as the teacher realised the student needed help to produce the utterance), the structure was provided after the animal and colour was produced separately and the teacher intervened to help with word order by providing the first letter of the structure ("v..."), or the student repeated after the teacher.
- "Completion": responses that came after another student had begun the answer or the teacher had started to answer and the student completed the phrase.

Table 1 includes the total number of responses each story elicited and the percentages of each kind of utterance (spontaneous, with help or completions, and whether the response involved the use of adjective + noun or not).

Table 1: Proportion of adjective + noun responses by story and response type

Story	Total responses	Total spontaneous responses	Responses with help or completions	No use of adj+noun (N)	Use of adj+noun (Y)	Use of adj+noun with help (Y with help)
1: The Grouchy Ladybug	12	75%	25%	33%	67%	0%
2: Brown Bear, Brown Bear	8	75%	25%	37.5%	50%	12.5%
3: I Went Walking	23	83%	17%	48%	43%	9%
4: The Very Busy Spider	7	100%	0%	43%	57%	0%

The ranking order

The data was analysed and a histogram was created to identify which story ranked higher and lower in terms of number of correct word order utterances. Figure 1 shows the proportion of responses for each story with reference to whether the response included the correct word order, incorrect word order or if the child required help to produce the structure.

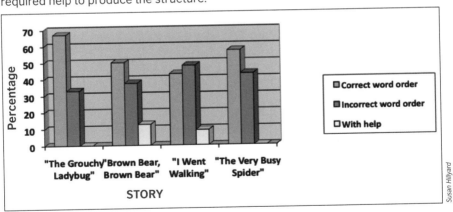

Figure 1: A comparison of proportions of response type across stories

Story number 1: *The Grouchy Ladybug*

The highest number of correct responses of adjective + noun word order were observed in *The Grouchy Ladybug* story. In this lesson, the pictures in the storybook were shown, but no rhythmic patterns were used. 75 per cent of the responses were spontaneous and the remaining 25 per cent needed help or were completions of others' utterances. 67 per cent of the responses involved the correct use of adjective + noun word order and the other 33 per cent of the responses did not contain the expected structure. Certain students were even able to produce a whole structure such as "it's a brown cheetah". Moreover, children produced the fewest incorrect answers with this story (see Appendix 4 for the data gathered for story number 1).

Story number 4: *The Very Busy Spider*

In *The Very Busy Spider* no rhythmic patterns were used, no illustrations were shown, and the story was acted out by the teacher with a puppet. 100 per cent of the responses were spontaneous, with 57 per cent being correct word order responses, 43 per cent of the answers did not include adjective-noun word order and no responses were produced with any type of help. Here, too, answers such as "it's a green bunny" were achieved.

Story number 2: *Brown Bear, Brown Bear*

Brown Bear, Brown Bear included both illustrations in the book and rhythmic patterns. Spontaneous responses amounted to 75 per cent and those with help or completions were the remaining 25 per cent. 50 per cent of the responses included the correct word order, 37.5 per cent did not produce the structure, and the remaining 12.5 per cent were able to produce the adjective + noun structure with help. However, certain students were able to produce the whole pattern: "green frog, green frog, what do you see? I see a purple cat looking at me".

Story number 3: *I Went Walking*

I Went Walking came last, with the smallest number of correct adjective-noun word order utterances. In this lesson the story was told using rhythmic patters, with the children being involved in acting out the story, but with no illustrations being shown. The amount of total spontaneous responses was 83 per cent, while the remaining 17 per cent were uttered with help or were completions. 43 per cent of the responses included the use of adjective-noun, 48 per cent did not, and nine per cent required help. Moreover, the children produced more incorrect word order structures than correct utterances (for instance: "a cat pink").

Analysis

A higher number of correct responses were produced in the stories that did not include rhythmic patterns. Therefore, this finding does not provide evidence to support the idea that the presence of rhyme in the story prose would facilitate correct adjective + noun word order.

Many other factors and conditions may have influenced the students' ease or difficulty in using correct adjective-noun word order:

- The pictures and colours in one book may have been more attractive than in another.
- The storytelling techniques used by the teacher may have influenced their understanding and enjoyment of the stories.
- The use of a puppet may have encouraged the children to answer more or less.
- One plot may have been more engaging than another.
- The way the children were involved in the stories when a response was required – interacting physically or visually – may have influenced their answers.

This interpretation could also be evidenced in the teacher-researcher's field notes. Each story seemed to have engaged the children in a different way. The field notes suggested that:

- The stories read with illustrations seemed to have been helpful because the colours of the images may have aided production in a visual way.
- The story which encouraged movement seemed to have engaged children in a physical way (acting out the animals, making animal noises and following the teacher around the classroom), although there was no aid for the production of colours.
- Children seemed motivated by the appearance of a spider puppet spinning its web in the last story, but again there were no visual images to aid the production of colours.

During the planning stage, the teacher-researcher was concerned that, after the first lesson, the students would have had exposure to the structure, and this factor was expected to influence children's production in subsequent stories, thus possibly affecting the validity of the data. However, it is surprising that the data does not necessarily reflect better results with subsequent exposure to the structure. Reflecting on this, it may be possible to infer that there are many other factors apart from exposure alone that influence learning, as argued in Murphy (2014). Furthermore, it may be interesting to note that in all cases except one (the third story, with rhythmic patterns and acted out), there were more successful word order utterances without help than incorrect ones.

Discussion

Although this Action Research project did not furnish conclusive results in showing whether rhythmic patterns in stories enhance acquisition of word order, it has provided some examples of how very young EFL learners are able to produce word order correctly, some alone and some with help, even if it is contrary to their use in their mother tongue.

Each story provided the framework for a repeated structure (adjective + noun) that allowed children to substitute words and share their own contributions to extend the content of a story. Therefore, this project supports the notion that children are able to grasp a given structure and use the framework provided in the story with the purpose of substituting vocabulary (e.g. substitute "black cat" with "brown cat"), personalising (e.g. providing their own contributions and suggestions) and using language creatively (e.g. "multicoloured cat").

The teacher-researcher's field notes showed that the children became engaged by the telling of stories and were motivated to produce the language successfully to be able to participate in the process of retelling. The repetitive phrases and the rhythm involved in the telling of the stories invited the children to interact spontaneously, producing the language in a safe context, due to the predictability of the expected utterances, which in turn allowed them to learn the structure "incidentally", in Brown's (1994: 66) terms, as opposed to through explicit instruction.

It must be considered that this small-scale investigation was limited to a reduced number of students in one school only and in one particular context. This class of 25 female four-year-olds had been having problems acquiring the correct word order structure in the foreign language. Therefore, the teacher carried out this Action Research project with the aim of trying to find ways to aid her students in learning this specific structure. As Kolsawalla (1999) claims, it may be interesting to carry out other systematic studies to research this area, as there seems to be a lack of research in this field.

This is of course only a very narrow analysis of descriptive data in a limited context and no statistical analysis has been carried out so as to furnish more conclusive results. However, the findings have been helpful for the practising teacher in her specific context, as one of the aims of Action Research is, in Elliott's (1991) terms, to be a professional development tool that provides practical judgment and enables the teacher to reflect on her practice.

References

Brewster, J, Ellis, G and Girard, D (2002) *The Primary English Teacher' Guide* (New Edition). Harlow: Pearson Education Limited.

Brown, HD (1994) *Principles of Language Learning and Teaching.* London: Prentice Hall.

Cameron, L (2001) *Teaching Languages to Young Learners.* Cambridge: Cambridge University Press.

Elliott, J (1991) *Action Research for Educational Change.* Buckingham: Open University Press.

Kolsawalla, H (1999) 'Teaching Vocabulary through Rhythmic Refrains in Stories', in Rixon, S (ed) *Young Learners of English: some research perspectives.* Harlow: Longman.

Lightbown, P and Spada, N (2006) *How Languages are Learned (3rd Edition).* Oxford: Oxford University Press.

Murphy, VA (2014) *Second language learning in the early school years: Trends and Contexts.* Oxford: Oxford University Press.

Roth, G (1998) *Teaching Very Young Children: Pre-school and Early Primary.* London: Richmond Publishing.

Appendix 1: Lesson Plans

Lesson	Steps
1 Monday 17th October, 2011 **Story with no rhythmic patterns + pictures**	Teacher pre-teaches some vocabulary that children may need to understand the story: friendly, grouchy, fight, ladybug, aphid, firefly with facial expressions, gestures and pictures. Teacher shows the cover of the book and reads the title. She asks children to predict what might happen and why the ladybug is a grouchy ladybug. Teacher tells *The Grouchy Ladybug* by Eric Carle, showing the pictures in the book. She will adapt the story so as to simplify some of the long sentences and to add colour+noun (e.g. brown gorilla/grey elephant). While reading, some questions will be asked: comprehension questions and prediction questions (What animal do you think she'll meet next?). Teacher asks some comprehension questions (perhaps in L1). The children help the teacher to retell the story (see how much vocabulary from the story they can produce and whether they can use the correct adjective-noun order).
2 Tuesday 18th October, 2011 **Story with rhythmic patterns + pictures**	Teacher pre-teaches some vocabulary: see, looking by asking the children what they can see around the room and at the end asking them to look at her because she's going to read a story. Teacher shows the cover of the book and reads the title. She asks children to predict what the story might be about. Teacher tells *Brown Bear, Brown Bear* by Eric Carle, showing the pictures in the book, making the rhythmic pattern salient. The children retell the story as a group (see how much vocabulary from the story they can produce and whether they can use the correct adjective-noun order).
3 Wednesday 19th October, 2011 **Story with rhythmic patterns but no pictures**	Teacher pre-teaches vocabulary: walking, following by making children follow her walking around the room. Teacher shows the cover of the book and reads the title. She asks children to predict what the story might be about and who will follow the boy. Teacher acts out *I Went Walking* by Sue Williams and Julie Rivas (acting out the different animals, making sounds, and walking around the room), without showing the pictures, but making the rhythmic pattern salient. The children create their own class story (see how much vocabulary from the story they can produce + other vocabulary they choose and whether they can use the correct adjective-noun order).
4 Thursday 20th October, 2011 **Story with no rhythmic patterns and no pictures**	Teacher pre-teaches vocabulary: spider, spider web, busy, owl, fly with facial expressions, sounds and pictures. Teacher shows the cover of the book and reads the title. She asks children to predict what the story might be about and why they think this is a busy spider. Teacher acts out *The Very Busy Spider* by Eric Carle (using a puppet of a spider spinning its web and acting out the different animals and making sounds), without showing the pictures. She will add colour+noun structure (e.g. white sheep, pink pig). The children create their own similar class story (see how much vocabulary from the story they can produce + other vocabulary they choose and whether they can use the correct adjective-noun order).

Appendix 2: Transcription selection

Transcription Code (adapted from Lightbown and Spada, 2006; Cameron, 2001; Nunan, 1991; and van Lier, 1988)

The conventions are as follows:

T	:	teacher
S1, S2, etc	:	identified student
Ss	:	several or all students simultaneously
T – Ss	:	teacher and students simultaneously
=	:	turn continues below, at the next identical symbol
(1.0)	:	pause of 1 second, etc.
?	:	rising intonation
!	:	strong emphasis
ok. now.	:	falling intonation
so, the next	:	low-rising intonation, suggesting continuation
m:, a::	:	extended syllable or phoneme
shall we start? ready?	:	overlapping or simultaneous talk
⌊yes		
((unint))	:	unintelligible
(T shows the picture)	:	non-verbal actions and comments
(singing)		
no-	:	abrupt cut-off
/pɪnɡuɪn/	:	phonetic transcription
te traje el cd	:	use of the mother tongue
[I brought the cd]	:	translation of the mother tongue

T:	First he found a? S8?
S23:	⌊Bee
S8:	bee
T:	what colour
S8:	yellow?
S24:	yellow and black
T:	a yellow and black bee
S24:	a yellow and black bee
T:	excellent. S5 (indicating to listen)
T:	and then a beetle
Ss:	beetle
T:	What colour?
S3:	beetle blue
S24:	blue
S23:	blue beetle
T:	a blue beetle S23 excellent (T gives s a high five). Then a grasshopper. A?
Ss:	green
S1:	grasshopper
S22:	green grasshu ((unint))
T:	green grasshopper
Ss:	green grasshe ((unint))
T:	excellent
S5:	a brown bird
T:	excellent. A lobster.
S14:	lobster green
S22:	a lobster green
T:	m::
S21:	es un cangrejo [it's a crab]

T: a lobster. What is a lobster

S5:   no un can- los cangrejos hacen asi [it's not a crab – crabs do this] (shows what crabs do with their hands) son mas   chiquitos y eso es una- [they're smaller and that's a-]

T: what colour is it?

S1:   green!

T: so it's a:? gr:?

S17:   green

S23:   lob

T: lobster. This is a skunk

S24:   skunk

S5:   it's a skunk blue

T: (indicates "no" with finger)

S22:   It's a:

T: S17?

S17:   It's a skunk

T: the other way round (indicating with hand)

S17:   a sku

S5:   a blue skunk

T: S5, yes! (high five) it's a blue skunk. It's a blue skunk. S6 and S7 (asking to pay attention)

S22:   (T turns the page, S22 puts hand up) yo! [me!]

T: yes, S22.

S22:   (4.0)

T: S22? It's a:?

S22:   snake

T: what colour?

Ss: green

S22:   green: (3.0) snake

T:	snake. It's a green snake. Yes. (S24 has her hand up) S24?
S24:	it's a brown?
S22:	it's a brown cheetah
T:	excellent. It's a brown cheetah
Ss:	cheetah
S5:	(T turns the page. S5 puts her hand up) It's a:?

Appendix 3: Field notes

1) Lesson 1: *The Grouchy Ladybug* (no rhythmic patterns + pictures)

Two ladybug images were helpful, children loved them. Understanding made clear of "friendly" and "grouchy". Great responses. Lots of production! And mostly spontaneous (not much help needed). S22 participated the most. Ss loved the story. Images must have helped production of colour, made it visual. Lesson went really well!

2) Lesson 2: *Brown Bear, Brown Bear* (rhythmic patterns + pictures)

Children love the pictures! Lots of spontaneous responses. Pictures made colour visual. Less adjective + noun than last class. However, many longer answers by using the whole structure ("green frog looking at me"). Able to include word order, replacing, in the whole structure.

3) Lesson 3: *I Went Walking* (rhythmic patterns + acting out)

Children enjoyed physical involvement and acting out the animals, making noises, following the teacher, etc. Very motivated to suggest their animal and colour. All were eager to participate. Lots of spontaneous responses, although not necessarily correct. Students didn't find it easy to include adjective + noun in the structure. About 50 per cent were successful. Not much visual information, maybe? Difficult for the Ss.

4) Lesson 4: *The Very Busy Spider* (no rhythmic patterns + acting out)

Loved the puppet, amazed that it was "really" spinning its web. About 50 per cent again. No visual aid again, perhaps? Pictures clearly help visually to produce a colour quickly. No colours, might mean Ss need to think a lot about it and it's easier to think of the animal and then give it a colour, unless the colour is presented (?).

Appendix 4: Data Analysis

Response Number	Student	Type of response	Utterance	Use of adj + noun (Y/N)
Lesson 1 Story: The Grouchy Ladybug				
1	24	Repetition after T	(a yellow and black bee)	N
2	3	Spontaneous	beetle blue	N
3	22	Spontaneous	green grasshu (grasshopper)	Y
4	5	Spontaneous	a brown bird	Y
5	14	Spontaneous	lobster green	N
6	5	Spontaneous	it's a skunk blue	N
7	22	Spontaneous	green: (pause) snake	Y
8	22	Completion of other S' response	it's a brown cheetah	Y
9	1	Completion of other S' response	it's a brown gorilla	Y
10	22	Spontaneous	it's a blue rhino	Y
11	12	Spontaneous	it's a blue elephant	Y
12	2	Spontaneous	it's a blue whale	Y

- Total responses: 12
- Total spontaneous responses: 9 (75%)
- Responses with help or completions: 3 (25%)
- No use of adj+noun (N): 4 (33%)
- Use of adj+noun (Y): 8 (67%)
- Use of adj+noun with help (Y with help): 0

4

Epilogue

4

Epilogue

Victoria A Murphy and Maria Evangelou, University of Oxford

The chapters in this volume highlight the diverse approaches and issues that underpin English language education through early childhood education and care (ECEC) settings. We would like to conclude with a few final thoughts on key issues and possible ways to move forward.

Early years teacher education, curriculum development and resources

We have seen from this volume that there is considerable variability with respect to the nature of the qualifications required to teach young children in pre-primary settings. We have also seen that there are particular issues with respect to language teaching in ECEC settings because, even where a teacher might have a relevant qualification, they may not have received any training on how to support English language learning (or vice versa). One of the ways this challenge is being addressed is through the collaborative teaching model – and a number of different and seemingly successful such models have been described in a few of the chapters of this volume. At the same time, we have also seen some examples that are less encouraging – notably those examples where the native speaker teacher, even with no qualifications whatsoever, is the dominant presence in the ECEC setting. Clearly, we need more research in this area to be able to develop appropriate guidance and support to language teaching professionals around the world.

Teacher education is also important in minority language learning contexts – where the child has a home language that is not English. A number of chapters illustrated how important it was that teachers are better equipped to handle the linguistic diversity inherent in many English-speaking early years settings, and that teacher education programmes should include more focus on the education of young English language learners. In the UK, for example, training on how to best support children with English as an Additional Language (EAL) does not figure as prominently in many Initial Teacher Education (ITE) programmes as we feel it could. In our view, all teachers are language teachers, and so a greater focus on this aspect in ITE is imperative.

Associated with the concerns around qualifications and training of teachers is the extent to which they themselves speak English. We have seen some examples where teachers themselves either do not have, or do not feel confident in, their own levels of English so as to teach it to young children. Teachers should therefore have support available to them for the development of their own English language learning, and ideally there would be some agreed-upon consistent norms as to minimum levels of proficiency required to teach English to young learners.

Evangelou, Sylva, Wild, Glenny and Kyriacou (2009) carried out a literature review that identified the most current evidence which speaks to the process of development for children from birth to age five. The main focus of this review was to identify the best supportive context for children's early learning and development. While their review was not directed towards English language education, many of their key findings relate directly to issues raised and discussed in this volume's chapters. With respect to curriculum development, a key finding relates to the importance of play in early years settings. Play can take many forms, be imaginative or pretend, physical and/or exploratory, but all of these are important in a child's development (Evangelou et al., 2009). Pretend play in particular can support language development, and by extension English language development in non-English speakers, because it involves interaction with adults, siblings and peers. Furthermore, it promotes thinking beyond the 'here and now', which is an important aspect of children's cognitive development. Adults have a key role in the development of children's play activities in early years settings. Adults can initiate games and help children become full partners, and eventually leaders, in different types of games. The important role of the adult in guided play activities underscores the importance of quality teacher education and training as discussed above.

The role of narrative is also exceedingly important in the development of children's language and can be extended to developing English language skills. Narrative is useful in building and maintaining communication, which in turn can have positive influences on literacy development. Play and narrative together help children experience linguistic interaction rather than just being exposed to language (Evangelou et al., 2009). As we continue to develop English language curricula for young children, we need to consider these features as key ingredients.

The resources available to teachers of young learners of English emerged as a common theme throughout this volume. The role of facilities, equipment and materials also emerged from Evangelou et al.'s (2009) review. They particularly note the importance of distinguishing between quality of the materials, and quality of use of the materials – something that can be enhanced through appropriate teacher education. Children can benefit from using everyday materials if there is facilitative, guided interaction on the part of an adult (parent or educator). Hence, while we do want to see good quality materials and resources available to teachers of young English language learners, just as important is what adults do with these materials in helping support and encourage English language skills.

Additionally, Evangelou et al. (2009) note the importance of time – something that also emerged in this volume. The issue is to ensure that appropriate amounts of time are allocated to different activities and, in particular, that adults should be led by the child's interests, rather than relying on their own perceptions of how much time is appropriate to spend on different types of linguistic tasks in class. So not only do children need enough time in English (a particular concern in EFL contexts), but they need appropriate amounts of time on different English language tasks (particularly literacy-based ones) to help them make connections between the activities they are engaged with and their own world.

First language support

A common theme from many of the contributions in this volume was the importance of developing the first language (L1). In both the minority language context and where English is a second or foreign language, ensuring that educational provision does not promote English at the cost of the L1 is paramount. Children need exposure to rich, complex language, and they also need to develop literacy skills in both their home language and in English. The importance of rich communication also emerged from the Evangelou et al. (2009) review. Rich conversations, notably between adults and children, provide important opportunities to support children's emotional and social relationships, enhance their self-esteem and, as is particularly relevant for English language learning, provide an invaluable source of linguistic input with which the young learner can engage.

The development of biliteracy skills can and should be mutually supportive, yet we have seen in this volume some examples where the home language of the student is either not factored in at all to the curriculum or where the implementation of EFL programmes overshadow the support for emerging L1 oral language and literacy skills. Many researchers have consistently demonstrated the importance of developing strong L1 skills and have also identified that spending time on L1 skills does not impede the development of the second language (e.g. Cummins, 1981; Genesee, this volume).

Parents and community

The role of the parent is another common theme throughout this volume. Parents are important contributors to the success of their children's educational achievement, and this is equally true if their child is receiving early years education through English. We need parents to work closely with schools and teachers, to support their work. However, we also need parents to have realistic expectations and help ensure that English language learning is fun and enjoyable for children, not just another academic achievement.

One of the key issues that emerged from Evangelou et al.'s (2009) review was the role of the home language environment (HLE) and the parents in general. They describe the important role that parents have in offering a secure and stable environment, intellectual stimulation, and parent–child interaction. The role of the HLE and parent emerged as some of the most powerful predictors of children's achievement. The importance of the home is just as important in the development of English language skills. Parents can be involved with and show an interest in the child's learning of English, which in turn will have an important, indirect facilitative effect on their English language outcomes. They encourage practitioners to 'acknowledge, value and support' the role that parents have in supporting their children's development by creating sufficient opportunities for all parents and carers to be involved. As Evangelou et al. (2009) note, 'what parents do is more important than who parents are' and research has shown that pre-schools that promote good interaction between parents and children are most beneficial. In summary, therefore, parents are important and, as we continue to research the area of ECEC through English for non-English speakers, we need to factor in the parents' involvement to enhance children's experiences and outcomes.

The need for more research

It may seem a truism – so self-evident as to be hardly worth mentioning – but we would like to highlight the need for more research in this area. We hope this volume serves in part as a metaphorical gauntlet to carry out more research in the English language learning and teaching of young children. Ultimately, we want to be able to feel confident in the provision we are implementing in contexts around the world. We feel this confidence can only be developed and nurtured through the gathering of evidence, and the use of that evidence to underpin decisions regarding policy, teacher education, curriculum design and development of resources and materials. We therefore are pleased to see the range of topics and approaches taken by the contributors to this volume and look forward to watching (and contributing to) the development of (English) language education in the early years. Taking the key findings from Evangelou et al.'s (2009) report, in combination with the themes that emerged from this volume, areas that need developing are: i) developing a skilled workforce through professional training, ii) developing quality environments in early years settings, and iii) the need for more research into children's development both within and across settings.

A final word

At the close of Genesee's chapter, he discusses (within the minority language learner context) how the current challenge is to reconceptualise strategies for educating young ELLs. We feel that this is equally true in all the contexts represented in this volume and we hope that, with continued scrutiny from all stakeholders, we will be able to further develop our understanding of how to best support multilingual development in young children throughout the world.

References

Cummins, J (1981) 'The role of the primary language development in promoting educational success for language minority students', in *Schooling and Language Minority Students: A Theoretical Framework*. Los Angeles, CA: California Department of Education.

Evangelou, M, Sylva, K, Wild, M, Glenny, G and Kyriacou, M (2009) *Early Years Learning and Development Literature Review*. Nottingham: DCSF Publications [DCSF RR 176].

5

Contributors

5

Contributors

Lynn Ang

Lynn Ang is Reader in Early Childhood at University College London (UCL), Institute of Education. Her research expertise includes the early years curriculum, issues of diversity, international early years policy, and early childhood care and education across cultures, particularly in Southeast Asia and the Asia-Pacific region. She has extensive methodological experience in evaluation, systematic reviews, ethnography, and qualitative and participatory methods in research. Lynn is particularly interested in the informal and formal contexts of children's learning and development, and the ways in which socially relevant research and advocacy for children and families are translated into practice and policy. She has worked on a number of research grants from major funding bodies including UNICEF, the British Academy, The National College for School Leadership (NCL), and the Economic and Social Research Council (ESRC). She is a Fellow of the Higher Education Academy (FHEA) and Fellow of the ESRC Peer Review College. She serves on the Editorial Board of the *International Journal of Early Years Education* and is also a supervisor of Masters and Doctoral students.

Fortidas Bakuza

Fortidas Bakuza works as a Lecturer at the Aga Khan University Institute for Educational Development, East Africa, where he teaches on the MA in areas of early years education and is engaged in a range of different outreach professional development courses for teachers, in particular in marginalised and hard to reach communities. He has more than 20 years of experience as a teacher, trainer and researcher working in early childhood development in areas of capacity building, research and documentation for advocacy and programme management, and has been the National Co-ordinator, Tanzania Early Childhood Development Network, a national network of organisations working in Tanzania to improve the lives of young children from birth to eight years. He has served in different associations and bodies nationally and internationally that advocate for early childhood development as a foundation to human development and is the ACEI (Association for Childhood Education International) Country Liaison for Tanzania. He has a PhD in Education Administration from the State University of New York, Buffalo, USA, in the area of early childhood education leadership and policy and their influences on ECE access, equity and quality, and he has also completed an MA, BA and several postgraduate professional courses on Children, Youth and Development.

Yvette Coyle

Yvette Coyle is an Associate Professor at the University of Murcia in Spain where she teaches future primary and pre-school teachers of EFL. Her research interests include vocabulary acquisition in young learners, classroom interaction processes and written feedback processing in children. She has published two books on teaching methodology, and several papers in journals such as *System, ELT Journal, Journal of Second Language Writing* and *Studies in Second Language Acquisition.*

Anne-Marie de Mejía

Anne-Marie de Mejía works at the Centro de Investigación y Formación en Educación at Universidad de los Andes, Bogotá, Colombia. She holds a PhD in Linguistics in the area of bilingual education from Lancaster University, UK. Her research interests include bilingual classroom interaction, the construction of bilingual curricula and processes of empowerment, and bilingual teacher development. She is the author of a number of books and articles in the area of bilingualism and bilingual education, both in Spanish and English.

Her latest publications include *Forging Multilingual Spaces* (2008); *Empowering Teachers across Cultures* (2011), jointly edited with Christine Hélot; *Bilingüismo en el Contexto Colombiano* and *Iniciativas y perspectivas en el Siglo XXI* (2011), edited with Alexis López and Beatriz Peña; and *Exploraciones sobre el aprendizaje de lenguas y contenidos en programas bilingües* (2012), edited with Beatriz Peña, María Cristina Arciniegas and Marta Luisa Montiel.

Sally Dixon

Sally Dixon is a PhD candidate at The Australian National University. Her research interests centre on language contact and multilingualism, particularly in the context of education. Outside of academia she has worked as a community linguist in the remote Pilbara, Australia, a professional mentor with the *Bridging the Language Gap Project* within Education Queensland, and developed multilingual curricula and resources in an Indigenous Education NGO in the Philippines.

Gail Ellis

Gail Ellis is Adviser, Young Learners and Quality, for the British Council and is based in Paris. Her publications include *Learning to Learn English, The Primary English Teacher's Guide* and *Tell it Again!* Her latest publication is *Teaching children how to learn*, co-authored with Nayr Ibrahim, published by Delta Publishing. Her main interests are children's literature, young learner ELT management and inclusive education.

Maria Evangelou

Maria Evangelou is Associate Professor in the Department of Education, University of Oxford. She is the Course Director for the MSc in Education, the Course Director for the MSc in Child Development and Education, and the Convenor of the FELL Research Group (Families Effective Learning and Literacy) at Oxford. She carries out extensive research in the areas of early childhood interventions, language and literacy development in the early years and methodological issues in research, and the role of evidence-based practices in education. She has published widely in leading educational journals.

Silke Fricke

Silke Fricke is a Speech and Language Therapist (SLT) and a Senior Lecturer in the Department of Human Communication Sciences at the University of Sheffield. As an SLT she specialised in children with speech, language and literacy difficulties, and she holds an MSc and PhD in Human Communication Sciences. Before joining the University of Sheffield as a lecturer she worked as a Post-Doctoral Researcher at the Department of Psychology, University of York. Her principal research interests lie in the field of speech, language, and literacy development and difficulties (including assessments) in monolingual and multilingual children, as well as the evaluation of intervention approaches.

Lauren Gawne

Lauren Gawne is an ELDP (Early Language Development Programme) Research Fellow at SOAS, University of London. Lauren was a member of the Aboriginal Child Language Acquisition Project (ACLA) in 2013. Lauren's other areas of research interest include Tibeto-Burman languages, language documentation methods and gesture in discourse.

Fred Genesee

Fred Genesee is Professor Emeritus in the Psychology Department at McGill University, Montreal. He has conducted extensive research on alternative forms of bilingual/immersion education for language minority and language majority students. His current research interests include language acquisition in pre-school bilingual children, internationally adopted children, second language reading acquisition, and the language and academic development of at-risk students in bilingual programmes. He has published numerous articles in scientific journals, professional books and magazines, and is the author of more than twelve books on bilingualism. He is the recipient of the Canadian Psychology Association Gold Medal Award, Paul Pimsler Award for Research in Foreign Language Education, Canadian Psychological Associate Award for Distinguished Contributions to Community or Public Service, California Association for Bilingual Education Award for Promoting Bilingualism and the le prix Adrien-Pinard.

Paul Gunashekar

Paul Gunashekar has been teaching English, training teachers of English and developing ELT instructional materials for over 40 years. Educated in Bangalore and London, he is a professor in the Department of Materials Development, Testing and Development, and Dean of Publications at the English and Foreign Languages University, Hyderabad, India. He has authored, co-authored and edited over 200 English teaching books — including coursebooks, workbooks, supplementary and literature readers, teachers' books and reading cards — for national and state agencies. He has conducted over 1,000 teacher education workshops in India, Nepal, Sri Lanka, UAE, Kuwait, Oman, Bahrain, Qatar, Saudi Arabia and Tanzania. He specialises in course design, teacher development and English for Specific Purposes. He edits the EFLU research journal *Languaging* and is the Indian English consultant to the *Oxford English Dictionary* and *Oxford Advanced Learner's Dictionary*.

Sarah Hillyard

Sarah Hillyard is a teacher of English and holds a Masters Degree in Teaching English to Young Learners from the University of York, UK. She has taught English in Kindergarten and is currently Kindergarten Co-ordinator at Florence Nightingale School in Buenos Aires, Argentina. She has also taught at secondary level and has been tutor of Children's Literature at the National Teacher Training College in the city of Buenos Aires. She spent two years travelling as an actress with The Performers (TIE – Theatre in Education). She now develops workshops and has published articles focusing on teaching English to very young learners.

Alberto Navarro Martínez

Alberto Navarro Martínez is an EFL teacher in a primary school in southern Spain. He holds a degree in Primary ELT and a Masters Degree in Educational Research and Innovation. He is interested in different approaches to teaching very young learners of English, and especially in the effectiveness of diverse strategies for developing phonemic awareness.

Gill Millard

Gill Millard is a speech and language therapist with over 10 years' experience working with children with speech, language and communication needs. Initially within the NHS, she worked with clients in clinics, early years settings, mainstream and special schools. Following this she spent time in a special needs centre in Guiyang, China, before working at ICAN's Dawn House School, a specialist school for primary- and secondary-aged children with severe and complex speech, language and communication needs. She subsequently brought her clinical experience to the field of research by joining the University of Sheffield as a Research Assistant on two oral language intervention projects.

Naashia Mohamed

Naashia Mohamed holds a PhD in Language Learning and Teaching from the University of Auckland. She has previously taught ESL to students of all levels and has led curriculum reform projects in the Maldives. She is currently a Senior Lecturer at the Maldives National University, teaching courses that relate to language, linguistics and research methods. Her research interests include language pedagogy, language policy and language teacher education.

Gemma Morales

Gemma Morales is a PhD student in the Linguistics and Applied Linguistics Department at the University of Melbourne, Australia. Gemma's research interests include language use by minority children and bilingual education. Her current research investigates the development of home language literacy skills in Indigenous children from remote Indigenous communities in the Northern Territory, Australia. Her work involves the creation of iPad apps designed to assess and train phonological awareness and letter knowledge in Indigenous Languages. Gemma is also working as a research assistant on the Aboriginal Child Language Acquisition Project (ACLA).

Sandie Mourão

Sandie Mourão is a freelance teacher educator, author and consultant specialising in early years language education and an invited assistant professor at Universidade Nova in Lisbon, Portugal. She is co-editor of *Early Years Second Language Education: International Perspectives on Theory and Practice* (Routledge) and the open access *Children's Literature in English Language Education* journal [http://clelejournal.org/], as well as author of a number of language learning courses and resource books. Her main research interests focus on early years language learning, picturebooks in language learning and classroom-based research.

Nipael Mrutu

Nipael Mrutu holds a Bachelor of Laws degree from Tumaini University, Iringa, Tanzania. She has worked as a Legal Officer for the United Law Chambers and as a Resident Magistrate in Dodoma, Tanzania. She has an MA in Anthropology specialising in child health and wellbeing from the University of Amsterdam (fully funded competitive scholarship) and is in the final stages of writing up her PhD thesis (fully funded competitive scholarship, University of Amsterdam) on Orphan Care and Support Transformations in the Context of HIV/AIDS in Tanzania. She has co-ordinated a number of health-related research projects in various regions of Tanzania, such as Arusha, Iringa, Kilimanjaro and Mwanza, most of which have focused on children's rights and wellbeing. She is currently a full-time Lecturer at the Aga Khan University, Institute for Educational Development, East Africa, where she has teaching responsibilities in areas of research and early years' education.

Victoria A Murphy

Victoria Murphy is Professor of Applied Linguistics in the Department of Education, University of Oxford. She is the Course Co-ordinator for the MSc in Applied Linguistics/Second Language Acquisition and carries out research in the area of child L2/FL development, EAL children's language and literacy development, and early years EAL and FL learning. She is the Convenor of the Research in English as an Additional Language (REAL) group at Oxford and has been published in a wide range of applied linguistics journals. She is the author of *Second Language Learning in the Early School Years: Trends and Contexts*, published by Oxford University Press in 2014.

Mei Lee Ng

Mei Lee Ng is an Assistant Professor and Associate Head of the Department of Early Childhood Education, Hong Kong Institute of Education. Dr Ng has completed her PhD studies at the Faculty of Education, Hong Kong University with her research topic on teaching English to kindergarteners in Hong Kong. She obtained her two Masters degrees on Teaching English as A Second Language and Early Childhood Education from the Institute of Education, London University. Combining her two specialisms, Dr Ng develops her particular interest in researching pre-schoolers' second language teaching and learning. In addition, her research interests also include early literacy and language development, parents' education and parental involvement.

Johanne Paradis

Johanne Paradis is a Professor in the Department of Linguistics at the University of Alberta. Before completing her PhD at McGill University, Paradis worked as a teacher of English as a second language. Paradis studies bilingual language acquisition, second language acquisition and specific language impairment in children. A primary focus of her research concerns children learning English as a second language: how these children approach native-speaker competence, what unique language development profiles they display, the factors explaining why some individual children learn English faster than others, and what language measures best differentiate English second language children with typical development from those with impairment. Paradis' research has been supported by funding from the Alberta Heritage Foundation for Medical Research, the Social Sciences and Humanities Research Council of Canada, the Canadian Language and Literacy Research Network, and the Alberta Centre for Child, Family and Community Research. Paradis is first author of the 2011 book *Dual Language Development and Disorders: A Handbook on Bilingualism and Second Language Learning* (2nd edition, Brookes Publishing). Paradis and colleagues have a website of resources for assessment with children learning English as a second language, the CHESL Centre (www.chesl.ualberta.ca).

Alan Pence

Alan Pence is UNESCO Chair for Early Childhood Education, Care and Development, and Professor, School of Child and Youth Care, University of Victoria. Dr Pence is the founder of the Early Childhood Development Virtual University (ECDVU), an ECD capacity-promoting programme active in Africa since 2001. The author of over 130 articles and chapters, two of his books that relate closely to this volume are *Africa's Future – Africa's Challenge: Early Childhood Care and Development in Sub-Saharan Africa* (edited with Garcia and Evans, 2008) and *Complexities, Capacities, Communities: Changing Development Narratives in ECD* (with Benner, 2015). He is the recipient of the International Education Leadership Award from the Canadian Bureau for International Education, the University of Victoria's inaugural Craigdarroch Research Award for 'societal benefit', and a finalist for the World Innovation Summit for Education (WISE) Award.

Susan Poetsch

Susan Poetsch is a PhD candidate at the Australian National University. Her research is on children's language acquisition and use in home and school contexts in a remote community in central Australia. She is also a lecturer in the Education Faculty at the University of Sydney, where she teaches units of study on morphology of Australian languages, language teaching methods and approaches, and curriculum development, in a programme for Indigenous Australian teachers.

Pauline Rea-Dickins

Pauline Rea-Dickins has worked for the Aga Khan University in East Africa, where she was Director, Institute for Educational Development, East Africa, and Principal, Tanzania Institute of Education. She has also held appointments at the University of Bristol, as Chair in Applied Linguistics in Education and Director of Research in the Graduate School of Education, and the Universities of Warwick, Lancaster and Dar es Salaam, Tanzania. She is currently affiliated with the Oxford University Centre for Assessment Studies. Pauline is an internationally recognised researcher and scholar in areas of language testing, classroom-based assessment, and language programme evaluation. She has successfully supervised over 30 doctoral students, several of whom have won international awards, and has an extensive record of successful research grants, most notably from the Economic and Social Science Council, the Department for International Development and the Department for Foreign Affairs, Trade and Development Canada. Pauline has worked extensively in a variety of capacities throughout her career in Sub-Saharan Africa, which has impacted on her profound belief that research should impact on the quality of educational experiences, especially for those learning in less privileged contexts.

Penelope Robinson

Penelope Robinson has worked in several countries as a schoolteacher, a teacher trainer and a university lecturer. She joined the School of Education at Leeds University in 2000 and specialised in language development and the teaching of languages to young learners. Her primary research interest is in the processes involved in the acquisition and learning of English as an additional and a foreign language, and the development of effective teaching practices that enable learners to understand and use English. She is also interested in the development of teacher knowledge and expertise through practitioner research, especially in the young learner classroom.

Julio Roca de Larios

Julio Roca de Larios is an Associate Professor at the Faculty of Education, University of Murcia, Spain. His research interests include L2 text generation processes, written feedback processing, and the analysis of interaction and learning processes in CLIL-oriented classrooms. He has published papers in journals such as *Language Learning, The Modern Language Journal, Journal of Second Language Writing, Learning and Instruction, Studies in Second Language Acquisition, Porta Linguarum* and *System*, as well as chapters in collective volumes edited by John Benjamins, Multilingual Matters or De Gruyter Mouton.

Kalyani Samantray

Kalyani Samantray has taught undergraduate and postgraduate courses in English language and literature in different colleges, and in the PG Department of English, Utkal University, Odisha, India, chairing the department for two years. She has an MA in Applied Linguistics from the University of London and a PhD in Phonology. Among her publications are ESL textbooks, textbooks on technical English and academic writing, teacher education materials, online learning materials and several research articles published by Oxford University Press, Cambridge University Press, Orient Blackswan, the National Council for Educational Research for Teachers, Government of India, IG National Open University, New Delhi, and State Councils for Higher Education. She has conducted more than 300 ELT workshops in India and abroad. She is an Article Editor for Sage One, Sage Publication Inc, USA; a certified TKT Trainer, British Council; and a Teacher Educator for Oxford University Press, University Grants Commission and NCERT, Government of India. She has worked as a consultant for UNICEF in developing ESL Primary Readers for tribal learners. Her current research interests are young learners and language learning, critical discourse analysis, focus-on-form grammar and intercultural communication.

K Padmini Shankar

K Padmini Shankar is a professor in the Department of ESL Studies, School of English Language Education, English and Foreign Languages University, Hyderabad, India, where she teaches on the Postgraduate Diploma in the Teaching of English (PGDTE), MA (TESL), and PhD (ELE) programmes at the university. Professor Shankar has presented papers at many seminars and conferences in India, and international conferences in Taiwan, Singapore, Malaysia, New Zealand, Thailand, and the UK. She has published research papers in national and international journals. She has edited coursebooks for grades 1–8, titled *Exploring English*, published by Harper Collins, India. Her research interests include teaching young learners, teacher education and teacher development, classroom-based research and psychology for language learning.

Shelina Walli

Shelina Walli graduated with an MEd in Teacher Education from the Aga Khan University, Institute for Educational Development, East Africa, where she now holds the position of Lecturer. She is currently enrolled in a doctoral programme at the University of Arizona, Department of Teaching Learning and Socio-cultural studies, with a Major in Early Childhood Education. She has over 25 years of experience in the field of early childhood care and education in varied capacities including classroom teaching, management and teacher education. Her research interests include integration of contextually relevant practices in early childhood practitioner preparation and the use of ICT in continuous professional development of place-bound early childhood practitioners. Shelina has been involved in several research projects at the Aga Khan University in blended learning initiatives and has been an online tutor on the Science of Early Childhood Development programme from Red River College.

Gillian Wigglesworth

Gillian Wigglesworth is professor and Deputy Dean of the Faculty of Arts at the University of Melbourne. She is a Chief Investigator and leader of the Melbourne node of the ARC Centre of Excellence for the Dynamics of Language. She is also Deputy Director of the Research Unit for Indigenous Language. She has an extensive background in first and second language acquisition and bilingualism, as well as language assessment. Her major research focus is on the multilingual communities in which Indigenous children in remote areas of Australia grow up, and how languages in these communities interact with English once children attend school.

Richard Wong Kwok Shing

Richard Wong Kwok Shing is Assistant Professor at the Department of Early Childhood Education of the Hong Kong Institute of Education. His research interests include consequences of becoming bilingual, teaching English as a second/foreign language and language education. He is also interested in creating picturebooks for young children. His English picturebook *Can you spot?* has been well received by parents in Hong Kong since its publication in 2013. For any enquiries relating to this article, please write to him at kswong@ied.edu.hk.

Yan Ling Zhou

Yan Ling Zhou is an Assistant Professor at the Department of Early Childhood Education of the Hong Kong Institute of Education. Prior to her PhD, she was a language teacher at primary and secondary schools for ten years. Her research interests lie in the field of developmental psychology, with an emphasis on the language and literacy development of Chinese and English as both L1 and L2 in typical children, or children with learning difficulties, in early educational settings, taking special account of factors including underlying mechanisms of literacy acquisition and parental influence, as well as teaching pedagogies of language education.

Acknowledgements

Victoria and Maria would like to thank all the contributors to the book for their enthusiasm and perseverance in putting this volume together. They would also like to thank Adrian Odell for his support and patience throughout the development of this volume. He was most calm and accommodating as deadlines flew past like leaves in the wind. Thanks also go to Charlotte Clancy for her help in the final stages of editing.